Fifteen years worth of
thanks to Ichigo, Rukia,
all the characters of *Bleach*
and to all the fans.

–Tite Kubo

BLEACH is author Tite Kubo's second title. Kubo made his debut
with *ZOMBIEPOWDER.*, a four-volume series for *WEEKLY SHONEN
JUMP*. To date, *BLEACH* has been translated into numerous
languages and has also inspired an animated TV series that
began airing in the U.S. in 2006. Beginning its serialization in
2001, *BLEACH* is still a mainstay in the pages of *WEEKLY SHONEN
JUMP*. In 2005, *BLEACH* was awarded the prestigious Shogakukan
Manga Award in the *shonen* (boys) category.

BLEACH
VOL. 74: DEATH & STRAWBERRY
SHONEN JUMP Manga Edition

STORY AND ART BY
TITE KUBO

Translation/Joe Yamazaki
Touch-up Art & Lettering/Mark McMurray
Design/Kam Li
Editor/Alexis Kirsch

Printed in the U.S.A.

Published by VIZ Media, LLC
P.O. Box 77010
San Francisco, CA 94107

10 9 8 7 6 5 4 3 2 1
First printing, October 2018

www.viz.com

THE WORLD'S
MOST POPULAR MANGA
SHONEN JUMP
www.shonenjump.com

Even without a form
We will never stop walking

BLEACH 74 | THE DEATH AND THE STRAWBERRY

Shonen Jump Manga

ALL STARS ★ AND

阿散井恋次
アバライレンジ

**RENJI
ABARAI**

**RUKIA
KUCHIKI**

朽木ルキア
クチキルキア

黒崎一護
クロサキイチゴ

**ICHIGO
KUROSAKI**

★ plot

Ichigo Kurosaki meets Soul Reaper Rukia Kuchiki and ends up helping her eradicate Hollows. After developing his powers as a Soul Reaper, Ichigo befriends many humans and Soul Reapers and grows as a person...

The war between the Soul Reapers and Quincies enters its final stage. Urahara reveals his Bankai for the first time and is able to take down Nakk Le Vaar with the help of Grimmjow. Meanwhile, as his allies are struggling in their fights against the remaining Quincies, Ichigo has reached Yhwach's throne room. The final battle has now begun!

BLEACH

YHWACH

石田雨竜
イシダウリュウ

ORIHIME
INOUE

ユーハバッハ

URYU
ISHIDA

井上織姫
イノウエオリヒメ

STORIES

BLEACH 74

THE DEATH AND THE STRAWBERRY

CONTENTS

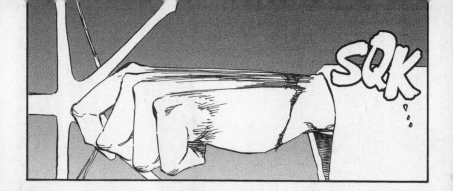

SQK

KR···K

MIND IF I ASK YOU SOME- THING...?

675. BLOOD FOR MY BONE

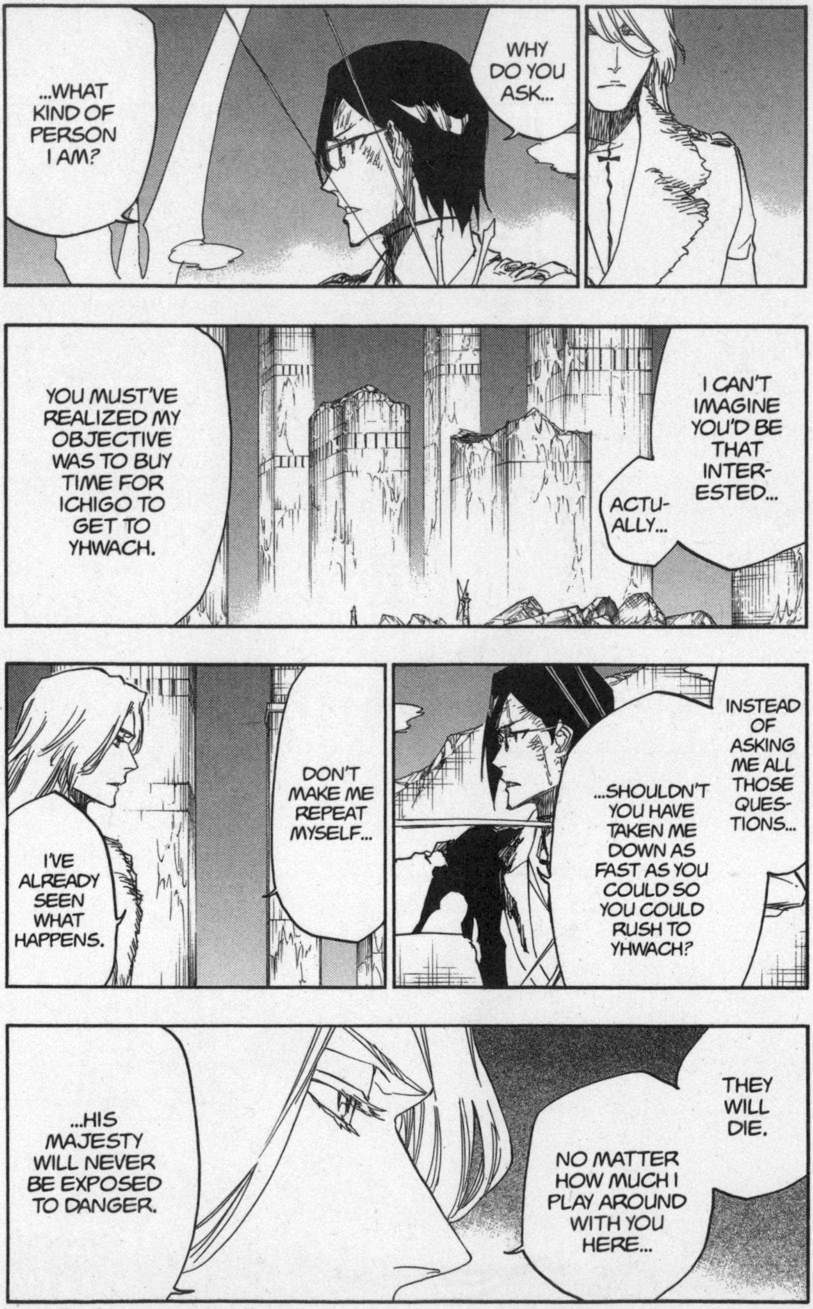
WHY DO YOU ASK...
...WHAT KIND OF PERSON I AM?
I CAN'T IMAGINE YOU'D BE THAT INTER-ESTED...
ACTU-ALLY...
YOU MUST'VE REALIZED MY OBJECTIVE WAS TO BUY TIME FOR ICHIGO TO GET TO YHWACH.
INSTEAD OF ASKING ME ALL THOSE QUES-TIONS...
...SHOULDN'T YOU HAVE TAKEN ME DOWN AS FAST AS YOU COULD SO YOU COULD RUSH TO YHWACH?
DON'T MAKE ME REPEAT MYSELF...
I'VE ALREADY SEEN WHAT HAPPENS.
THEY WILL DIE.
NO MATTER HOW MUCH I PLAY AROUND WITH YOU HERE...
...HIS MAJESTY WILL NEVER BE EXPOSED TO DANGER.

READ THIS WAY

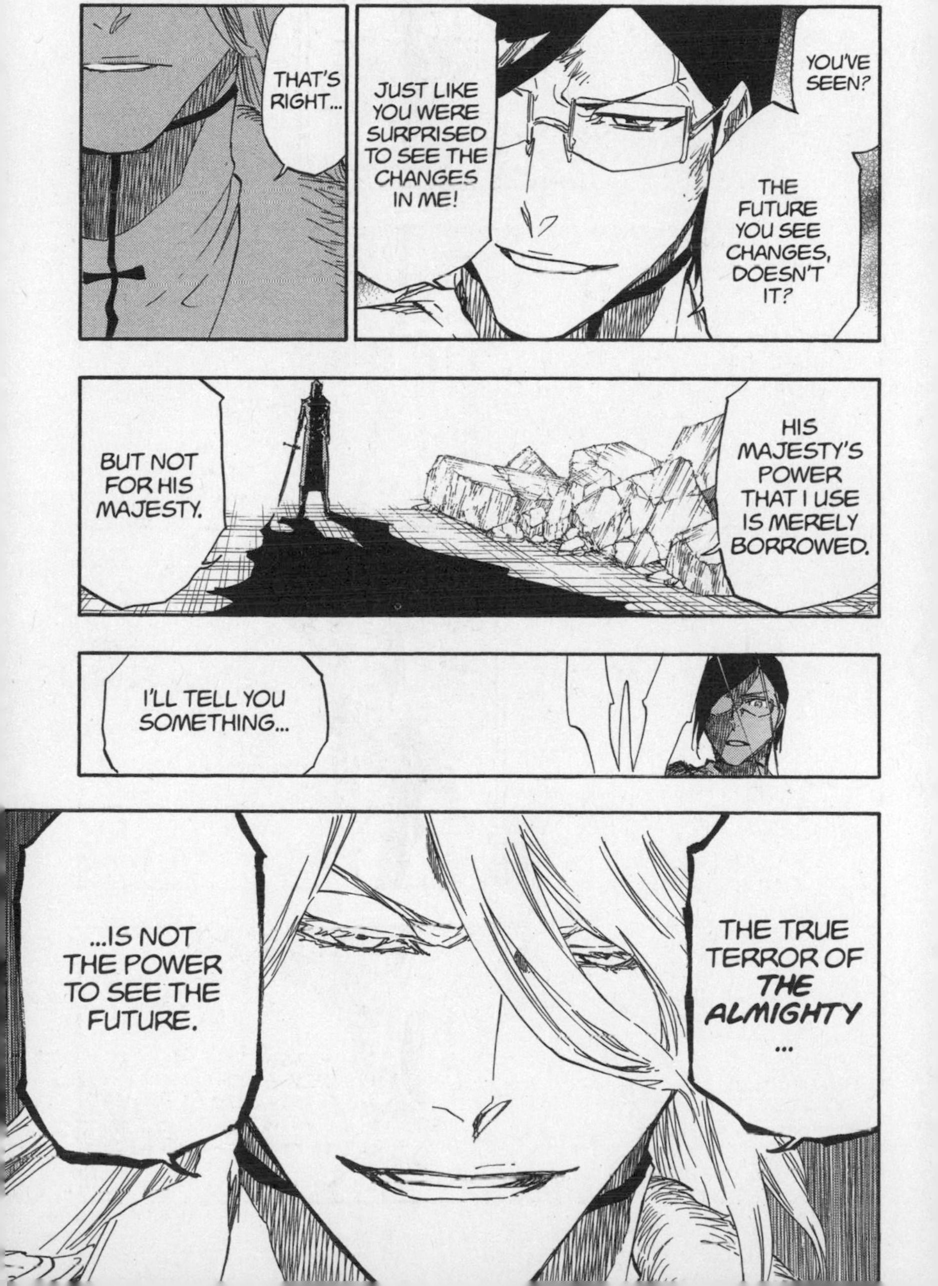
YOU'VE SEEN?
THE FUTURE YOU SEE CHANGES, DOESN'T IT?
JUST LIKE YOU WERE SURPRISED TO SEE THE CHANGES IN ME!
THAT'S RIGHT...
HIS MAJESTY'S POWER THAT I USE IS MERELY BORROWED.
BUT NOT FOR HIS MAJESTY.
I'LL TELL YOU SOMETHING...
THE TRUE TERROR OF *THE ALMIGHTY* ...
...IS NOT THE POWER TO SEE THE FUTURE.

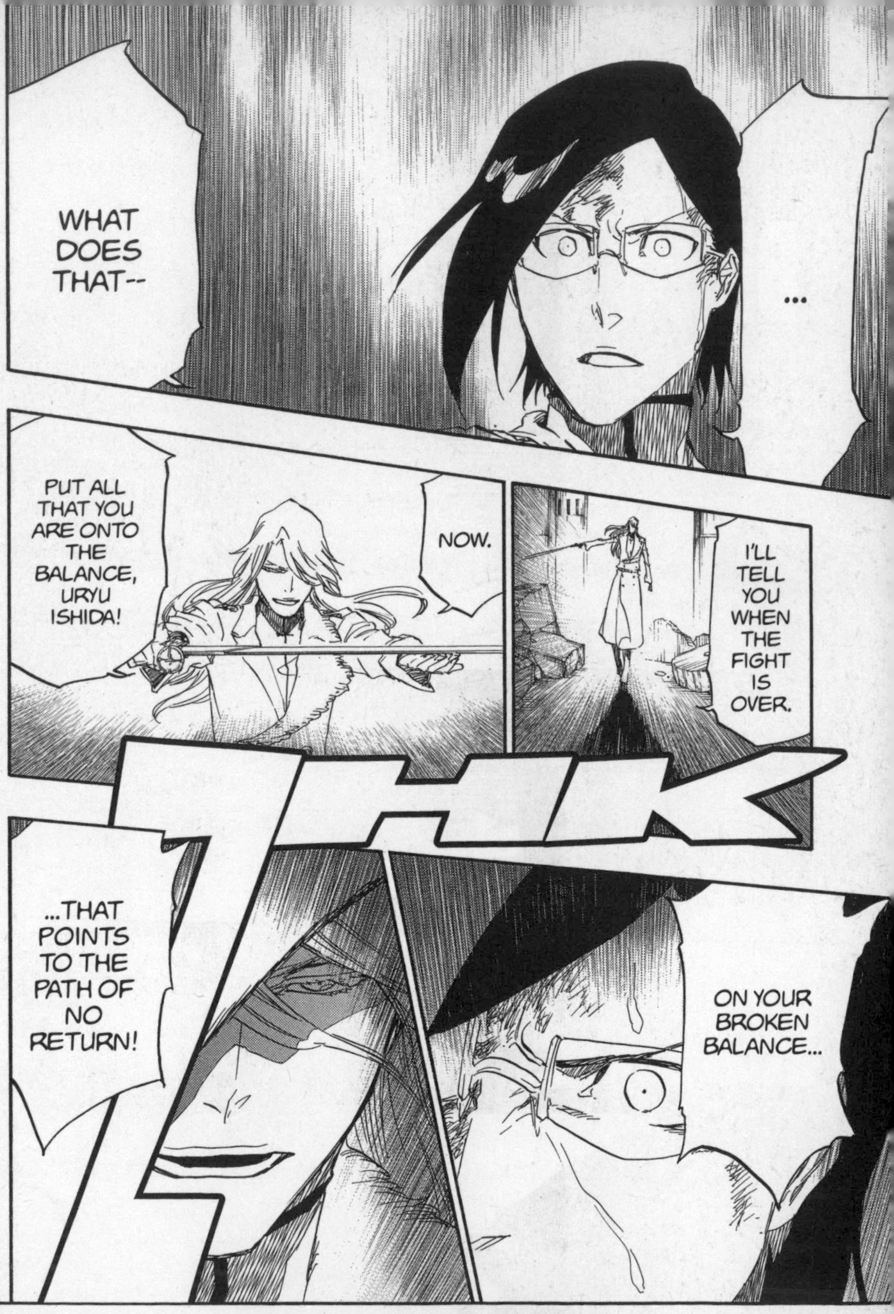
...
WHAT DOES THAT--
I'LL TELL YOU WHEN THE FIGHT IS OVER.
NOW.
PUT ALL THAT YOU ARE ONTO THE BALANCE, URYU ISHIDA!
JHK
ON YOUR BROKEN BALANCE...
...THAT POINTS TO THE PATH OF NO RETURN!

BLEACH 675.

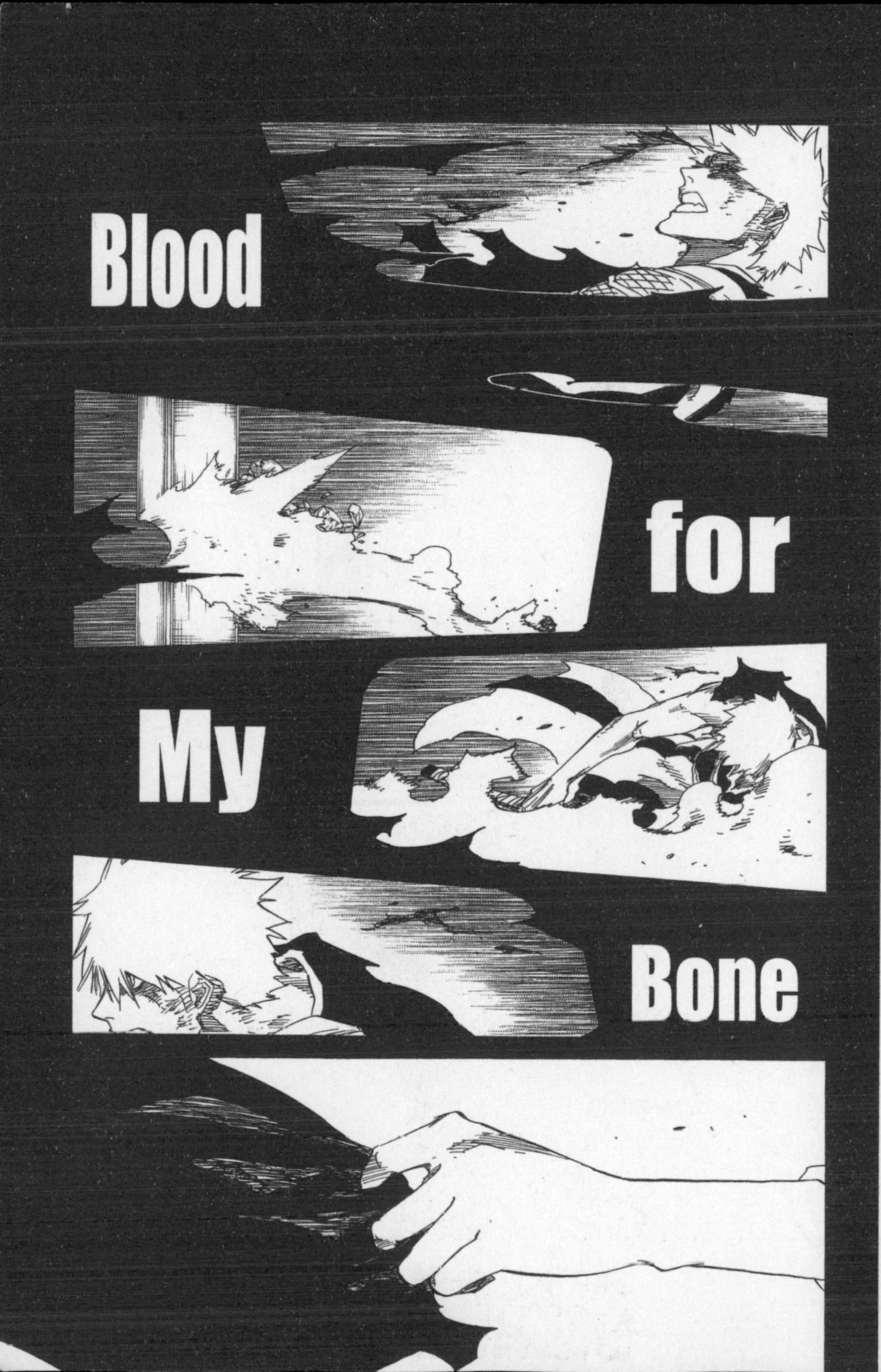
Blood
for
My
Bone

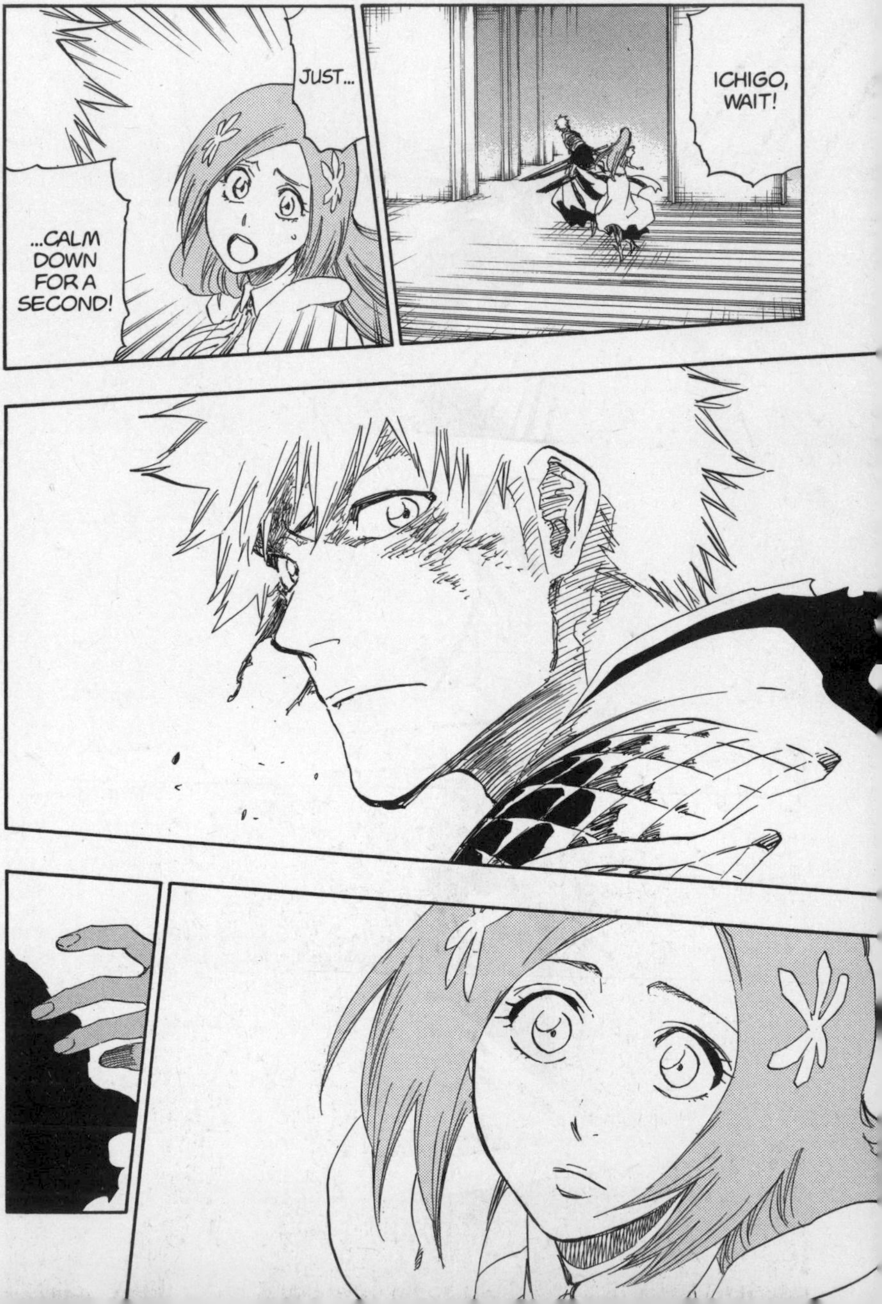
ICHIGO, WAIT!
JUST...
...CALM DOWN FOR A SECOND!

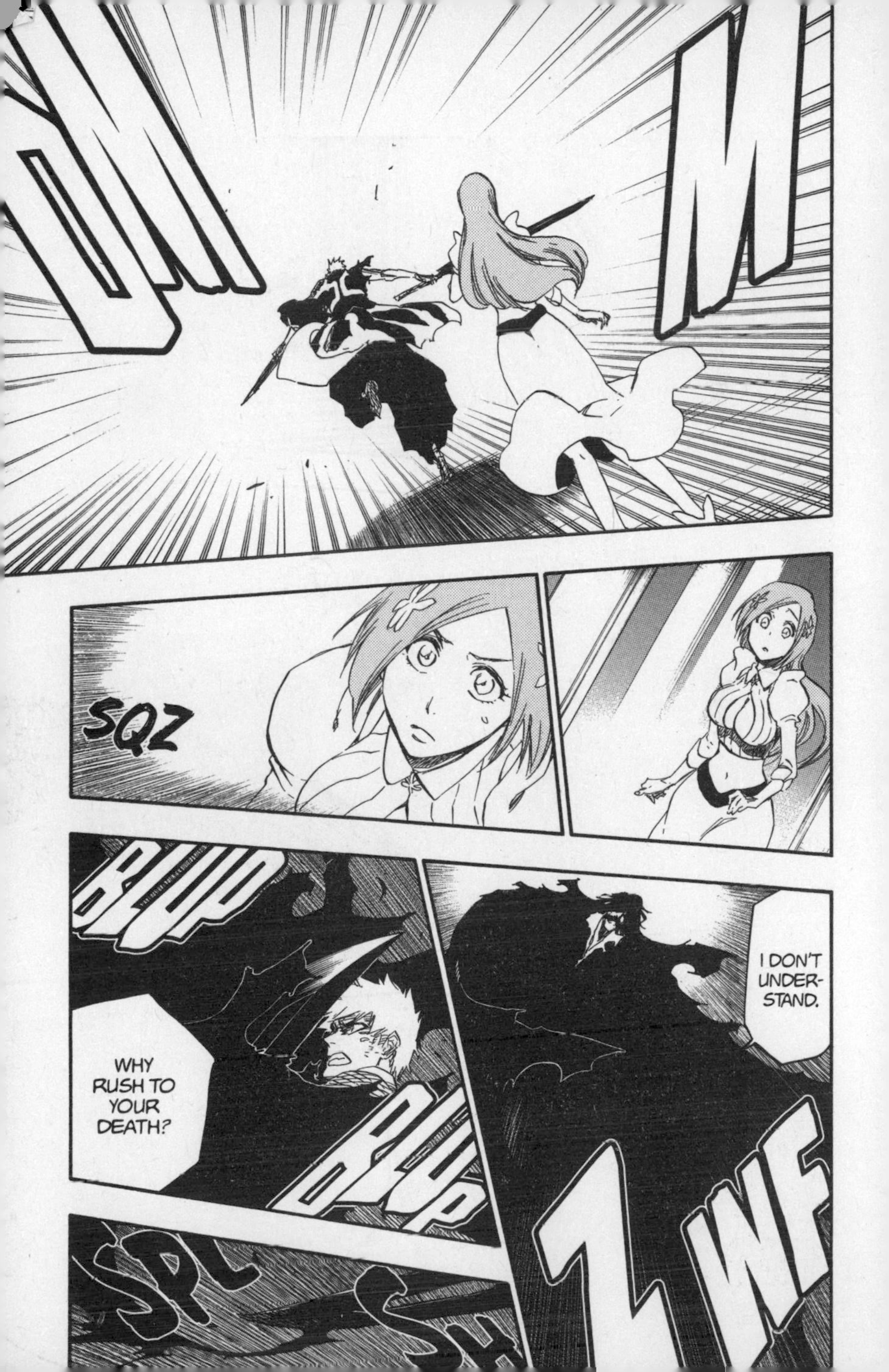
SQZ
I DON'T UNDER-STAND.
WHY RUSH TO YOUR DEATH?

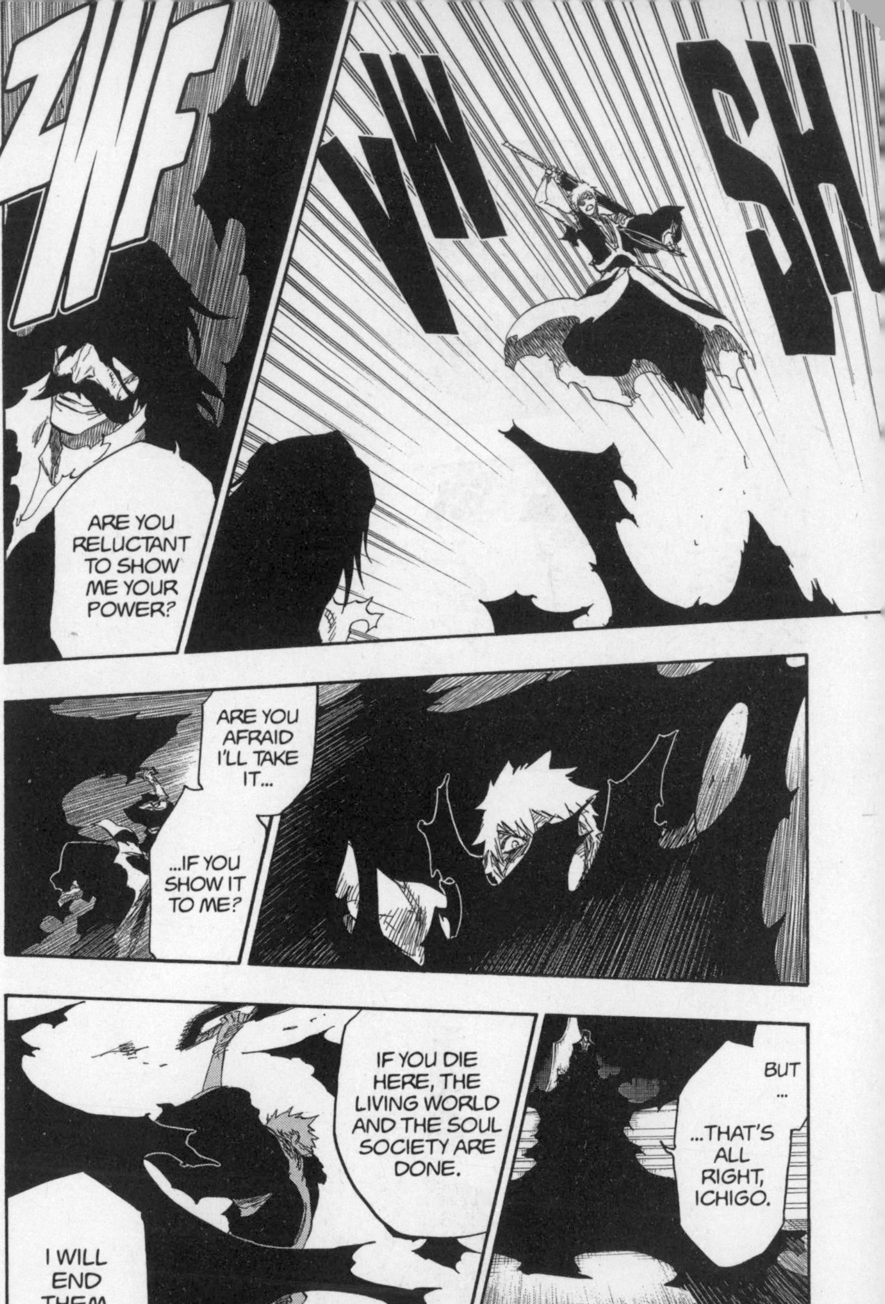
SH
ZWF
ARE YOU RELUCTANT TO SHOW ME YOUR POWER?
ARE YOU AFRAID I'LL TAKE IT...
...IF YOU SHOW IT TO ME?
BUT ...
...THAT'S ALL RIGHT, ICHIGO.
IF YOU DIE HERE, THE LIVING WORLD AND THE SOUL SOCIETY ARE DONE.
I WILL END THEM.

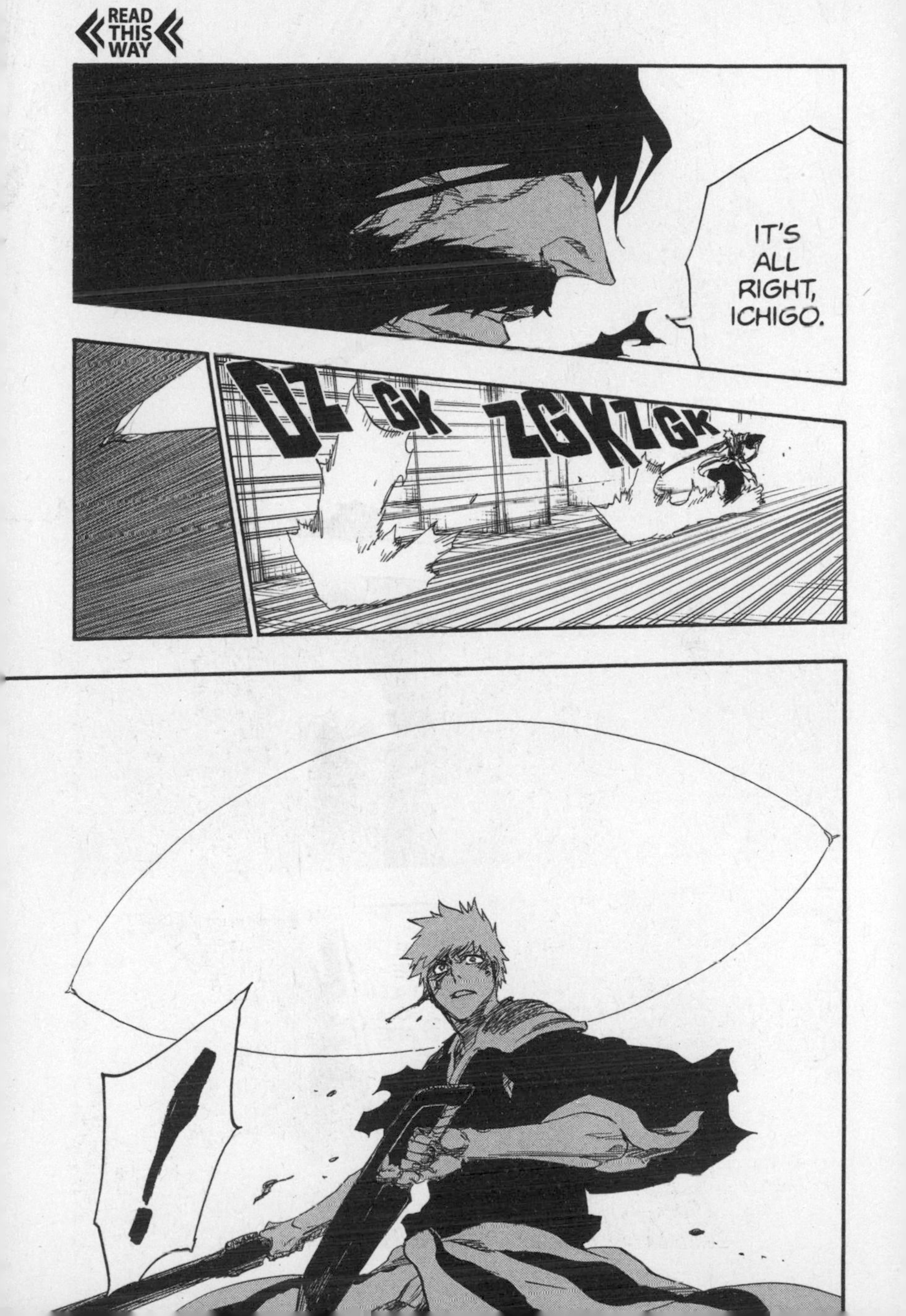
READ THIS WAY
IT'S ALL RIGHT, ICHIGO.
DZ GK ZGKZGK
!

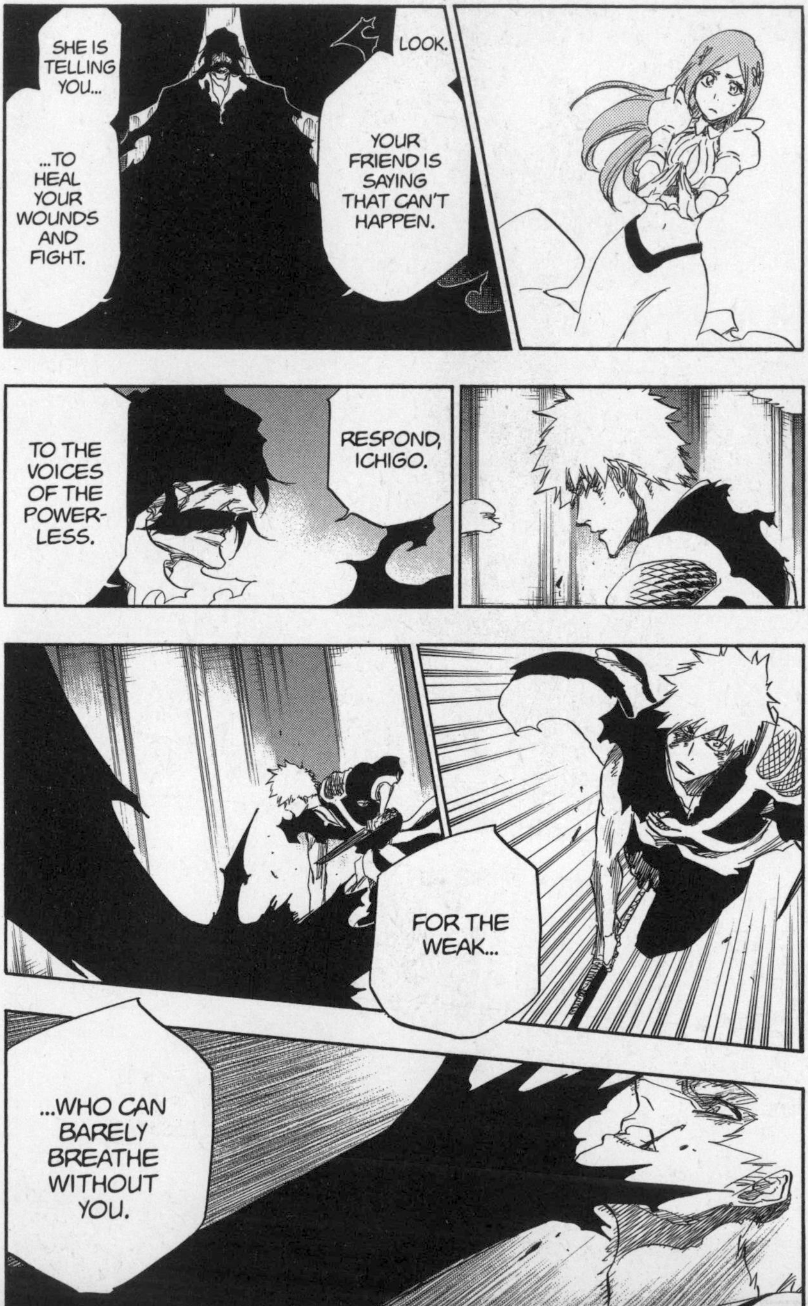
LOOK.
YOUR FRIEND IS SAYING THAT CAN'T HAPPEN.
SHE IS TELLING YOU...
...TO HEAL YOUR WOUNDS AND FIGHT.
RESPOND, ICHIGO.
TO THE VOICES OF THE POWERLESS.
FOR THE WEAK...
...WHO CAN BARELY BREATHE WITHOUT YOU.

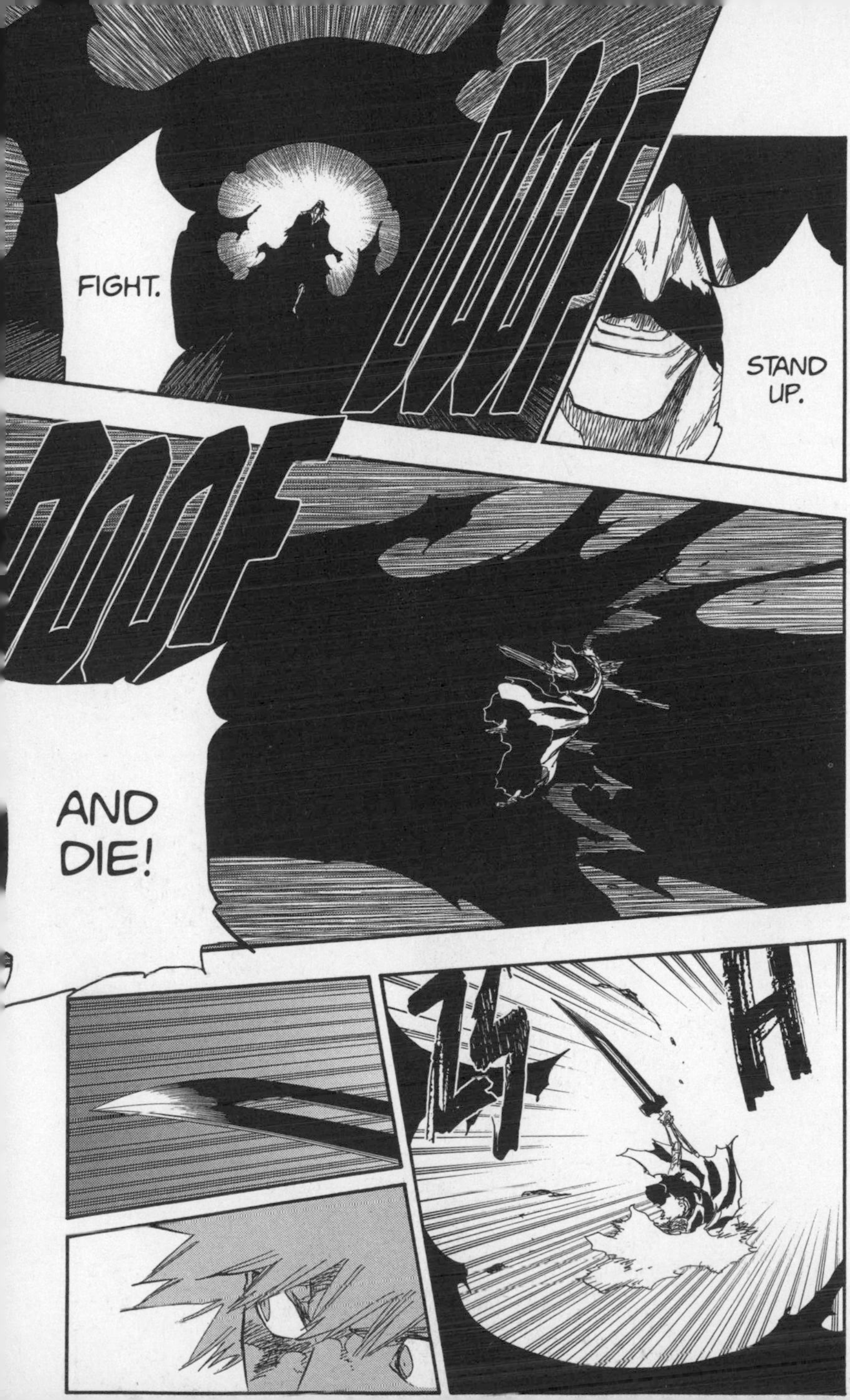
STAND UP.
FIGHT.
AND DIE!

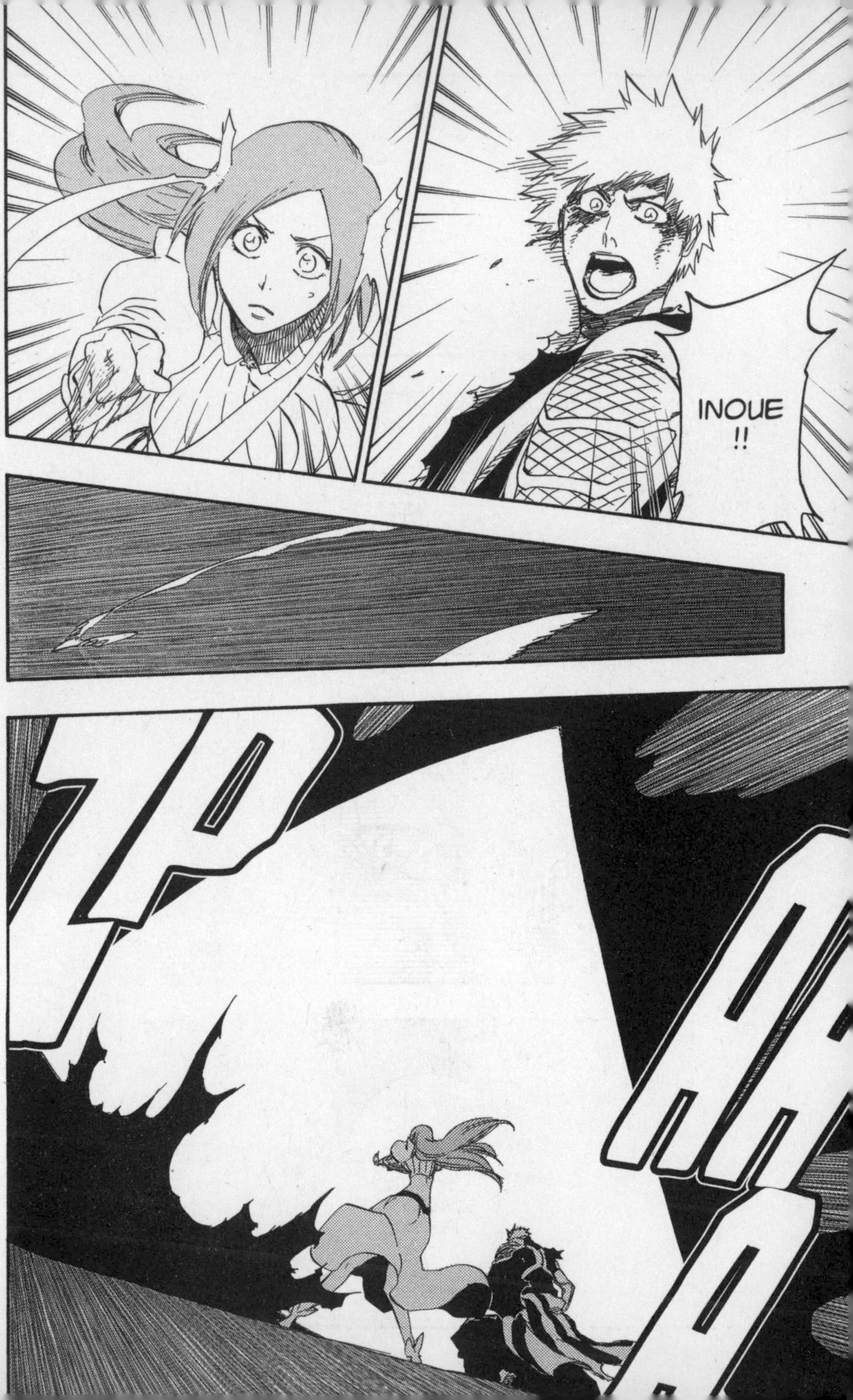
INOUE !!

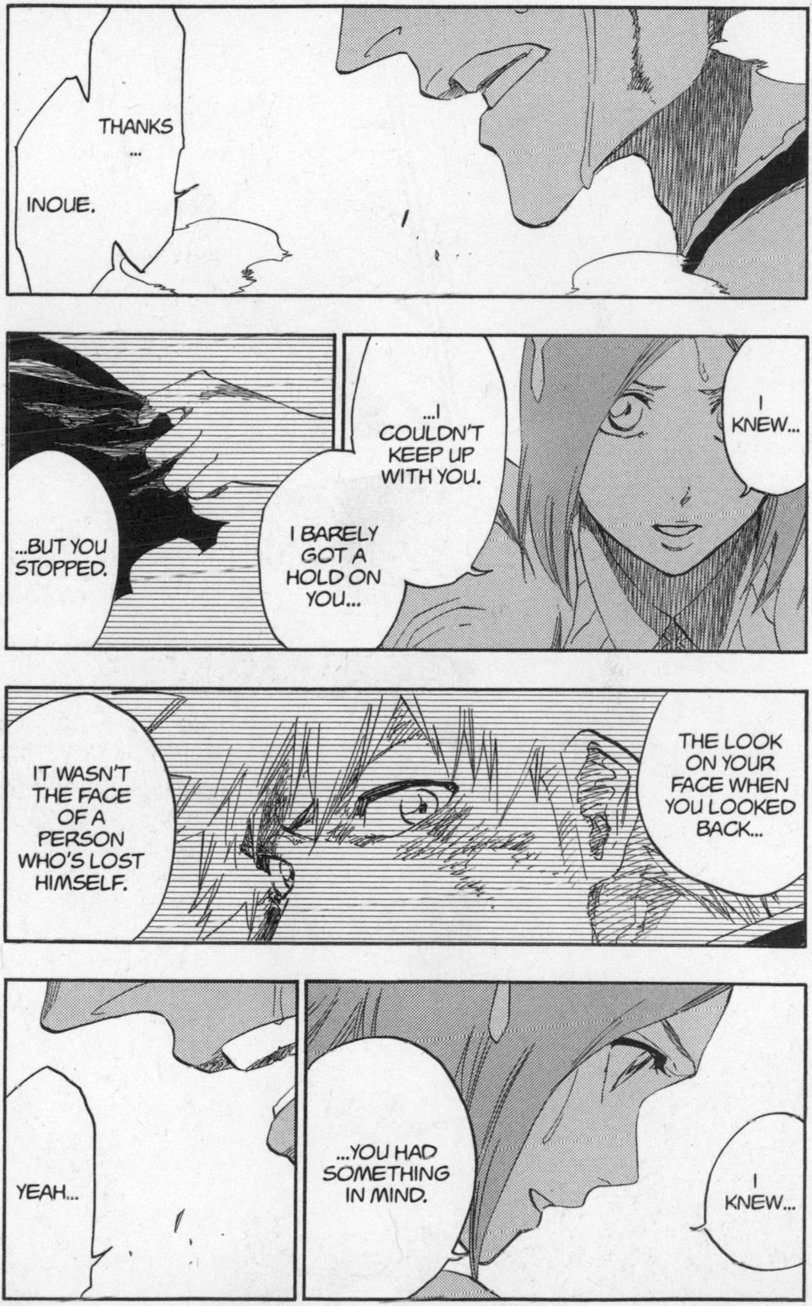
THANKS ... INOUE.
I KNEW...
...I COULDN'T KEEP UP WITH YOU.
I BARELY GOT A HOLD ON YOU...
...BUT YOU STOPPED.
THE LOOK ON YOUR FACE WHEN YOU LOOKED BACK...
IT WASN'T THE FACE OF A PERSON WHO'S LOST HIMSELF.
I KNEW...
...YOU HAD SOMETHING IN MIND.
YEAH...

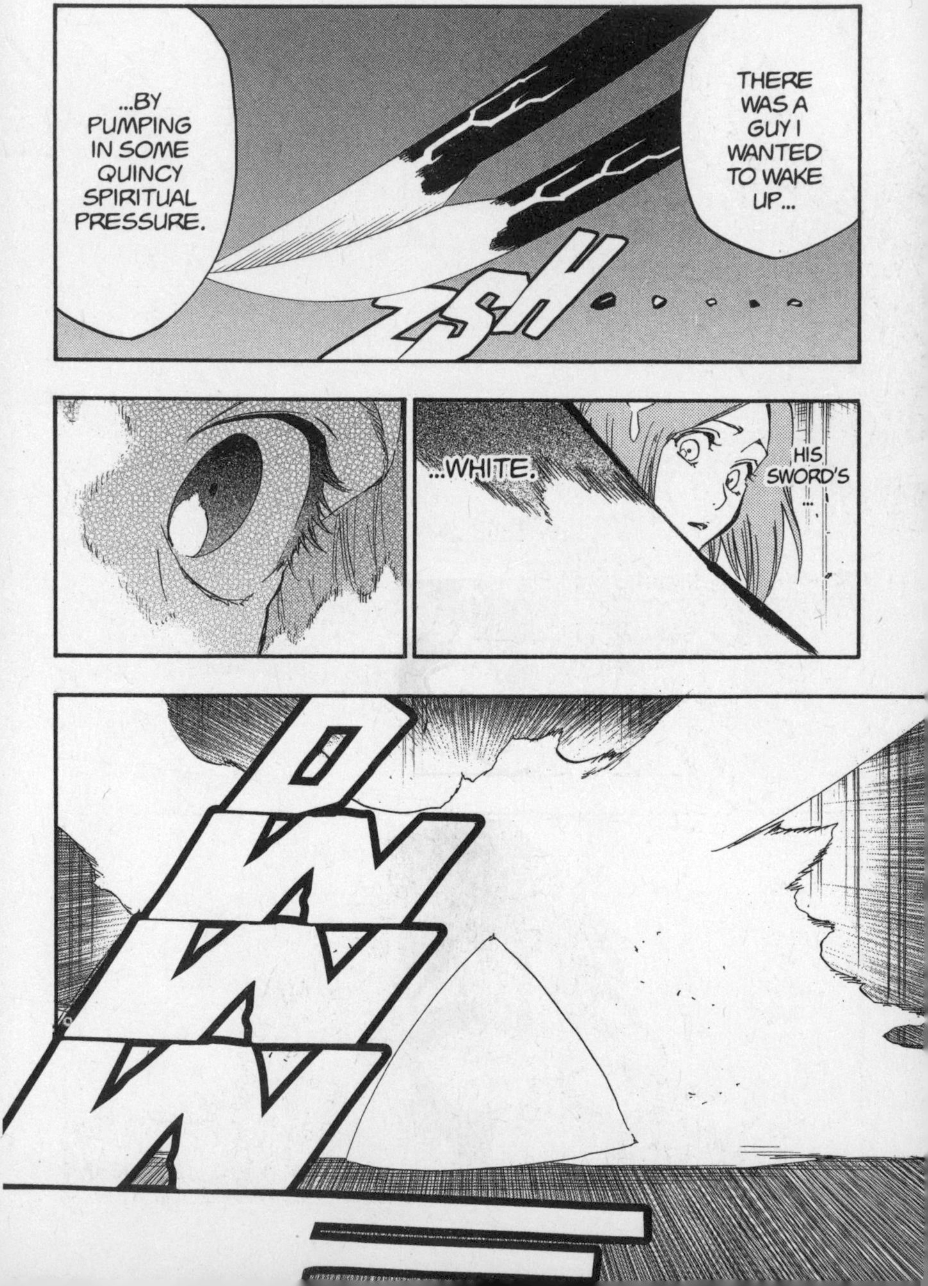
THERE WAS A GUY I WANTED TO WAKE UP...
...BY PUMPING IN SOME QUINCY SPIRITUAL PRESSURE.
ZSH
HIS SWORD'S...
...WHITE.

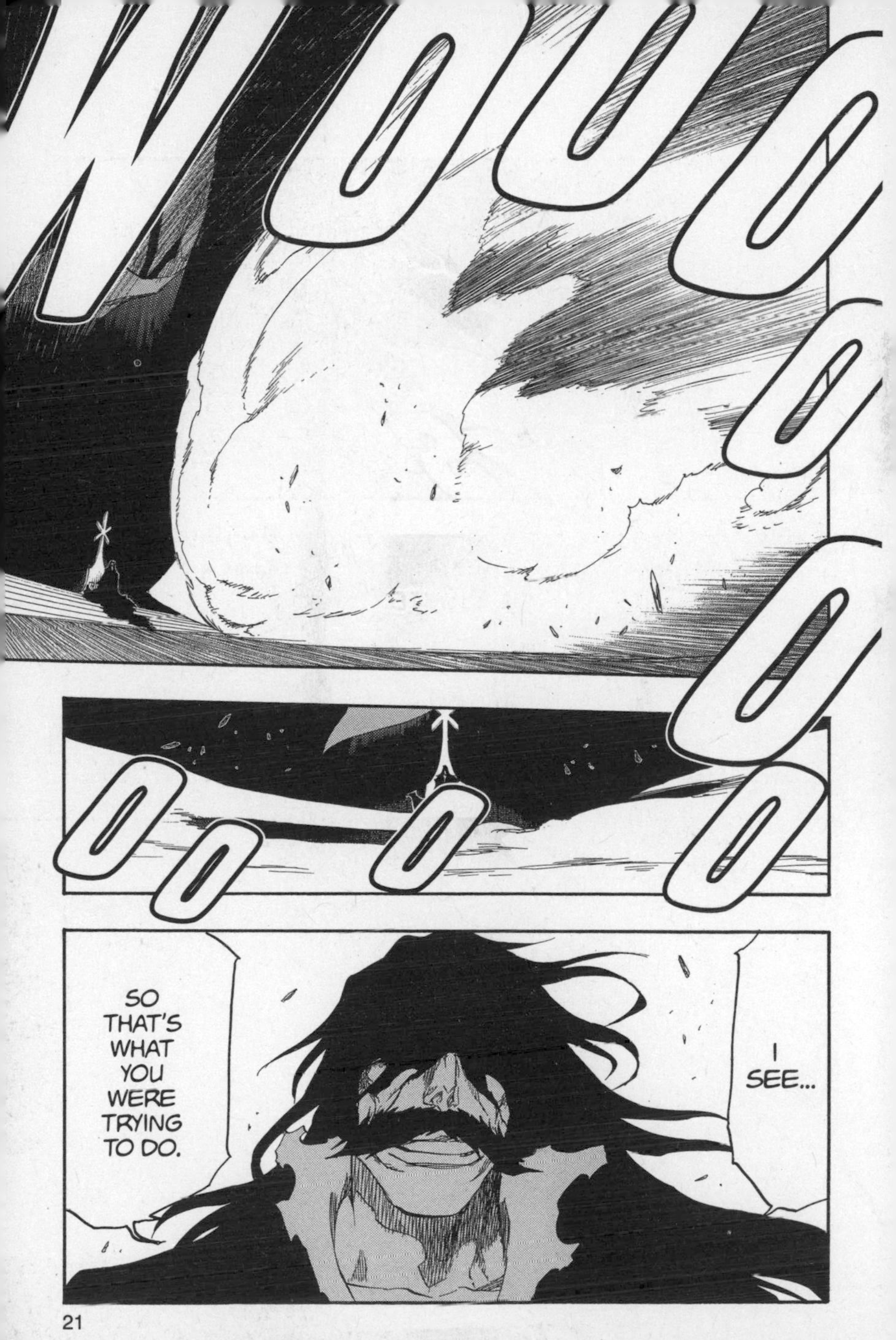
I SEE...
SO THAT'S WHAT YOU WERE TRYING TO DO.

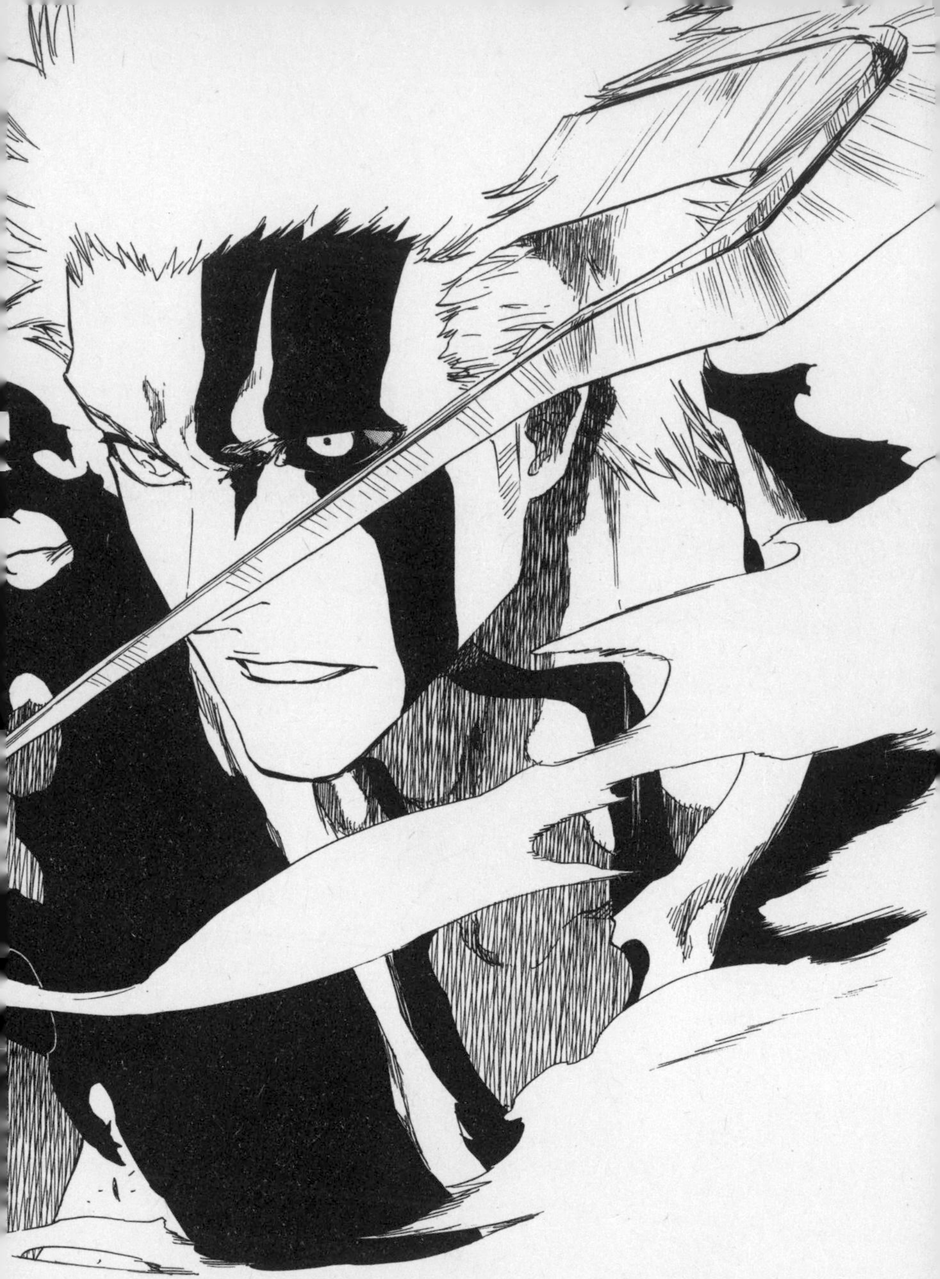

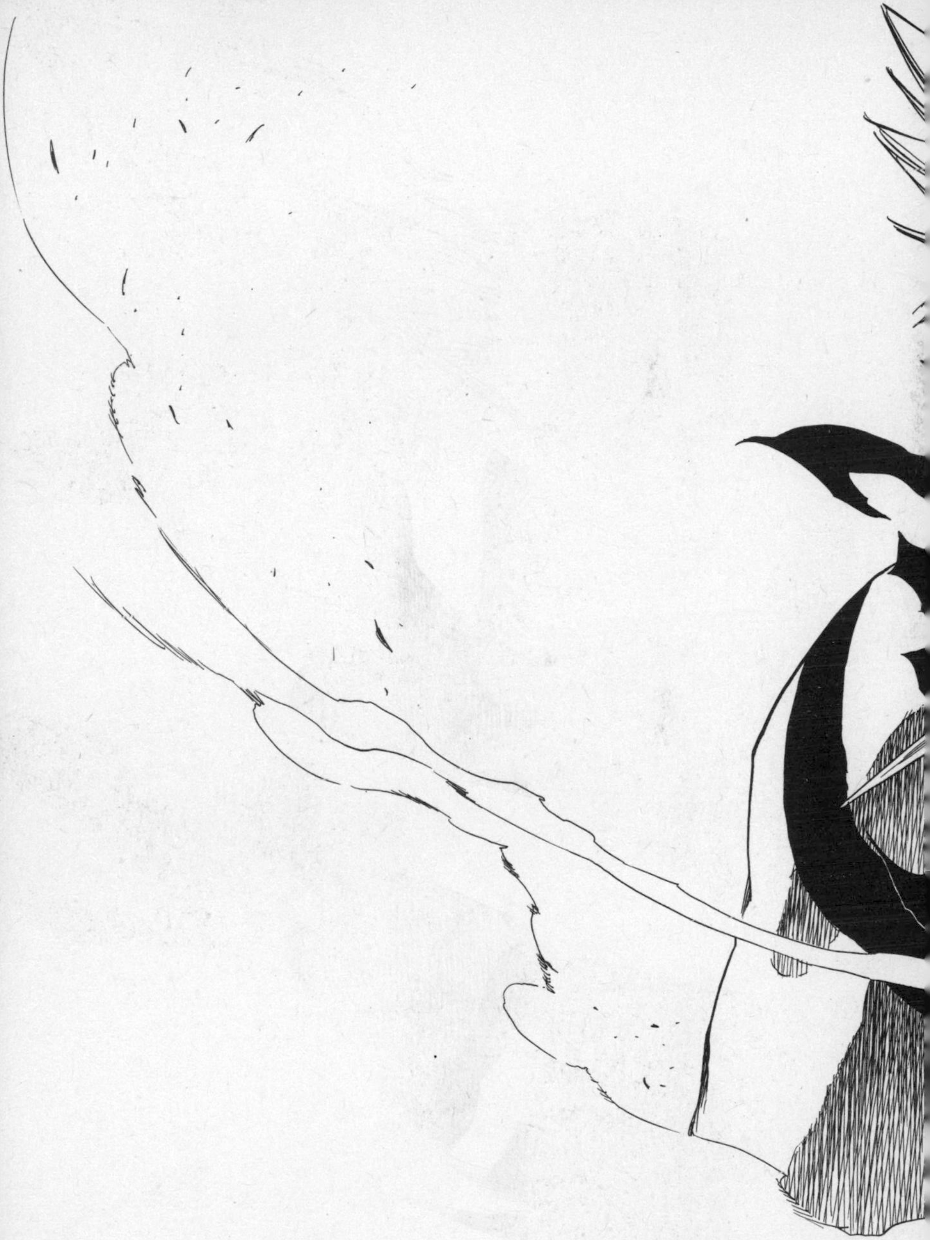

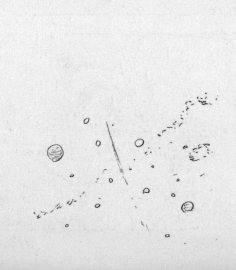

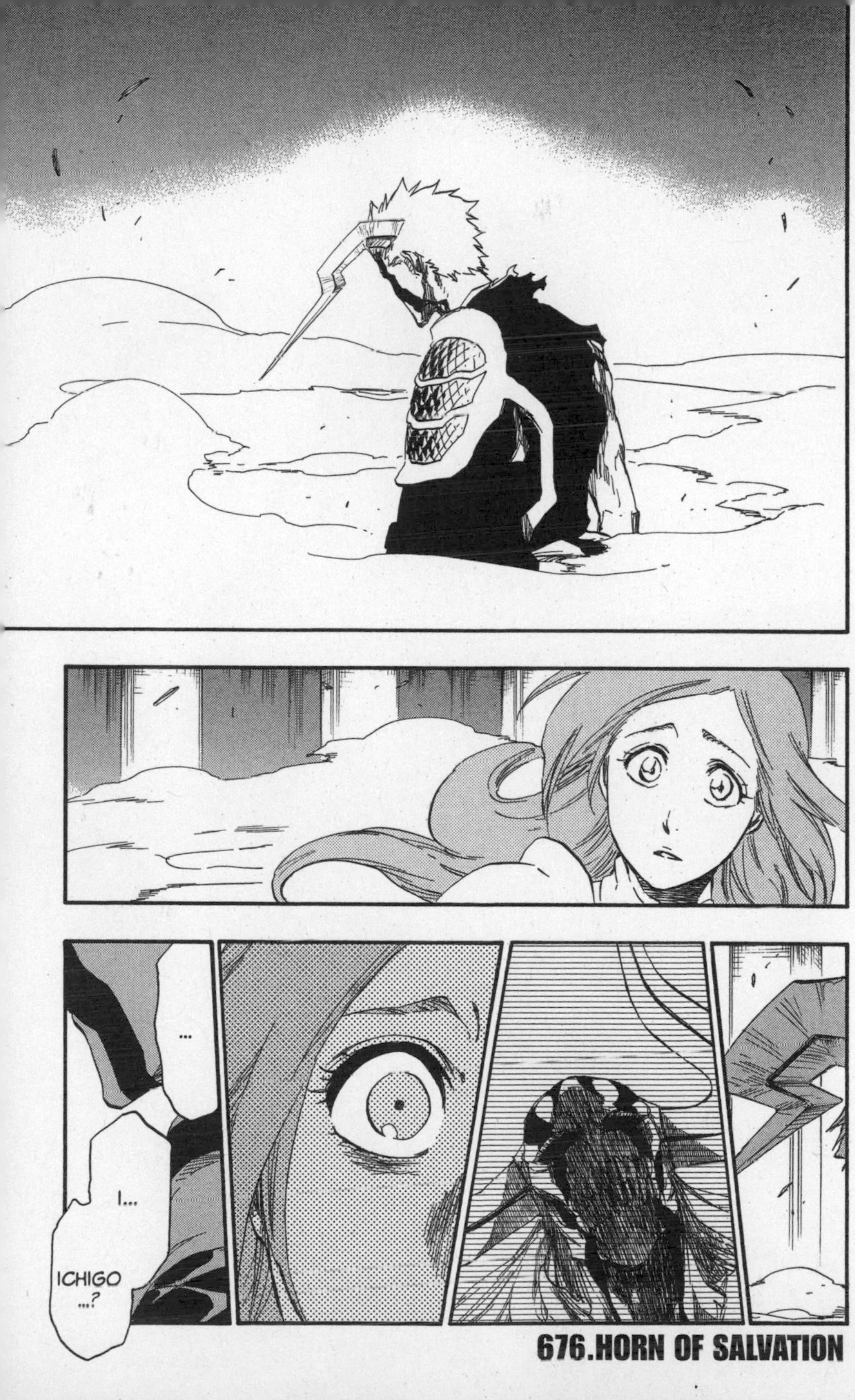
...
I...
ICHIGO ...?

676.HORN OF SALVATION

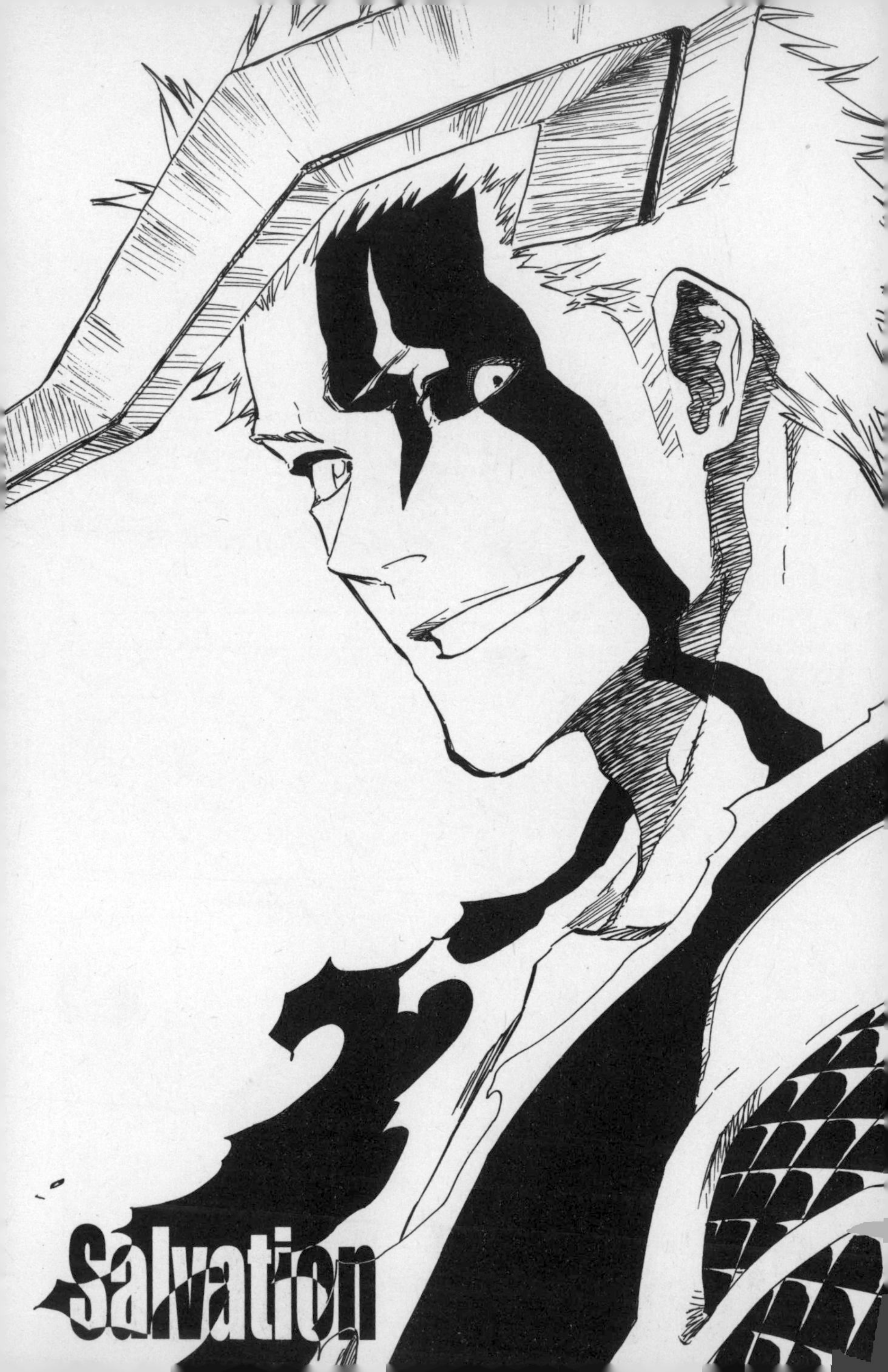
Salvation

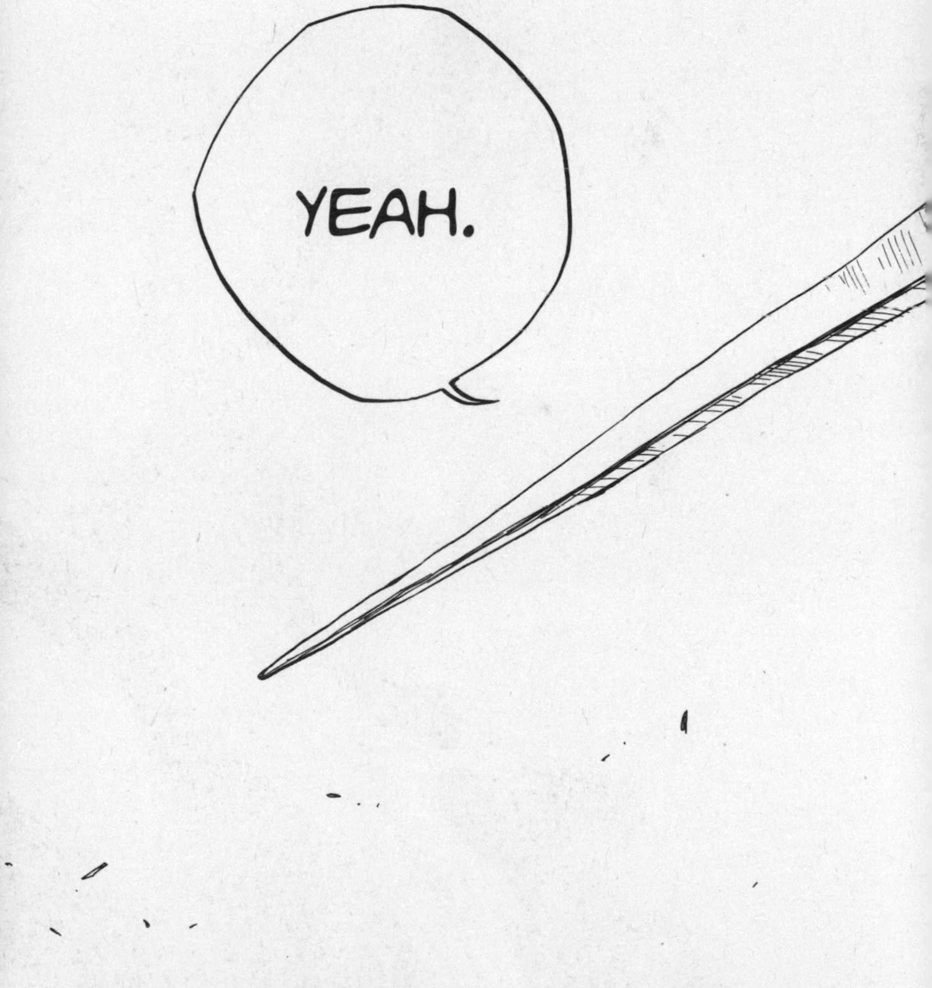
YEAH.

BLEACH 676. Horn of

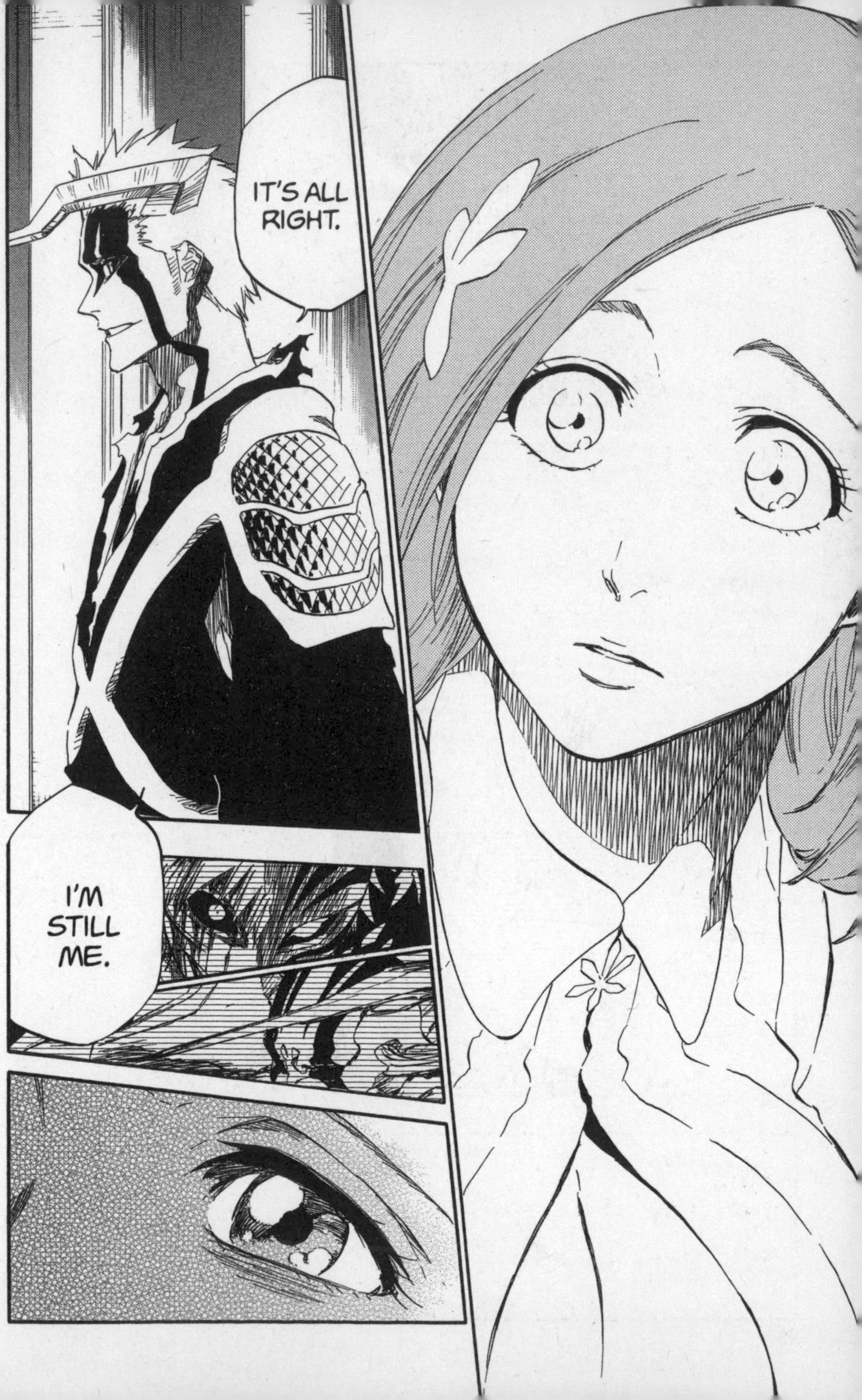
IT'S ALL RIGHT.
I'M STILL ME.

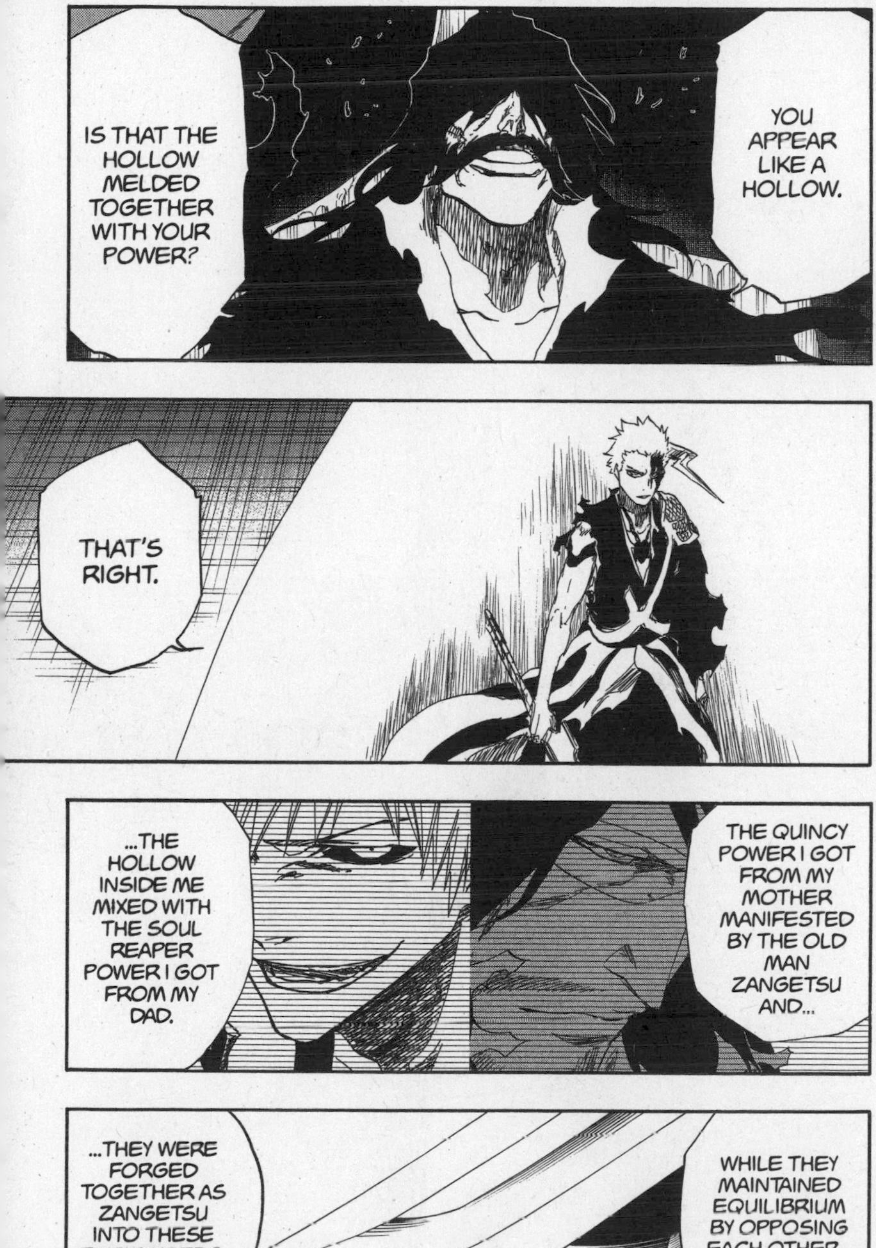
YOU APPEAR LIKE A HOLLOW.
IS THAT THE HOLLOW MELDED TOGETHER WITH YOUR POWER?
THAT'S RIGHT.
THE QUINCY POWER I GOT FROM MY MOTHER MANIFESTED BY THE OLD MAN ZANGETSU AND...
...THE HOLLOW INSIDE ME MIXED WITH THE SOUL REAPER POWER I GOT FROM MY DAD.
WHILE THEY MAINTAINED EQUILIBRIUM BY OPPOSING EACH OTHER...
...THEY WERE FORGED TOGETHER AS ZANGETSU INTO THESE TWO SWORDS.

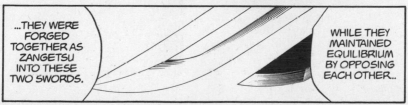

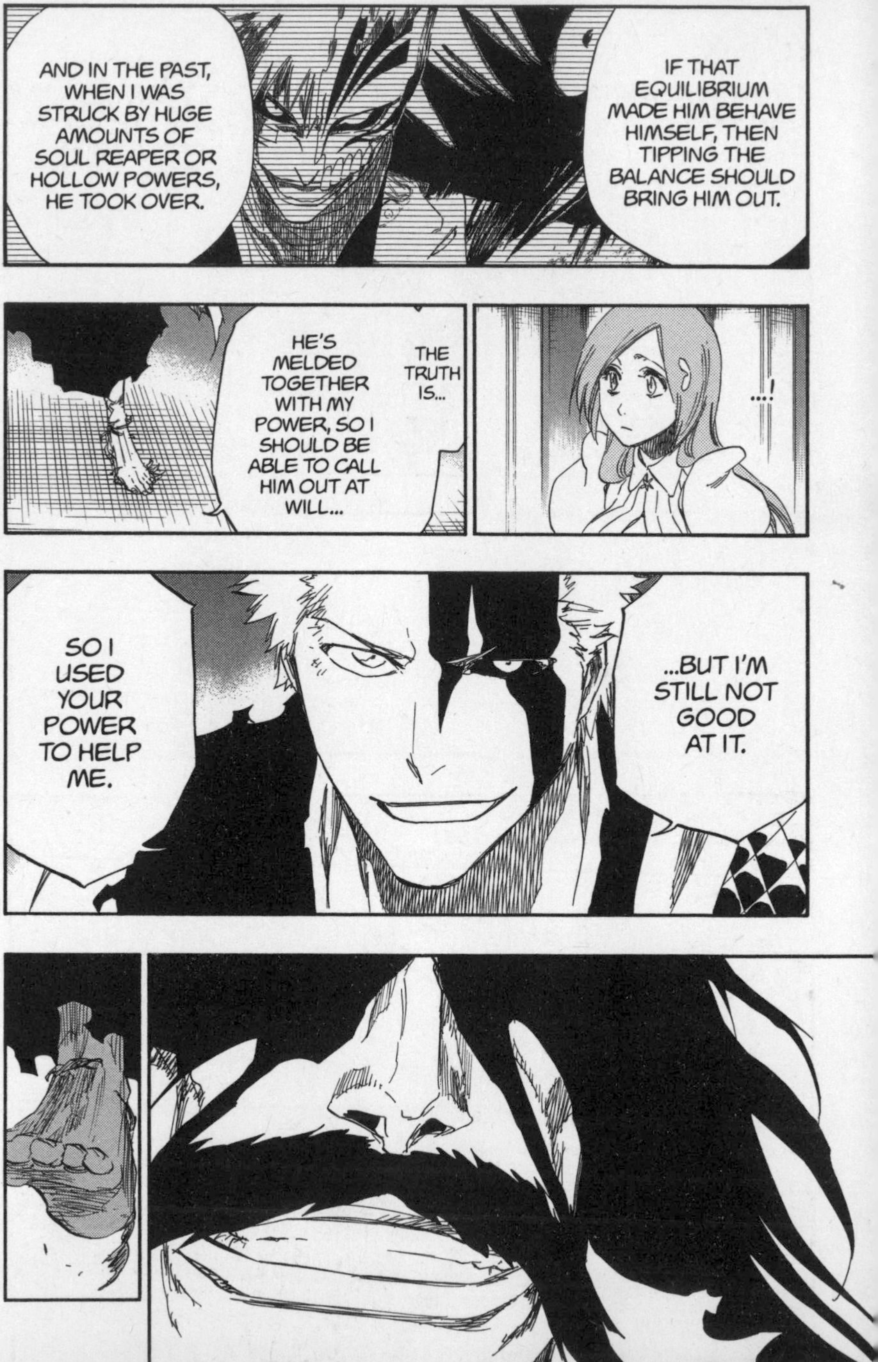
IF THAT EQUILIBRIUM MADE HIM BEHAVE HIMSELF, THEN TIPPING THE BALANCE SHOULD BRING HIM OUT.
AND IN THE PAST, WHEN I WAS STRUCK BY HUGE AMOUNTS OF SOUL REAPER OR HOLLOW POWERS, HE TOOK OVER.
...!
THE TRUTH IS...
HE'S MELDED TOGETHER WITH MY POWER, SO I SHOULD BE ABLE TO CALL HIM OUT AT WILL...
...BUT I'M STILL NOT GOOD AT IT.
SO I USED YOUR POWER TO HELP ME.

READ THIS WAY

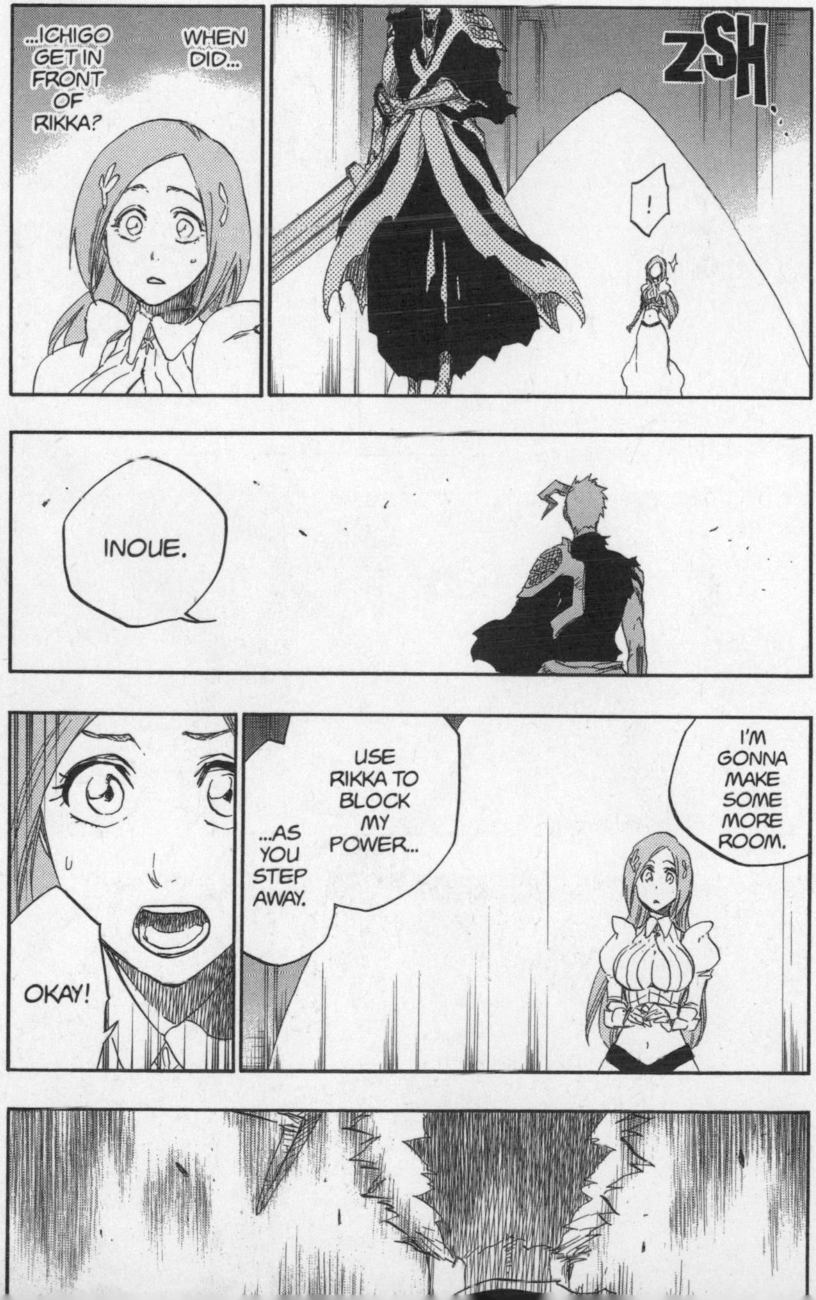
ZSH
!
WHEN DID...
...ICHIGO GET IN FRONT OF RIKKA?
INOUE.
I'M GONNA MAKE SOME MORE ROOM.
USE RIKKA TO BLOCK MY POWER...
...AS YOU STEP AWAY.
OKAY!

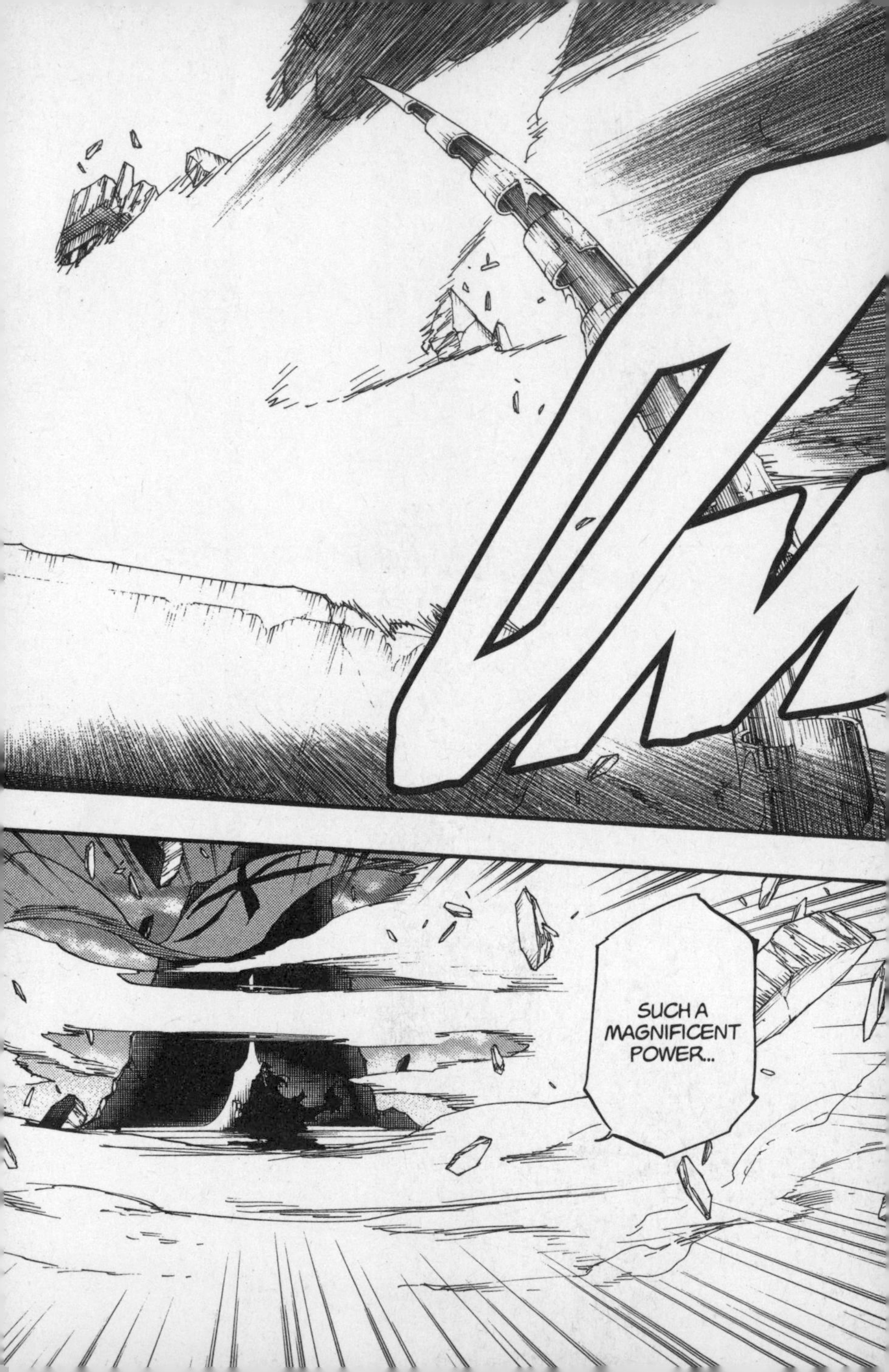
SUCH A MAGNIFICENT POWER...

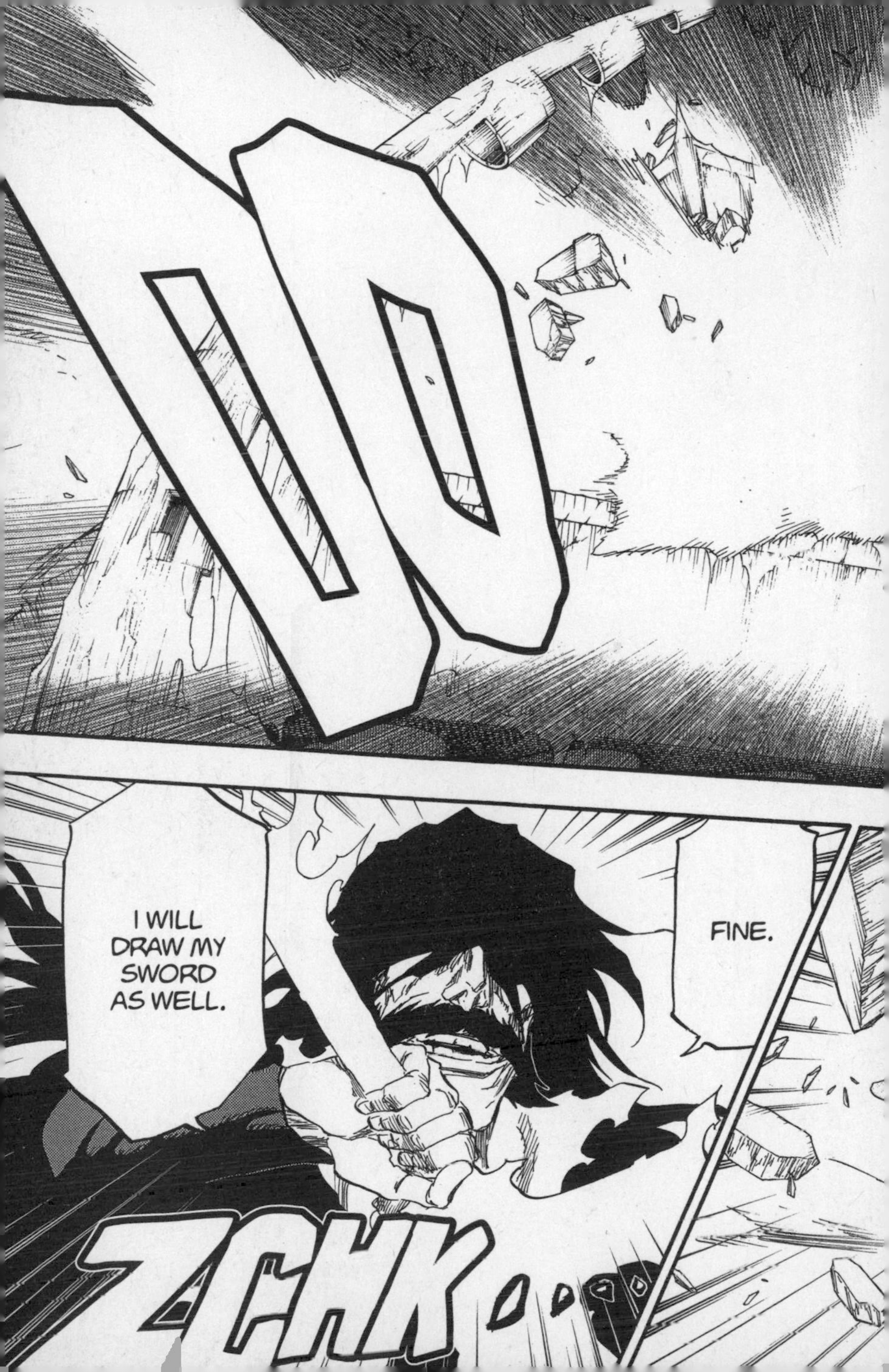
FINE.
I WILL DRAW MY SWORD AS WELL.
ZCHK..

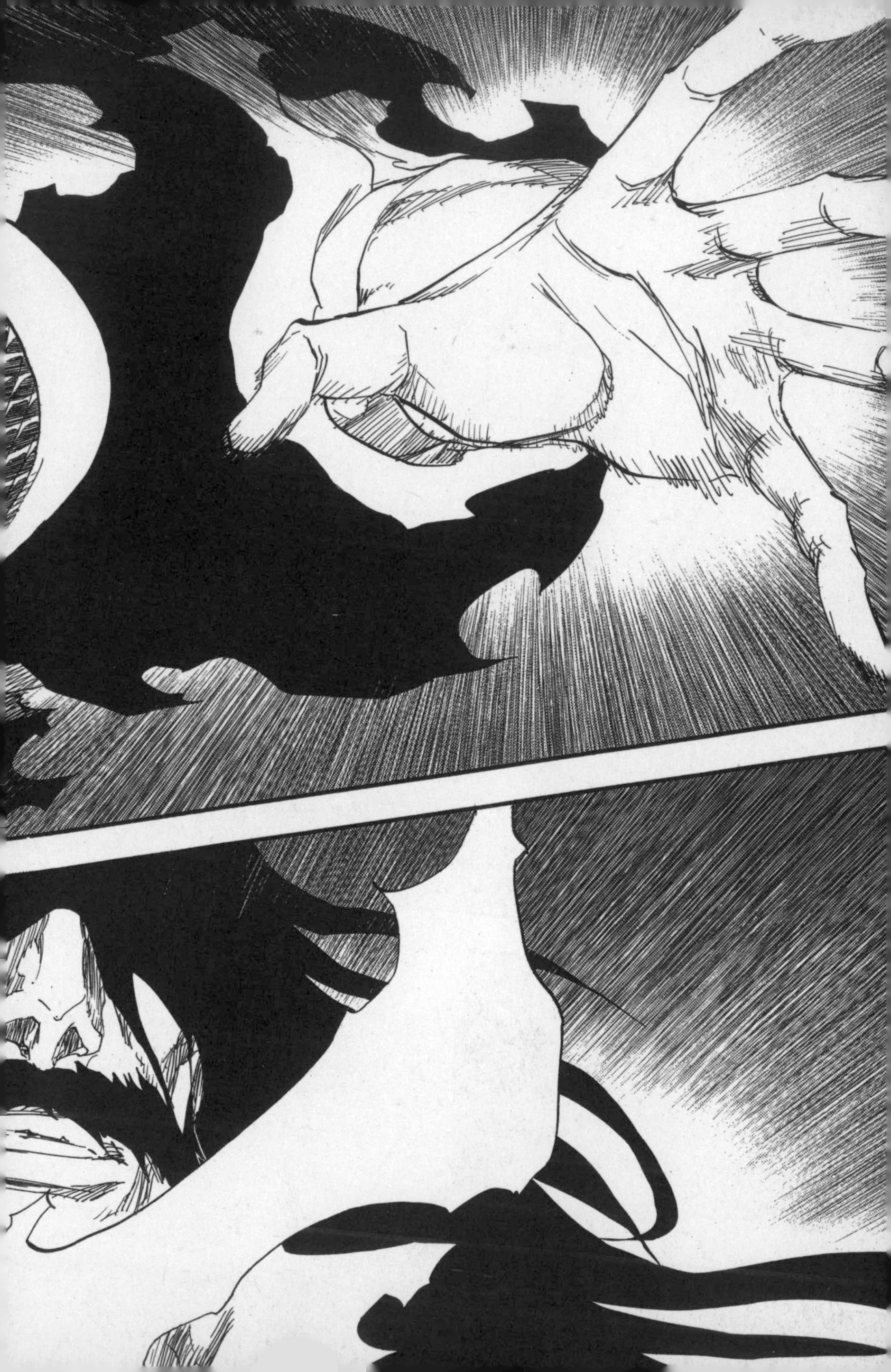

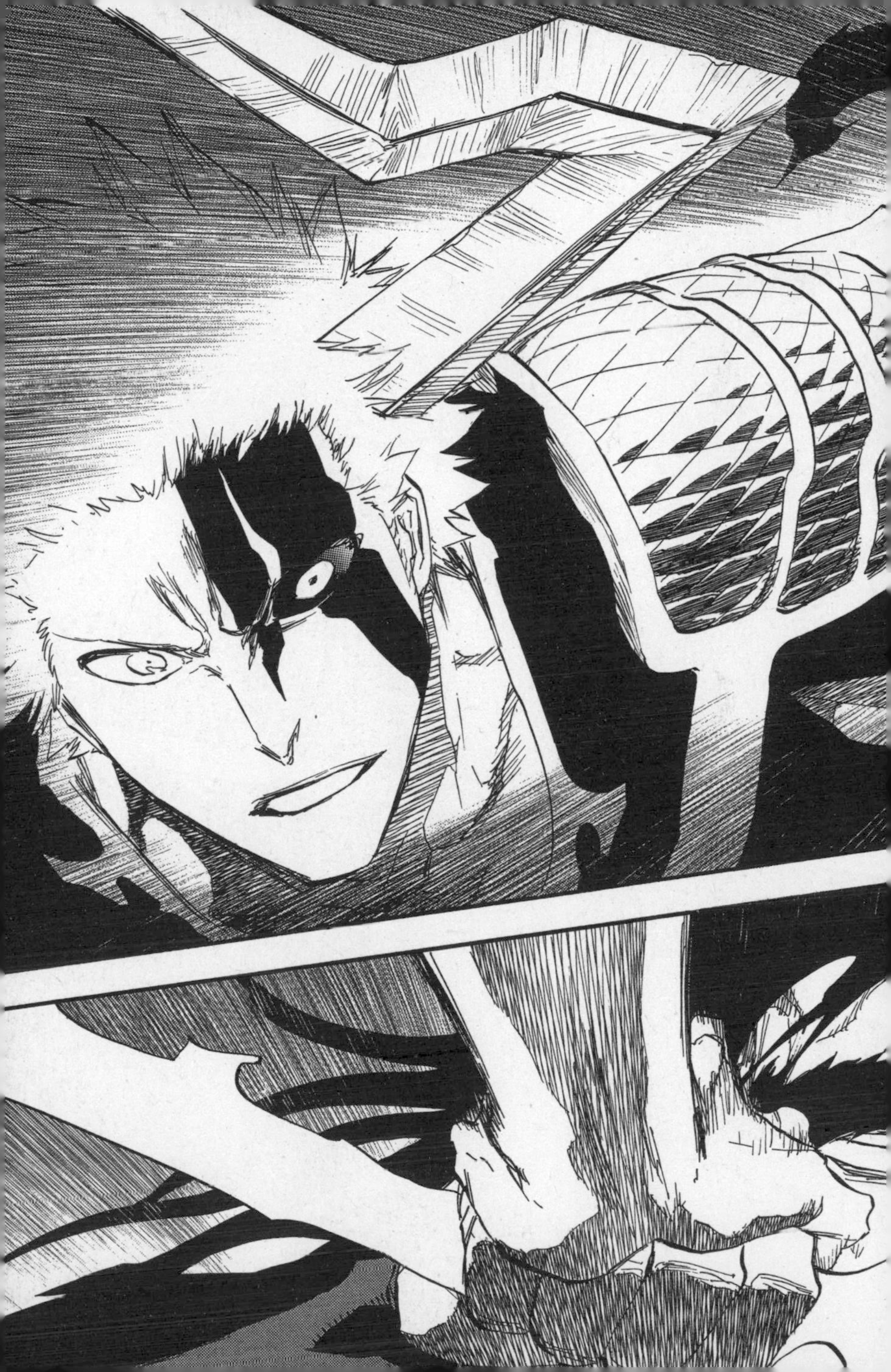

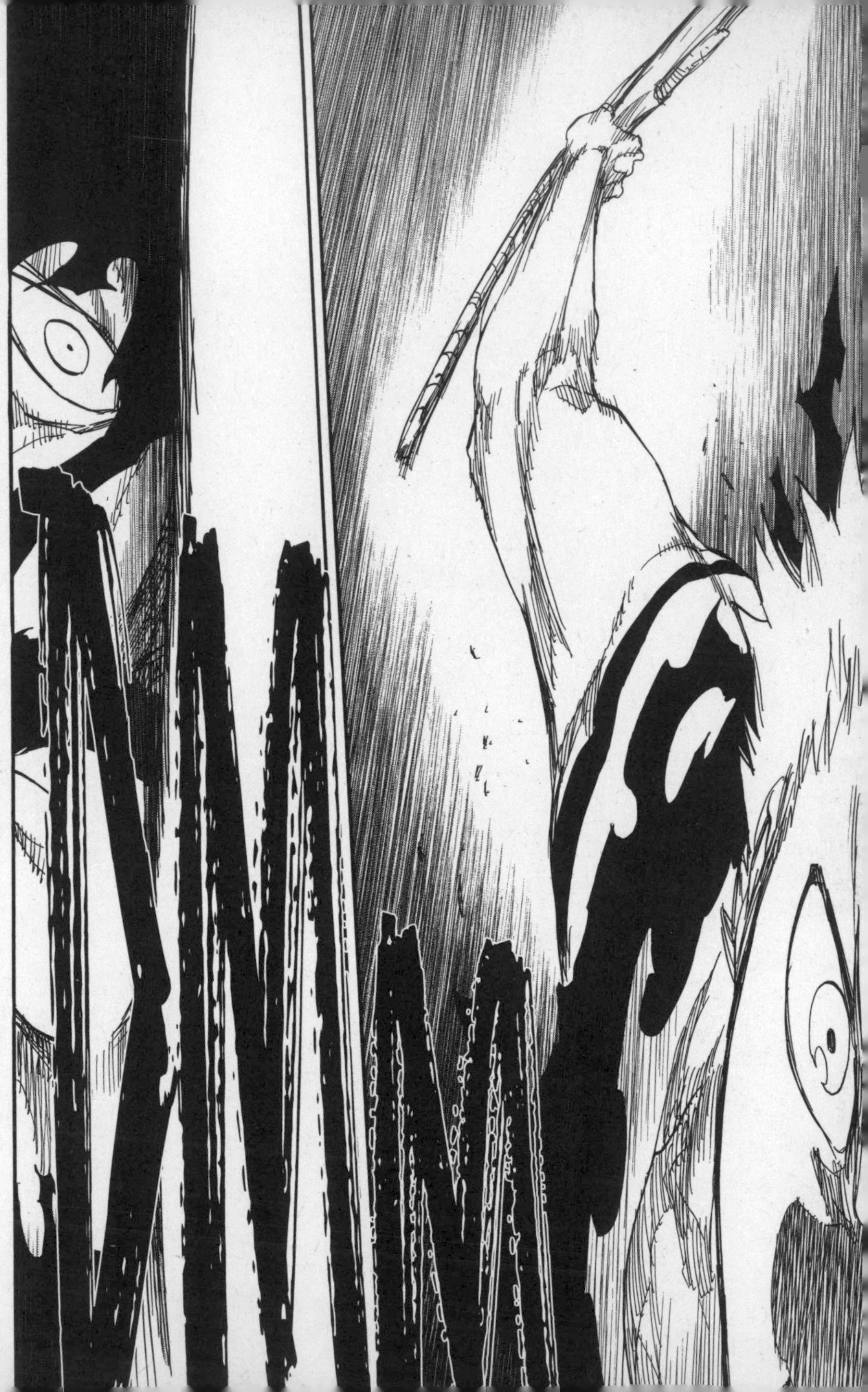

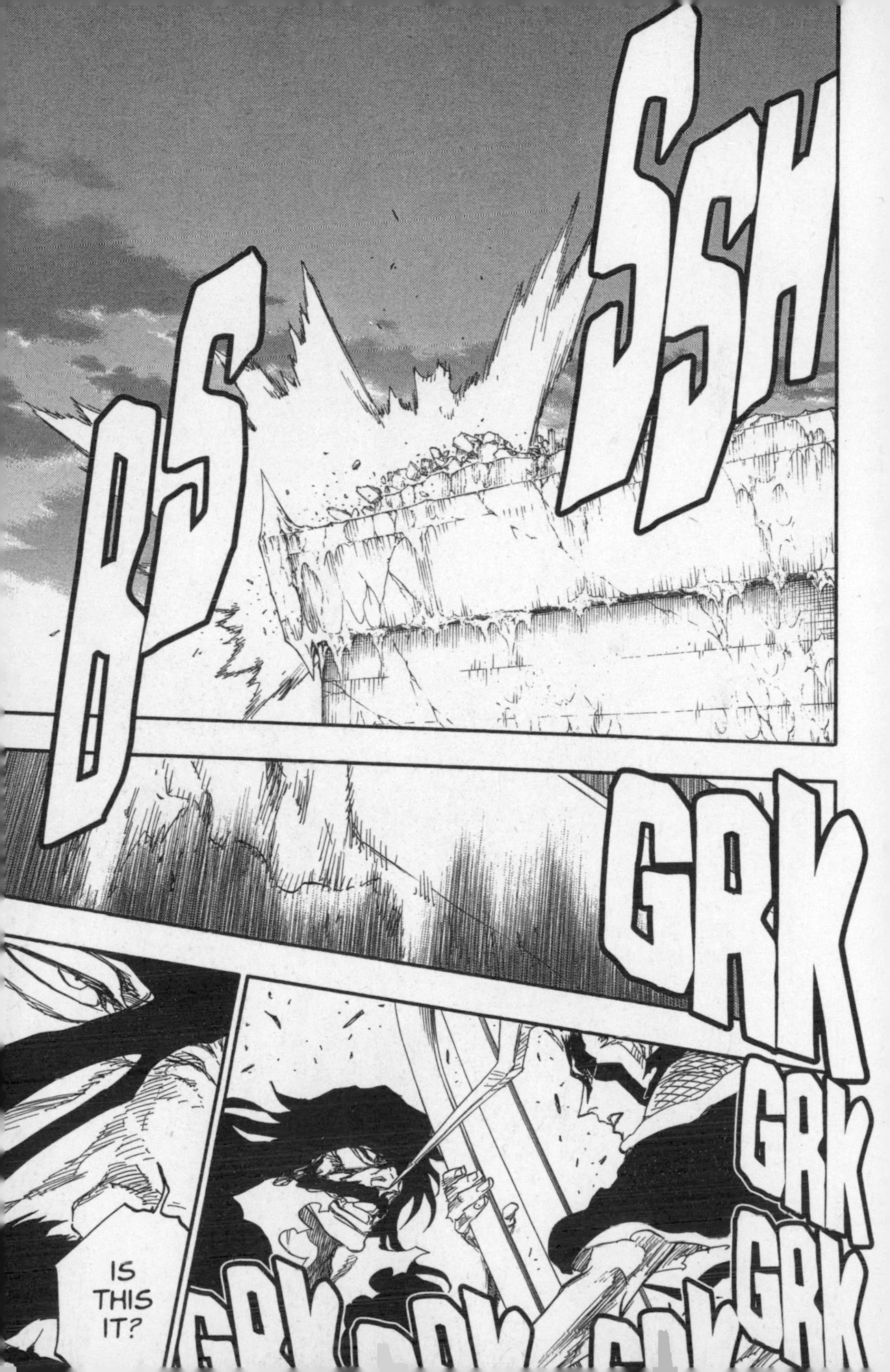
SSH
BS
GRK
GRK
GRK
IS THIS IT?

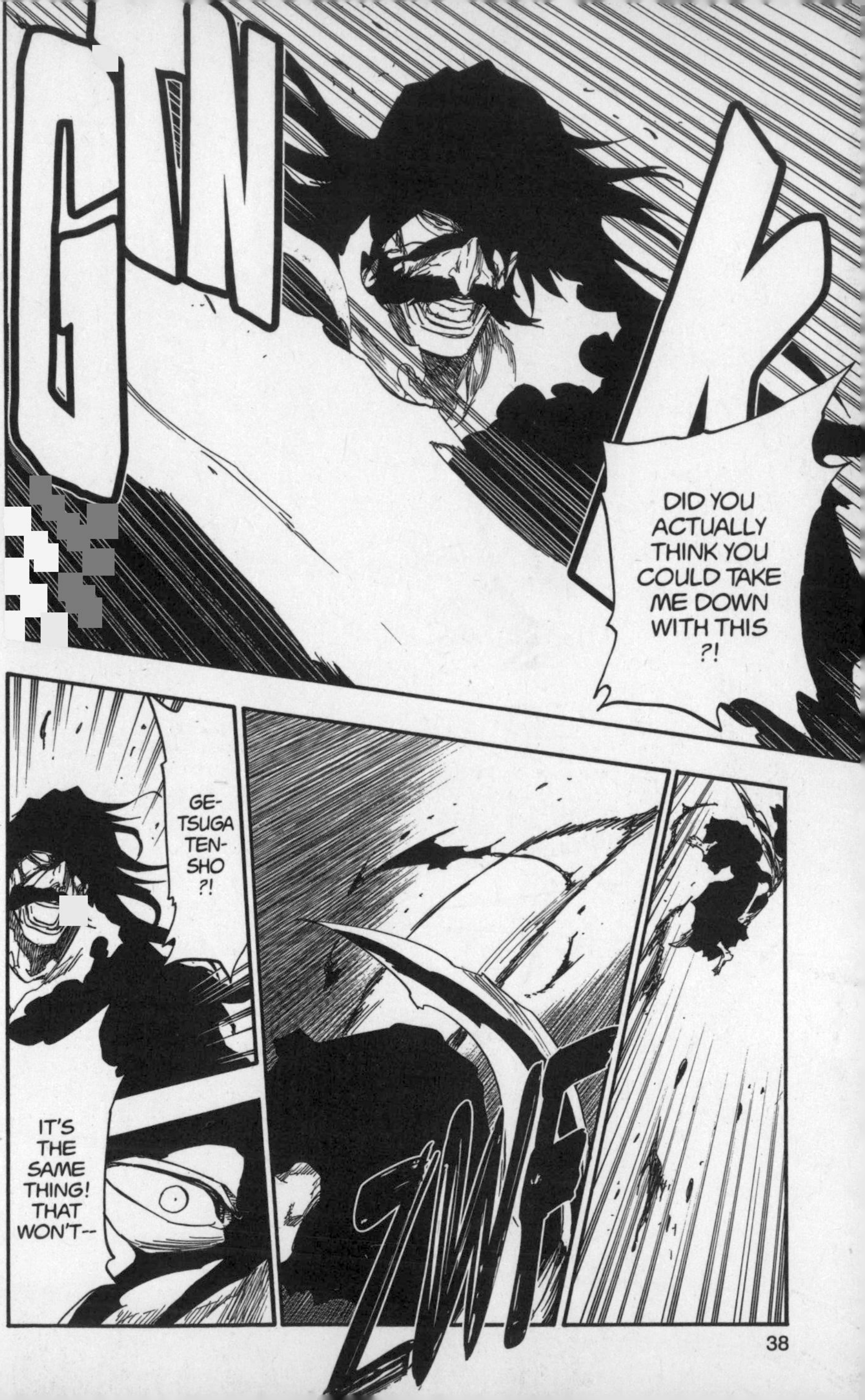
DID YOU ACTUALLY THINK YOU COULD TAKE ME DOWN WITH THIS ?!
GE-TSUGA TEN-SHO ?!
IT'S THE SAME THING! THAT WON'T--

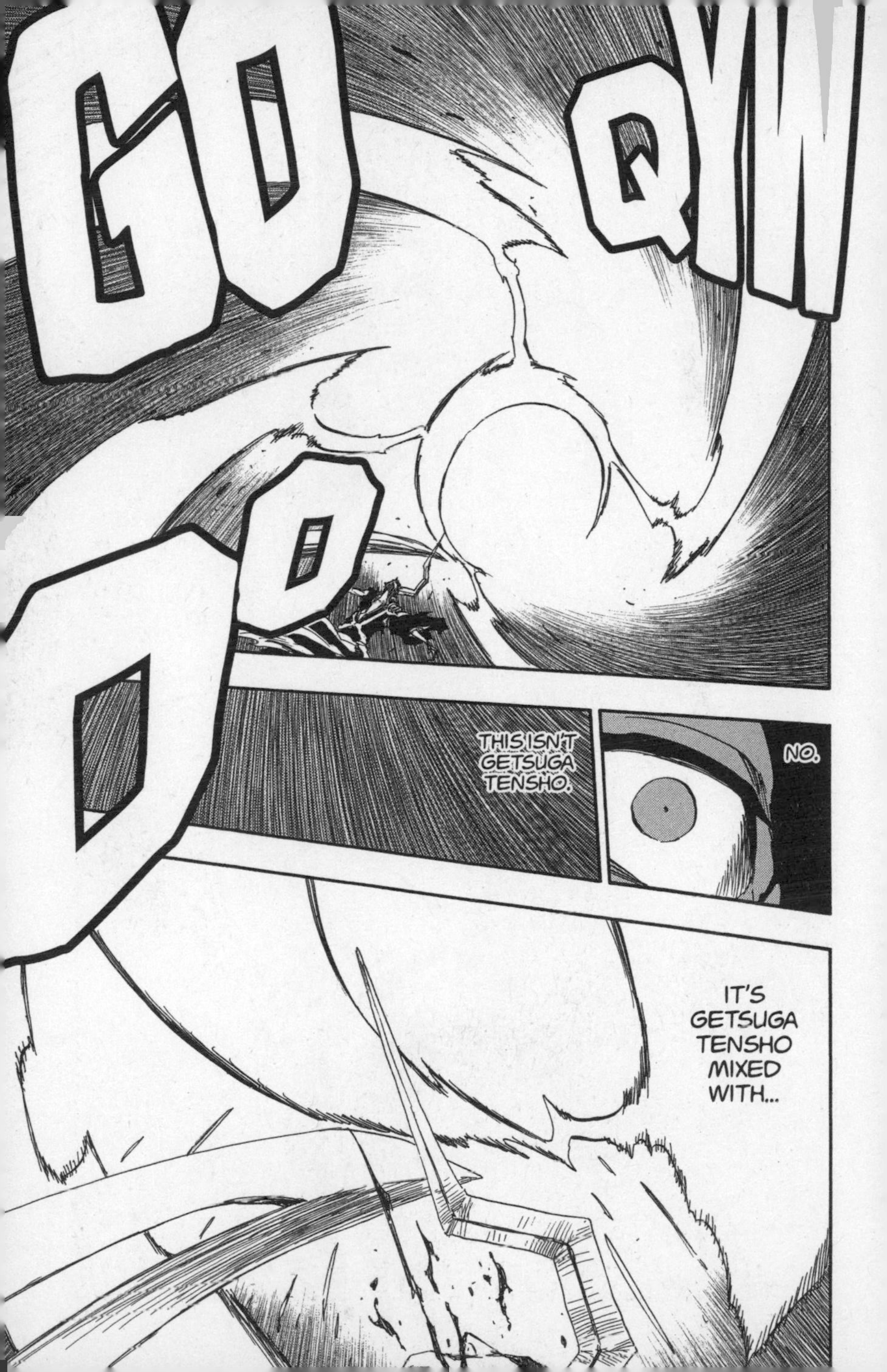
NO.
THIS ISN'T GETSUGA TENSHO.
IT'S GETSUGA TENSHO MIXED WITH...

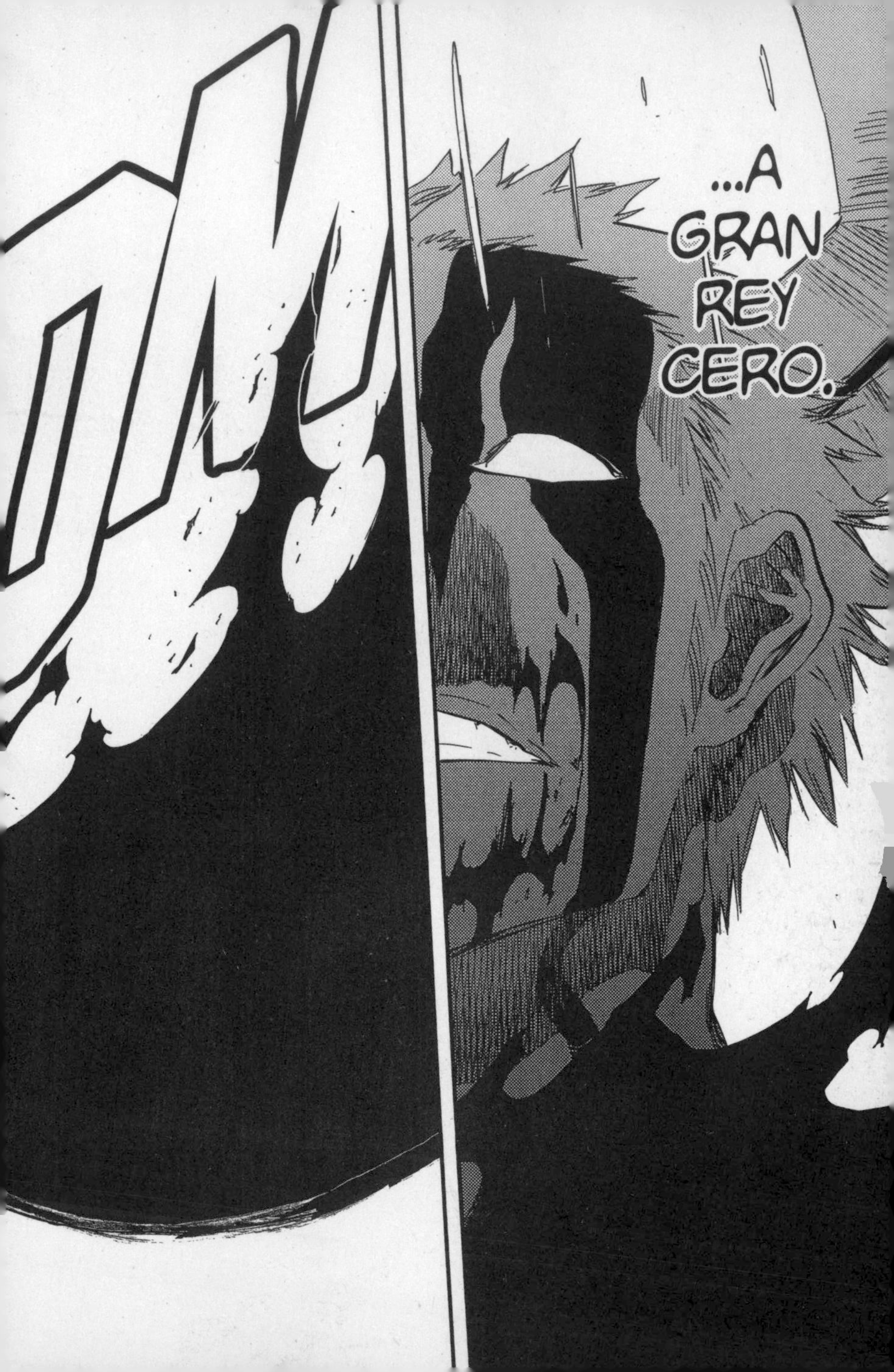
...A GRAN REY CERO.

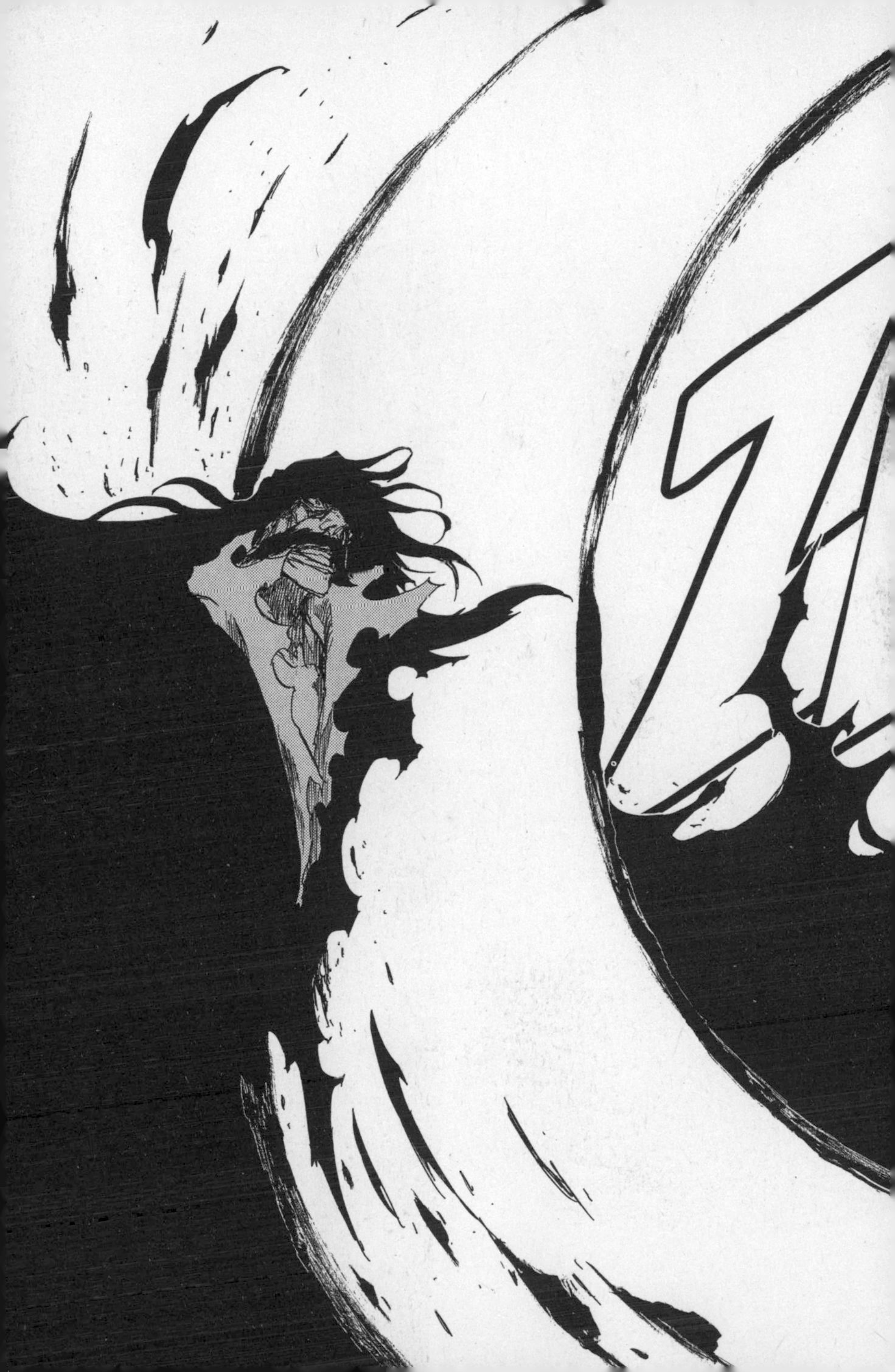

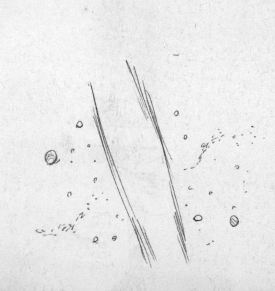

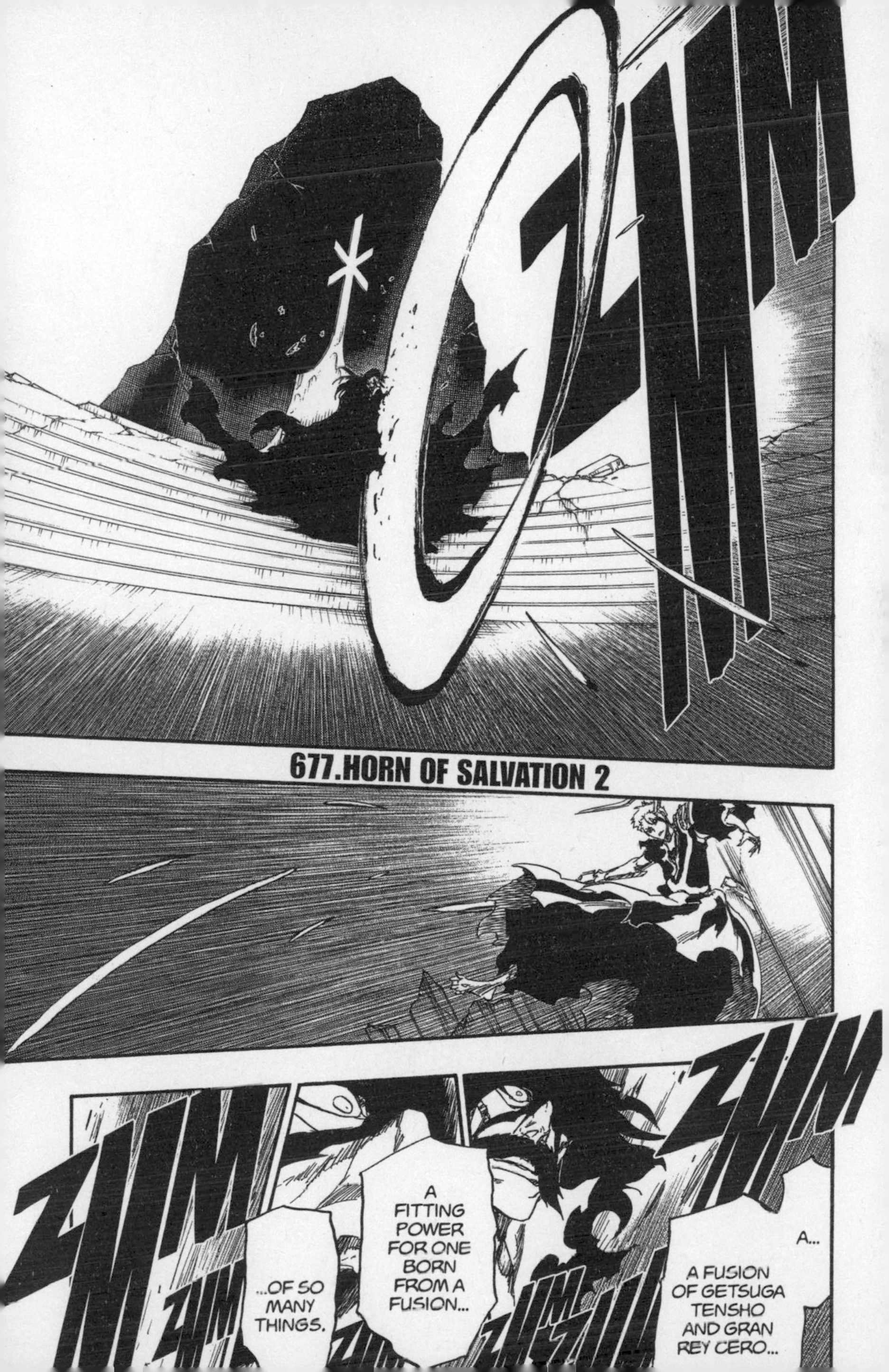
677.HORN OF SALVATION 2
A...
A FUSION OF GETSUGA TENSHO AND GRAN REY CERO...
A FITTING POWER FOR ONE BORN FROM A FUSION...
...OF SO MANY THINGS.

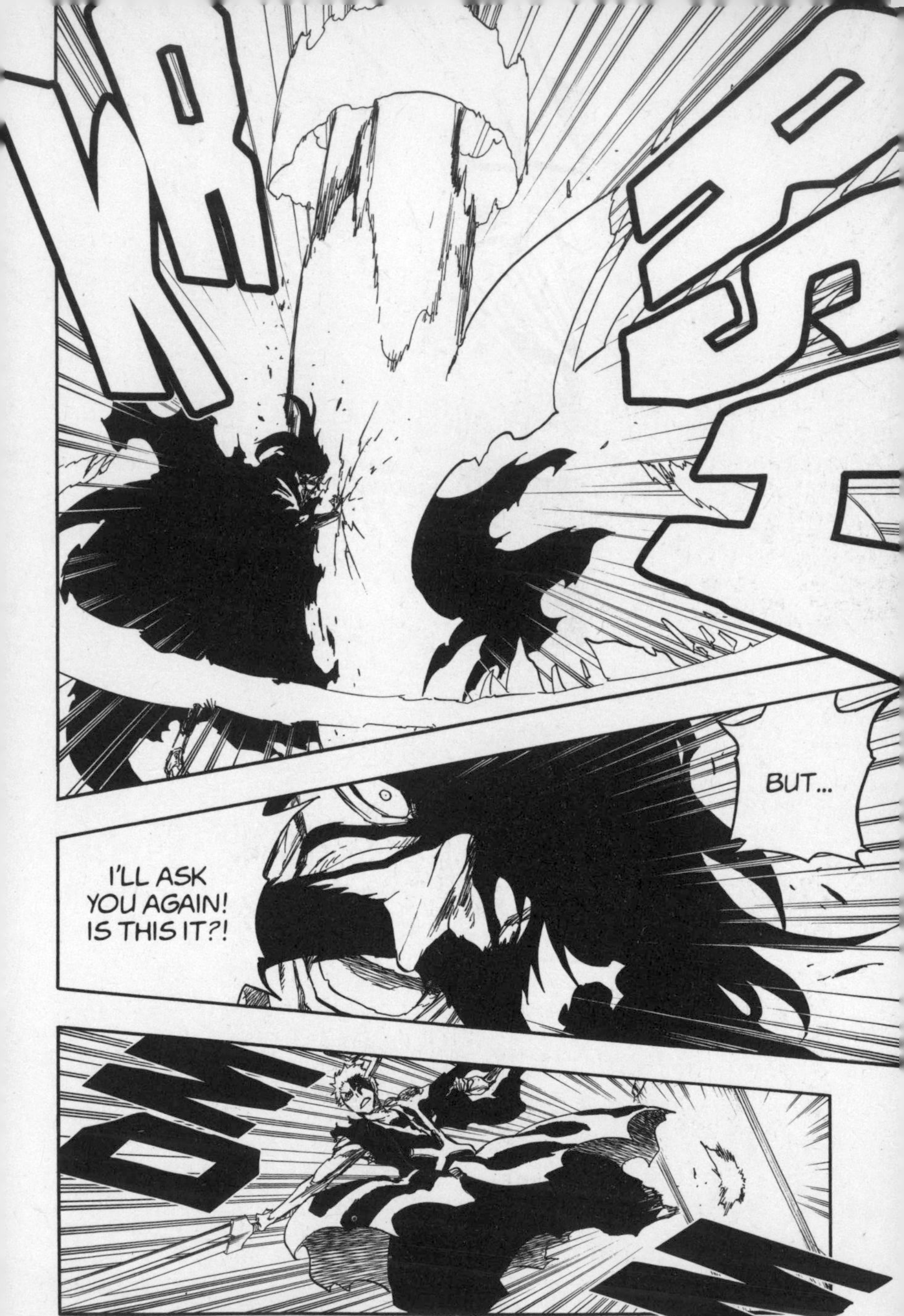
BUT...
I'LL ASK YOU AGAIN! IS THIS IT?!

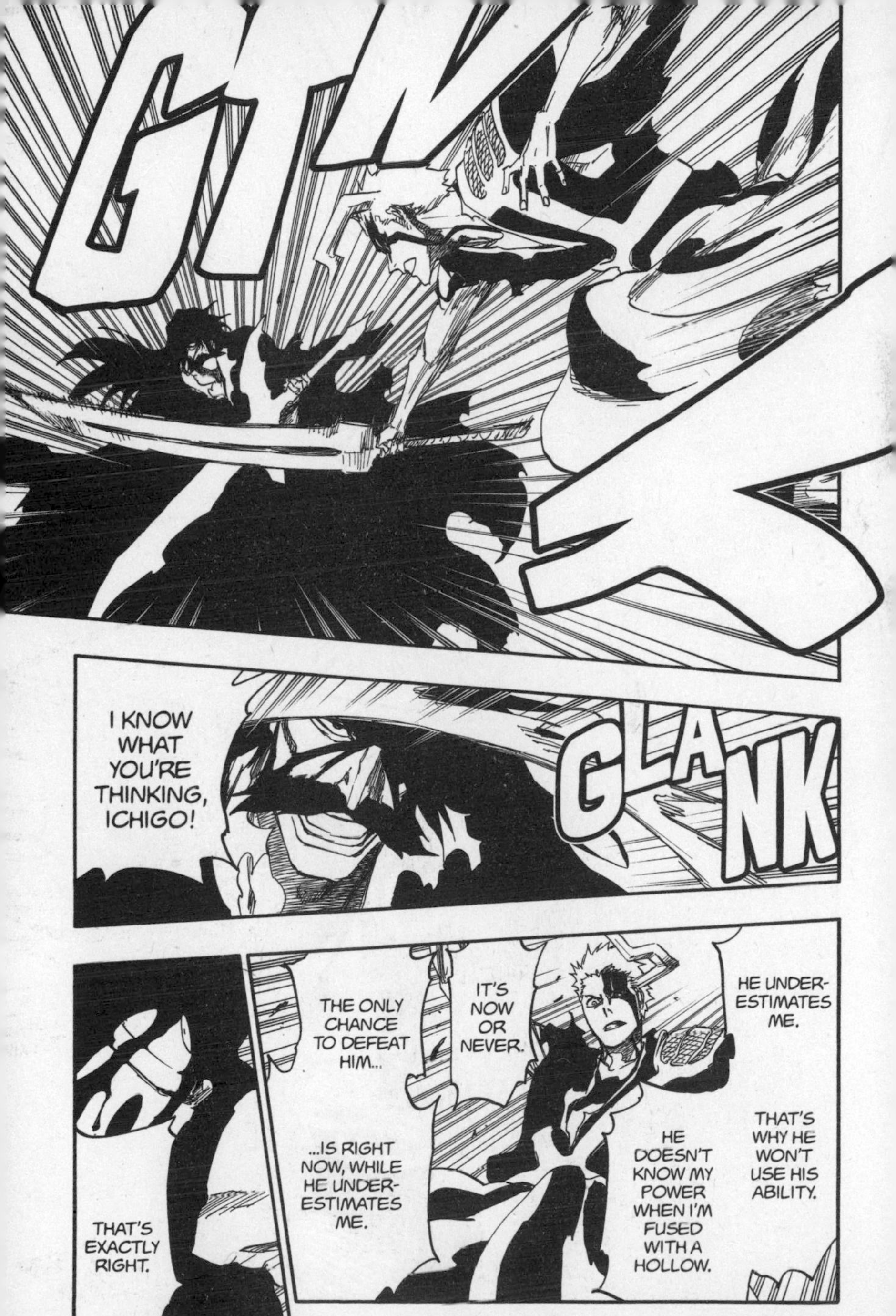
GIN
GLANK
I KNOW WHAT YOU'RE THINKING, ICHIGO!
HE UNDER-ESTIMATES ME.
THAT'S WHY HE WON'T USE HIS ABILITY.
HE DOESN'T KNOW MY POWER WHEN I'M FUSED WITH A HOLLOW.
IT'S NOW OR NEVER.
THE ONLY CHANCE TO DEFEAT HIM...
...IS RIGHT NOW, WHILE HE UNDER-ESTIMATES ME.
THAT'S EXACTLY RIGHT.

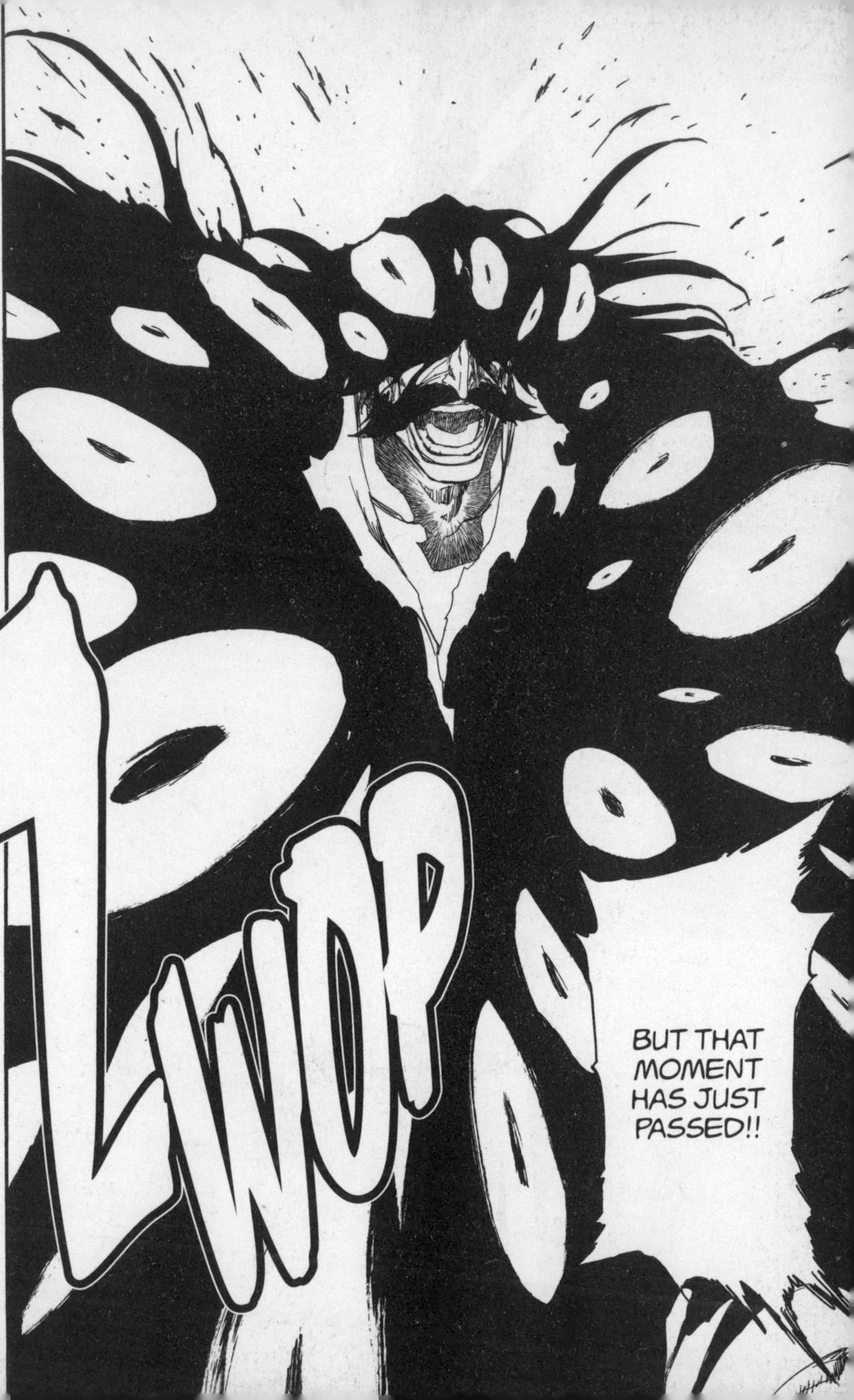
BUT THAT MOMENT HAS JUST PASSED!!

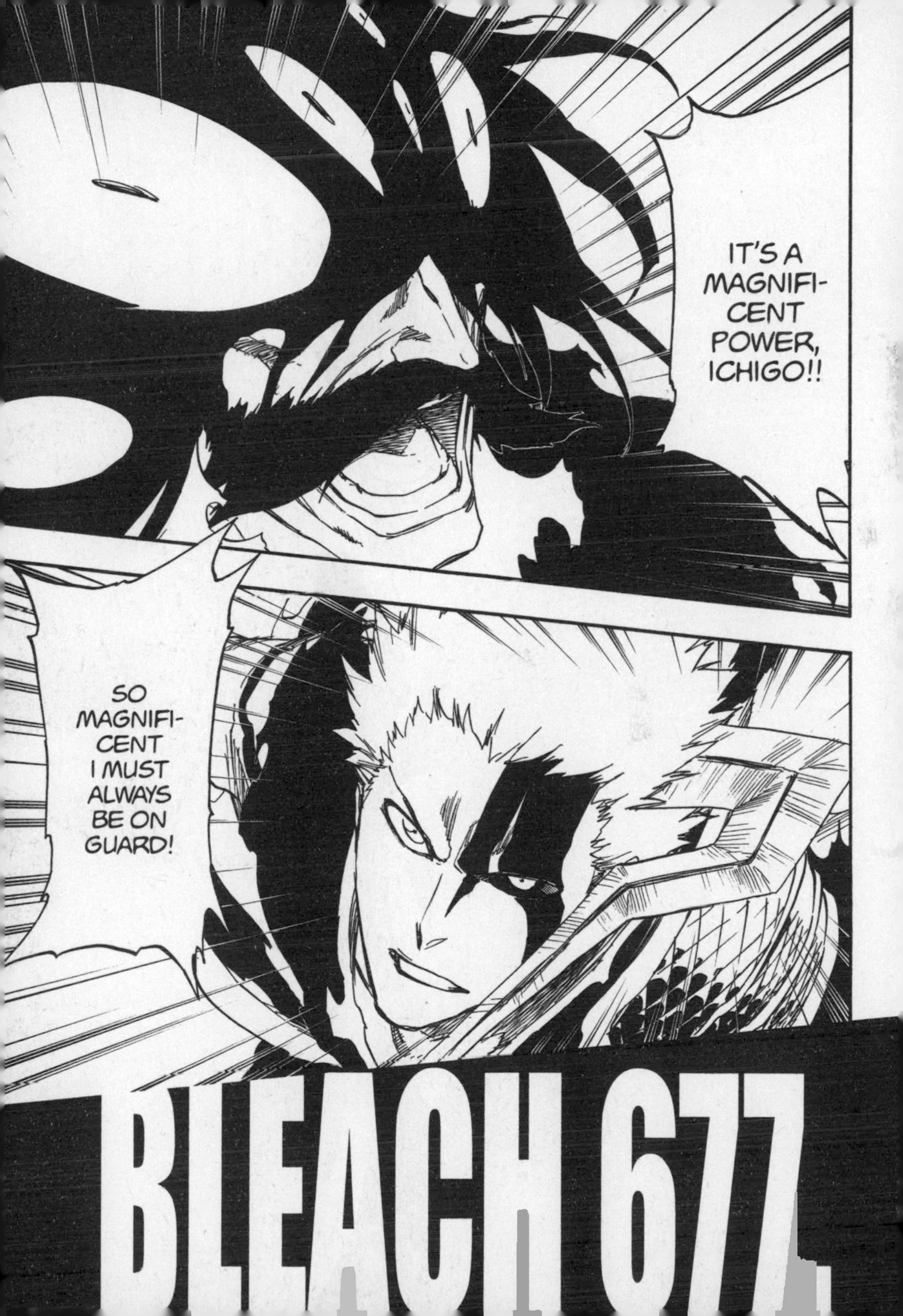
IT'S A MAGNIFI-CENT POWER, ICHIGO!!
SO MAGNIFI-CENT I MUST ALWAYS BE ON GUARD!
BLEACH 677.

Horn of Salvation 2

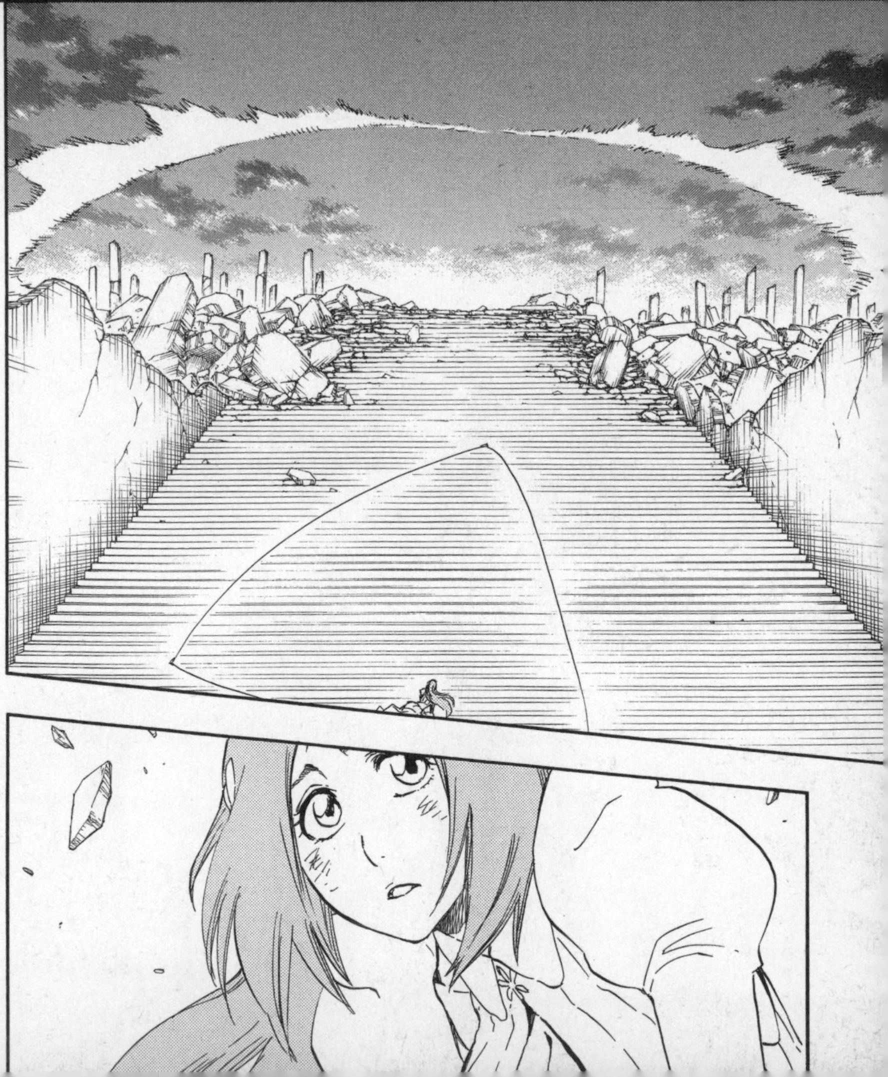

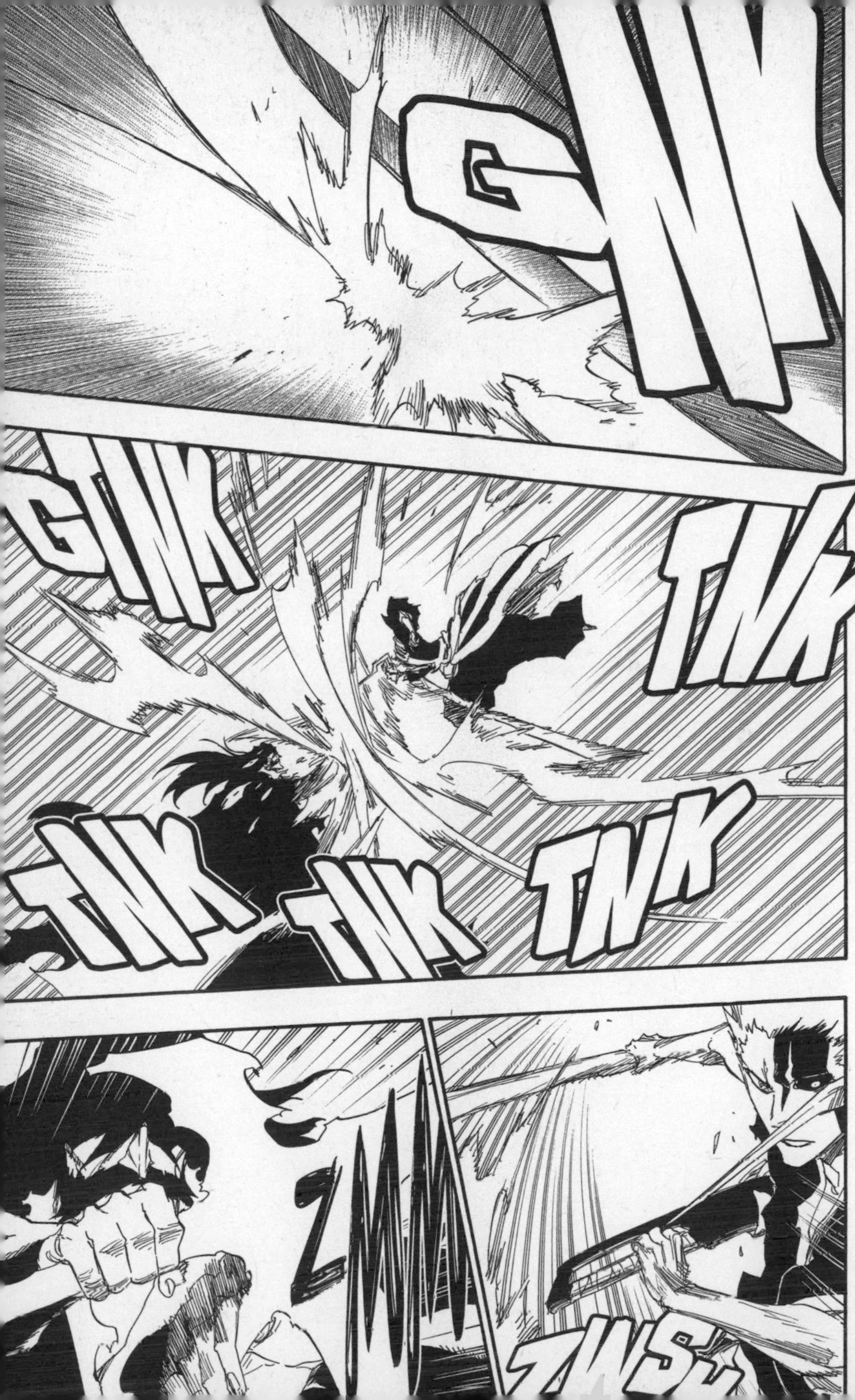
GINN
TINK
GINK
TINK
TINK
TINK
ZWSH

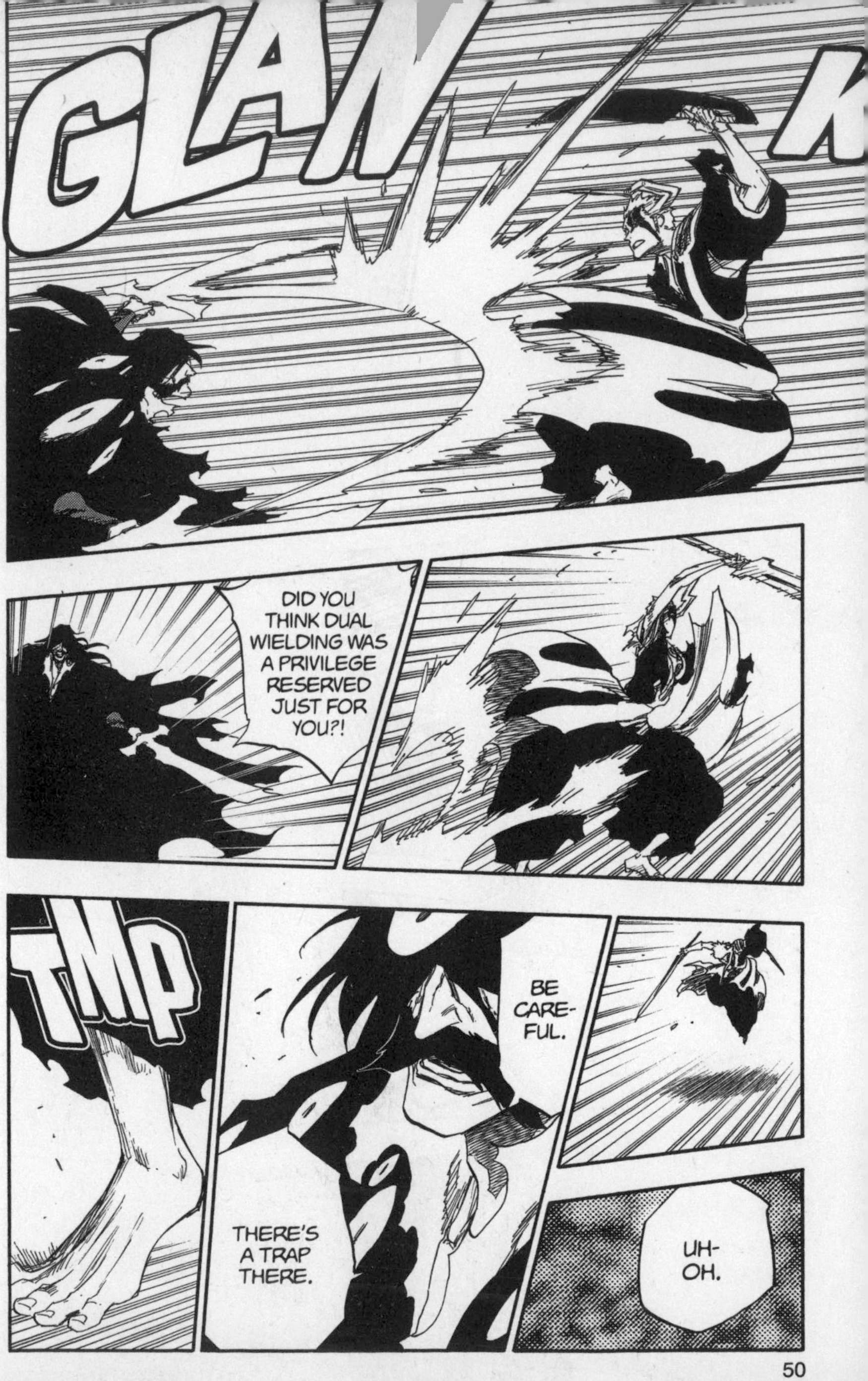

CLAN K
DID YOU THINK DUAL WIELDING WAS A PRIVILEGE RESERVED JUST FOR YOU?!
UH-OH.
BE CAREFUL.
THERE'S A TRAP THERE.
TMP

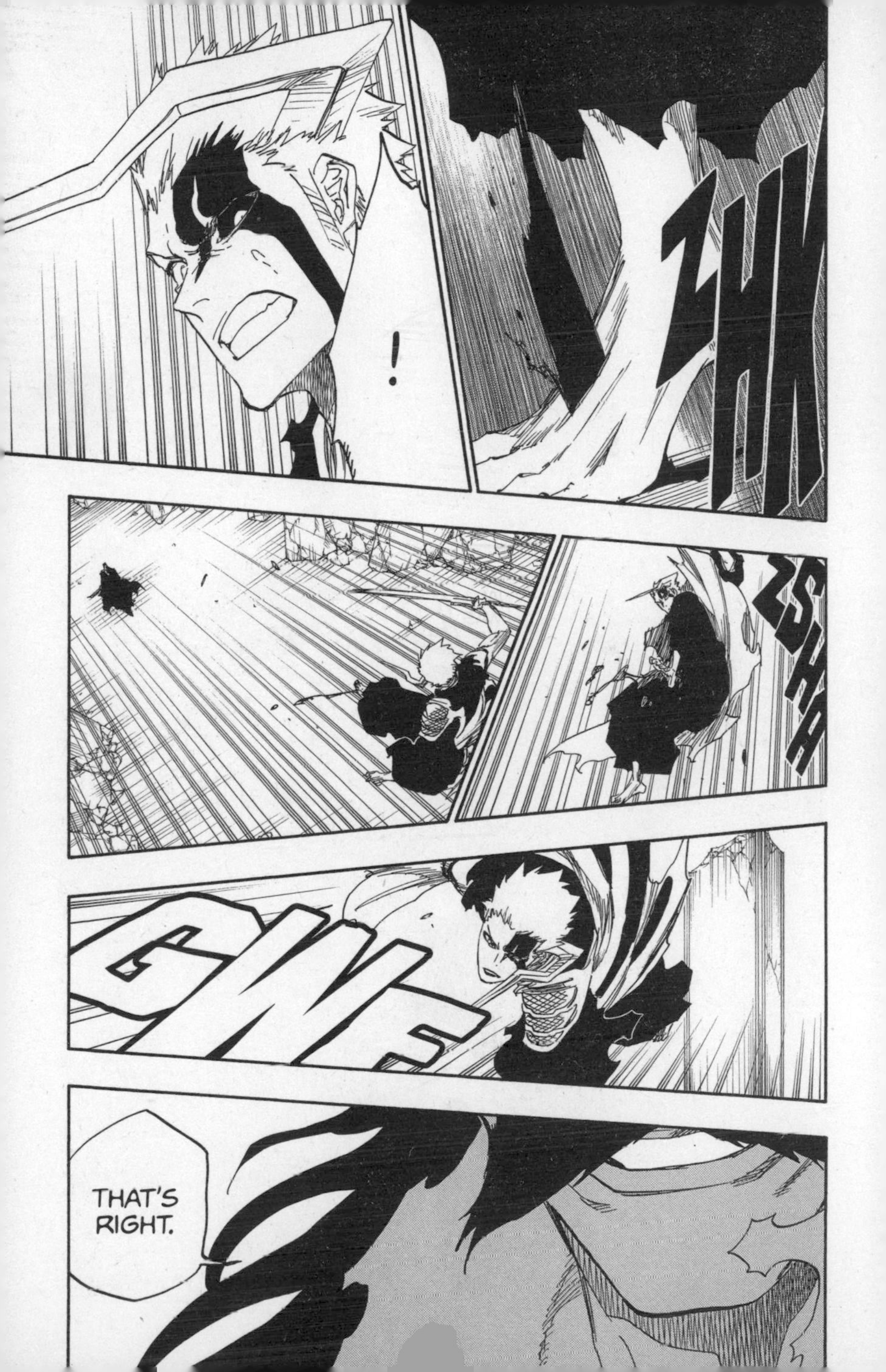
ZHK
!
ZSHA
GWE
THAT'S RIGHT.

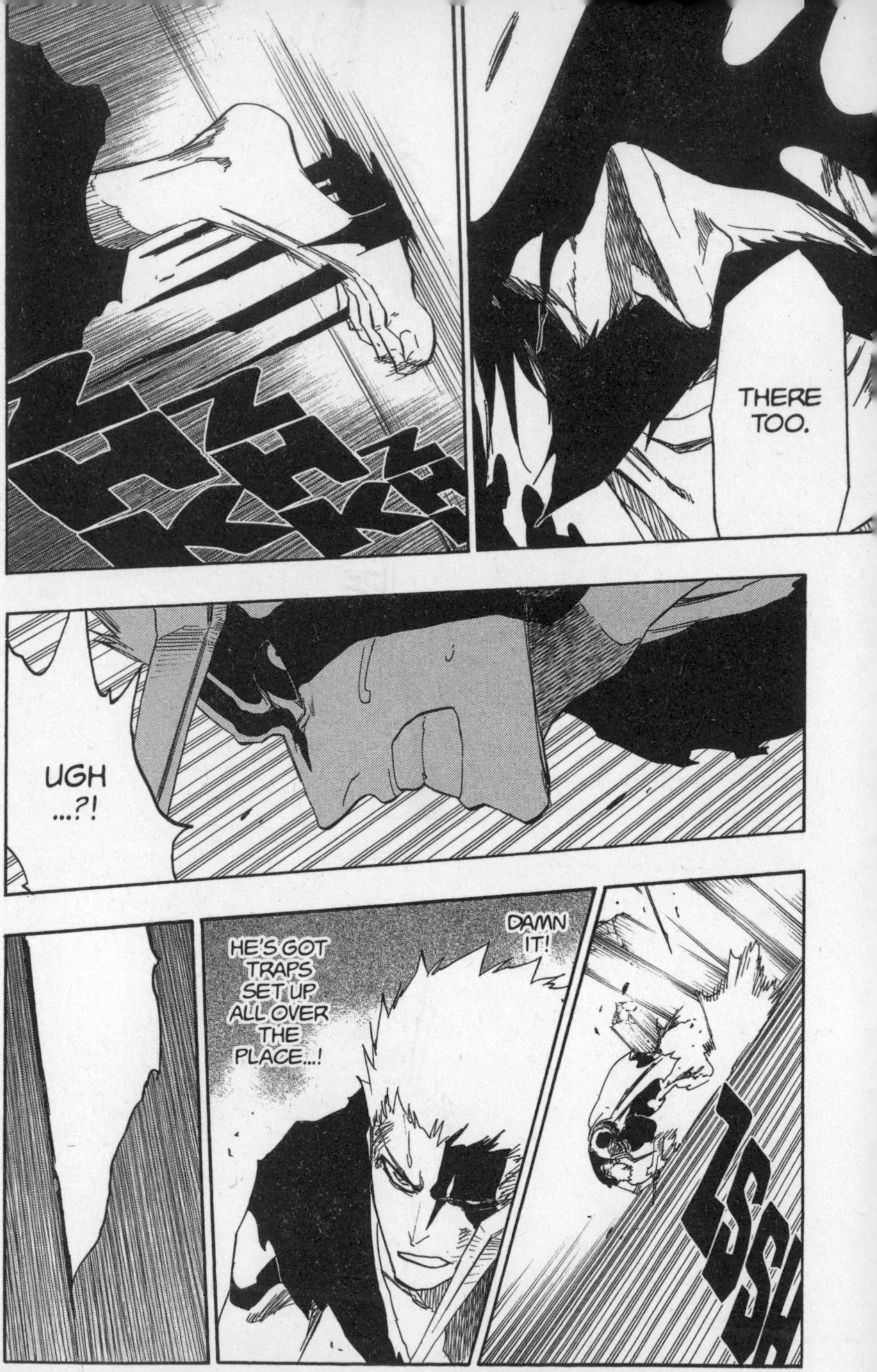
THERE TOO.
UGH ...?!
DAMN IT!
HE'S GOT TRAPS SET UP ALL OVER THE PLACE...!

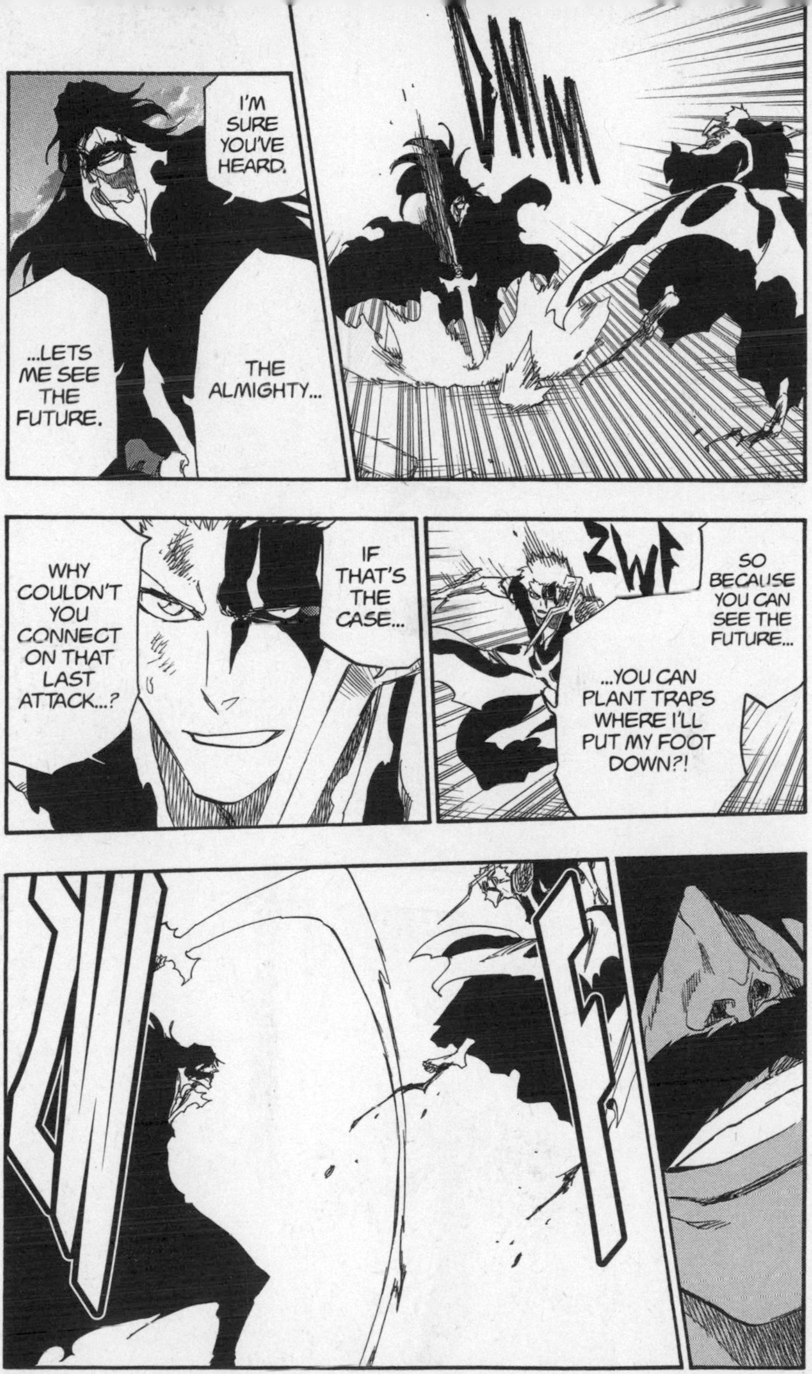
DMM
I'M SURE YOU'VE HEARD.
THE ALMIGHTY...
...LETS ME SEE THE FUTURE.
ZWF
SO BECAUSE YOU CAN SEE THE FUTURE...
...YOU CAN PLANT TRAPS WHERE I'LL PUT MY FOOT DOWN?!
IF THAT'S THE CASE...
WHY COULDN'T YOU CONNECT ON THAT LAST ATTACK...?

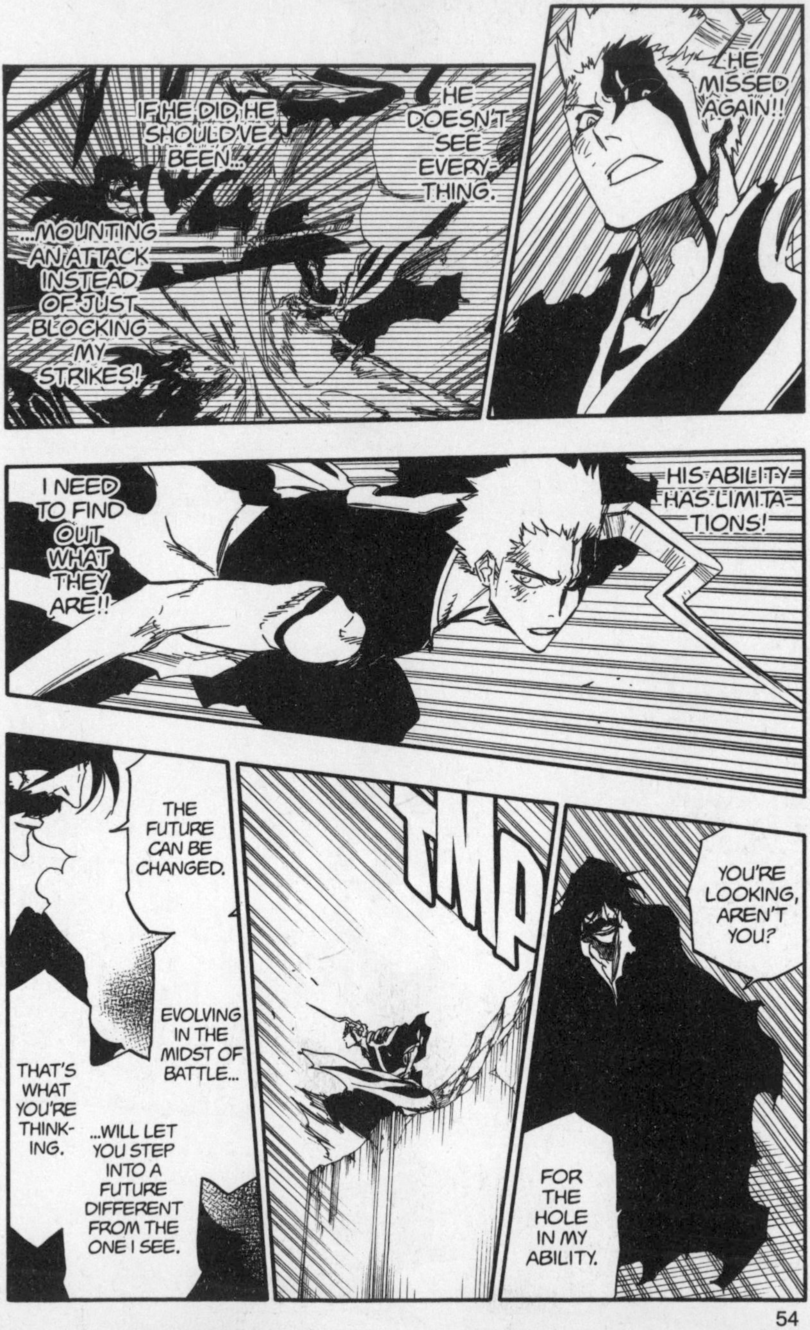
HE MISSED AGAIN!!
HE DOESN'T SEE EVERYTHING.
IF HE DID HE SHOULD'VE BEEN...
...MOUNTING AN ATTACK INSTEAD OF JUST BLOCKING MY STRIKES!
HIS ABILITY HAS LIMITATIONS!
I NEED TO FIND OUT WHAT THEY ARE!!
YOU'RE LOOKING, AREN'T YOU?
FOR THE HOLE IN MY ABILITY.
TMP
THE FUTURE CAN BE CHANGED.
EVOLVING IN THE MIDST OF BATTLE...
...WILL LET YOU STEP INTO A FUTURE DIFFERENT FROM THE ONE I SEE.
THAT'S WHAT YOU'RE THINKING.

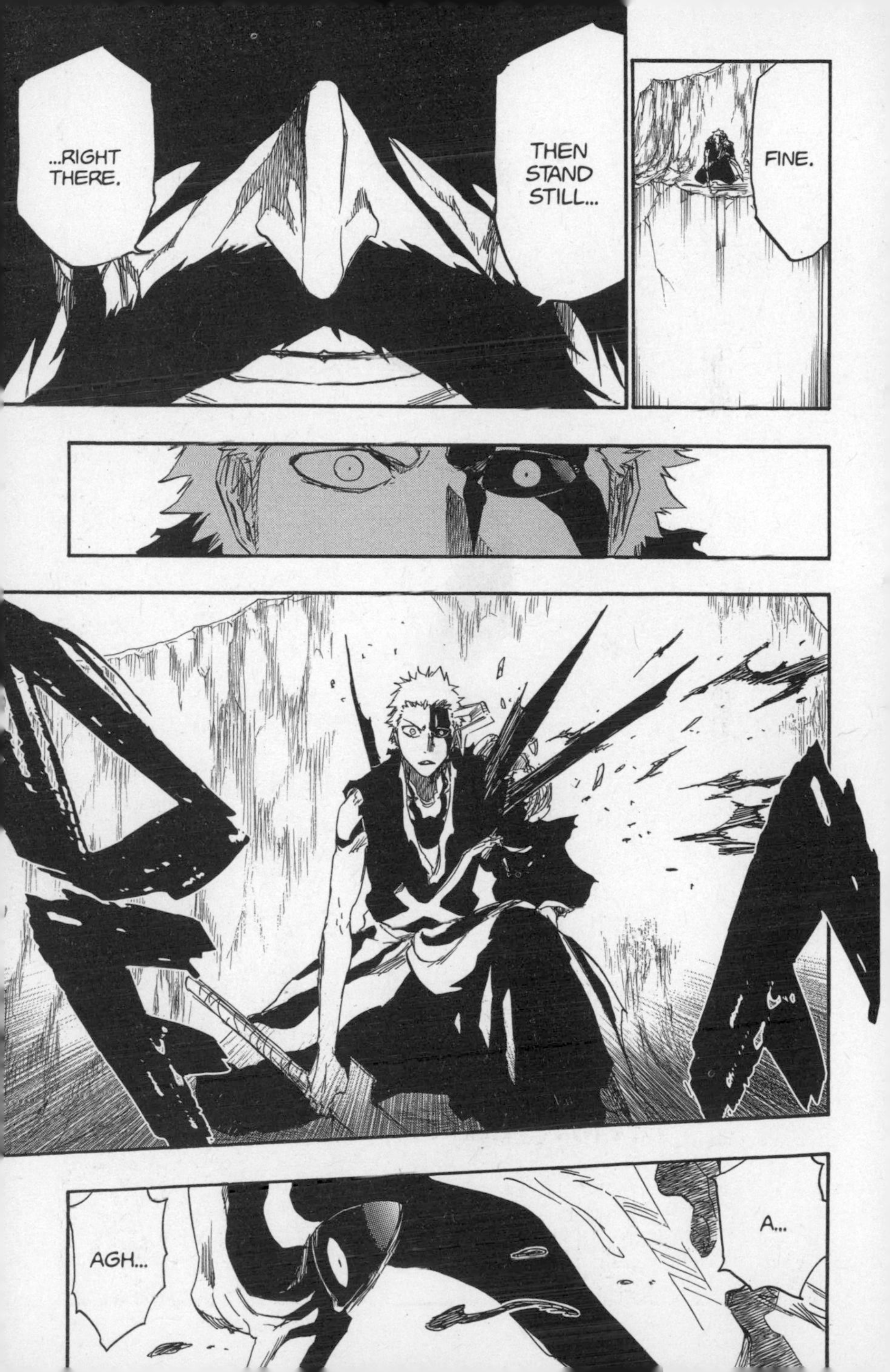
FINE.
THEN STAND STILL...
...RIGHT THERE.
A...
AGH...

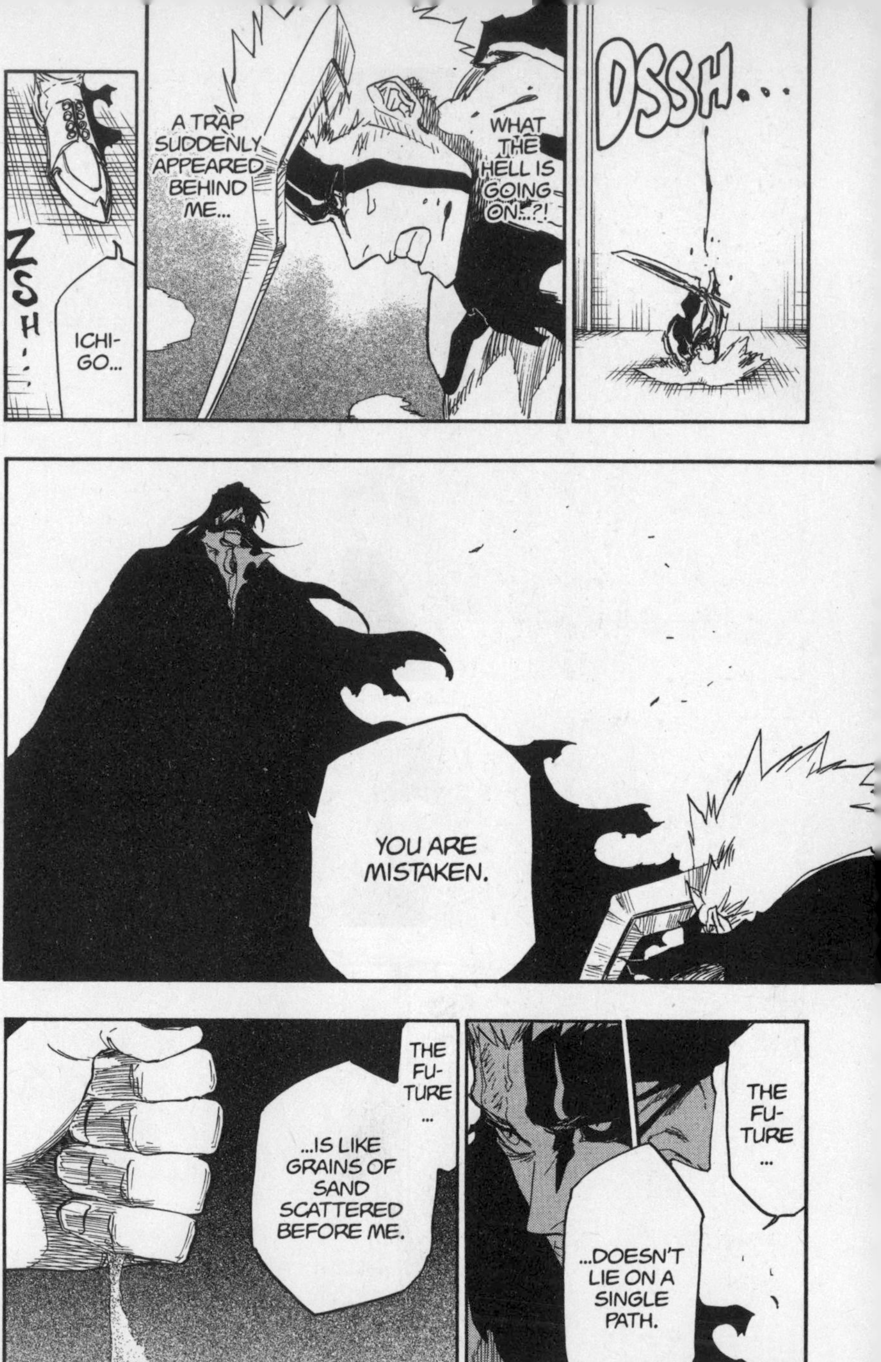
DSSH...
WHAT THE HELL IS GOING ON...?!
A TRAP SUDDENLY APPEARED BEHIND ME...
ZSH...
ICHIGO...
YOU ARE MISTAKEN.
THE FUTURE...
...DOESN'T LIE ON A SINGLE PATH.
THE FUTURE...
...IS LIKE GRAINS OF SAND SCATTERED BEFORE ME.

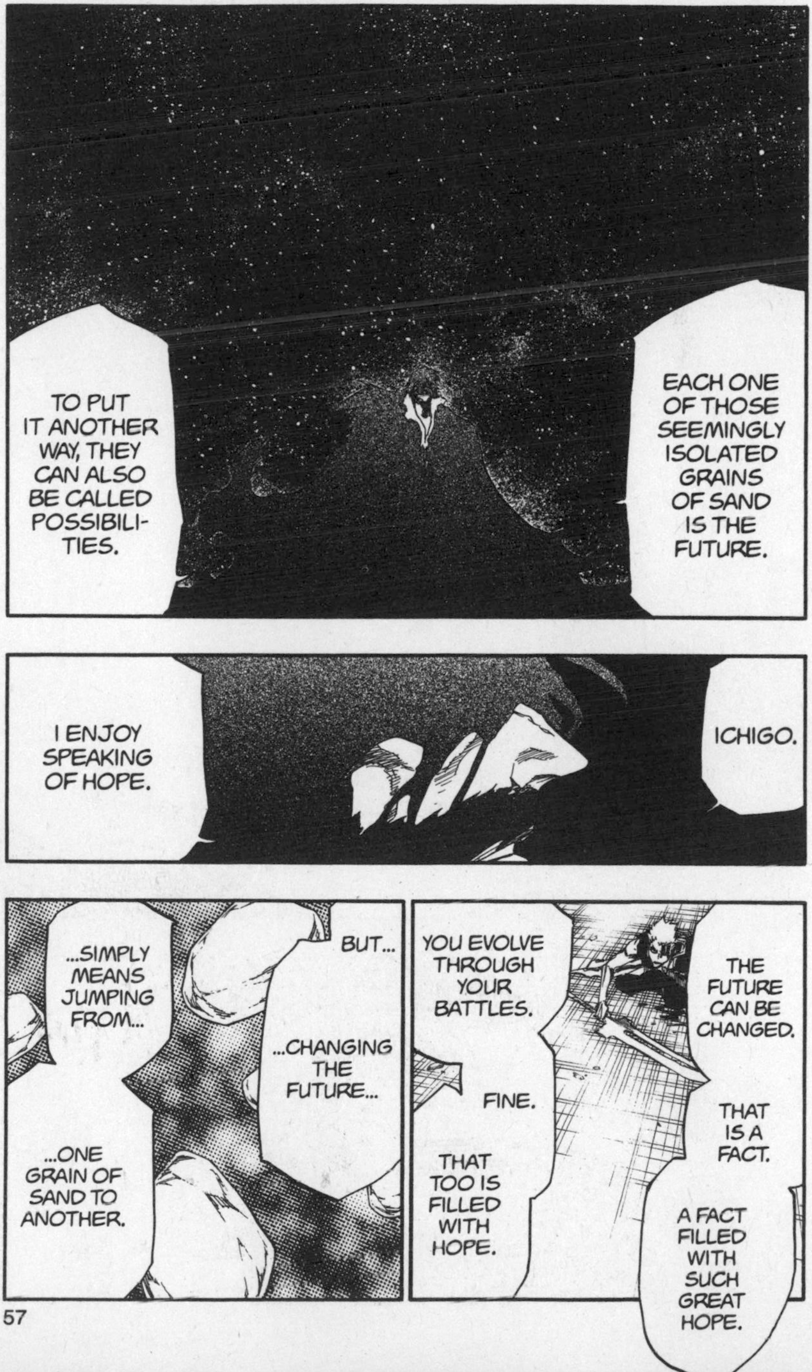
EACH ONE OF THOSE SEEMINGLY ISOLATED GRAINS OF SAND IS THE FUTURE.
TO PUT IT ANOTHER WAY, THEY CAN ALSO BE CALLED POSSIBILI-TIES.
ICHIGO.
I ENJOY SPEAKING OF HOPE.
THE FUTURE CAN BE CHANGED.
THAT IS A FACT.
A FACT FILLED WITH SUCH GREAT HOPE.
YOU EVOLVE THROUGH YOUR BATTLES.
FINE.
THAT TOO IS FILLED WITH HOPE.
BUT...
...CHANGING THE FUTURE...
...SIMPLY MEANS JUMPING FROM...
...ONE GRAIN OF SAND TO ANOTHER.

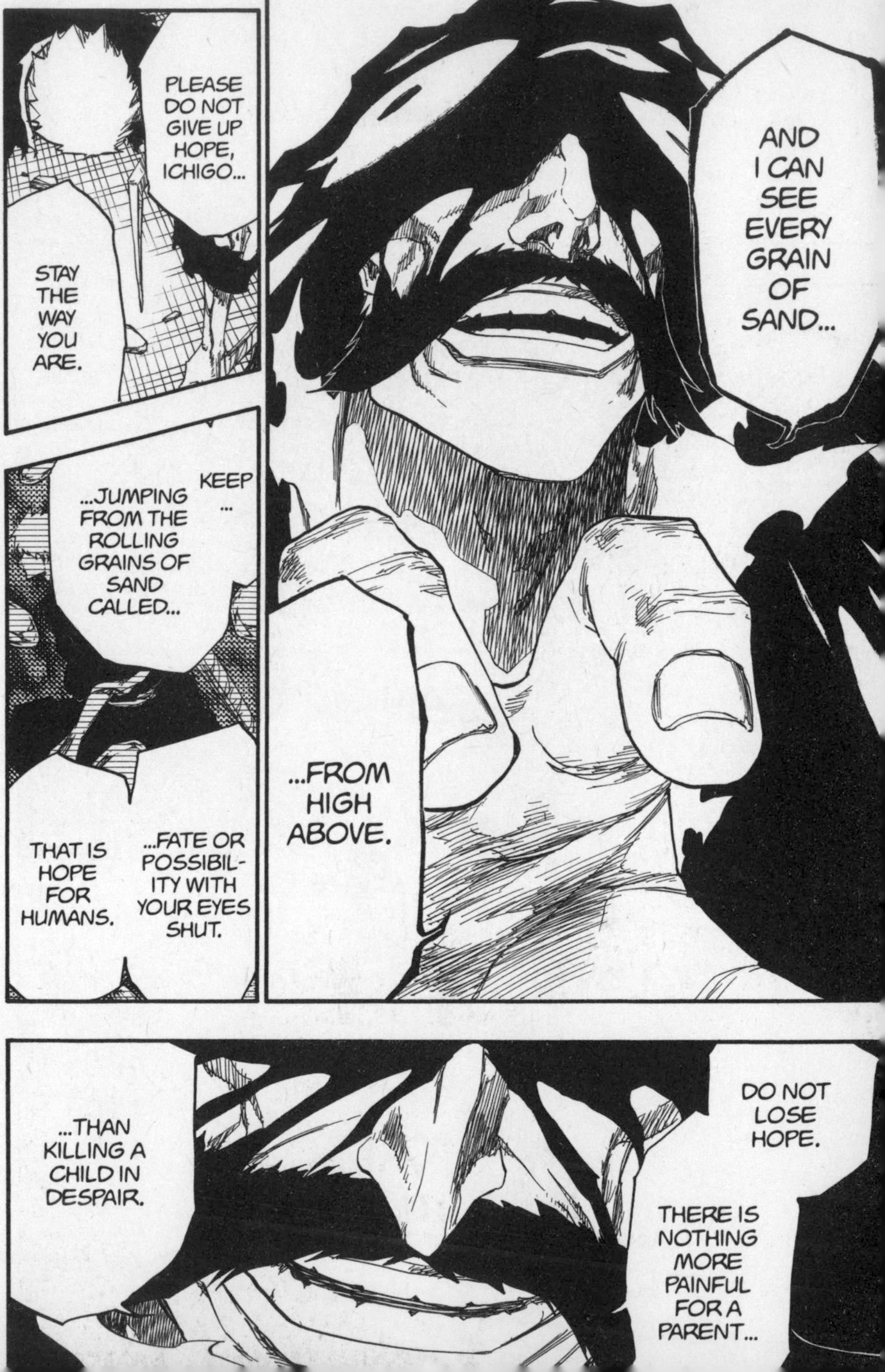
AND I CAN SEE EVERY GRAIN OF SAND...
...FROM HIGH ABOVE.
PLEASE DO NOT GIVE UP HOPE, ICHIGO...
STAY THE WAY YOU ARE.
KEEP...
...JUMPING FROM THE ROLLING GRAINS OF SAND CALLED...
...FATE OR POSSIBIL-ITY WITH YOUR EYES SHUT.
THAT IS HOPE FOR HUMANS.
DO NOT LOSE HOPE.
THERE IS NOTHING MORE PAINFUL FOR A PARENT...
...THAN KILLING A CHILD IN DESPAIR.

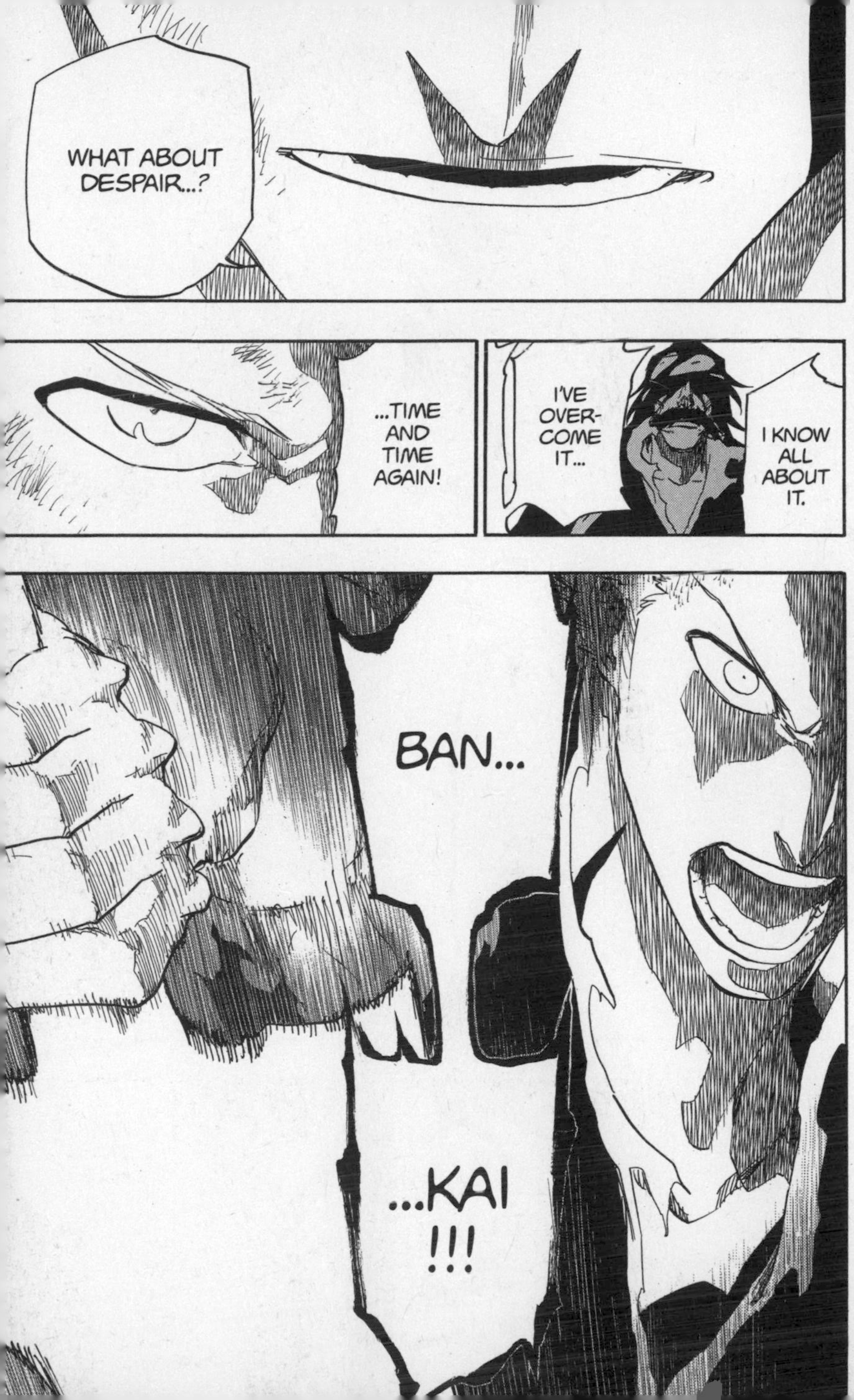
WHAT ABOUT DESPAIR...?
I KNOW ALL ABOUT IT.
I'VE OVERCOME IT...
...TIME AND TIME AGAIN!
BAN...
...KAI !!!

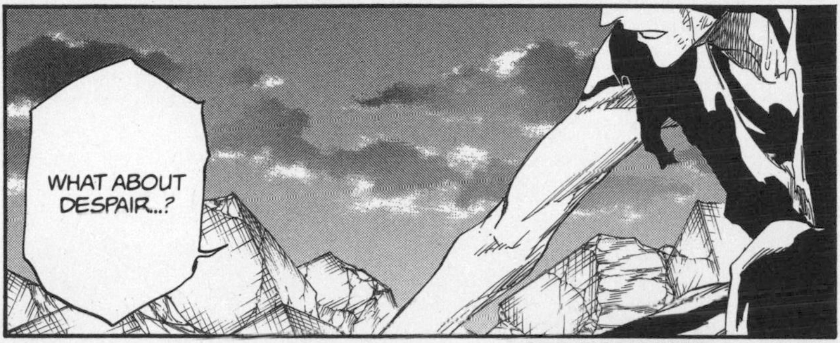
WHAT ABOUT DESPAIR...?

678. THE FUTURE BLACK

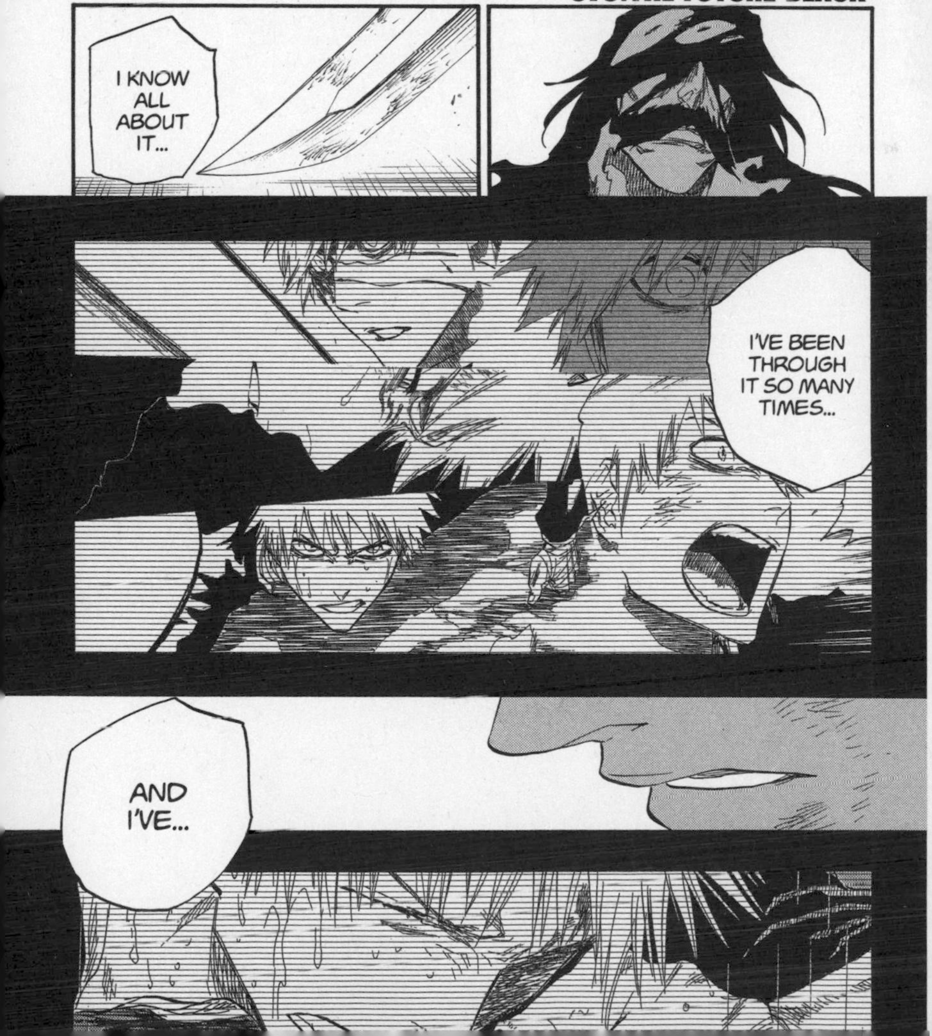
I KNOW ALL ABOUT IT...
I'VE BEEN THROUGH IT SO MANY TIMES...
AND I'VE...

BLEACH 678.

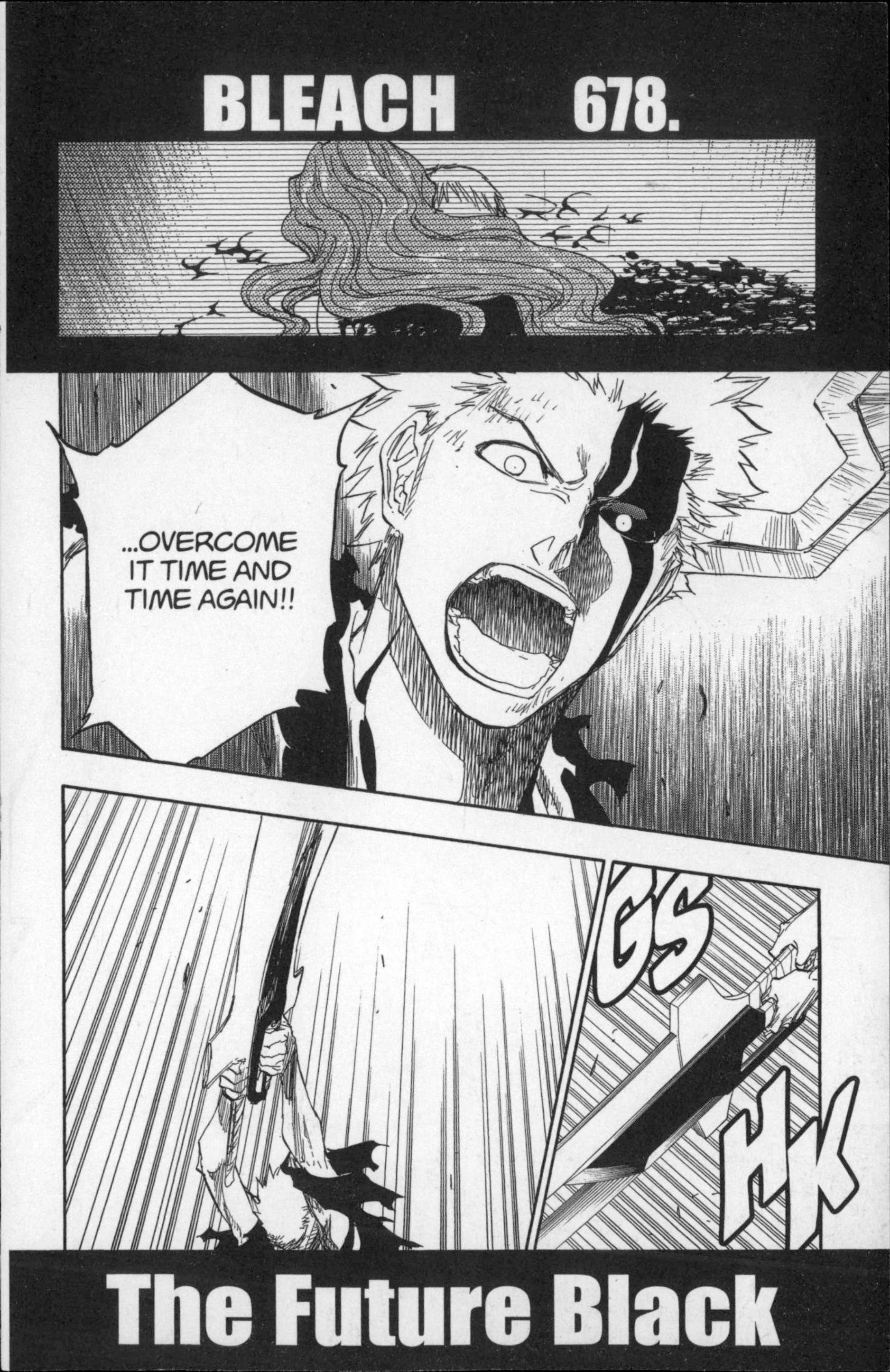
...OVERCOME IT TIME AND TIME AGAIN!!
GS
HK

The Future Black

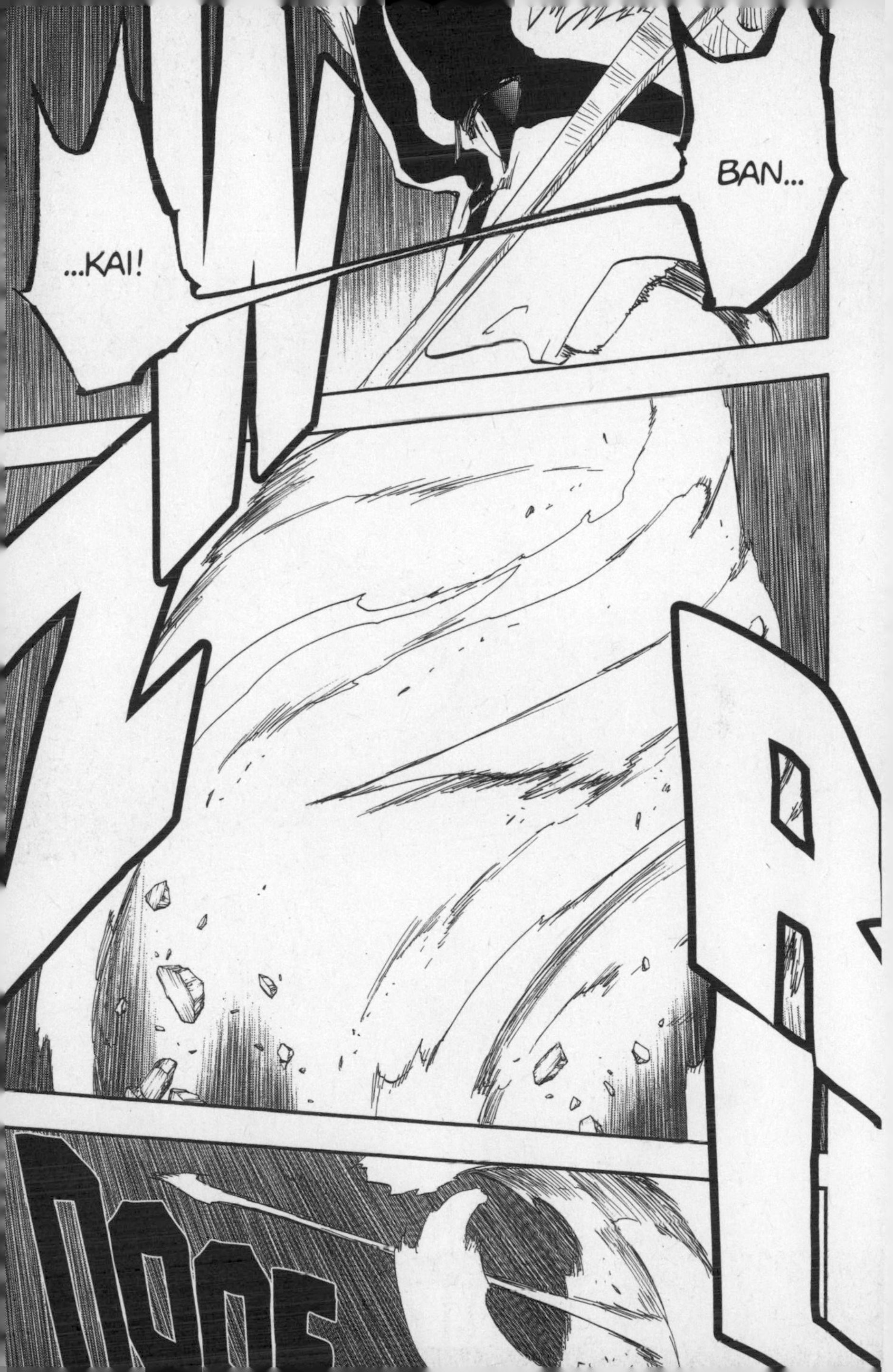
BAN...
...KAI!

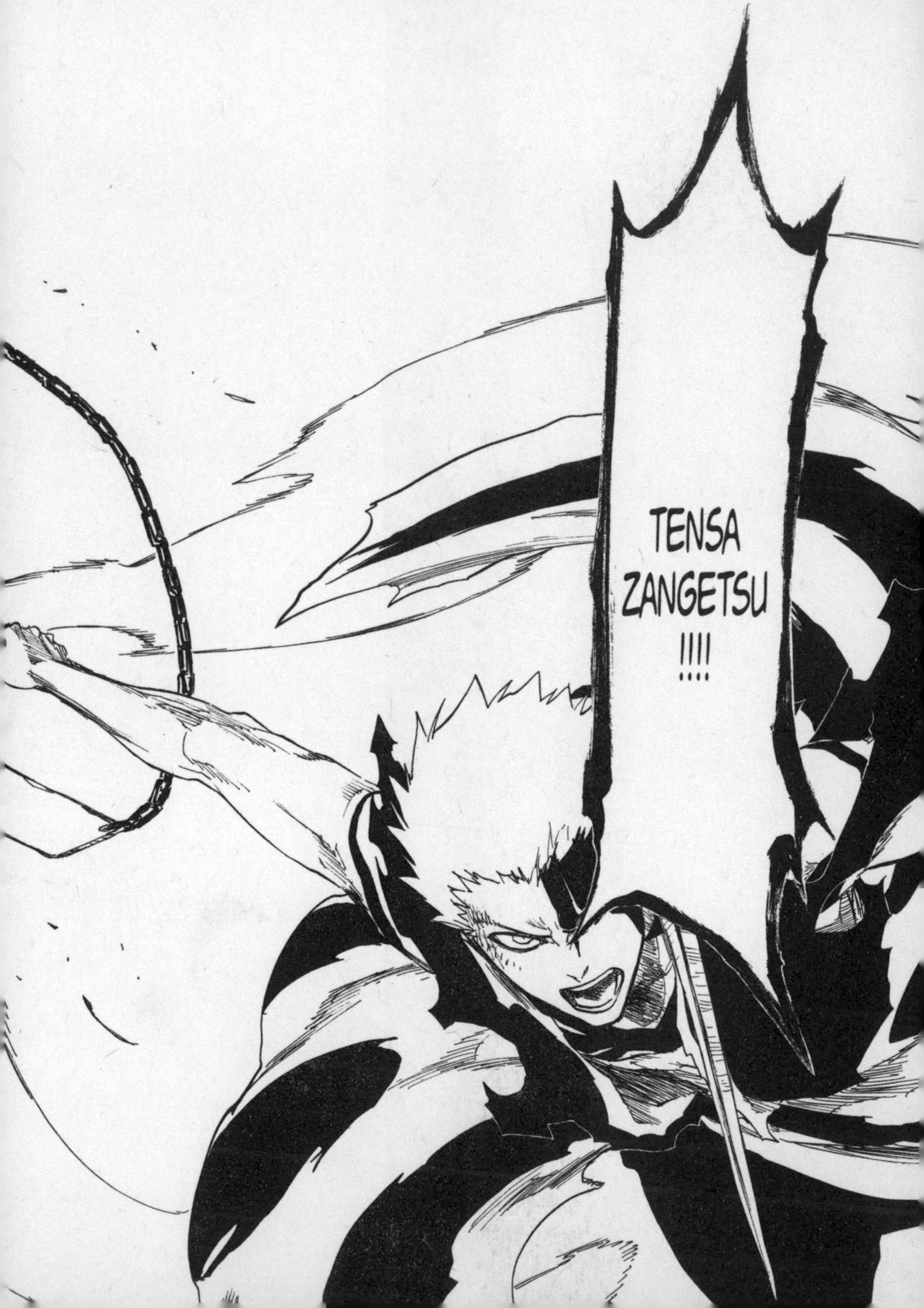
TENSA ZANGETSU !!!!

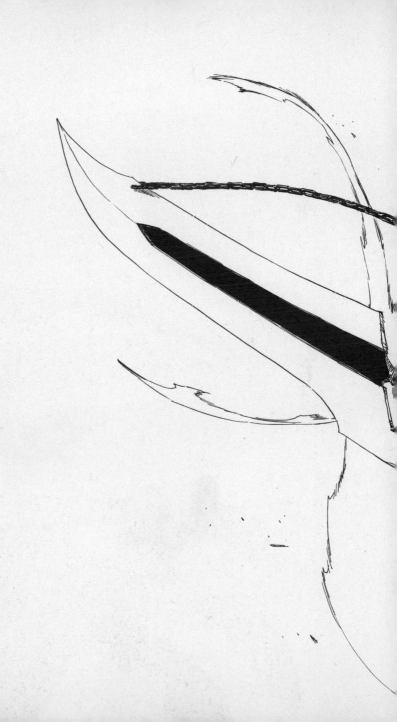

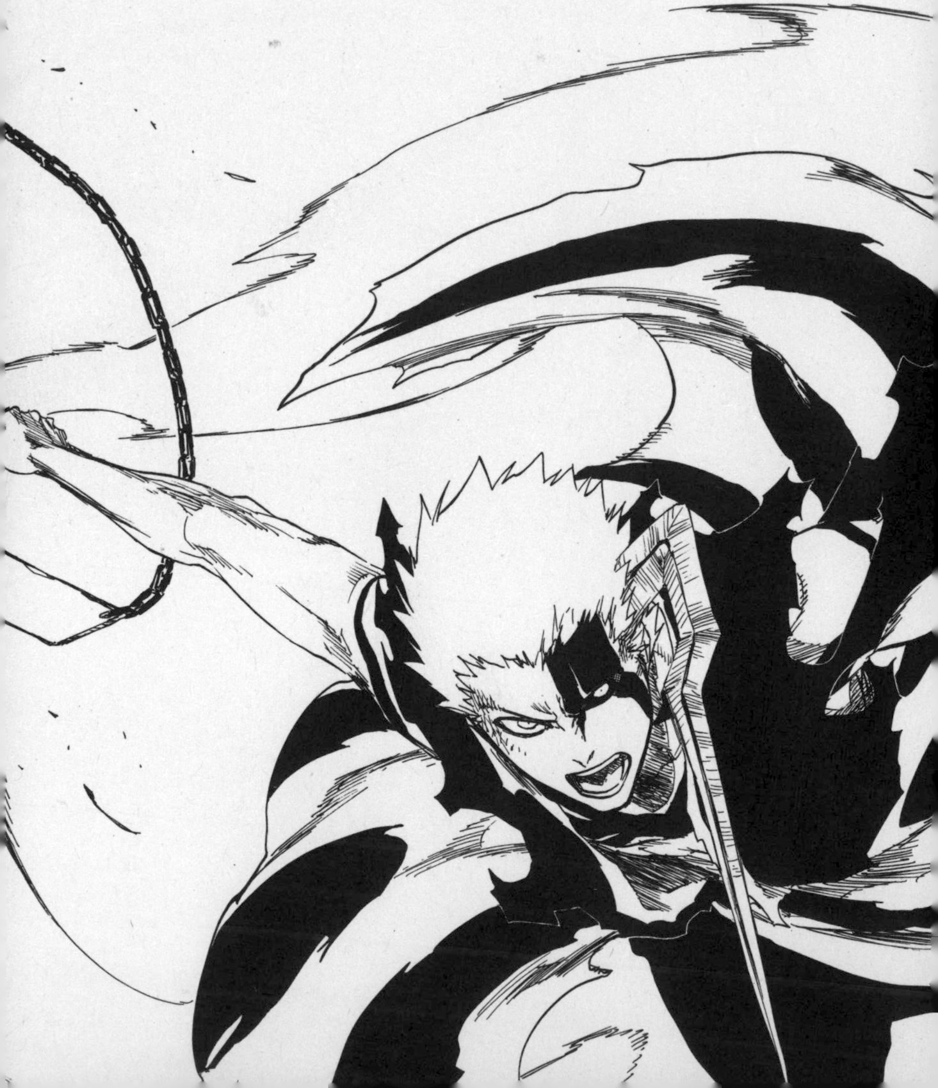

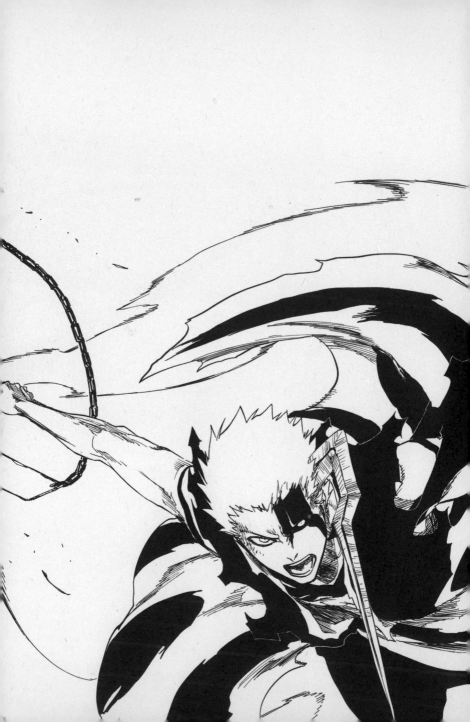

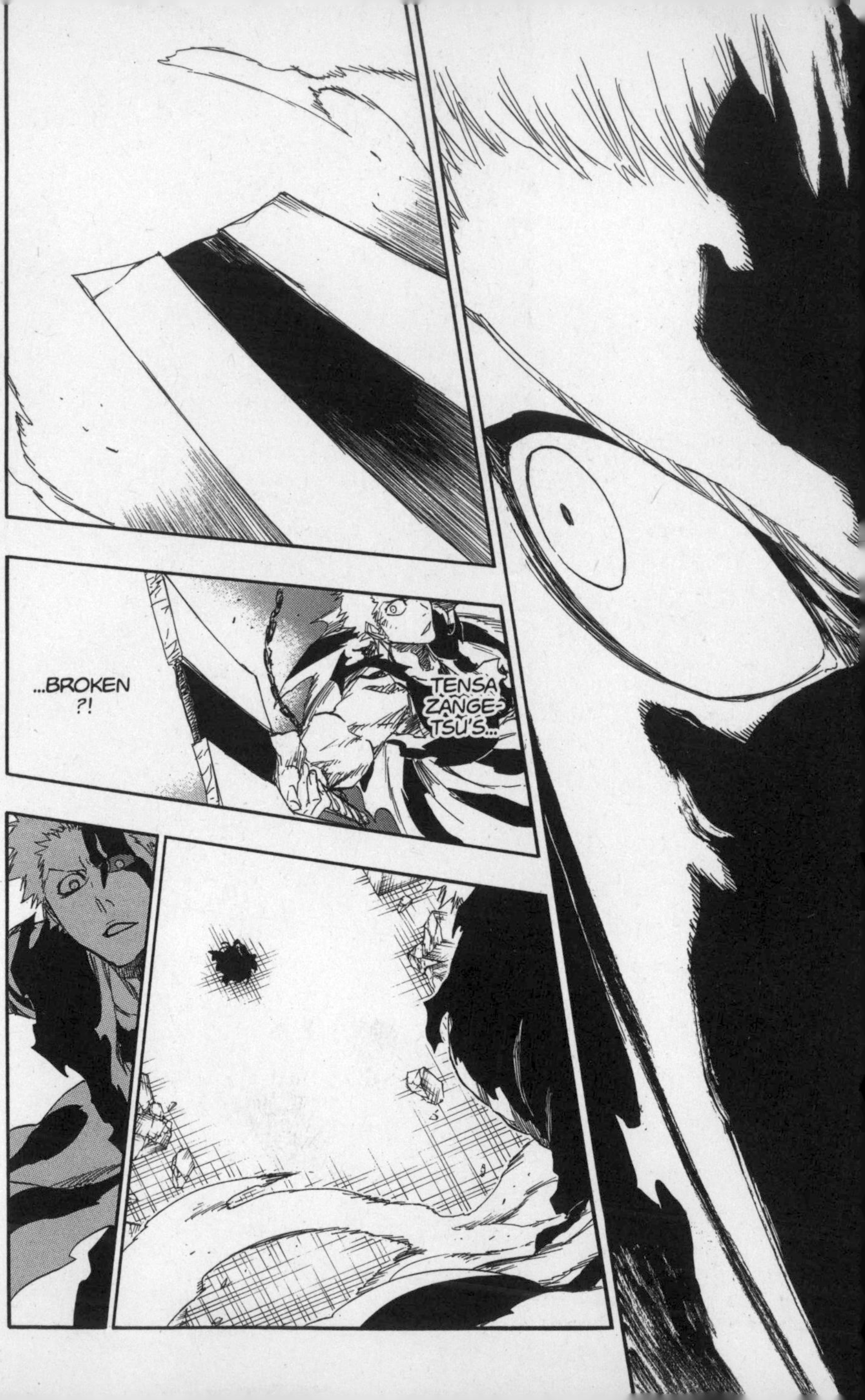
TENSA ZANGETSU'S...
...BROKEN ?!

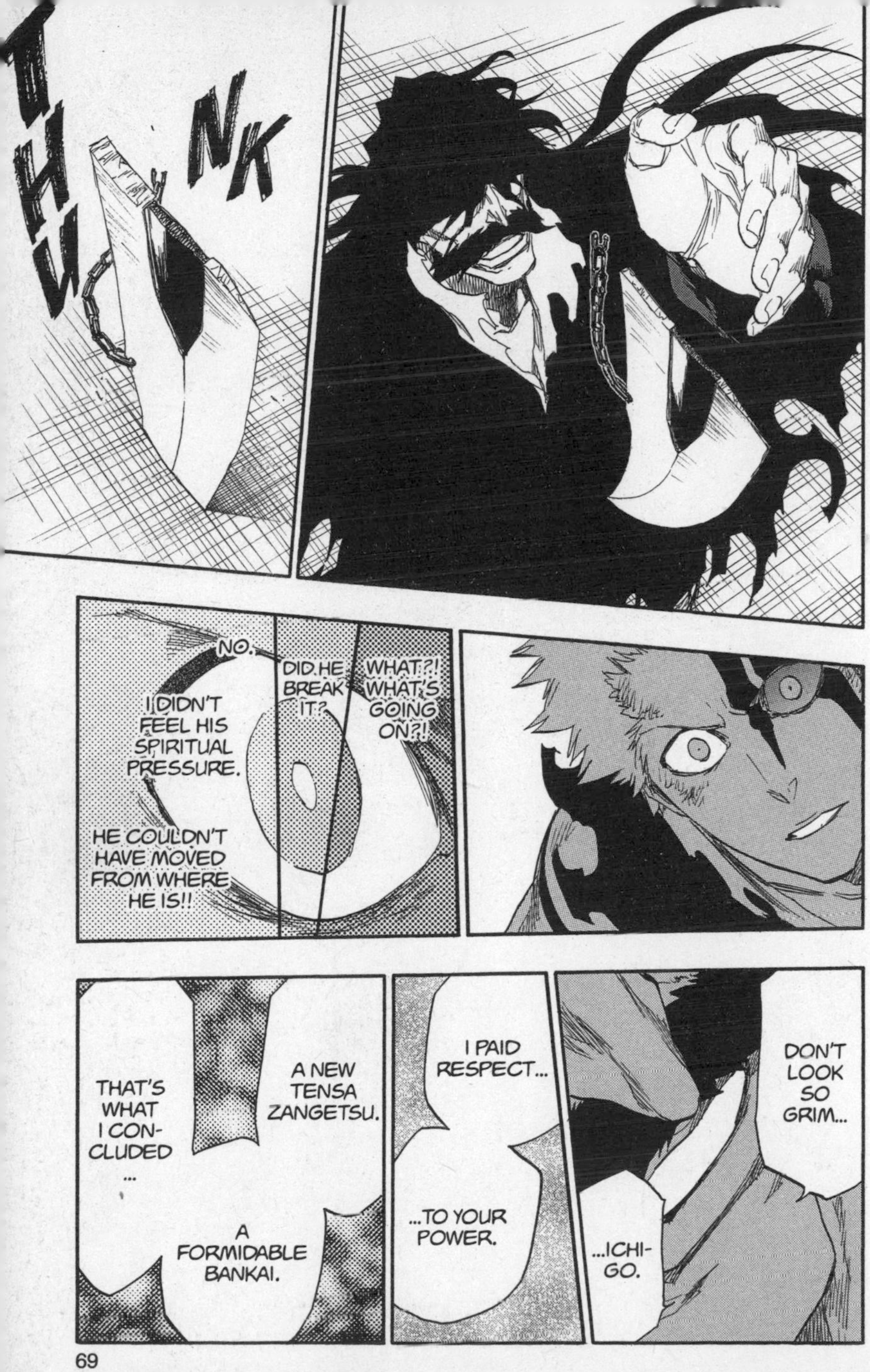
THUNK
WHAT?!
WHAT'S
GOING
ON?!
DID HE
BREAK
IT?
NO.
I DIDN'T
FEEL HIS
SPIRITUAL
PRESSURE.
HE COULDN'T
HAVE MOVED
FROM WHERE
HE IS!!
DON'T
LOOK
SO
GRIM...
...ICHI-
GO.
I PAID
RESPECT...
...TO YOUR
POWER.
A NEW
TENSA
ZANGETSU.
A
FORMIDABLE
BANKAI.
THAT'S
WHAT
I CON-
CLUDED
...

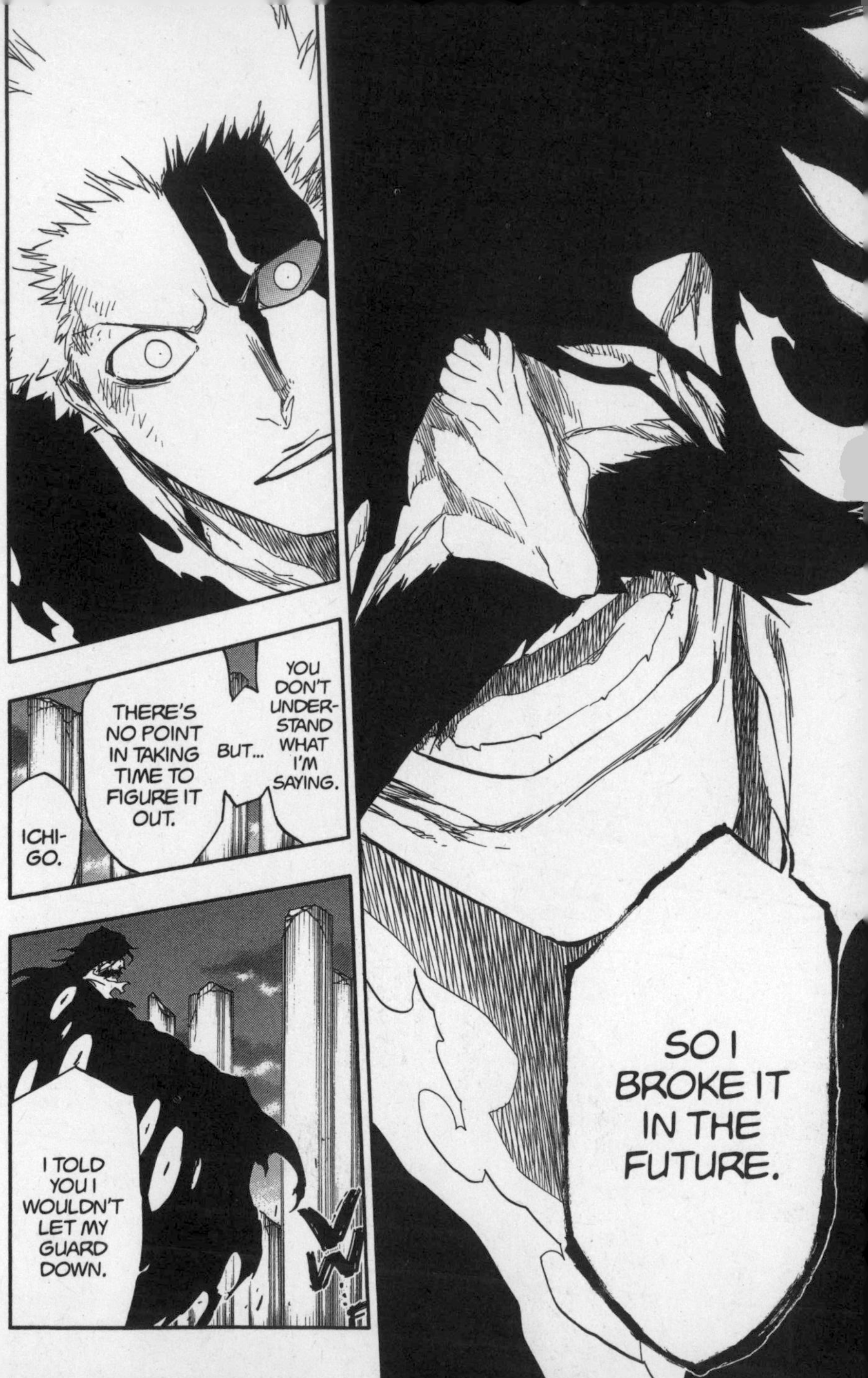
SO I BROKE IT IN THE FUTURE.
YOU DON'T UNDER-STAND WHAT I'M SAYING.
BUT...
THERE'S NO POINT IN TAKING TIME TO FIGURE IT OUT.
ICHI-GO.
I TOLD YOU I WOULDN'T LET MY GUARD DOWN.

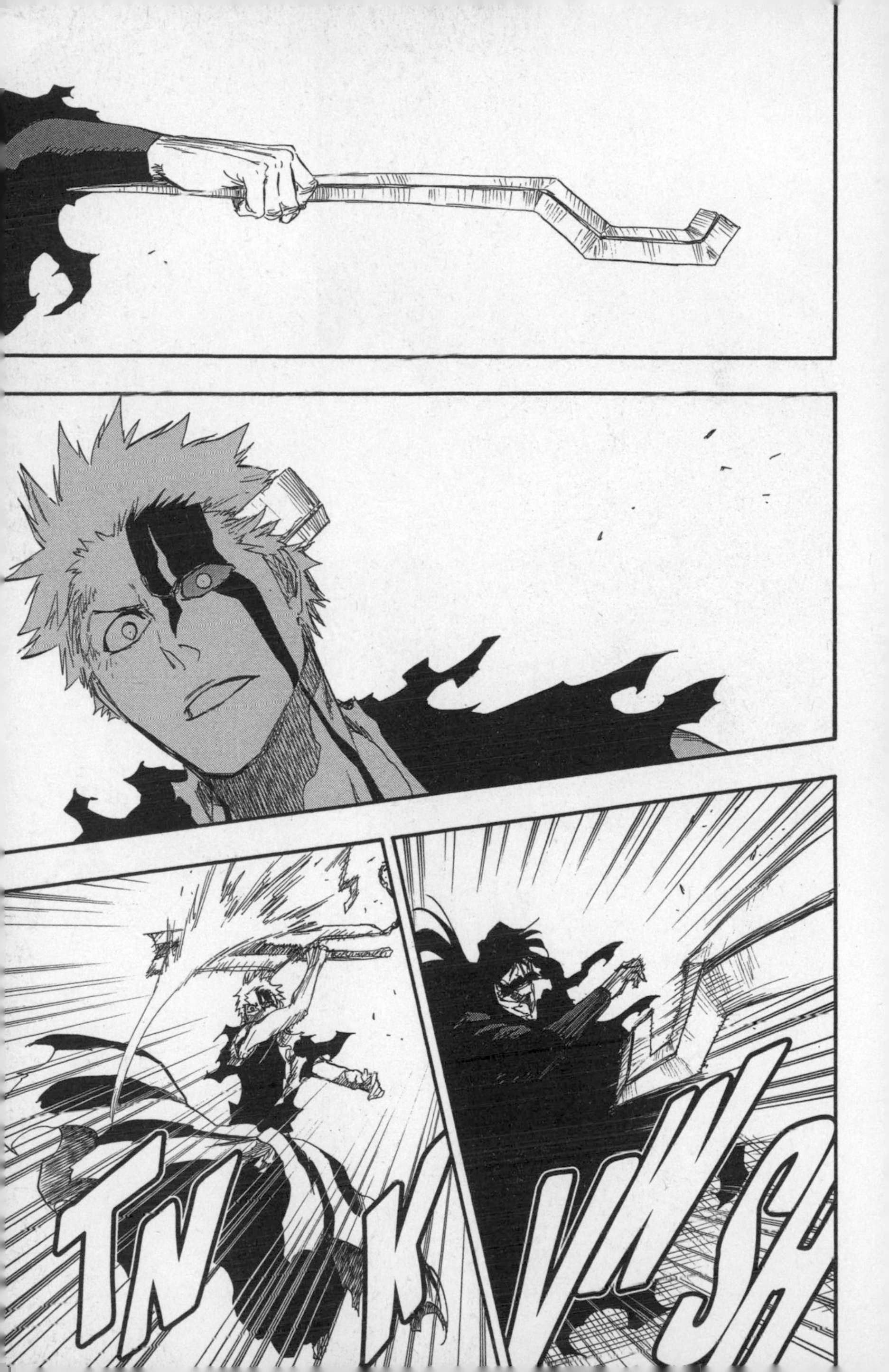
VWSH
TNK

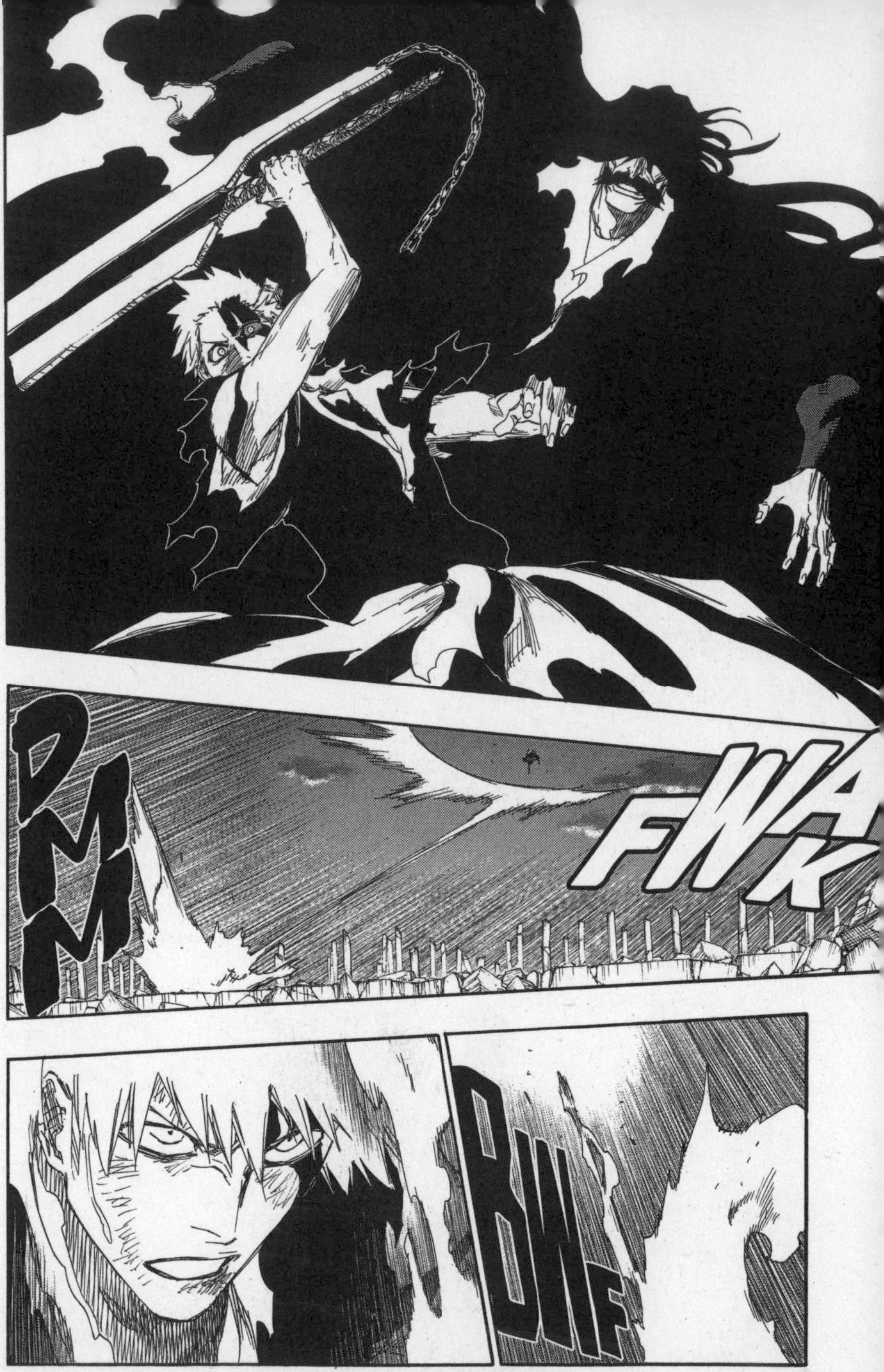
FWAK
DMM
BWF

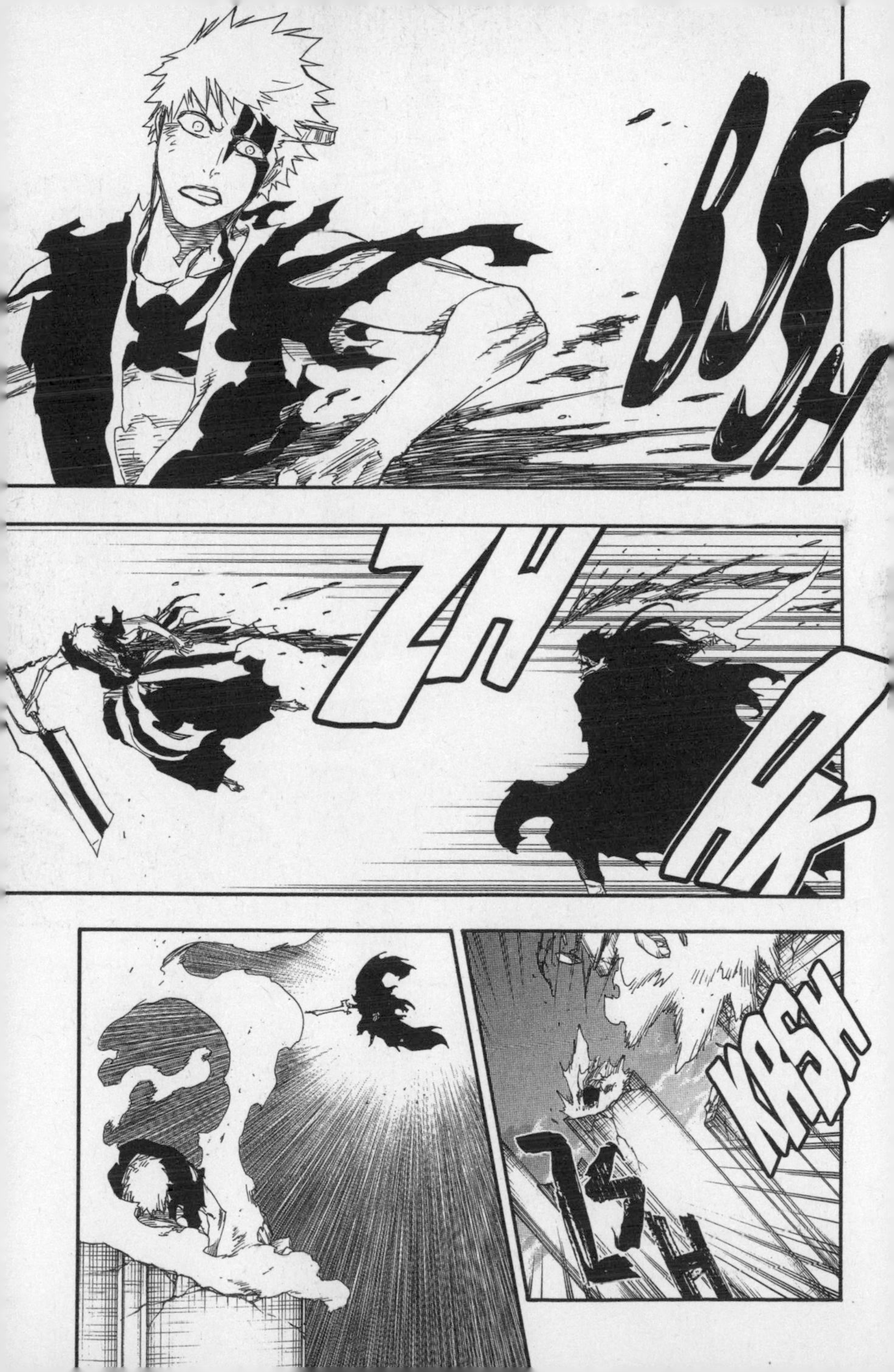
BSSH
ZHAK
KRSH
ZSH

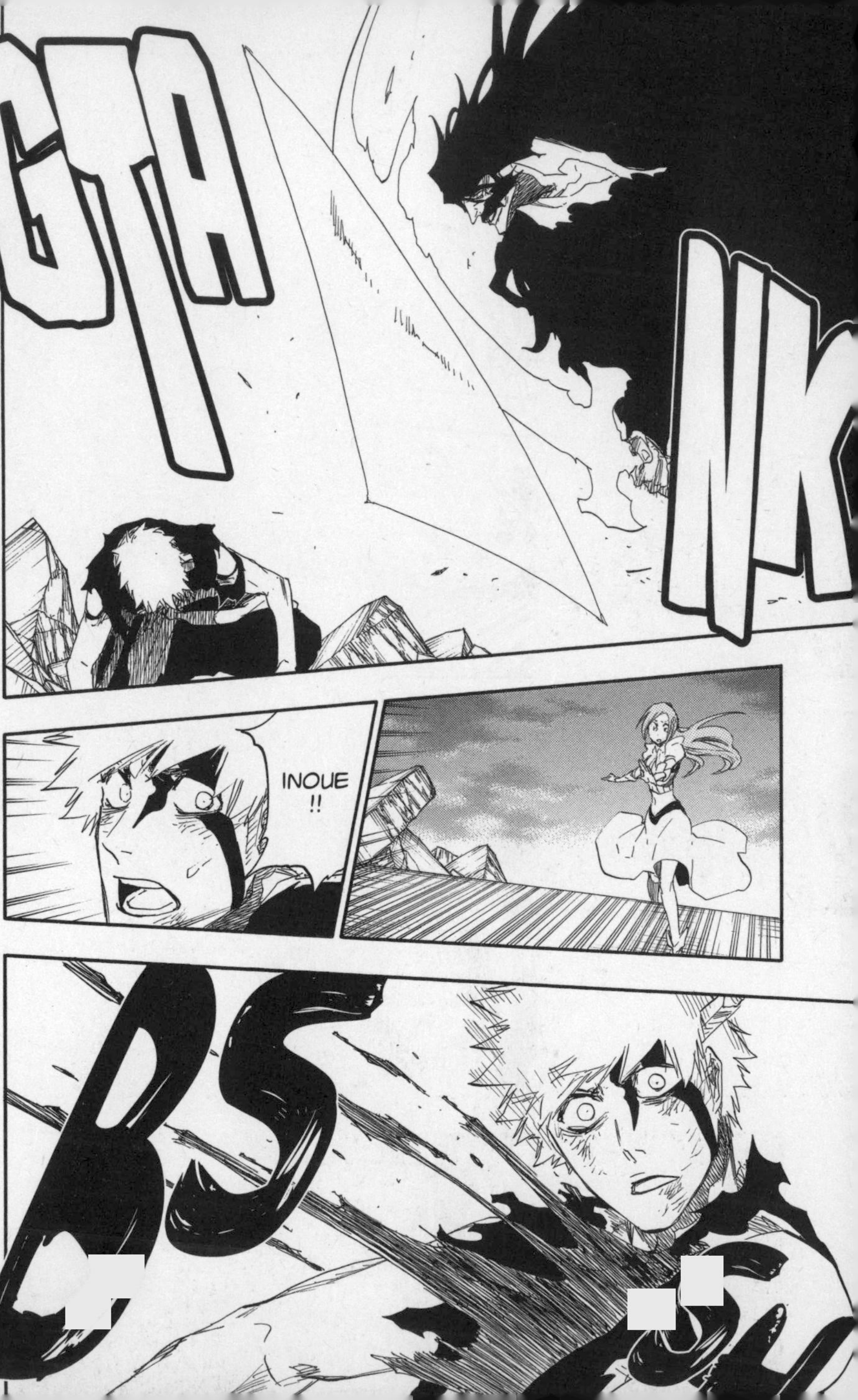
INOUE
!!

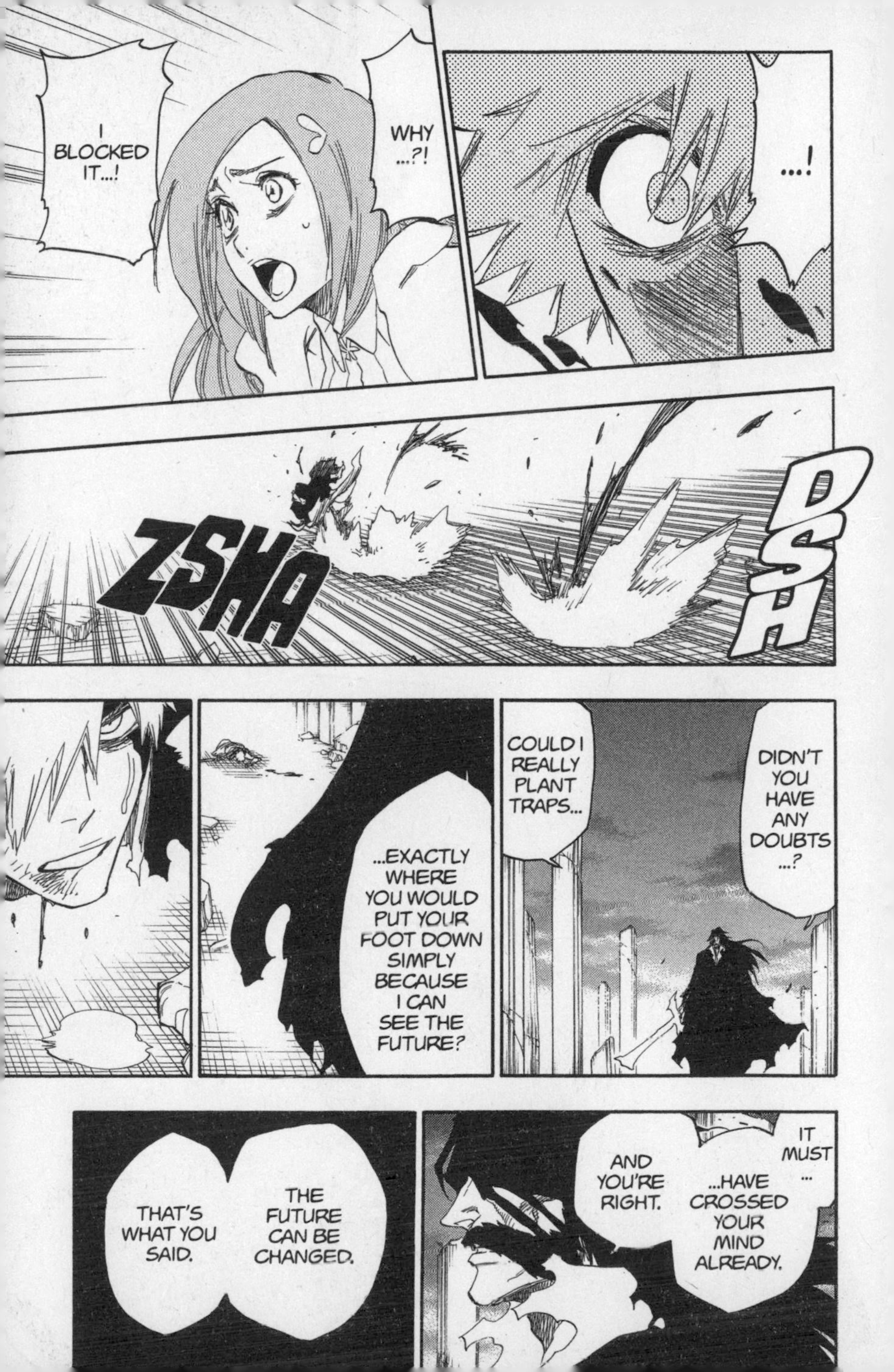
...!
WHY ...?!
I BLOCKED IT...!
DSH
ZSHA
DIDN'T YOU HAVE ANY DOUBTS ...?
COULD I REALLY PLANT TRAPS...
...EXACTLY WHERE YOU WOULD PUT YOUR FOOT DOWN SIMPLY BECAUSE I CAN SEE THE FUTURE?
IT MUST ...
...HAVE CROSSED YOUR MIND ALREADY.
AND YOU'RE RIGHT.
THE FUTURE CAN BE CHANGED.
THAT'S WHAT YOU SAID.

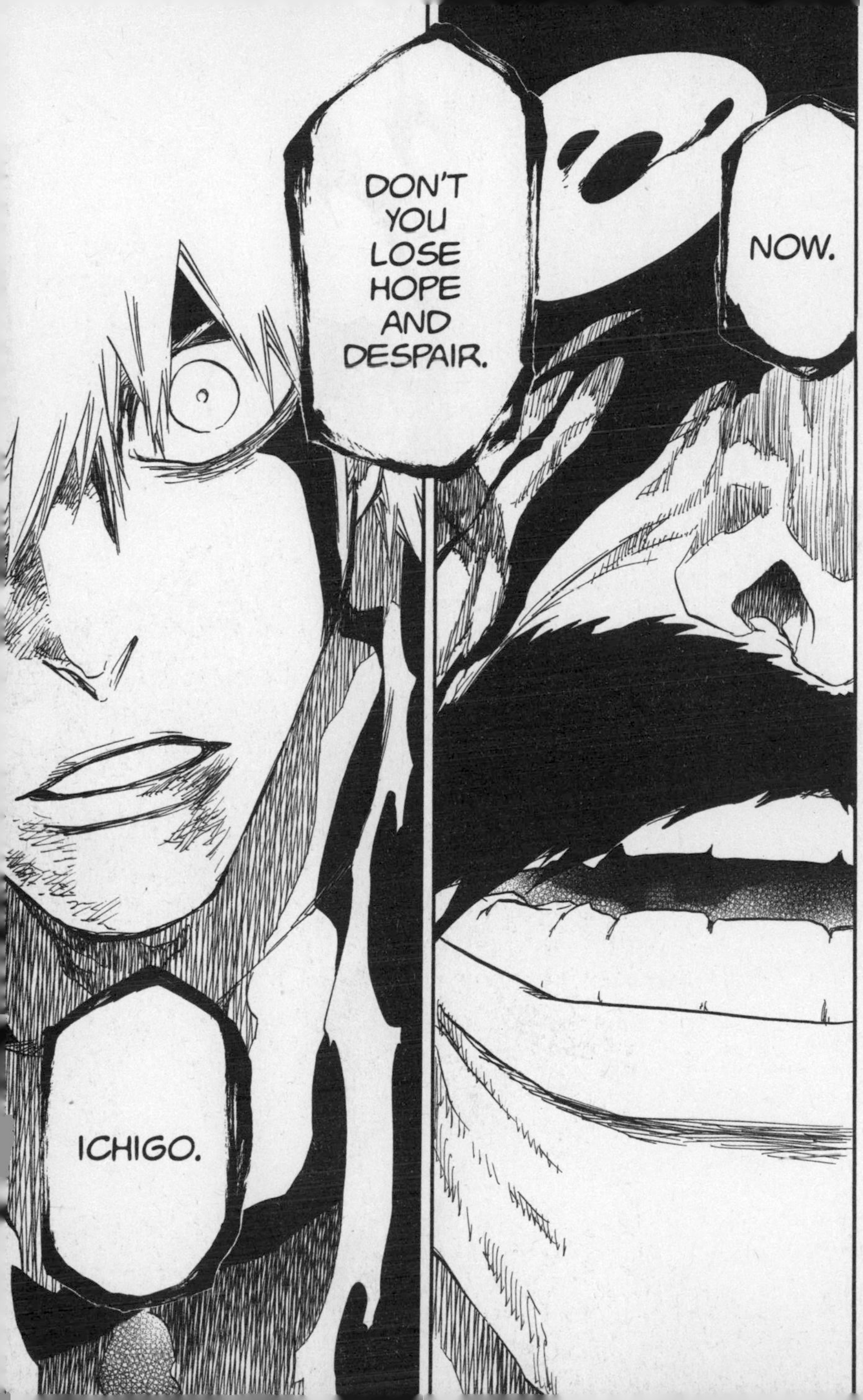
NOW.
DON'T YOU LOSE HOPE AND DESPAIR.
ICHIGO.

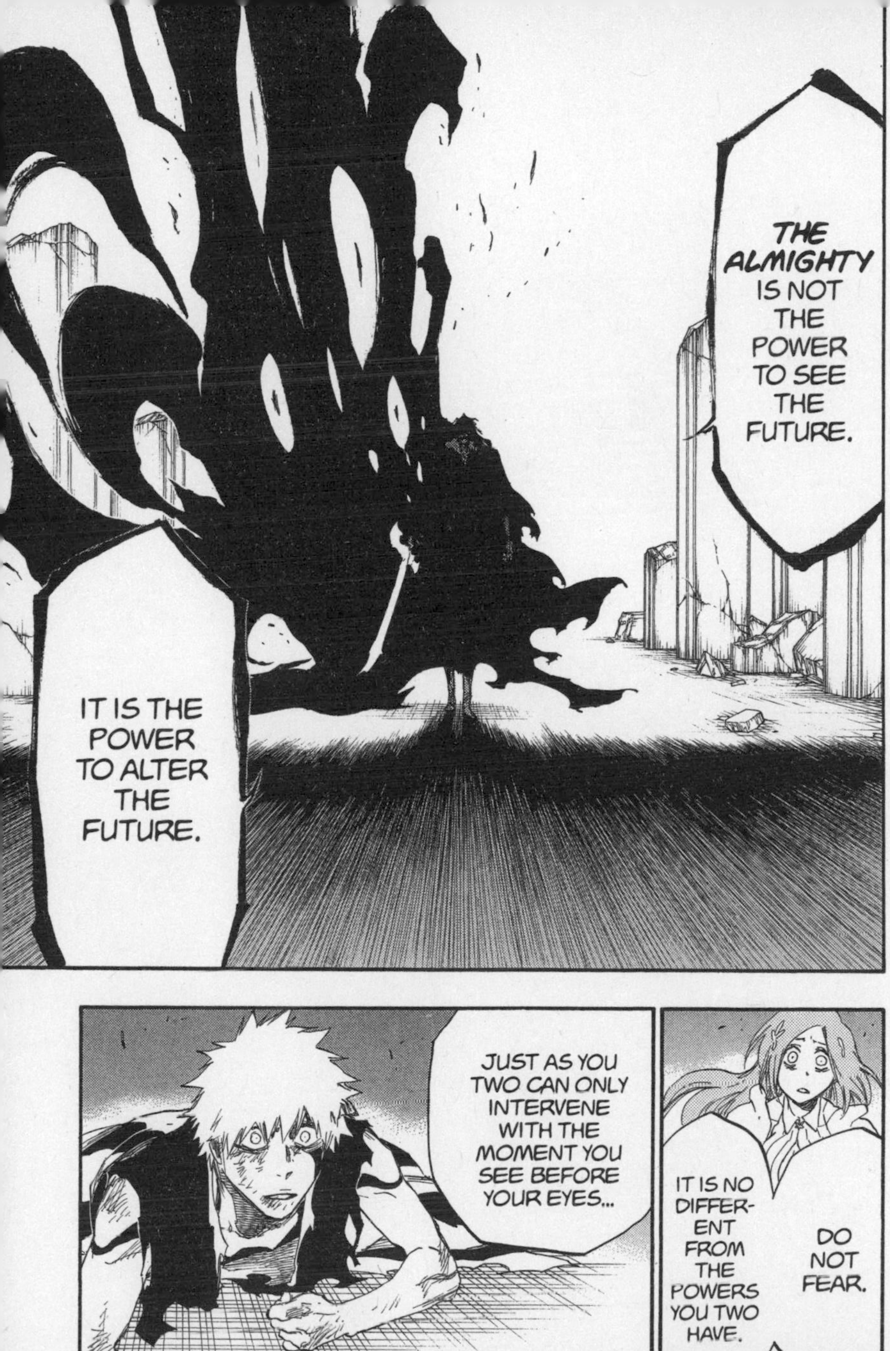
THE ALMIGHTY IS NOT THE POWER TO SEE THE FUTURE.
IT IS THE POWER TO ALTER THE FUTURE.
DO NOT FEAR.
IT IS NO DIFFER-ENT FROM THE POWERS YOU TWO HAVE.
JUST AS YOU TWO CAN ONLY INTERVENE WITH THE MOMENT YOU SEE BEFORE YOUR EYES...

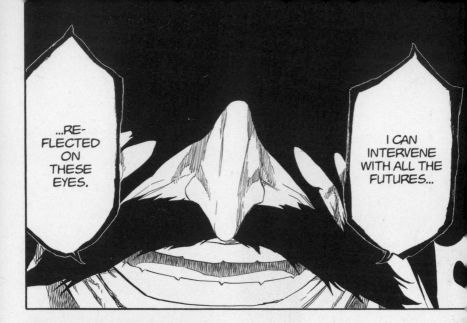

I CAN INTERVENE WITH ALL THE FUTURES...
...RE-FLECTED ON THESE EYES.
ICHI-GO.
YOU HAVE OVER-COME DESPAIR...
...AND CHANGED THE FUTURE COUNTLESS TIMES.
DO YOU KNOW WHY YOU WERE ABLE TO DO THAT?
IT'S BE-CAUSE ...
...I WASN'T THERE.

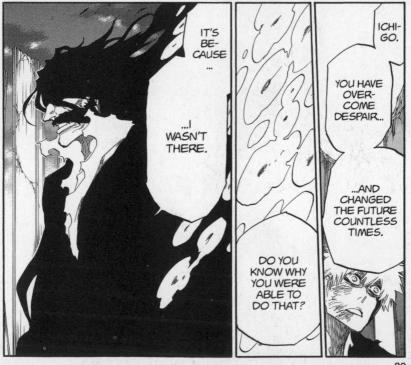

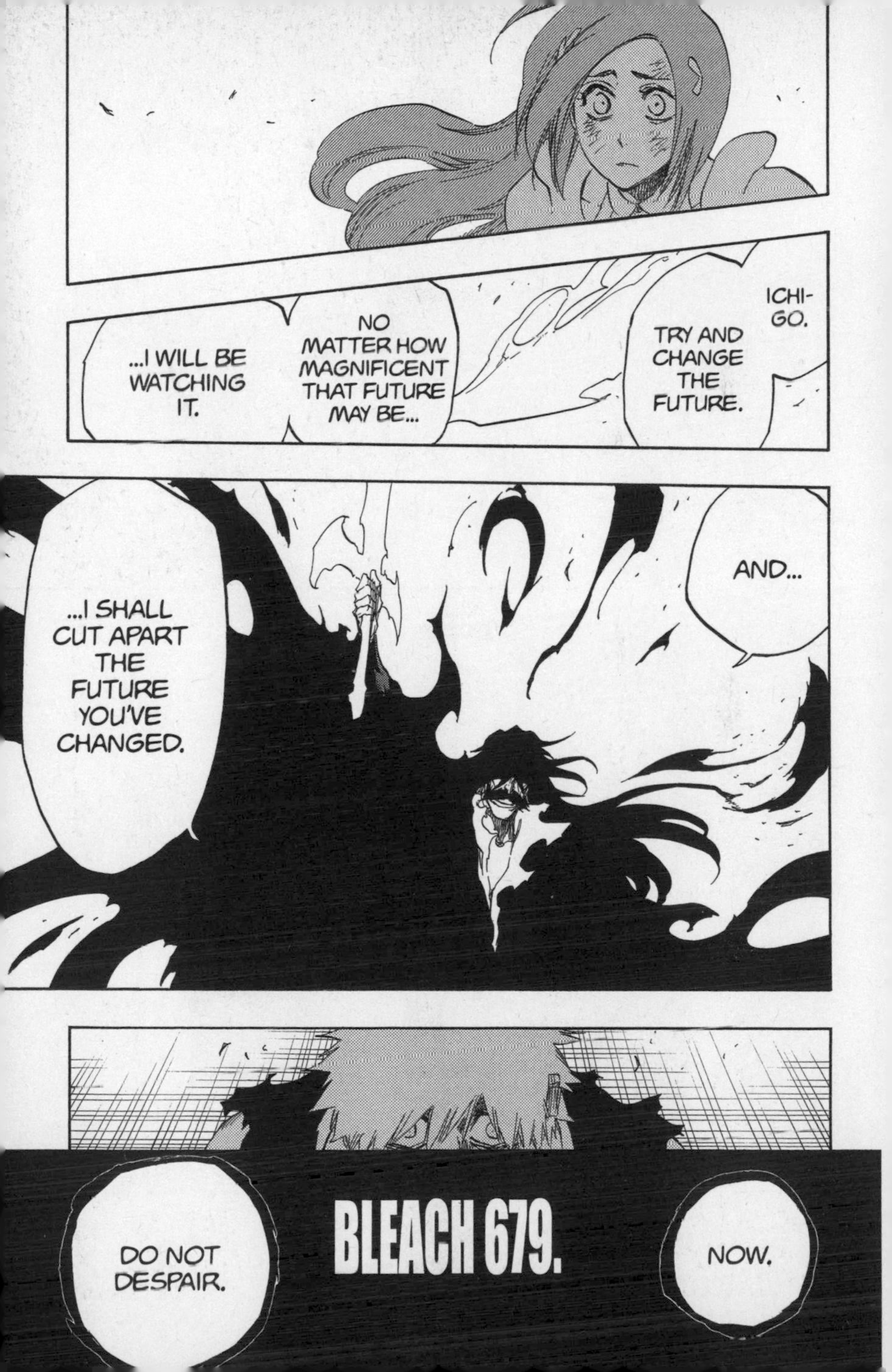
ICHI-GO.
TRY AND CHANGE THE FUTURE.
NO MATTER HOW MAGNIFICENT THAT FUTURE MAY BE...
...I WILL BE WATCHING IT.
AND...
...I SHALL CUT APART THE FUTURE YOU'VE CHANGED.
NOW.
BLEACH 679.
DO NOT DESPAIR.

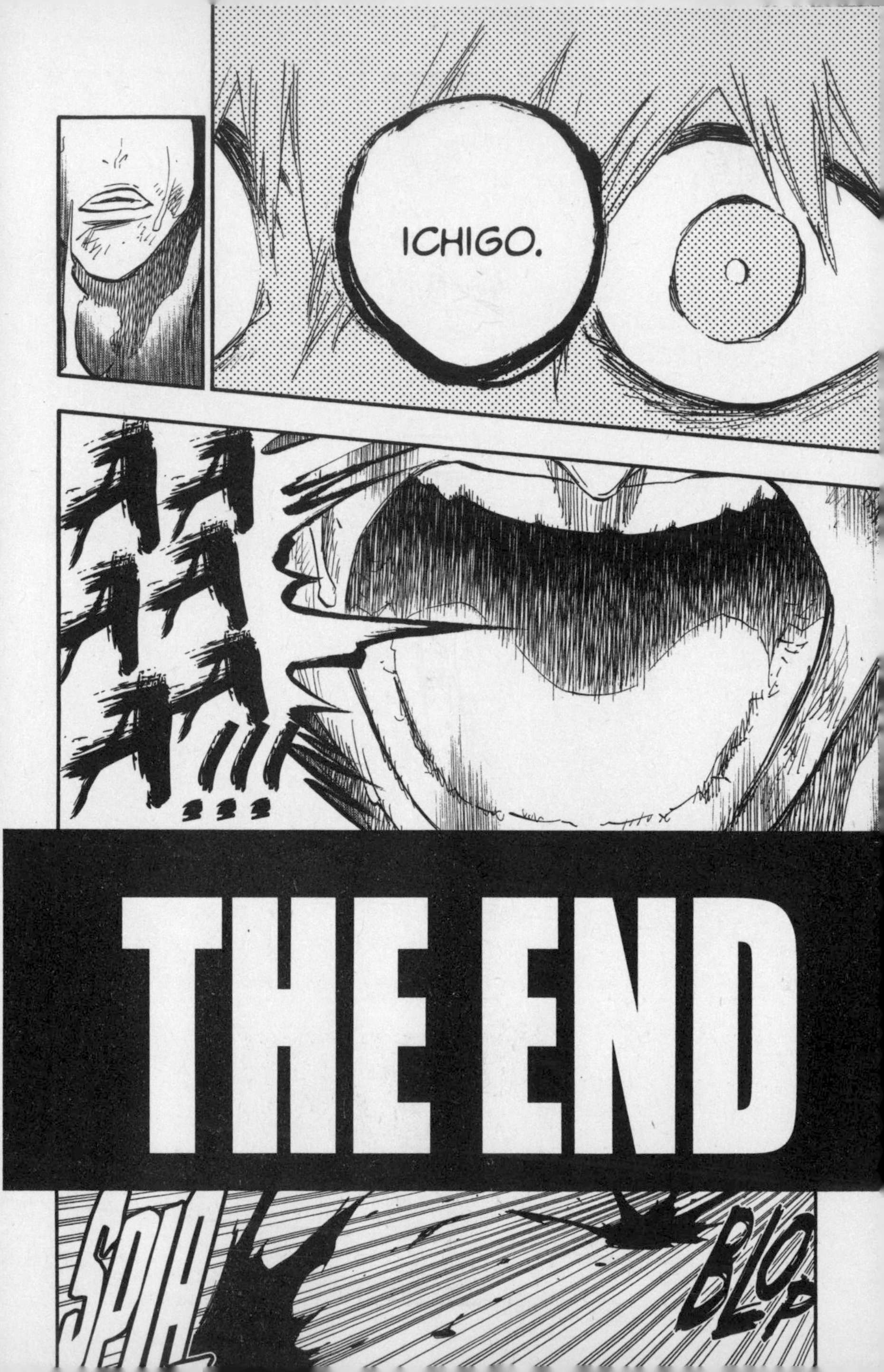
ICHIGO.
THE END

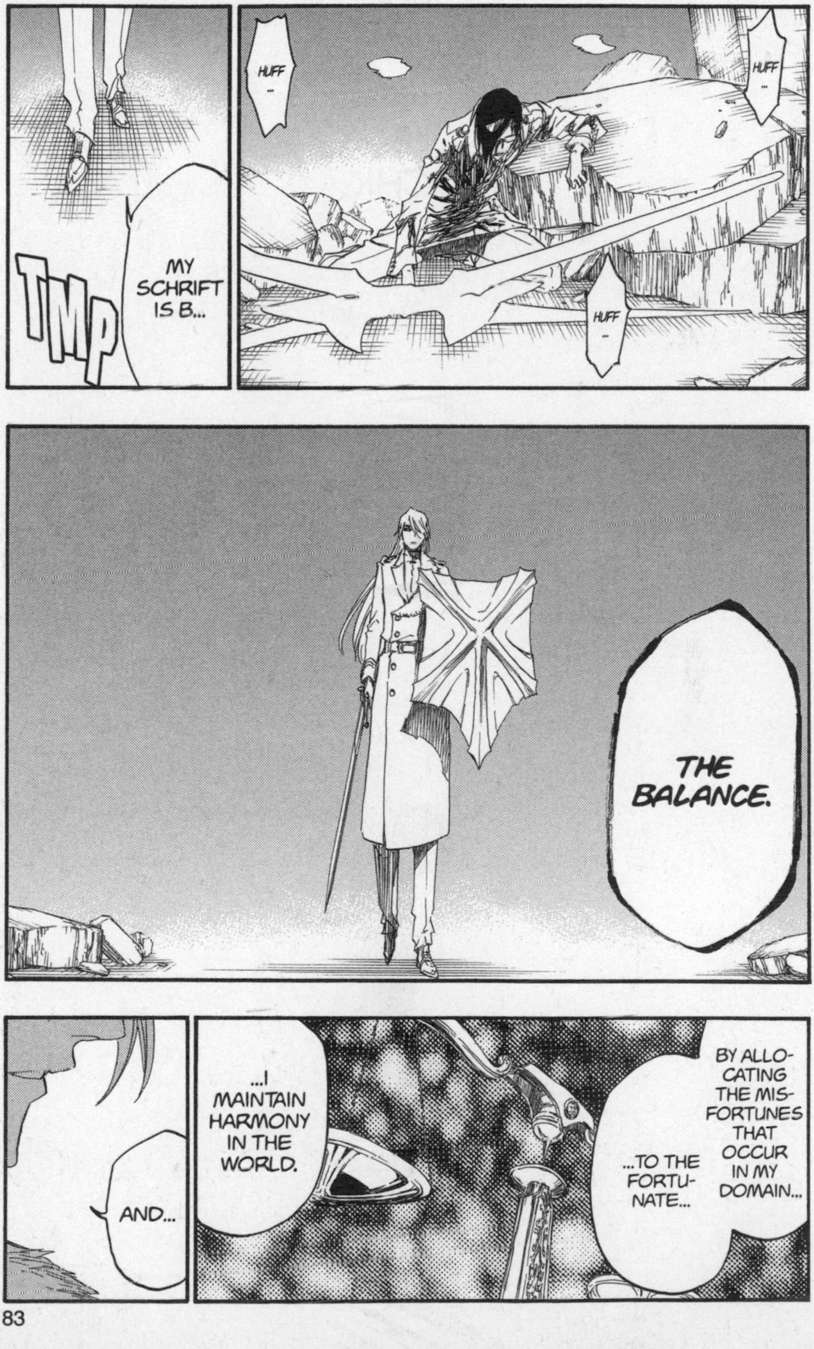
HUFF...
HUFF...
HUFF...
MY SCHRIFT IS B...
TMP
THE BALANCE.
BY ALLO-CATING THE MIS-FORTUNES THAT OCCUR IN MY DOMAIN...
...TO THE FORTU-NATE...
...I MAINTAIN HARMONY IN THE WORLD.
AND...

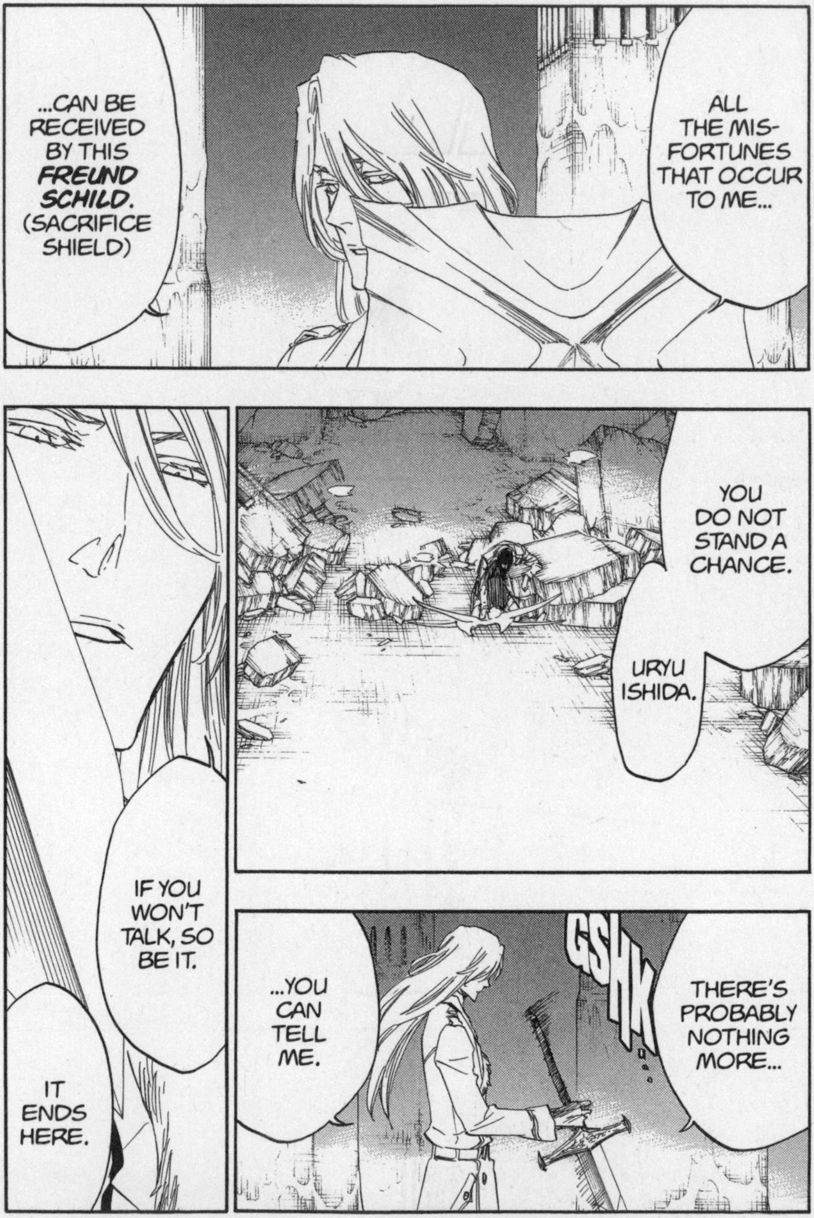
ALL THE MIS-FORTUNES THAT OCCUR TO ME...
...CAN BE RECEIVED BY THIS **FREUND SCHILD.** (SACRIFICE SHIELD)
YOU DO NOT STAND A CHANCE.
URYU ISHIDA.
THERE'S PROBABLY NOTHING MORE...
GSHK
...YOU CAN TELL ME.
IF YOU WON'T TALK, SO BE IT.
IT ENDS HERE.

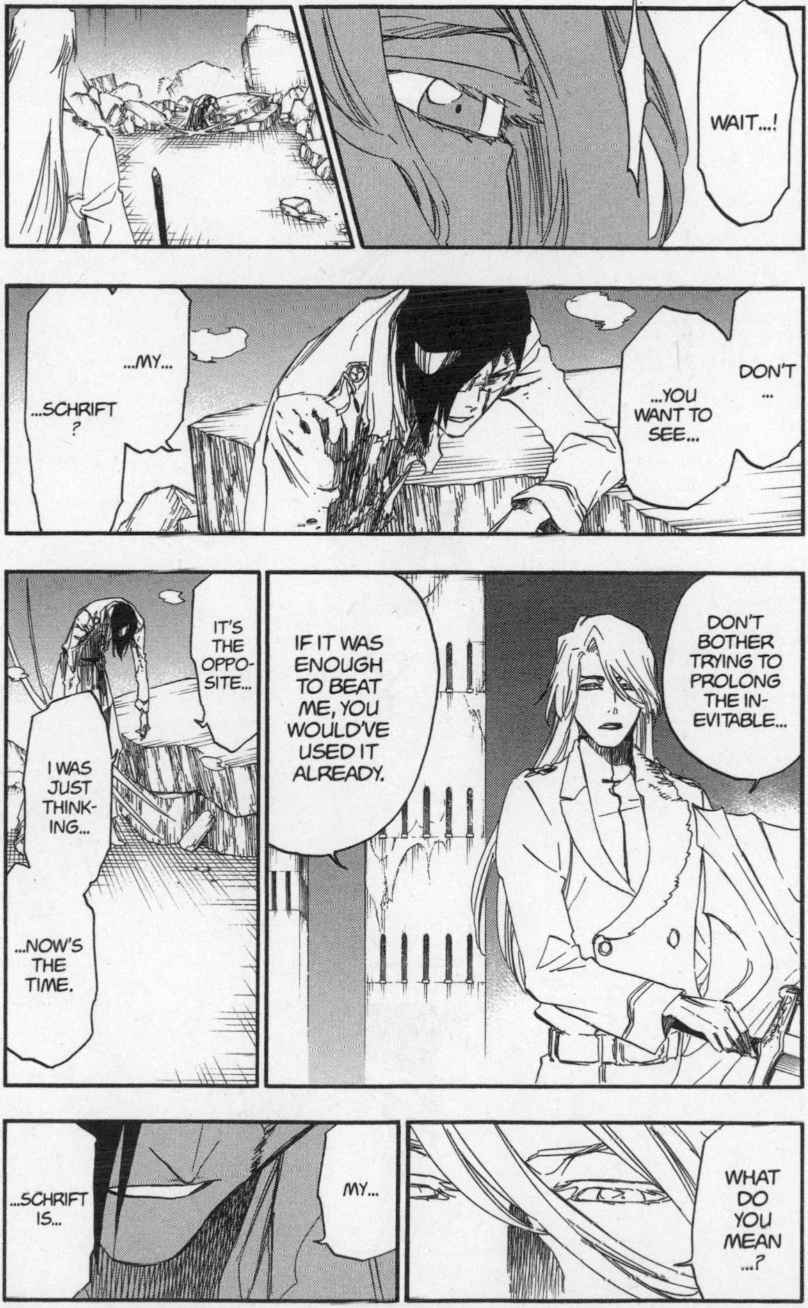
WAIT...!
DON'T ...
...YOU WANT TO SEE...
...MY...
...SCHRIFT ?
DON'T BOTHER TRYING TO PROLONG THE IN-EVITABLE...
IF IT WAS ENOUGH TO BEAT ME, YOU WOULD'VE USED IT ALREADY.
IT'S THE OPPO-SITE...
I WAS JUST THINK-ING...
...NOW'S THE TIME.
WHAT DO YOU MEAN ...?
MY...
...SCHRIFT IS...

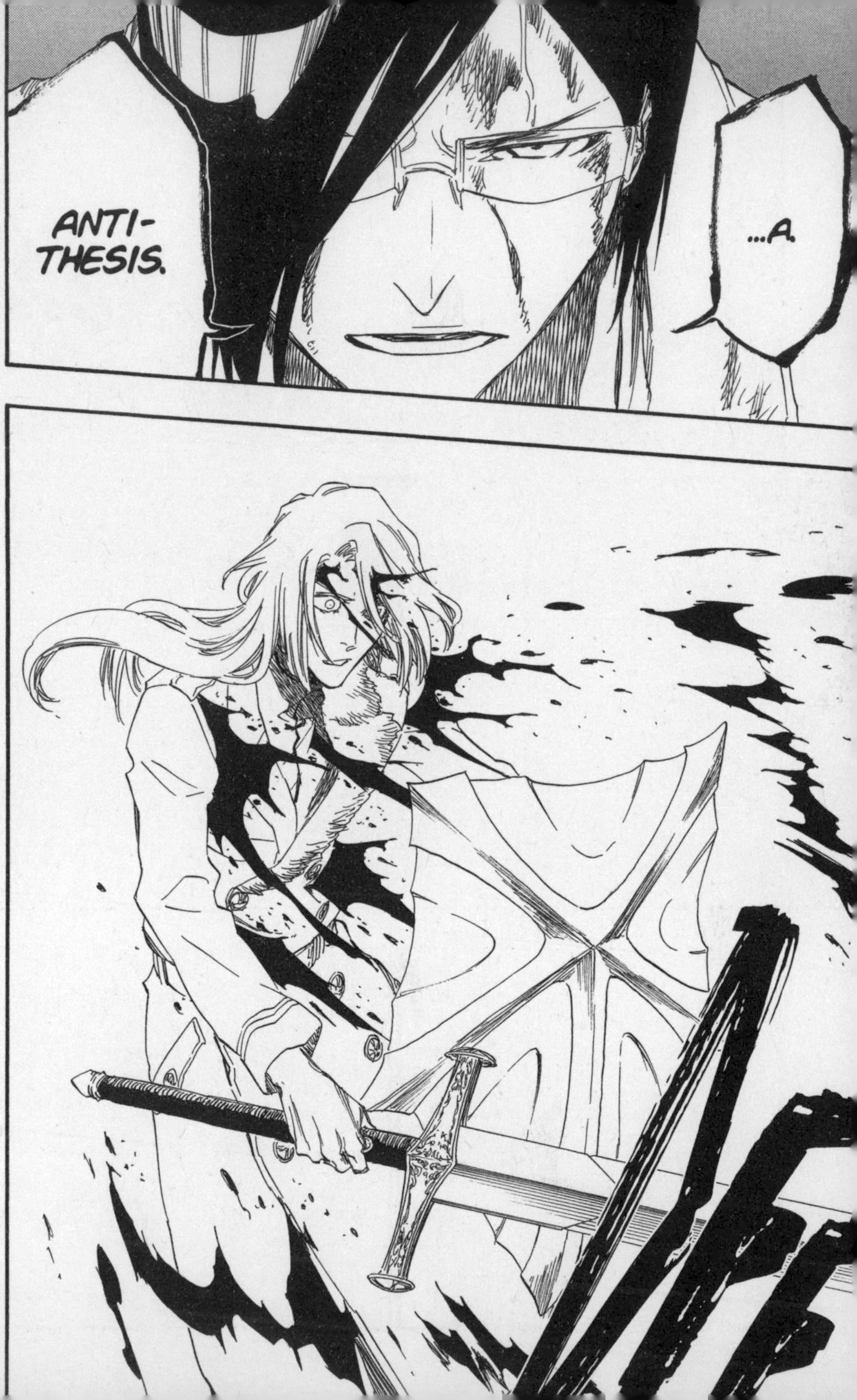
...A.
ANTI-
THESIS.

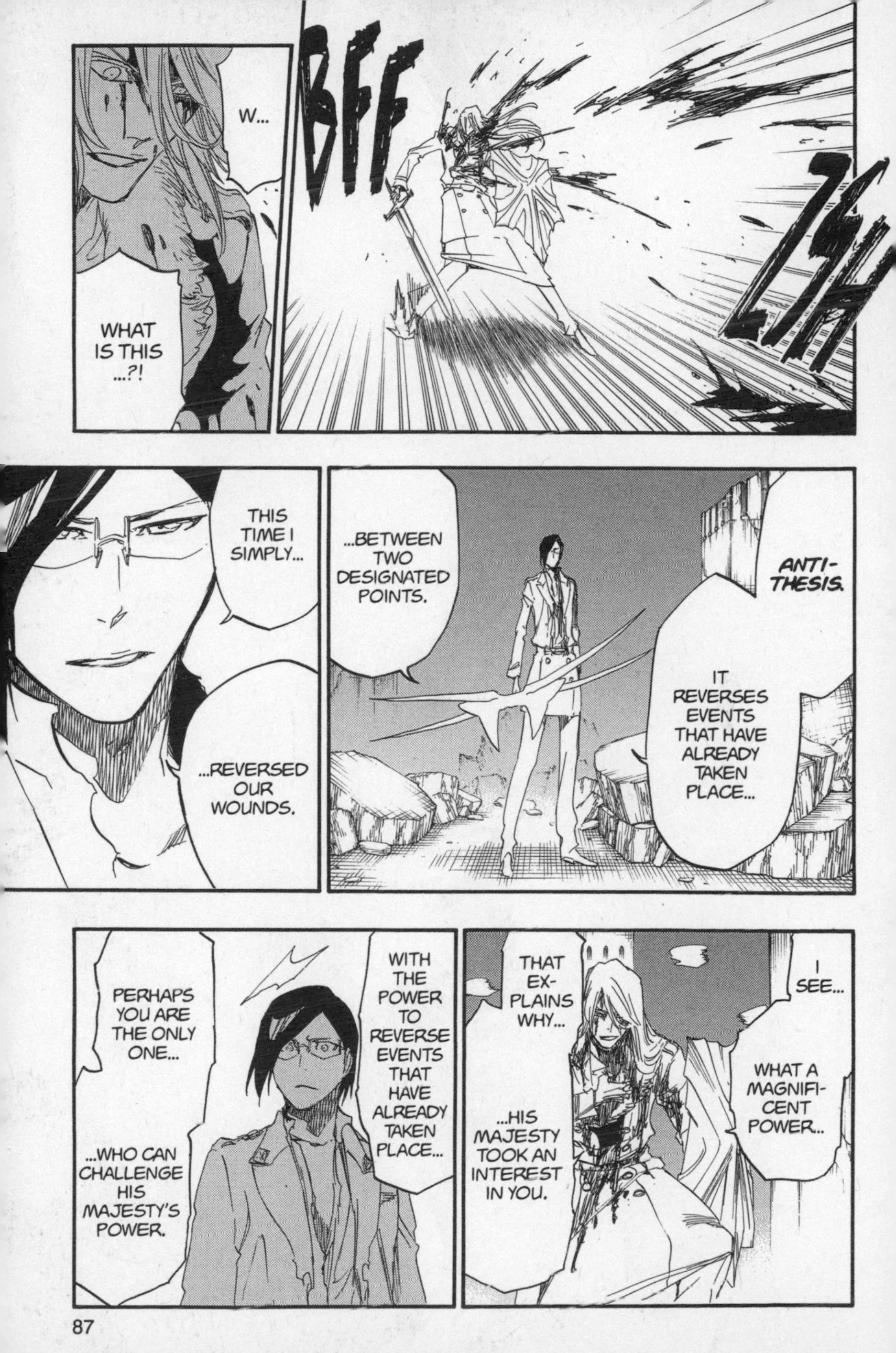
BFF
ZSH
W...
WHAT IS THIS ...?!
ANTITHESIS.
IT REVERSES EVENTS THAT HAVE ALREADY TAKEN PLACE...
...BETWEEN TWO DESIGNATED POINTS.
THIS TIME I SIMPLY...
...REVERSED OUR WOUNDS.
I SEE...
WHAT A MAGNIFICENT POWER...
THAT EXPLAINS WHY...
...HIS MAJESTY TOOK AN INTEREST IN YOU.
WITH THE POWER TO REVERSE EVENTS THAT HAVE ALREADY TAKEN PLACE...
PERHAPS YOU ARE THE ONLY ONE...
...WHO CAN CHALLENGE HIS MAJESTY'S POWER.

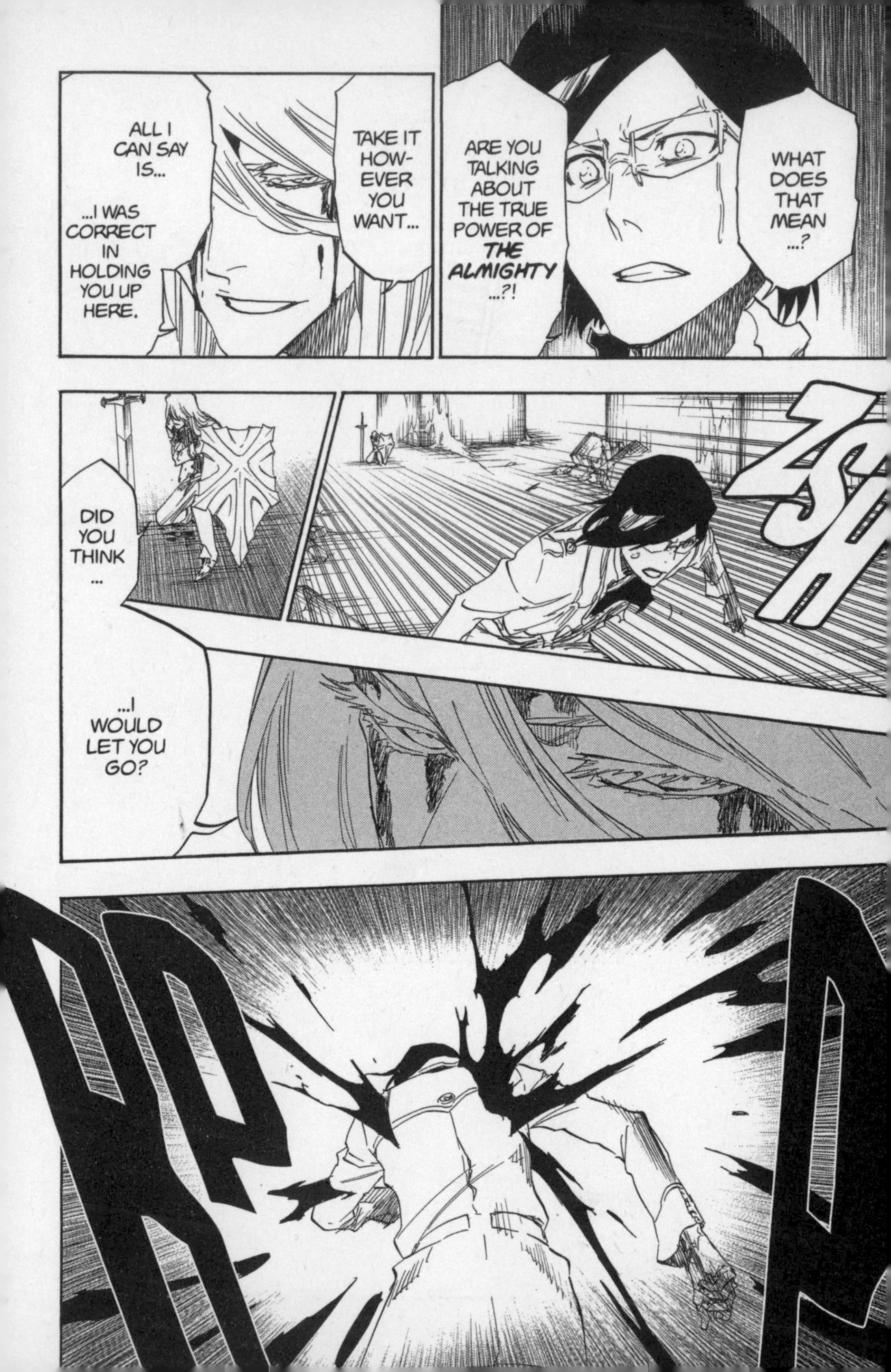
WHAT DOES THAT MEAN ...?
ARE YOU TALKING ABOUT THE TRUE POWER OF THE ALMIGHTY ...?!
TAKE IT HOW- EVER YOU WANT...
ALL I CAN SAY IS...
...I WAS CORRECT IN HOLDING YOU UP HERE.
ZSH
DID YOU THINK ...
...I WOULD LET YOU GO?

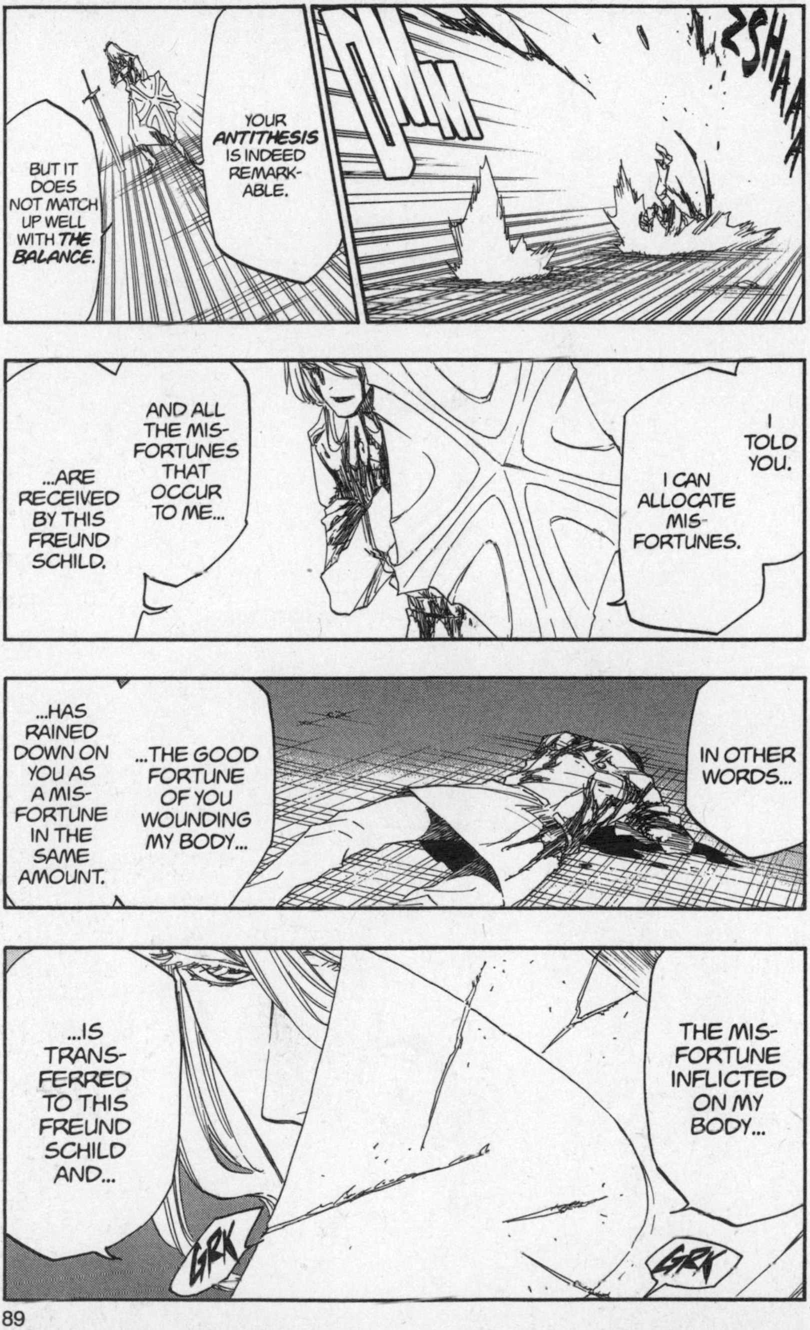
YOUR ANTITHESIS IS INDEED REMARKABLE.
BUT IT DOES NOT MATCH UP WELL WITH THE BALANCE.
I TOLD YOU.
I CAN ALLOCATE MISFORTUNES.
AND ALL THE MISFORTUNES THAT OCCUR TO ME...
...ARE RECEIVED BY THIS FREUND SCHILD.
IN OTHER WORDS...
...THE GOOD FORTUNE OF YOU WOUNDING MY BODY...
...HAS RAINED DOWN ON YOU AS A MISFORTUNE IN THE SAME AMOUNT.
THE MISFORTUNE INFLICTED ON MY BODY...
GRK
...IS TRANSFERRED TO THIS FREUND SCHILD AND...
GRK

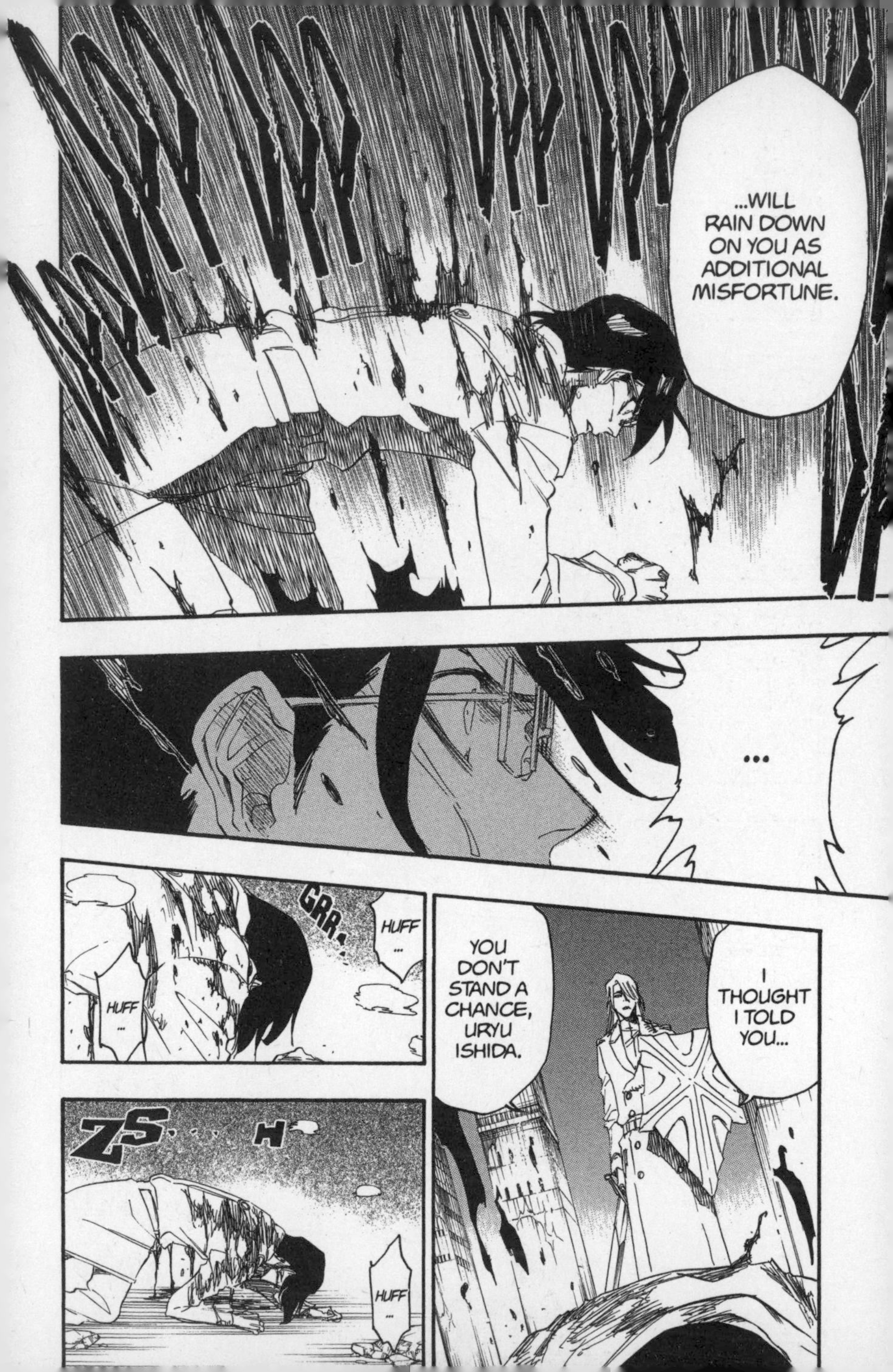
...WILL RAIN DOWN ON YOU AS ADDITIONAL MISFORTUNE.
...
GRR
HUFF ...
HUFF ...
I THOUGHT I TOLD YOU...
YOU DON'T STAND A CHANCE, URYU ISHIDA.
ZSH
HUFF ...

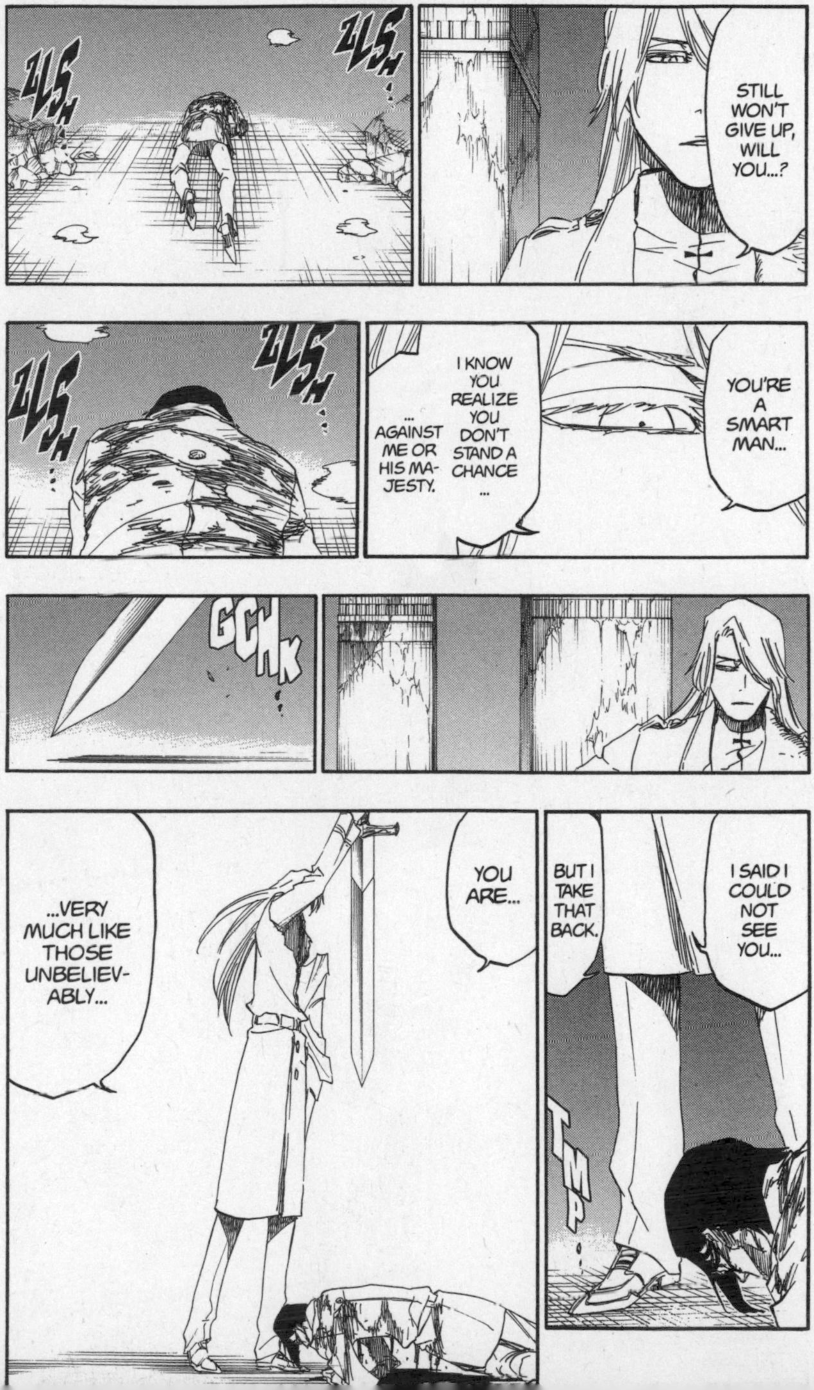
STILL WON'T GIVE UP, WILL YOU...?
ZLSH
ZLSH
YOU'RE A SMART MAN...
I KNOW YOU REALIZE YOU DON'T STAND A CHANCE ...
... AGAINST ME OR HIS MAJESTY.
ZLSH
ZLSH
GCHK
I SAID I COULD NOT SEE YOU...
BUT I TAKE THAT BACK.
TMP
YOU ARE...
...VERY MUCH LIKE THOSE UNBELIEVABLY...

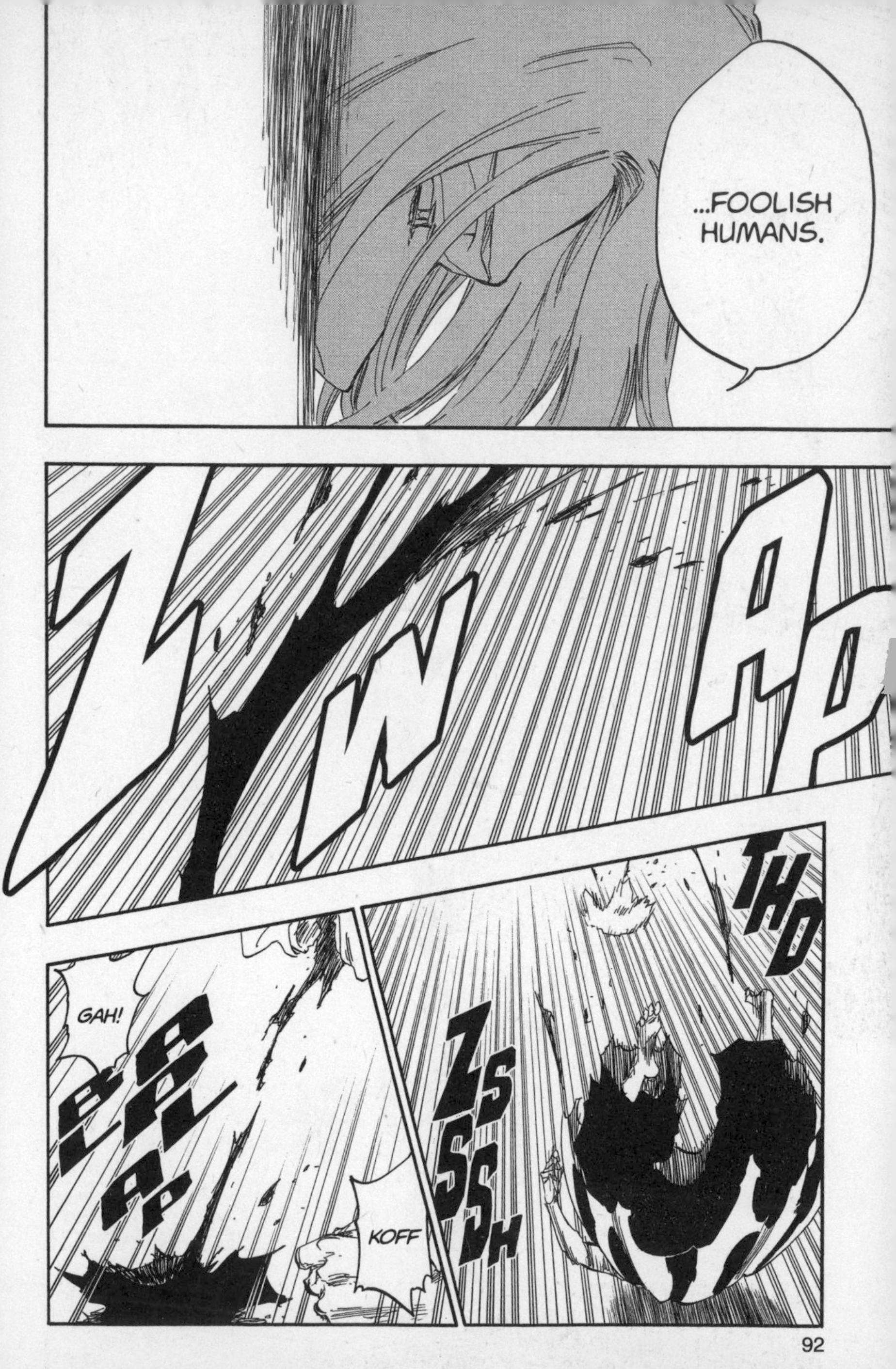
...FOOLISH HUMANS.
ZWAP
THD
ZSSSH
GAH!
KOFF

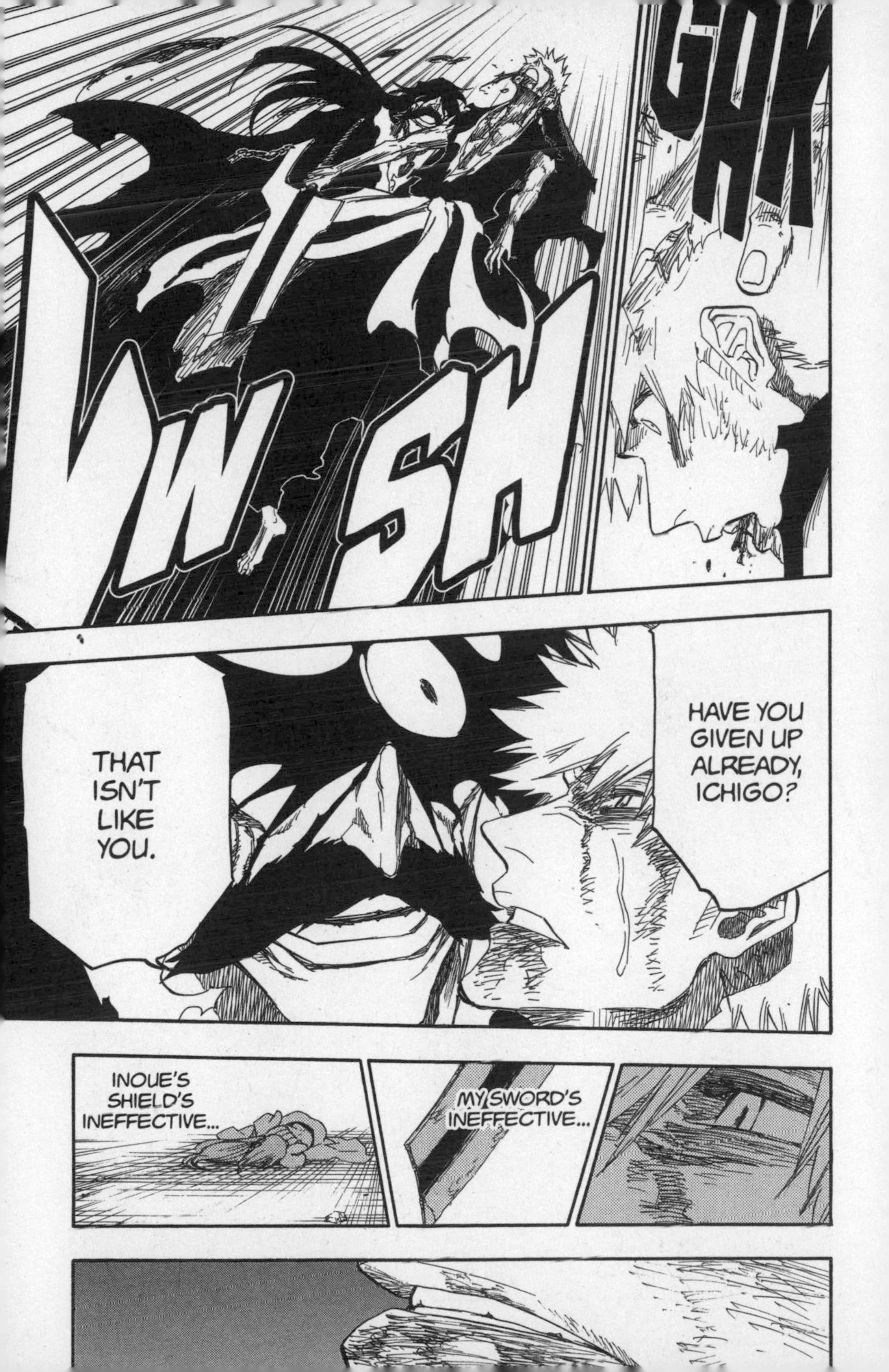
GAK
HAVE YOU GIVEN UP ALREADY, ICHIGO?
THAT ISN'T LIKE YOU.
MY SWORD'S INEFFECTIVE...
INOUE'S SHIELD'S INEFFECTIVE...

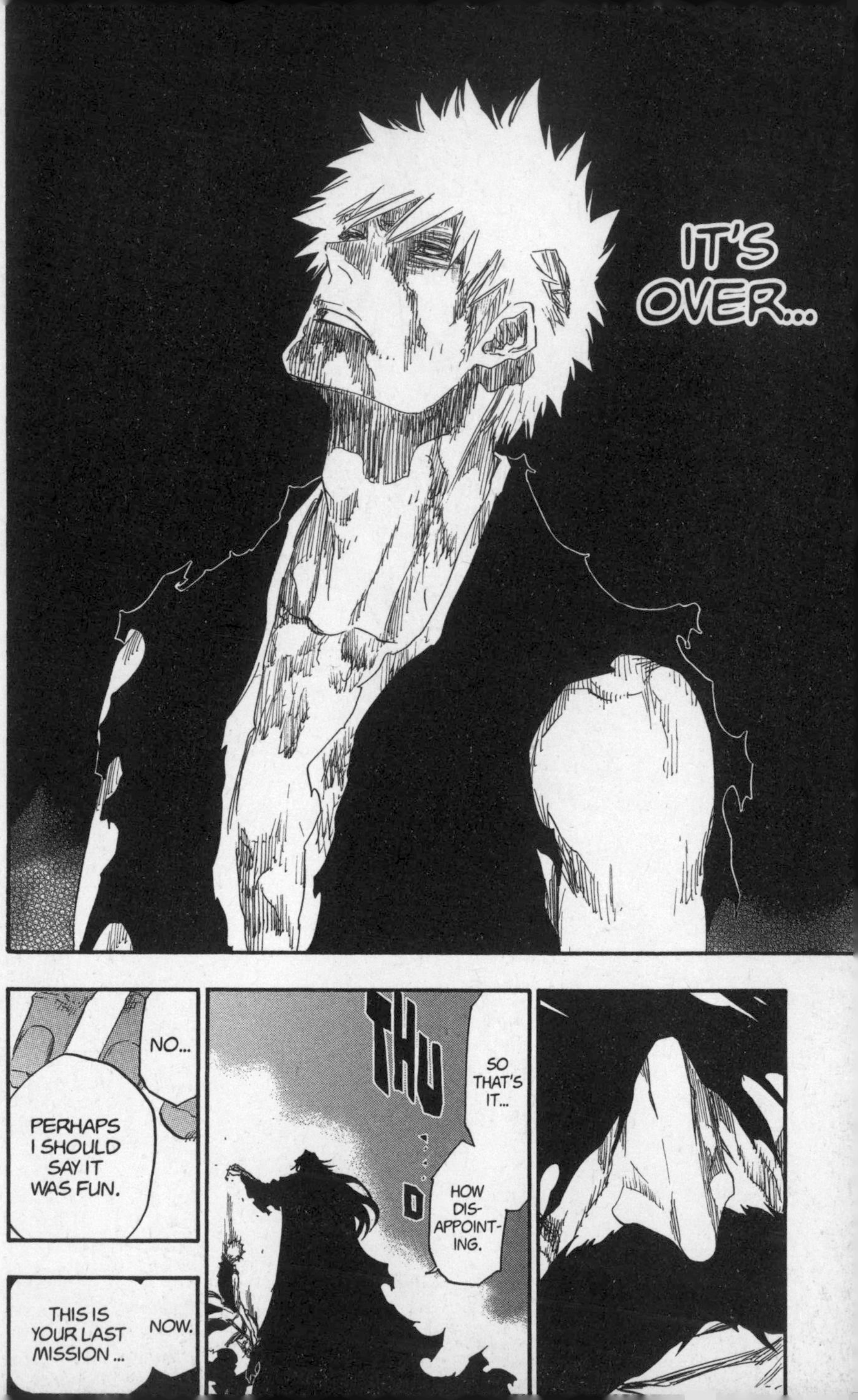
IT'S OVER...
THU
D
SO THAT'S IT...
HOW DIS-APPOINT-ING.
NO...
PERHAPS I SHOULD SAY IT WAS FUN.
NOW.
THIS IS YOUR LAST MISSION ...

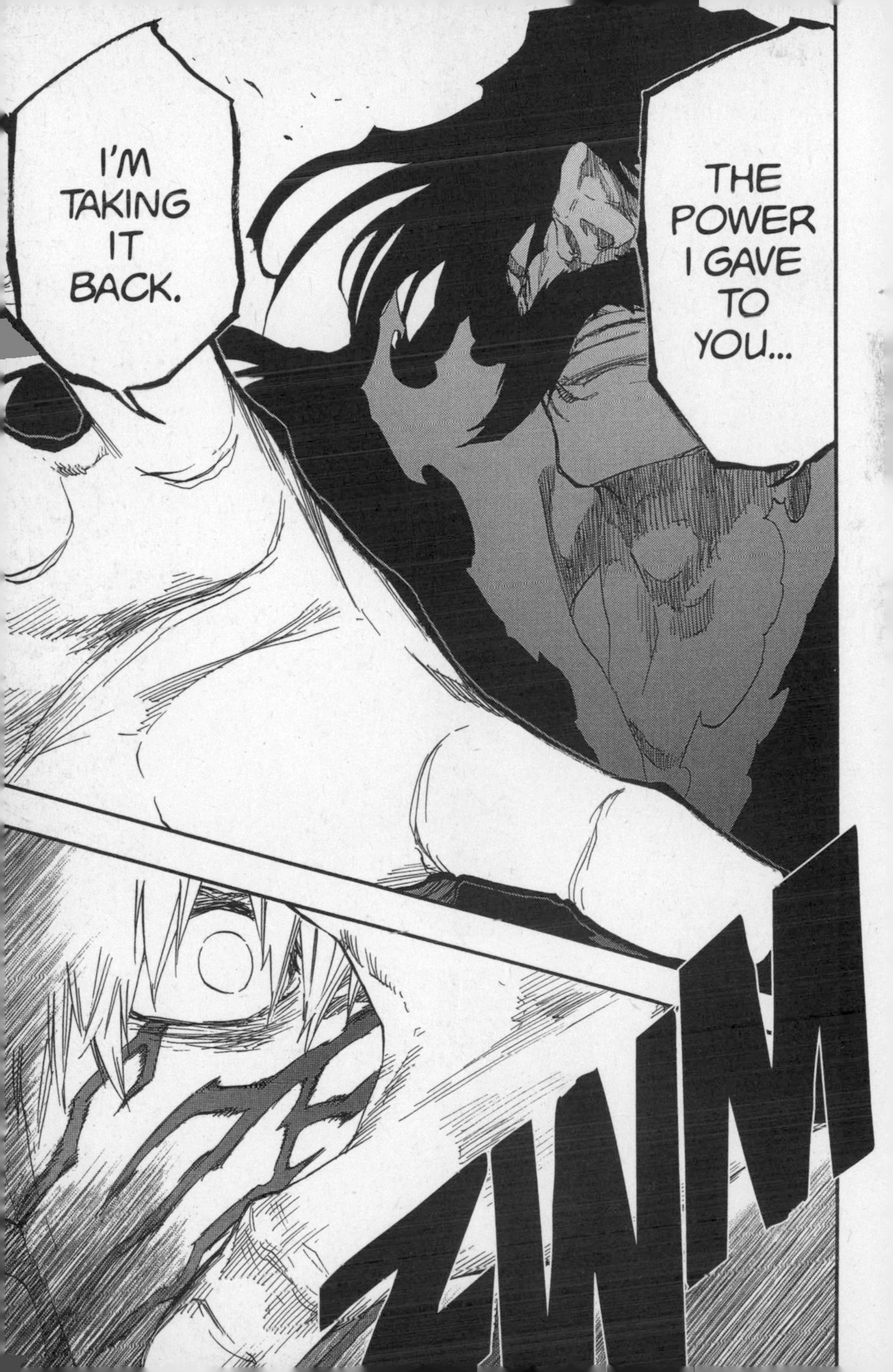
THE POWER I GAVE TO YOU...
I'M TAKING IT BACK.
ZNNN

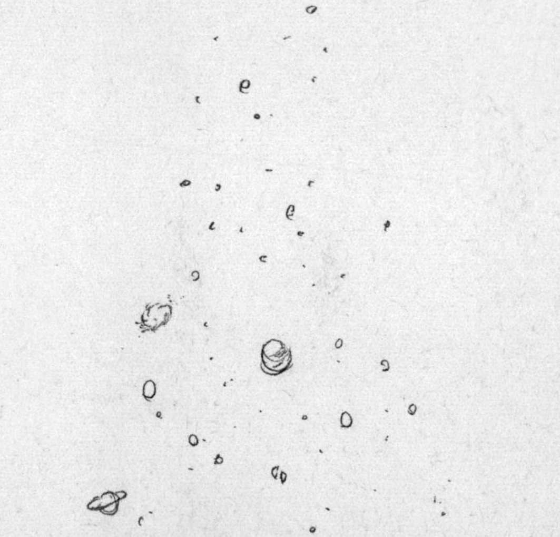

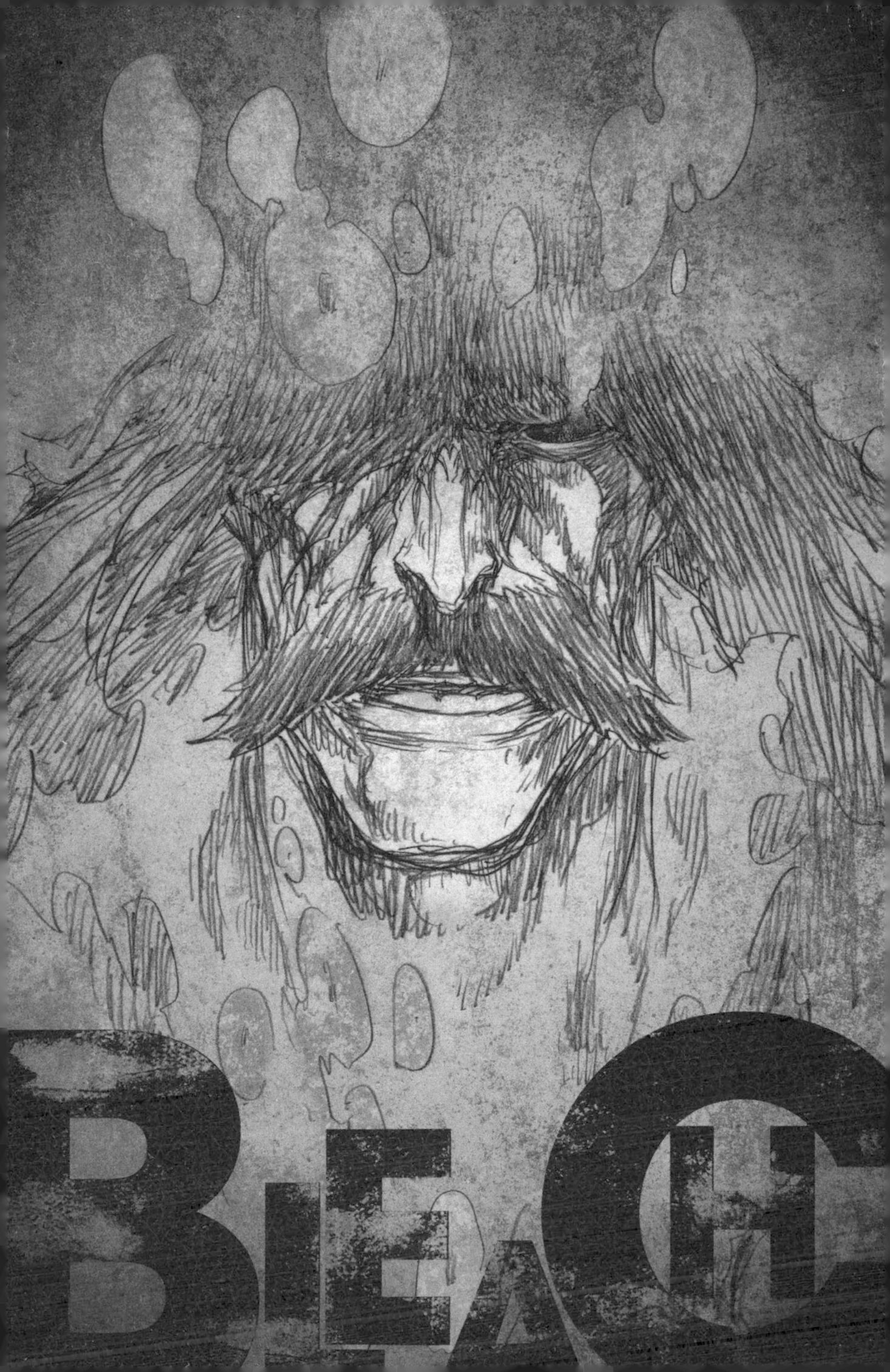
BLEACH

BLEACH
ブリーチ

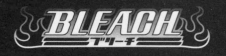

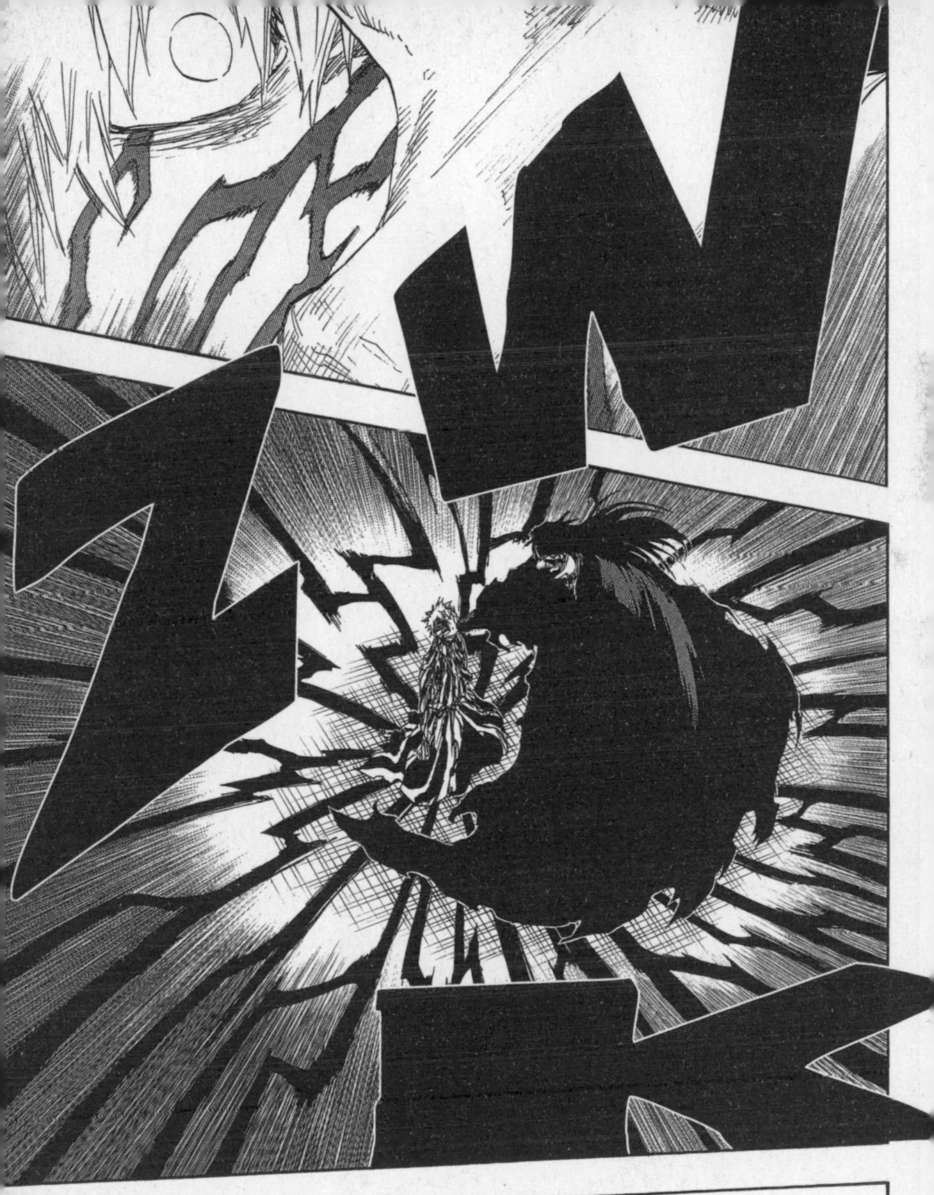

OH...

IT'S GOING AWAY...

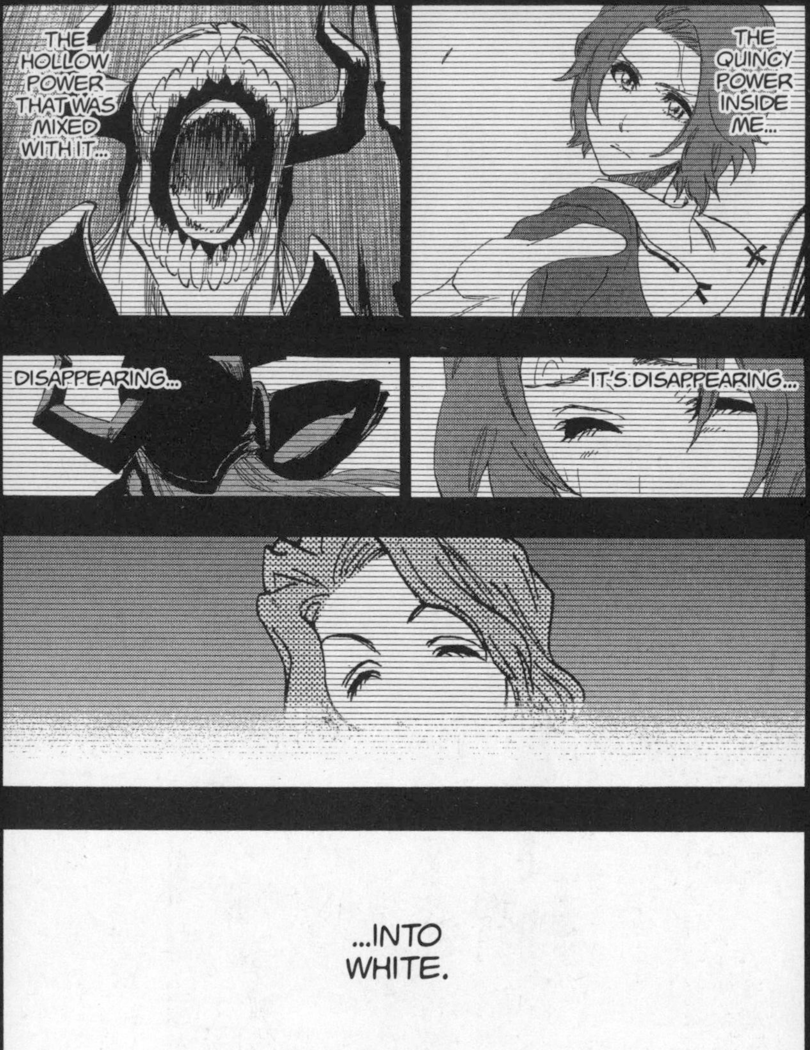
THE QUINCY POWER INSIDE ME...
THE HOLLOW POWER THAT WAS MIXED WITH IT...
IT'S DISAPPEARING...
DISAPPEARING...
...INTO WHITE.

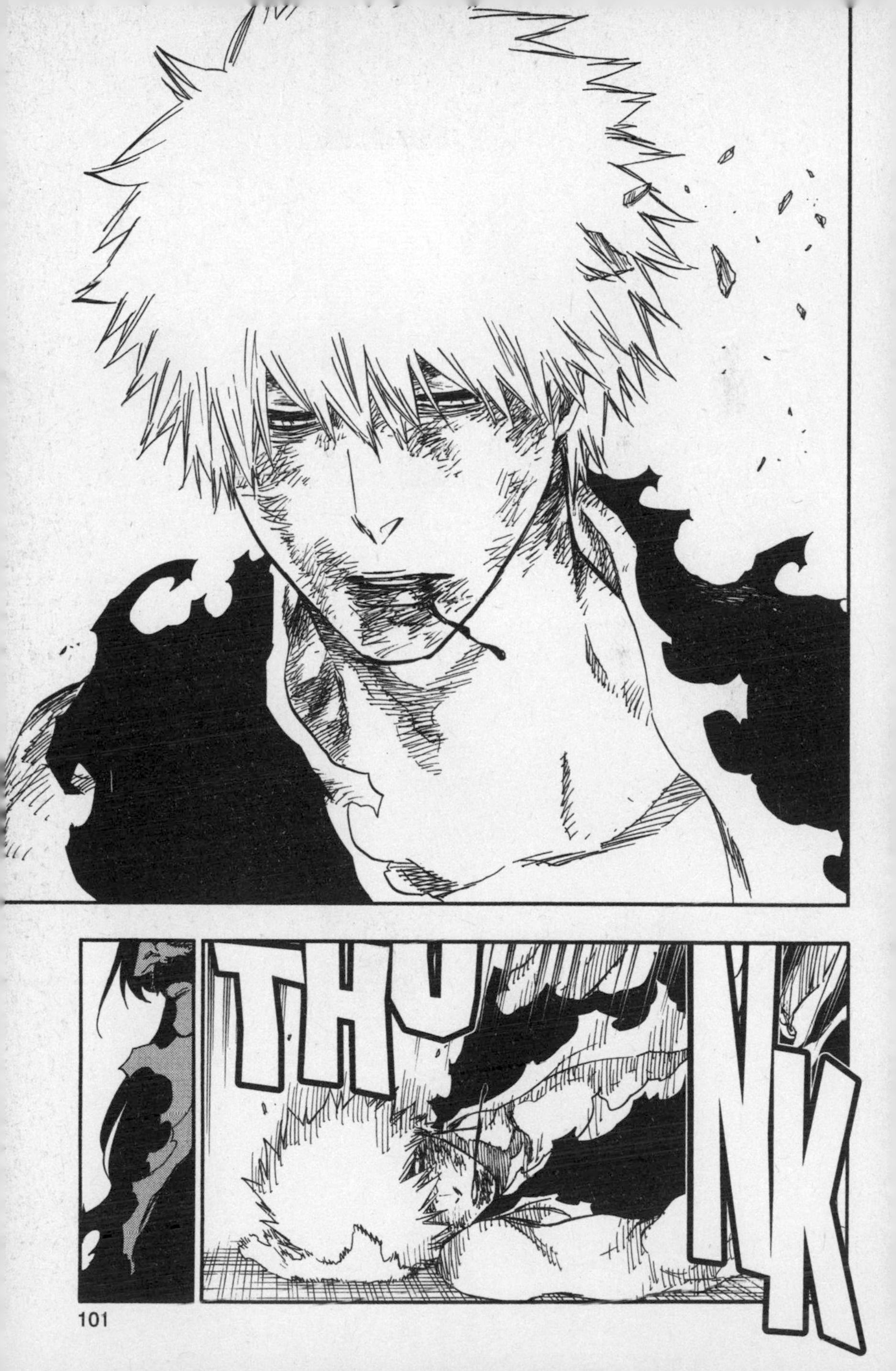
THUNK

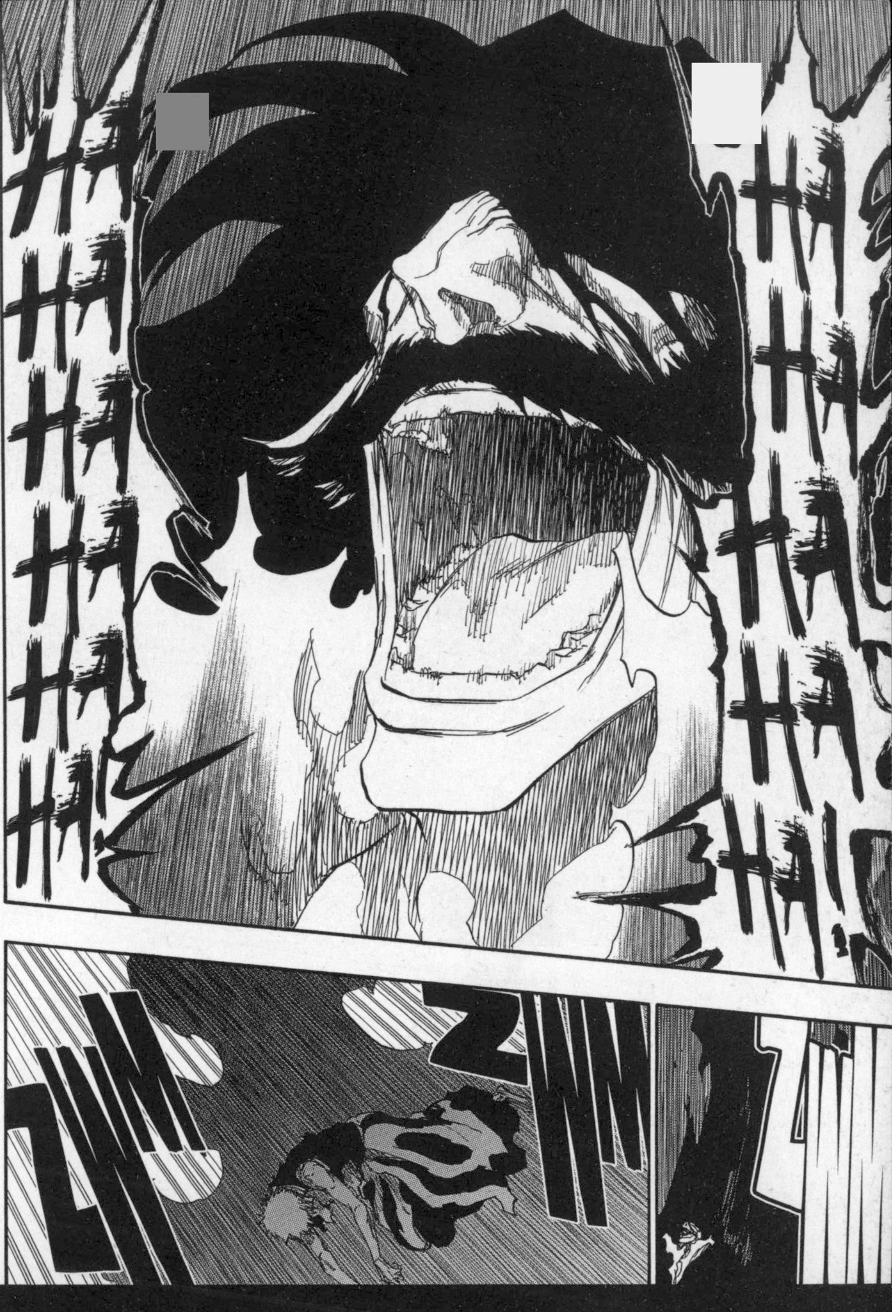
HA HA HA HA HA HA!
HA HA HA HA HA HA

BLEACH 680.

THE END
2

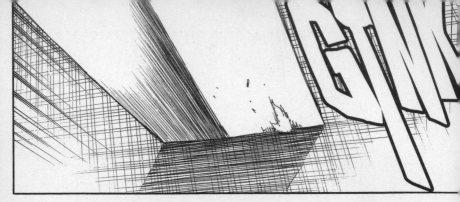

HUFF...

HUFF...

I'M...

...LIKE THEM?

HUFF...

SO YOU CAN STILL MOVE...

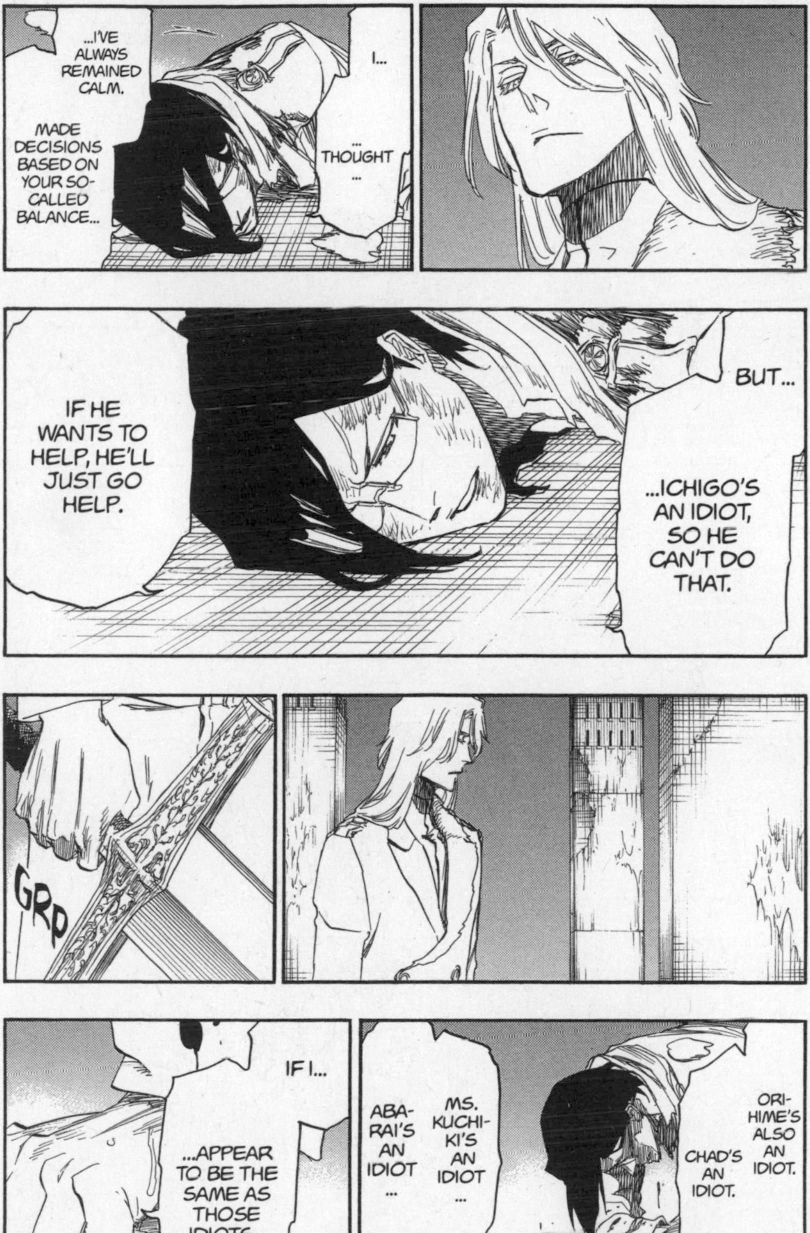
I...
...THOUGHT...
...I'VE ALWAYS REMAINED CALM.
MADE DECISIONS BASED ON YOUR SO-CALLED BALANCE...
BUT...
...ICHIGO'S AN IDIOT, SO HE CAN'T DO THAT.
IF HE WANTS TO HELP, HE'LL JUST GO HELP.
GRP
ORI-HIME'S ALSO AN IDIOT.
CHAD'S AN IDIOT.
MS. KUCHI-KI'S AN IDIOT...
ABA-RAI'S AN IDIOT...
IF I...
...APPEAR TO BE THE SAME AS THOSE IDIOTS...

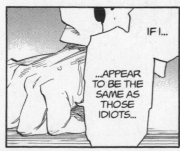

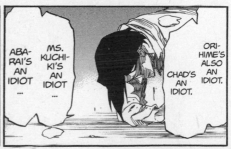

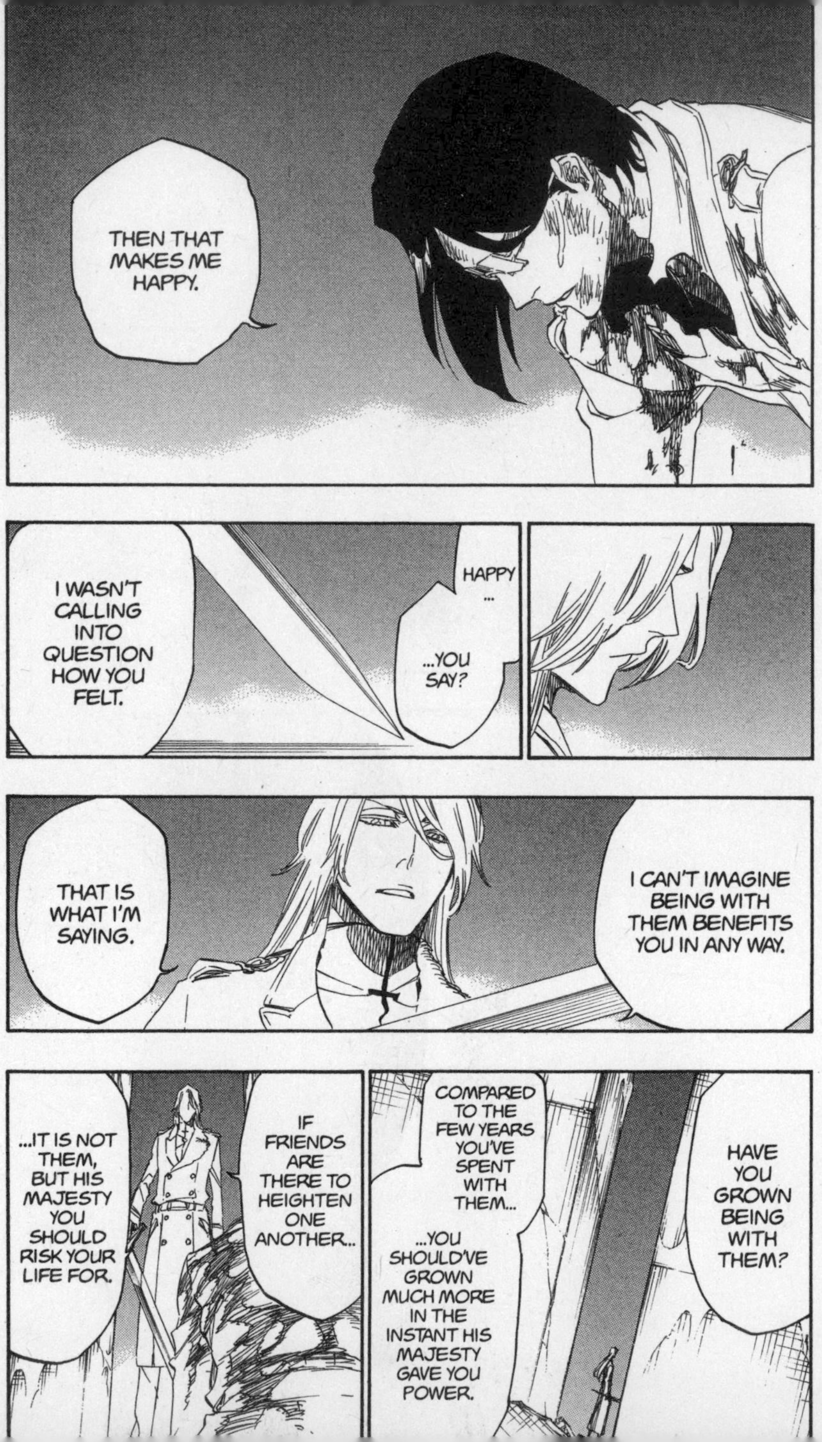
THEN THAT MAKES ME HAPPY.
HAPPY ...
...YOU SAY?
I WASN'T CALLING INTO QUESTION HOW YOU FELT.
I CAN'T IMAGINE BEING WITH THEM BENEFITS YOU IN ANY WAY.
THAT IS WHAT I'M SAYING.
HAVE YOU GROWN BEING WITH THEM?
COMPARED TO THE FEW YEARS YOU'VE SPENT WITH THEM...
...YOU SHOULD'VE GROWN MUCH MORE IN THE INSTANT HIS MAJESTY GAVE YOU POWER.
IF FRIENDS ARE THERE TO HEIGHTEN ONE ANOTHER...
...IT IS NOT THEM, BUT HIS MAJESTY YOU SHOULD RISK YOUR LIFE FOR.

READ THIS WAY

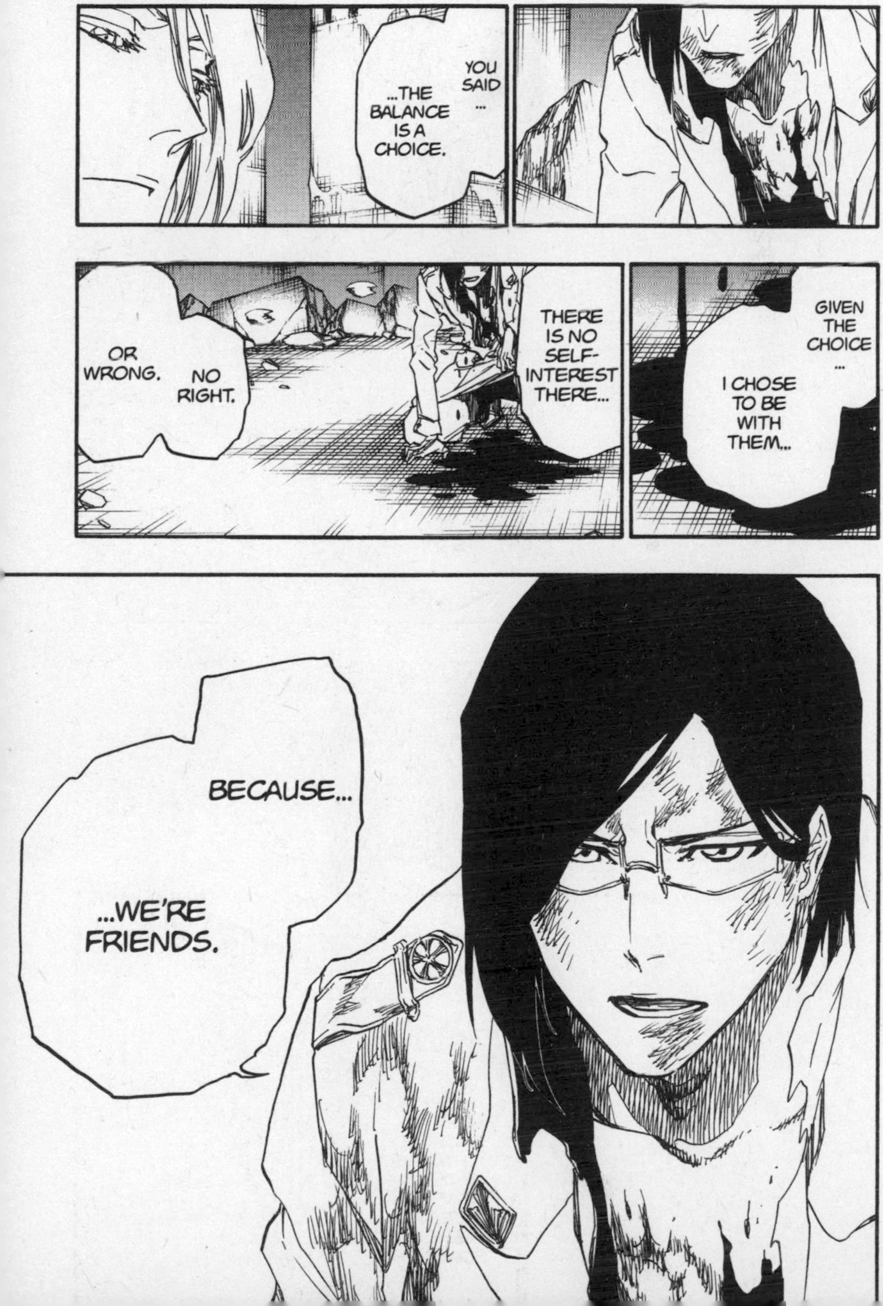
YOU SAID ...
...THE BALANCE IS A CHOICE.
GIVEN THE CHOICE ...
I CHOSE TO BE WITH THEM...
THERE IS NO SELF-INTEREST THERE...
NO RIGHT.
OR WRONG.
BECAUSE...
...WE'RE FRIENDS.

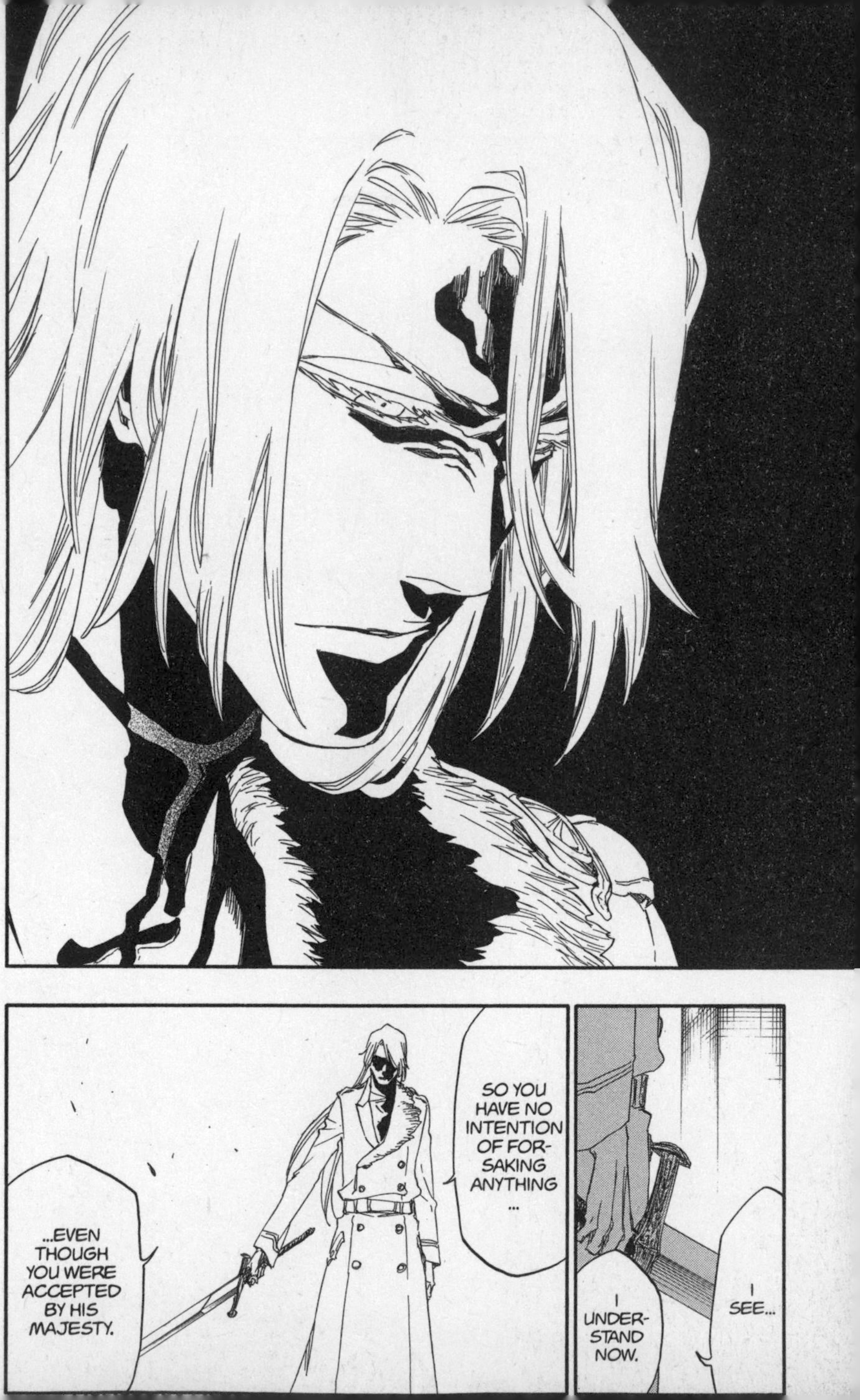
I SEE...
I UNDER-STAND NOW.
SO YOU HAVE NO INTENTION OF FOR-SAKING ANYTHING ...
...EVEN THOUGH YOU WERE ACCEPTED BY HIS MAJESTY.

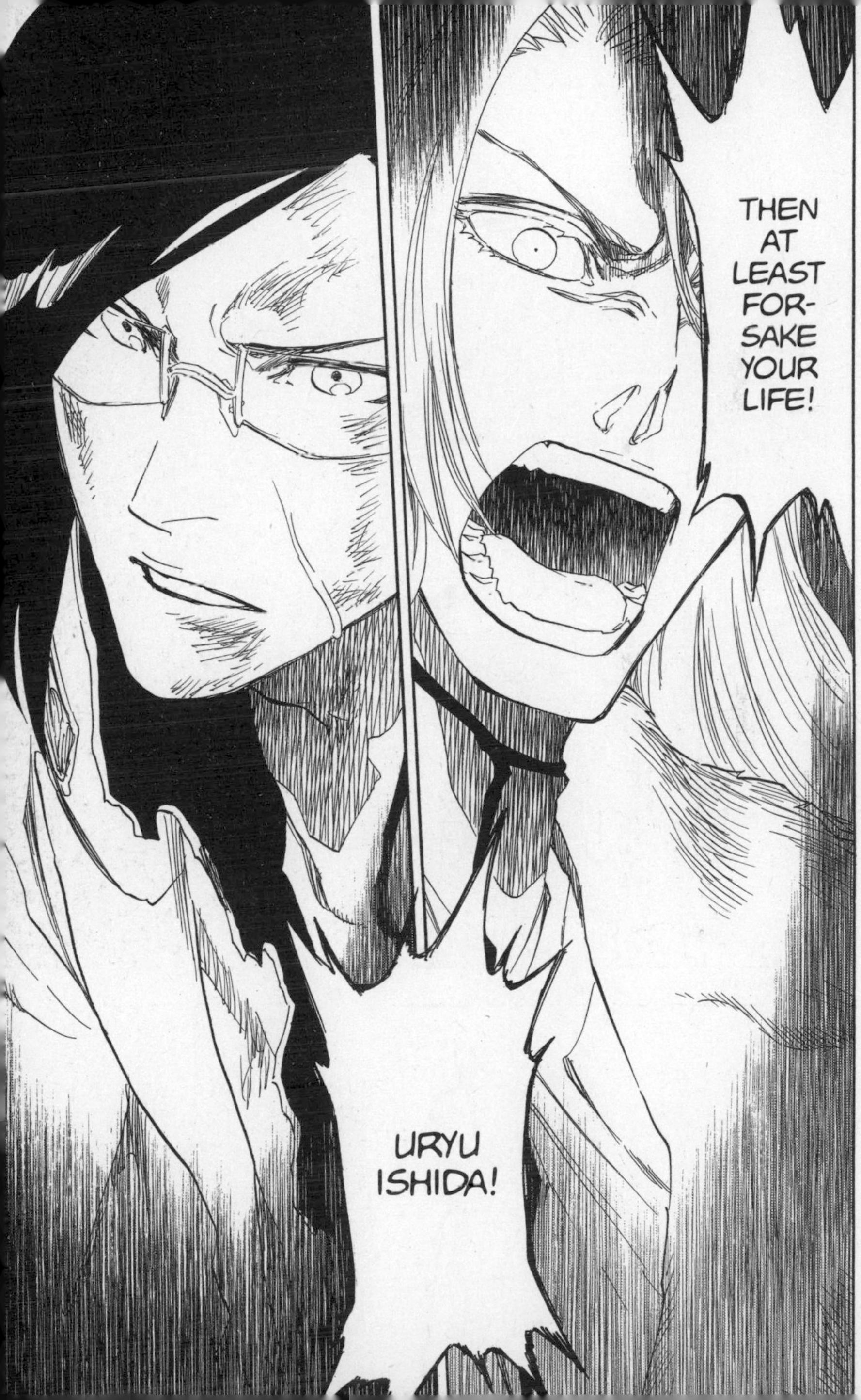
THEN AT LEAST FOR-SAKE YOUR LIFE!
URYU ISHIDA!

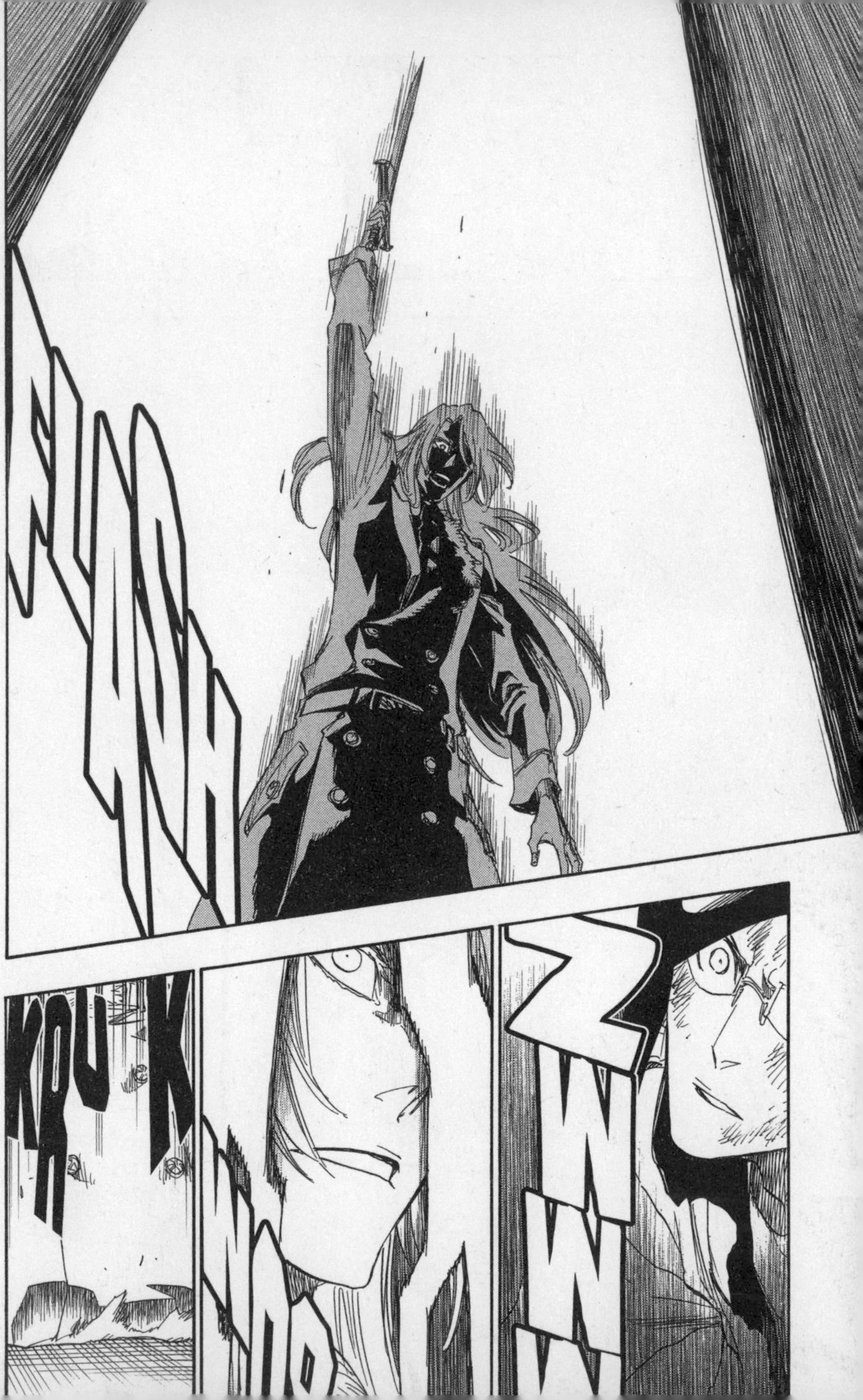
CLASH

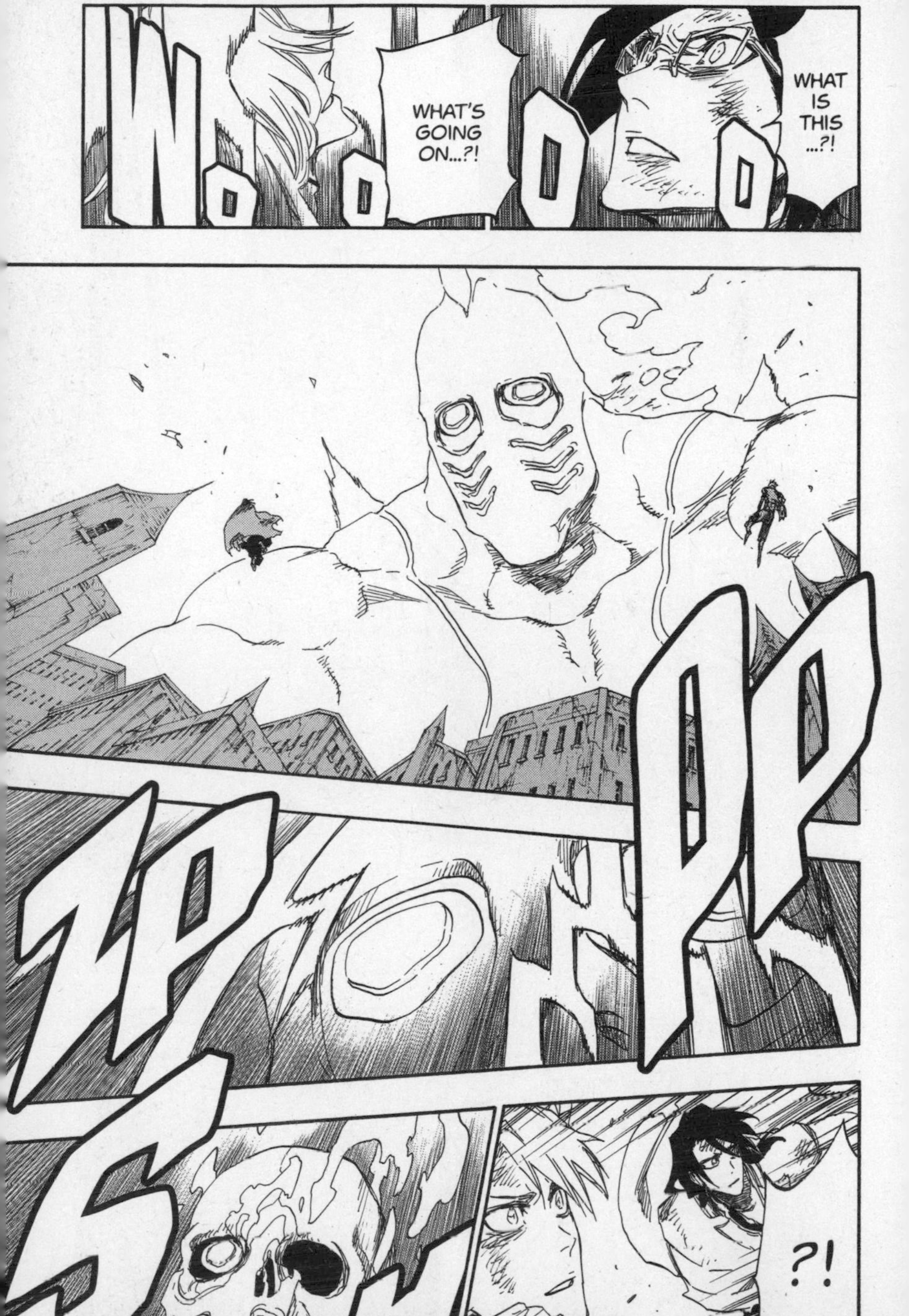

WHAT IS THIS ...?!
WHAT'S GOING ON...?!
?!

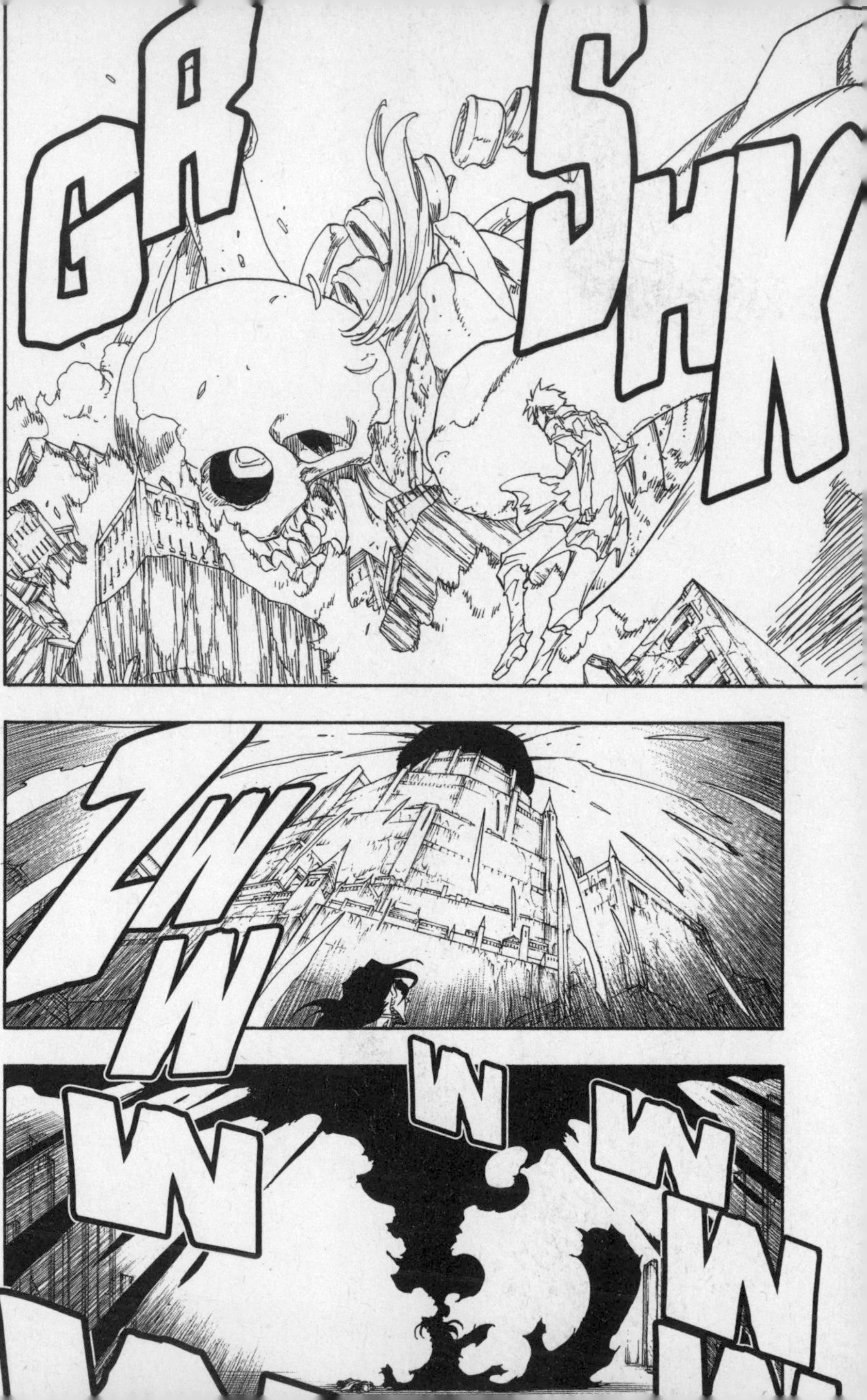
CRSHK
ZWWWWWW

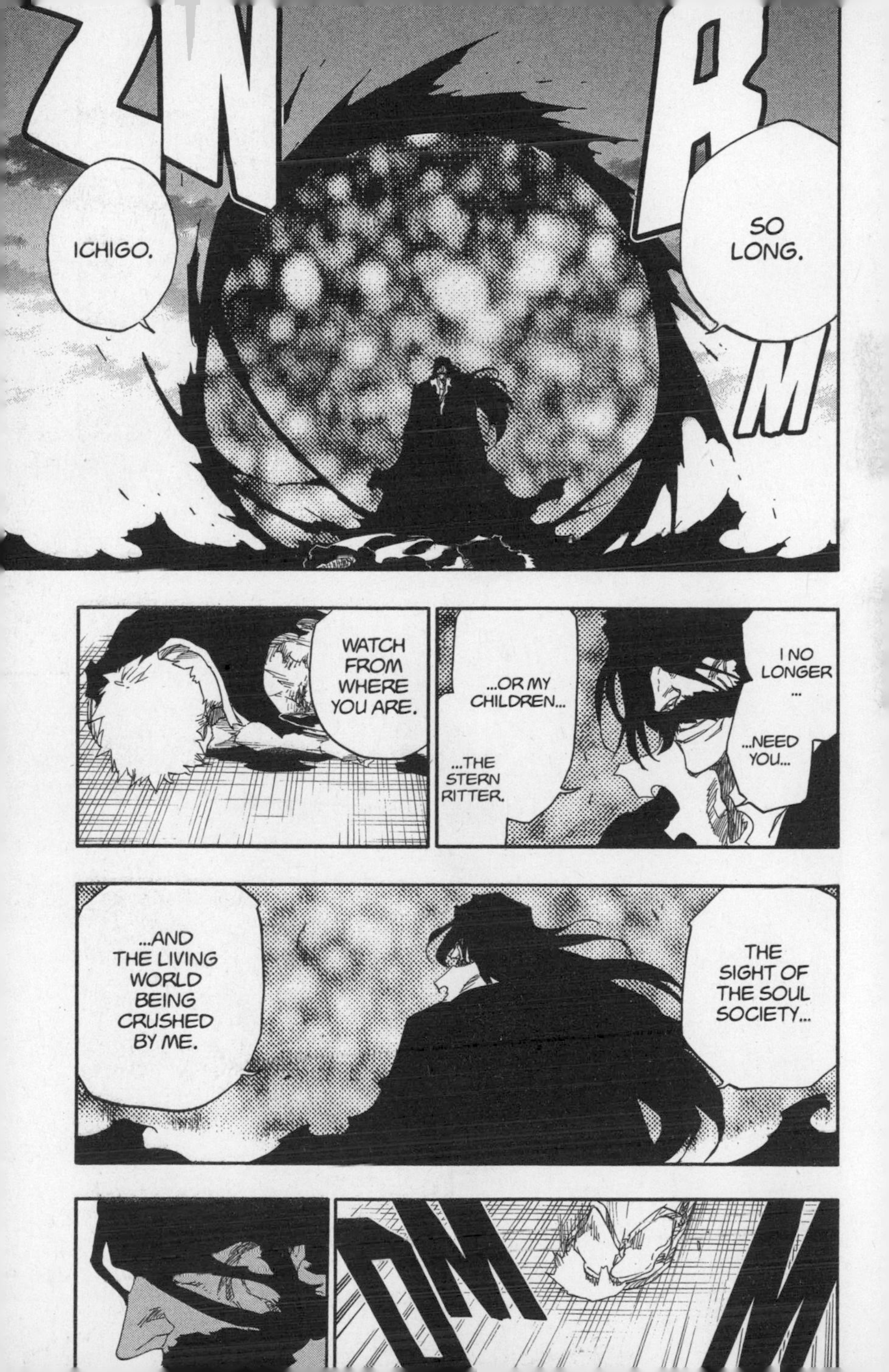
SO LONG.
ICHIGO.
I NO LONGER ...
...NEED YOU...
...THE STERN RITTER.
...OR MY CHILDREN...
WATCH FROM WHERE YOU ARE.
THE SIGHT OF THE SOUL SOCIETY...
...AND THE LIVING WORLD BEING CRUSHED BY ME.

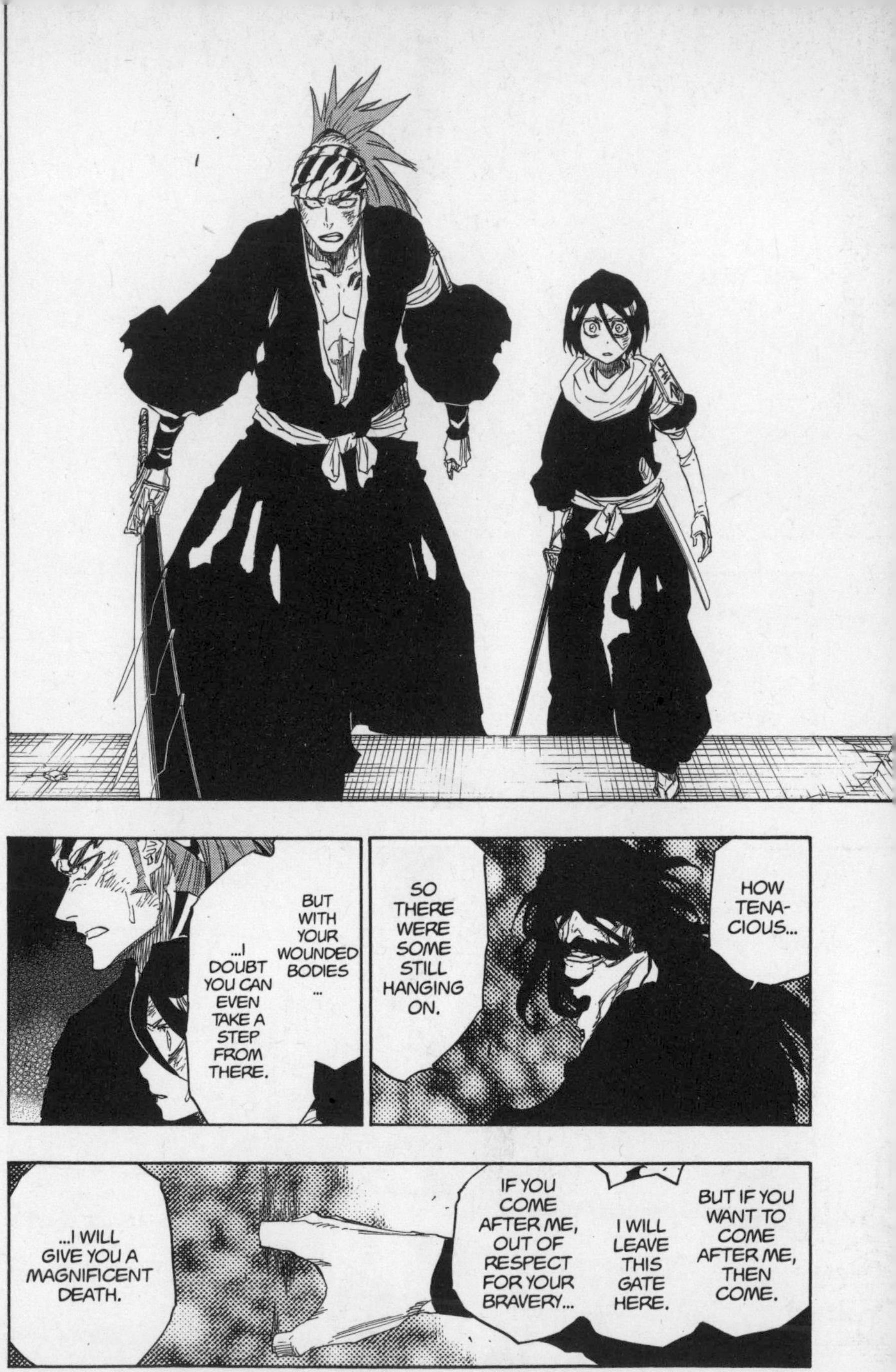
HOW TENACIOUS...
SO THERE WERE SOME STILL HANGING ON.
BUT WITH YOUR WOUNDED BODIES...
...I DOUBT YOU CAN EVEN TAKE A STEP FROM THERE.
BUT IF YOU WANT TO COME AFTER ME, THEN COME.
I WILL LEAVE THIS GATE HERE.
IF YOU COME AFTER ME, OUT OF RESPECT FOR YOUR BRAVERY...
...I WILL GIVE YOU A MAGNIFICENT DEATH.

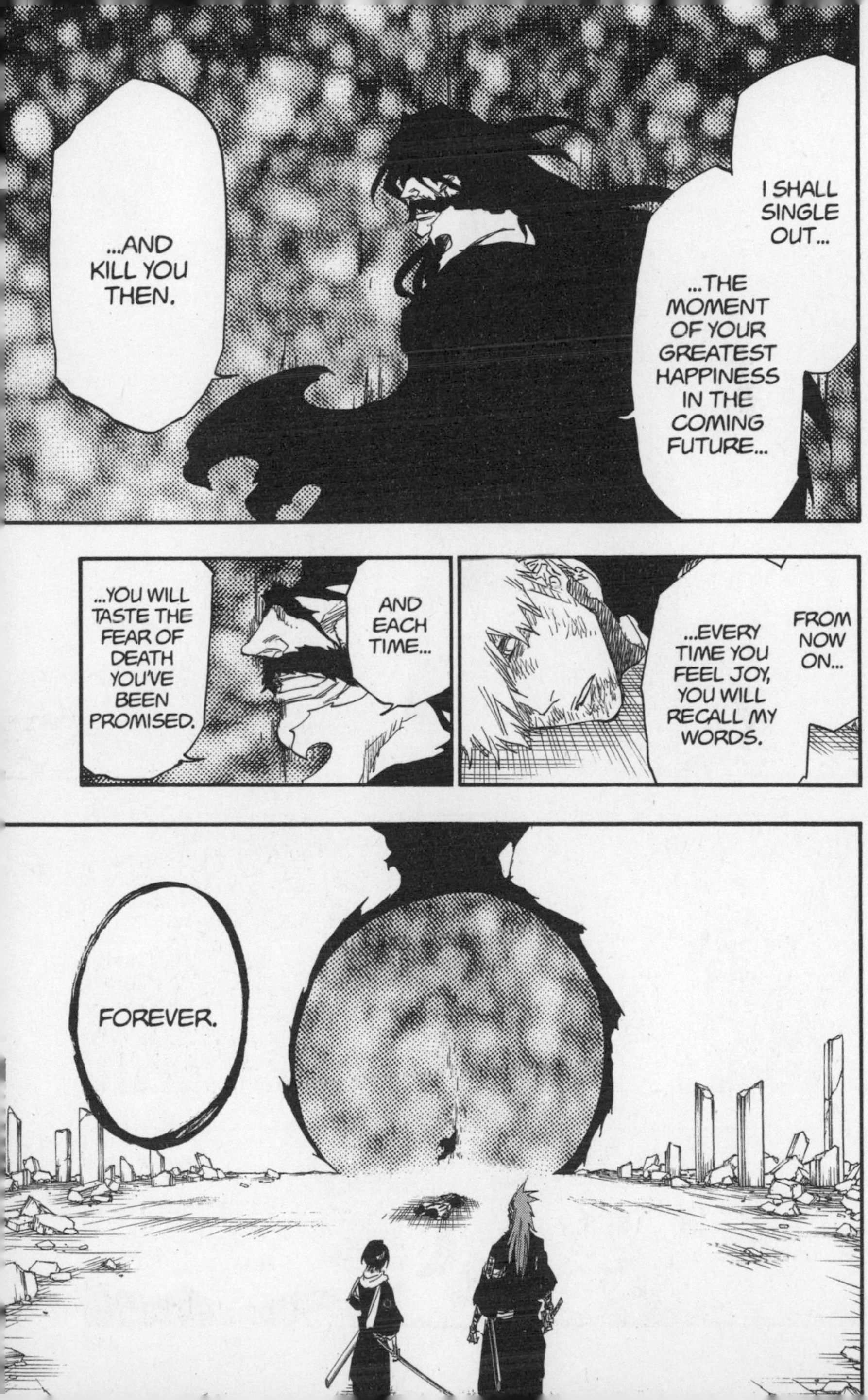
I SHALL SINGLE OUT...
...THE MOMENT OF YOUR GREATEST HAPPINESS IN THE COMING FUTURE...
...AND KILL YOU THEN.
FROM NOW ON...
...EVERY TIME YOU FEEL JOY, YOU WILL RECALL MY WORDS.
AND EACH TIME...
...YOU WILL TASTE THE FEAR OF DEATH YOU'VE BEEN PROMISED.
FOREVER.

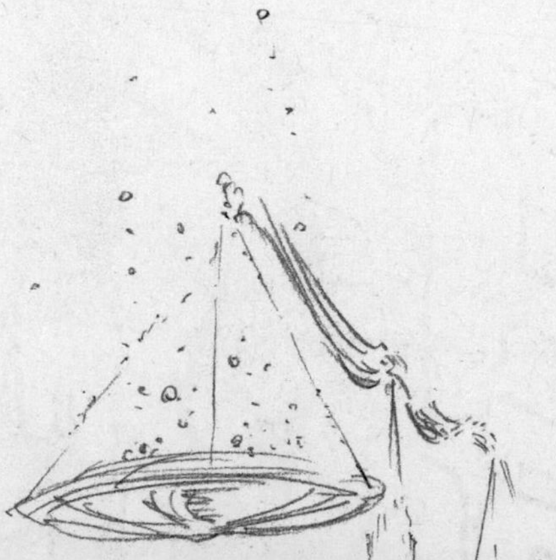

681. THE END TWO WORLD

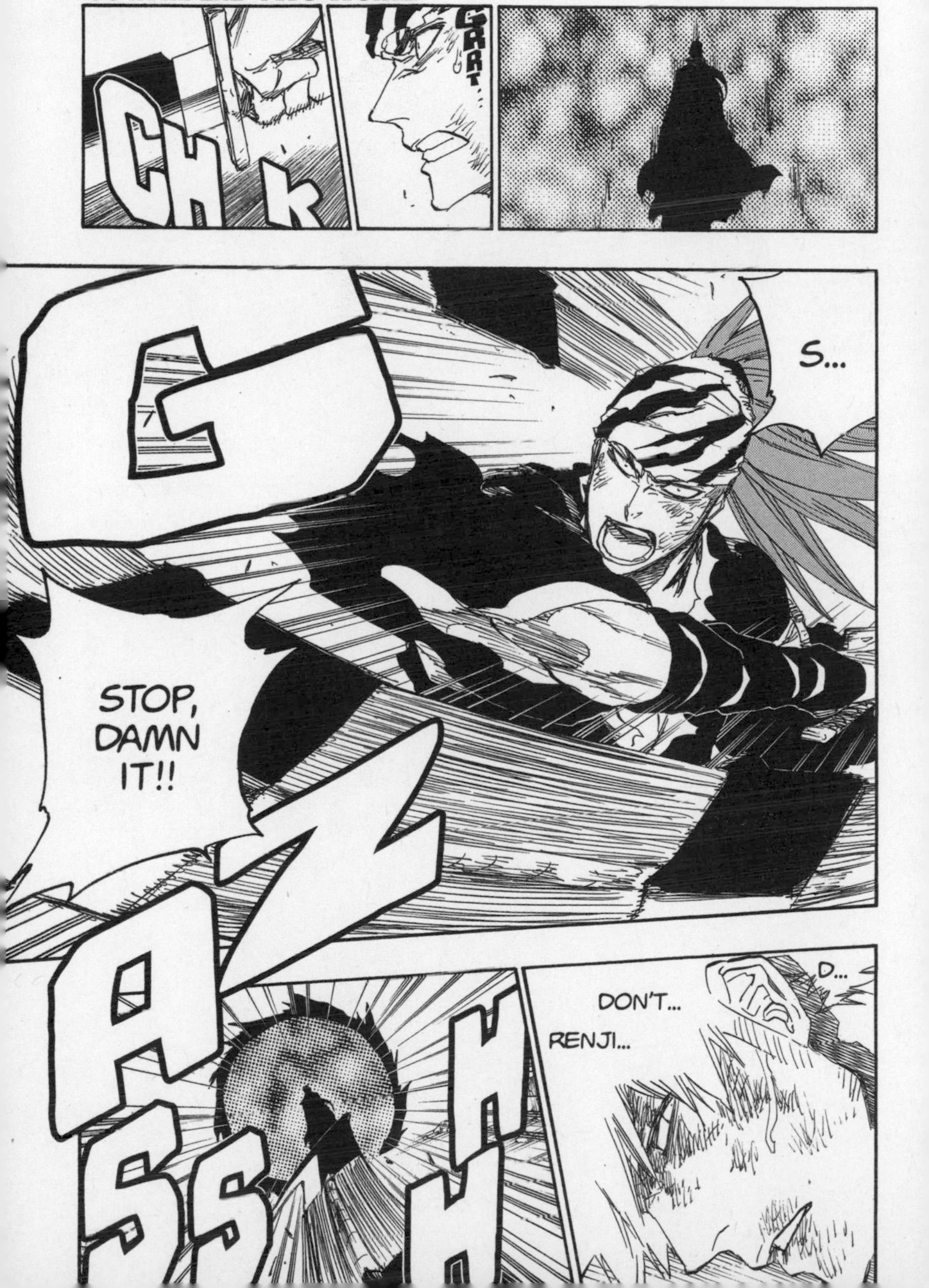
GRRRT
CHK
S...
STOP, DAMN IT!!
D...
DON'T...
RENJI...

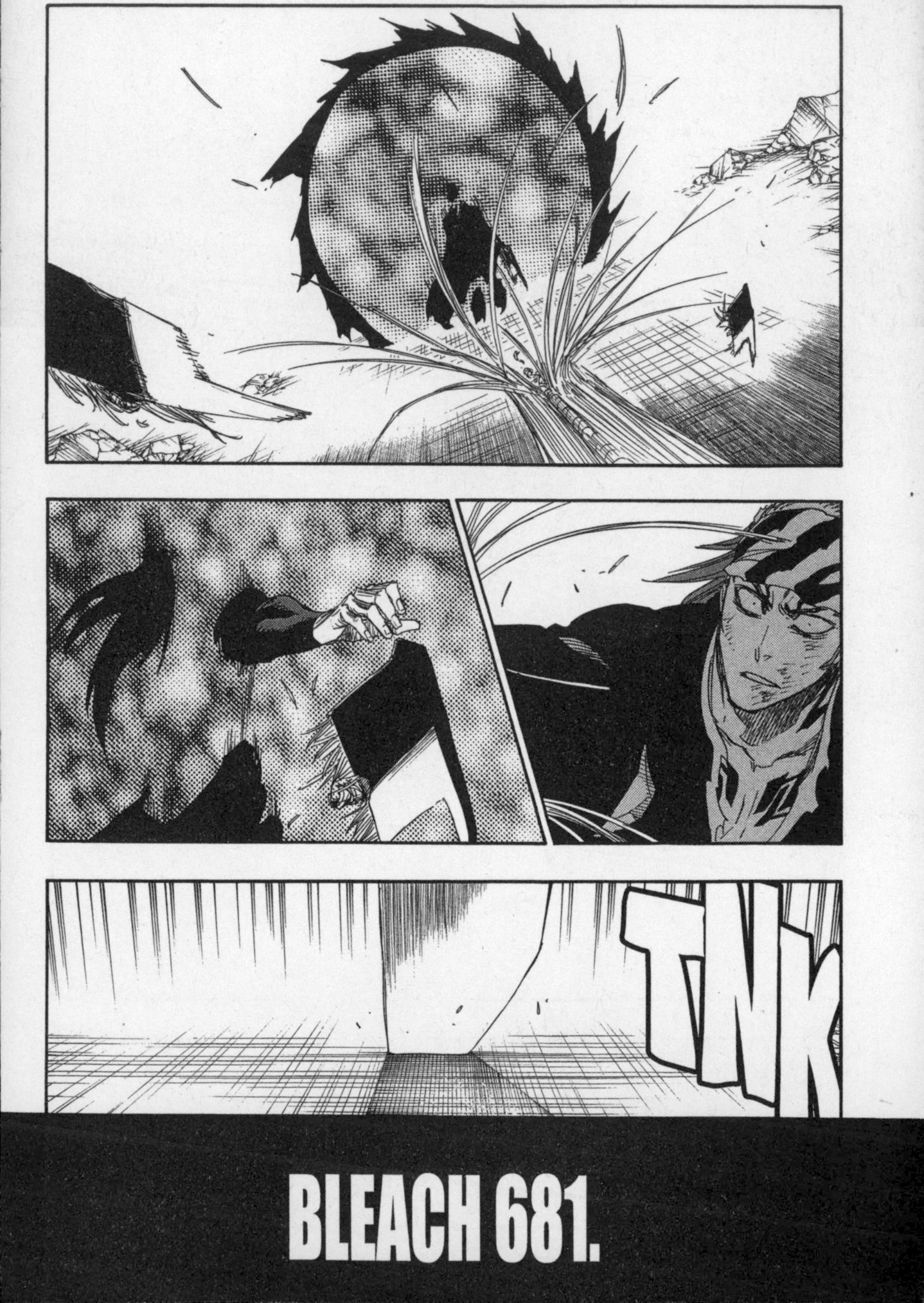
TNK

BLEACH 681.

THE END TWO WORLD

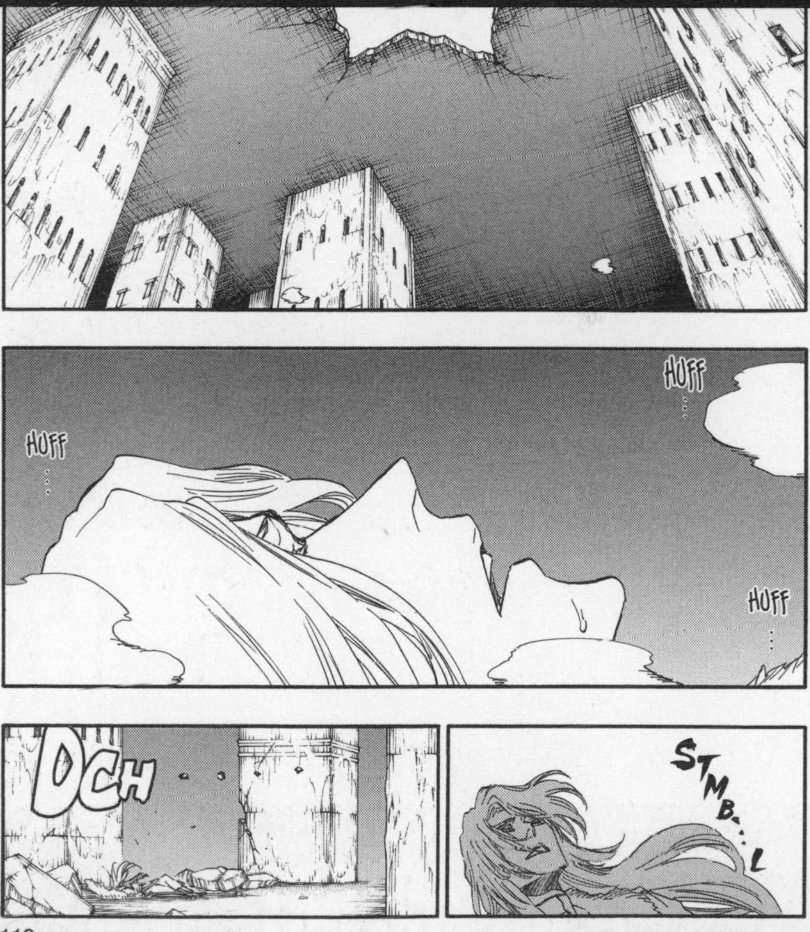
HUFF...
HUFF...
HUFF...
STMB...L
DCH

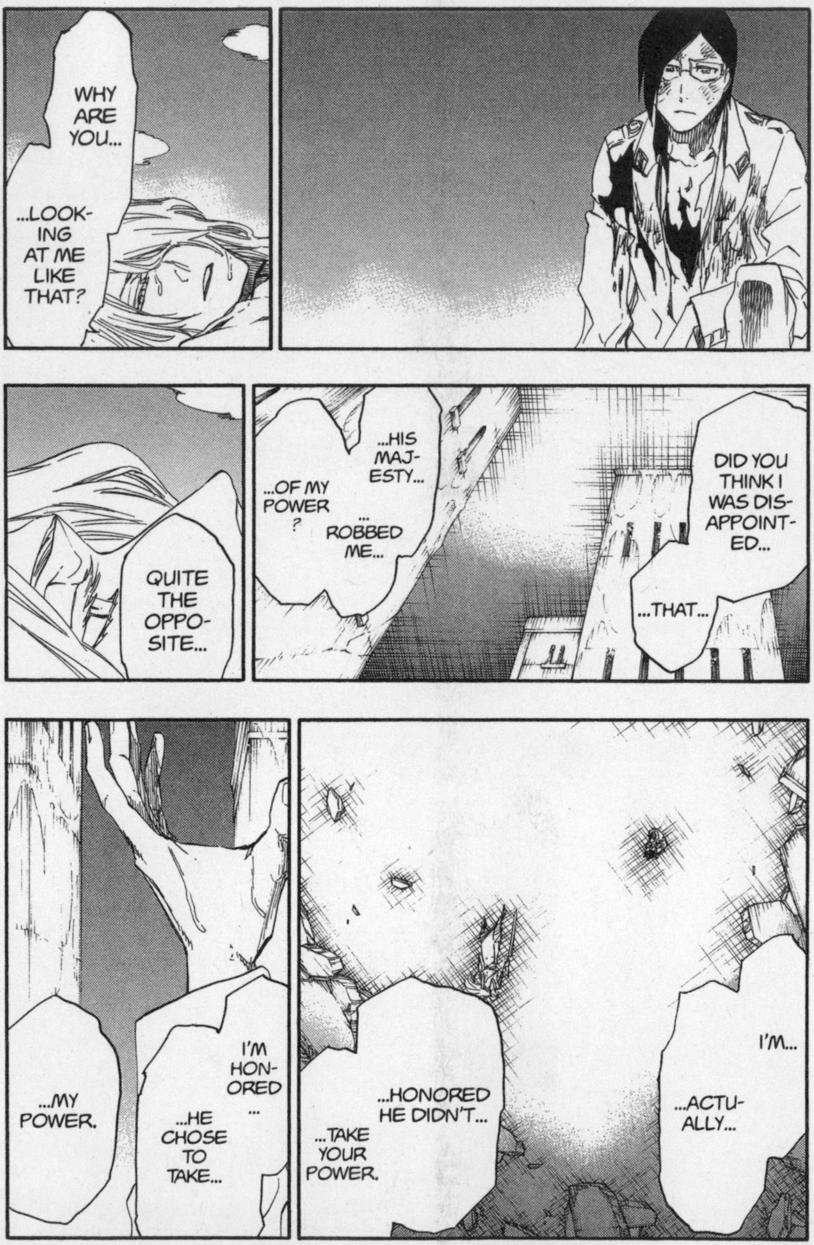
WHY ARE YOU...
...LOOKING AT ME LIKE THAT?
DID YOU THINK I WAS DISAPPOINTED...
...THAT...
...HIS MAJESTY...
...ROBBED ME...
...OF MY POWER?
QUITE THE OPPOSITE...
I'M...
...ACTUALLY...
...HONORED HE DIDN'T...
...TAKE YOUR POWER.
I'M HONORED...
...HE CHOSE TO TAKE...
...MY POWER.

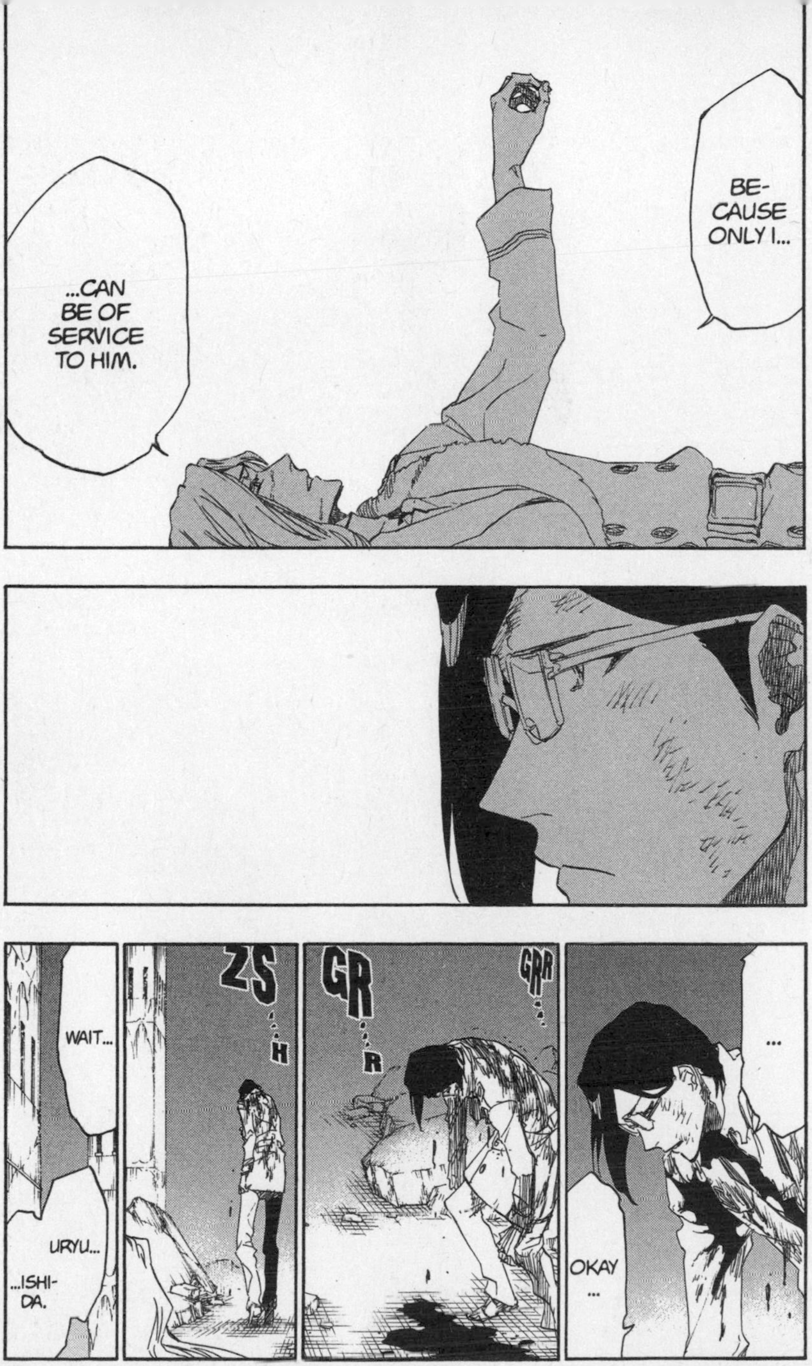
BE-CAUSE ONLY I...
...CAN BE OF SERVICE TO HIM.
...
OKAY ...
GRR
GR...R
ZS...H
WAIT...
URYU...
...ISHI-DA.

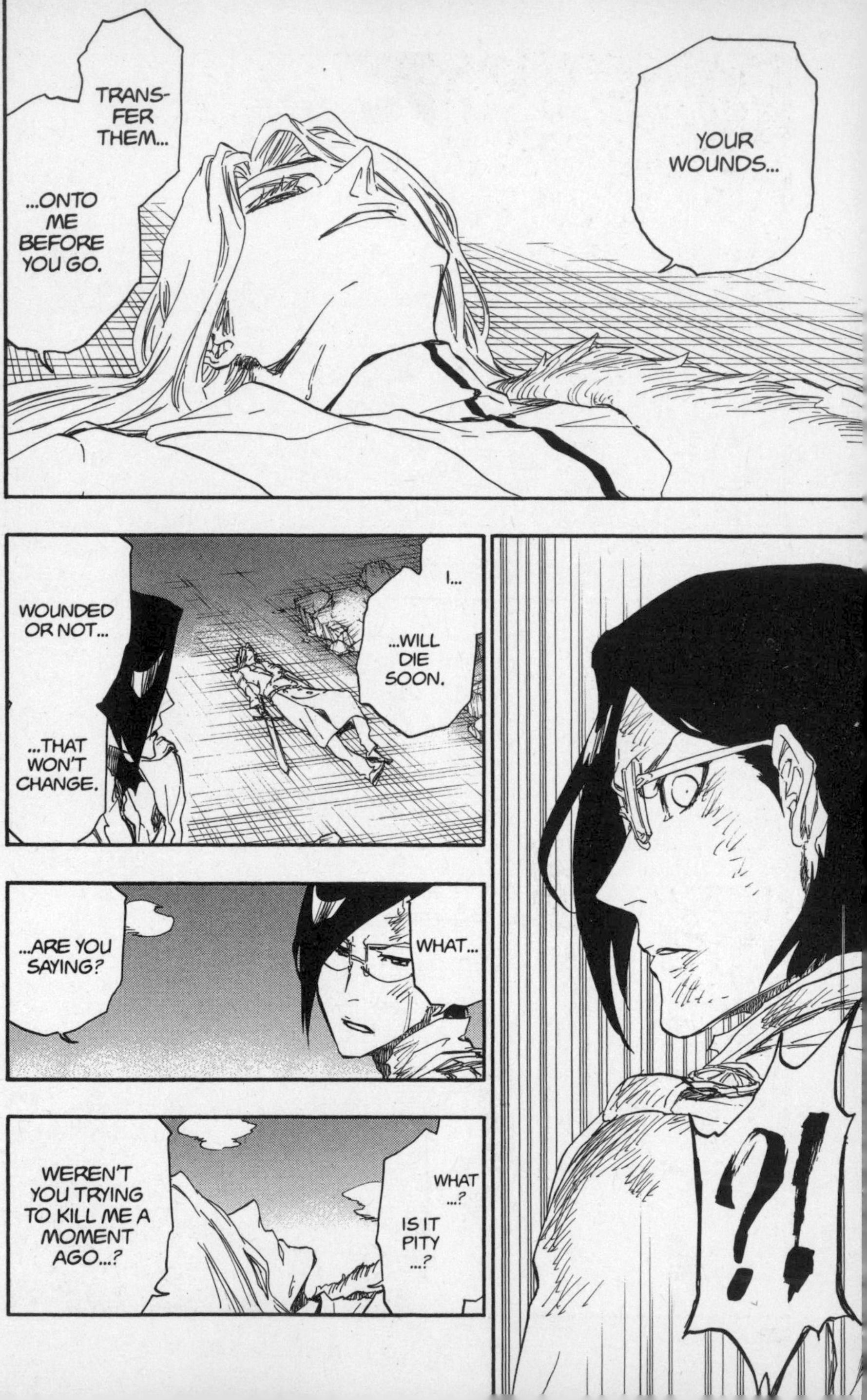
YOUR WOUNDS...
TRANSFER THEM...
...ONTO ME BEFORE YOU GO.
?!
I...
...WILL DIE SOON.
WOUNDED OR NOT...
...THAT WON'T CHANGE.
WHAT...
...ARE YOU SAYING?
WHAT ...?
IS IT PITY ...?
WEREN'T YOU TRYING TO KILL ME A MOMENT AGO...?

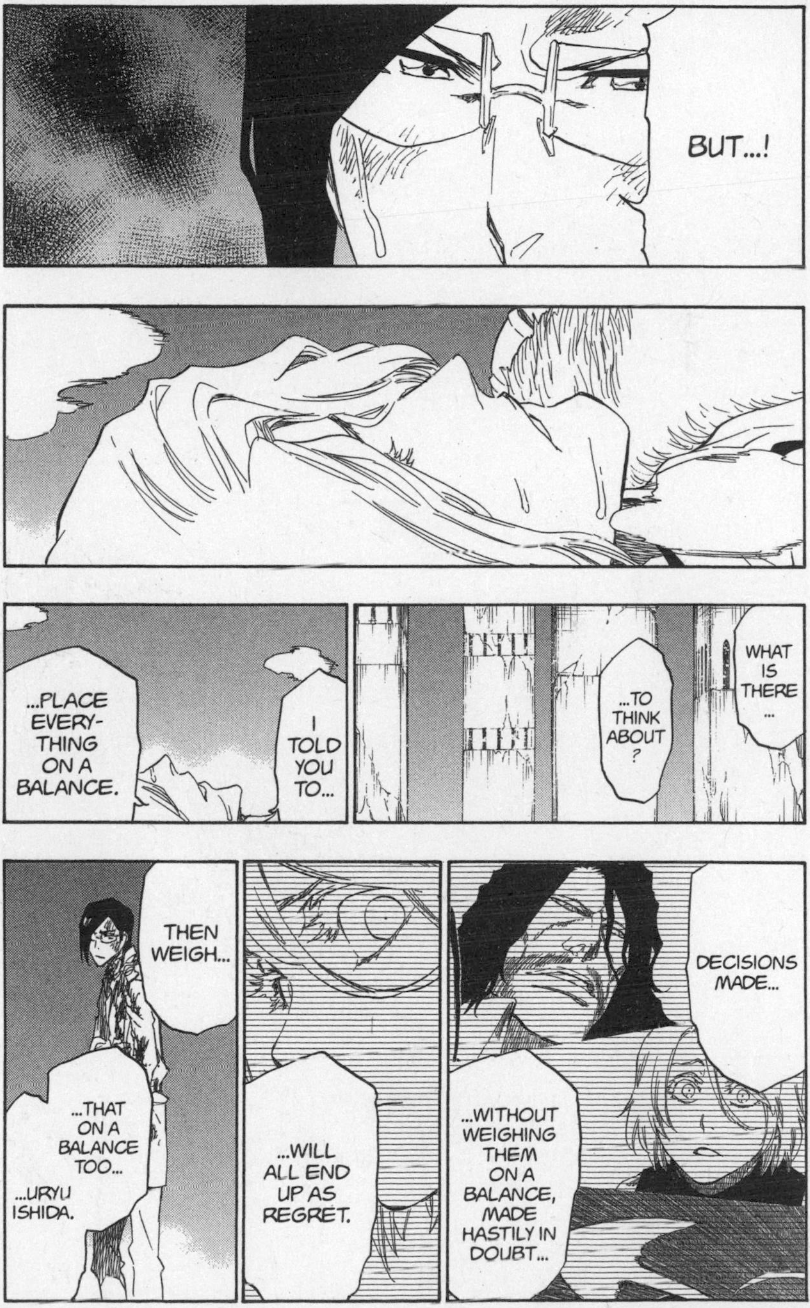
BUT...!
WHAT IS THERE...
...TO THINK ABOUT?
I TOLD YOU TO...
...PLACE EVERY-THING ON A BALANCE.
DECISIONS MADE...
...WITHOUT WEIGHING THEM ON A BALANCE, MADE HASTILY IN DOUBT...
...WILL ALL END UP AS REGRET.
THEN WEIGH...
...THAT ON A BALANCE TOO...
...URYU ISHIDA.

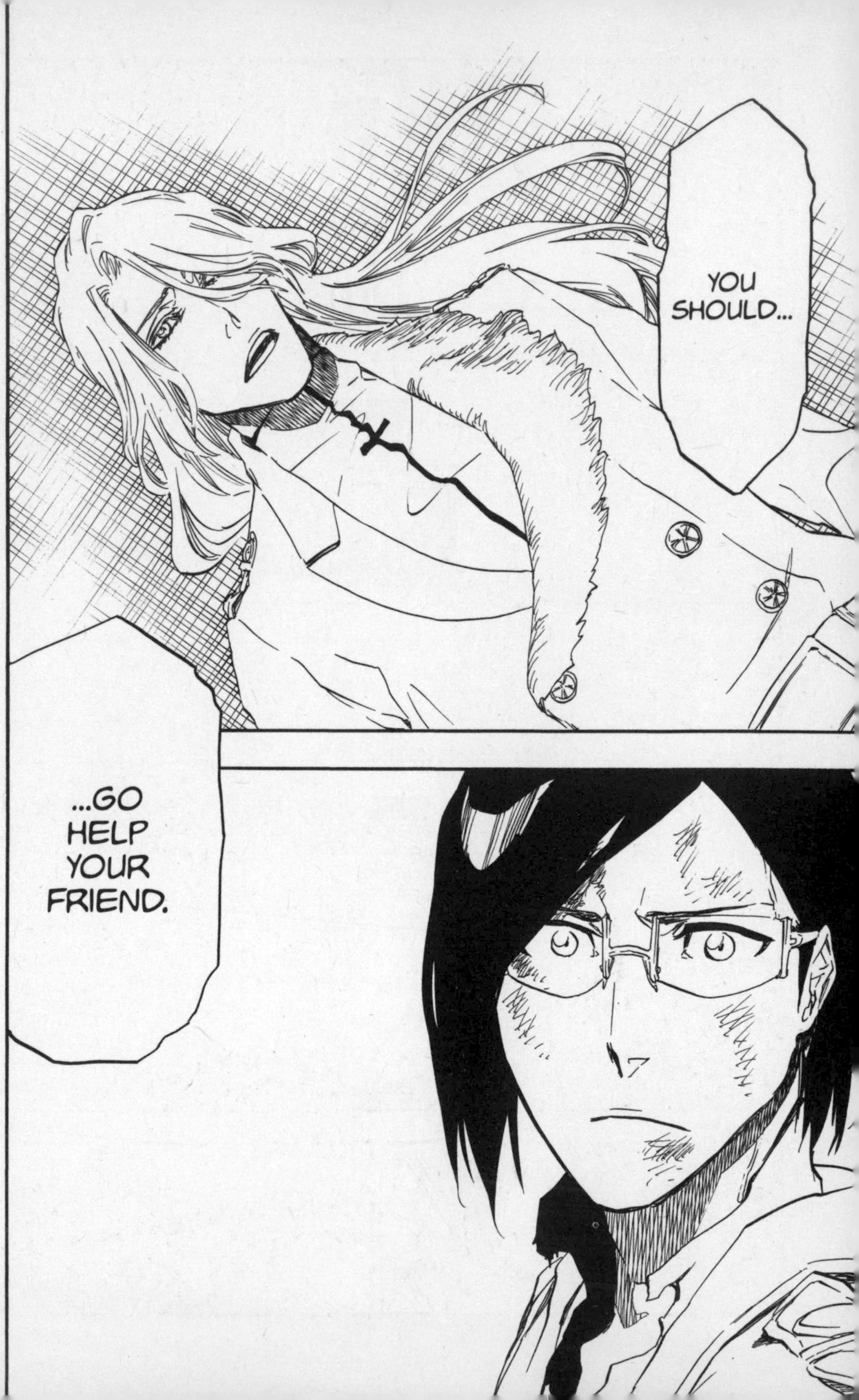
YOU SHOULD...
...GO HELP YOUR FRIEND.

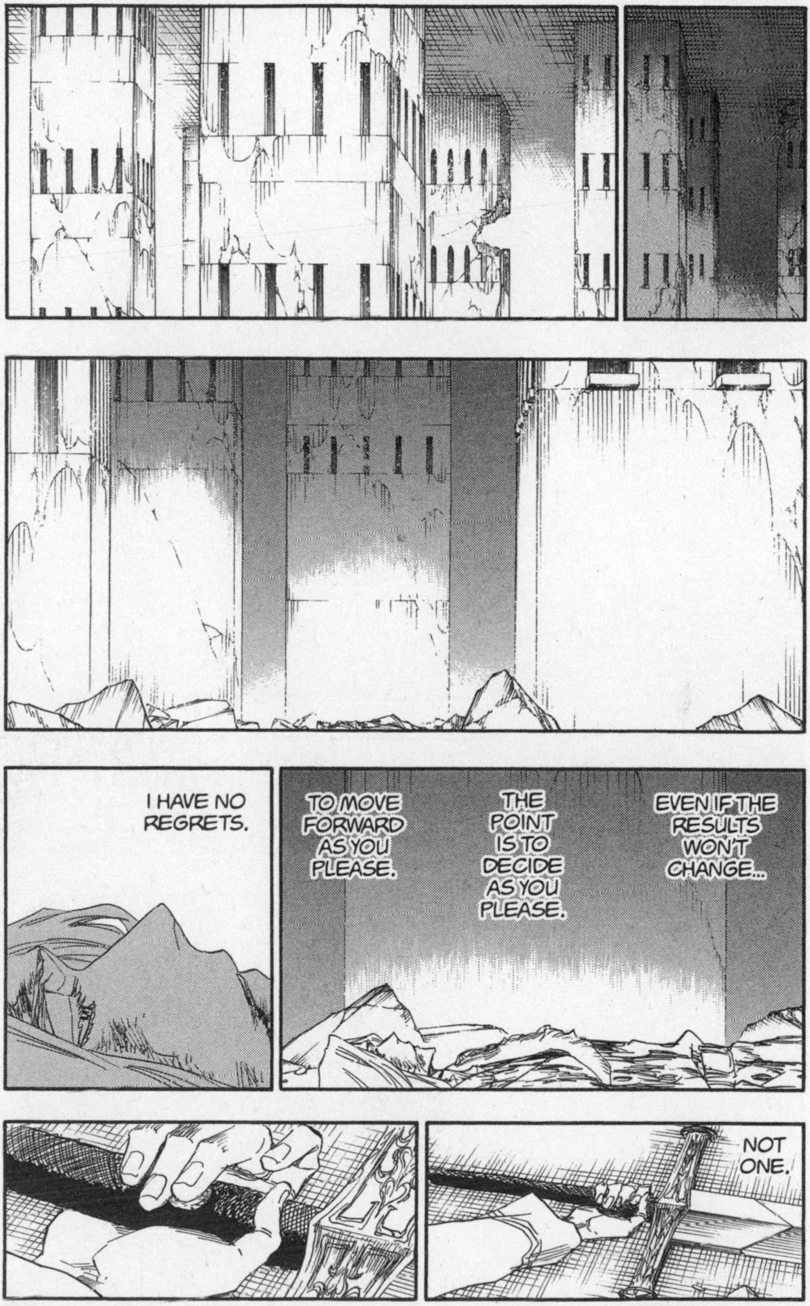
EVEN IF THE RESULTS WON'T CHANGE...
THE POINT IS TO DECIDE AS YOU PLEASE.
TO MOVE FORWARD AS YOU PLEASE.
I HAVE NO REGRETS.
NOT ONE.

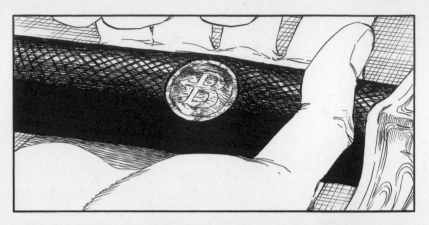

WHAT...

...KIND OF
POWER IS
THAT?

READ THIS WAY

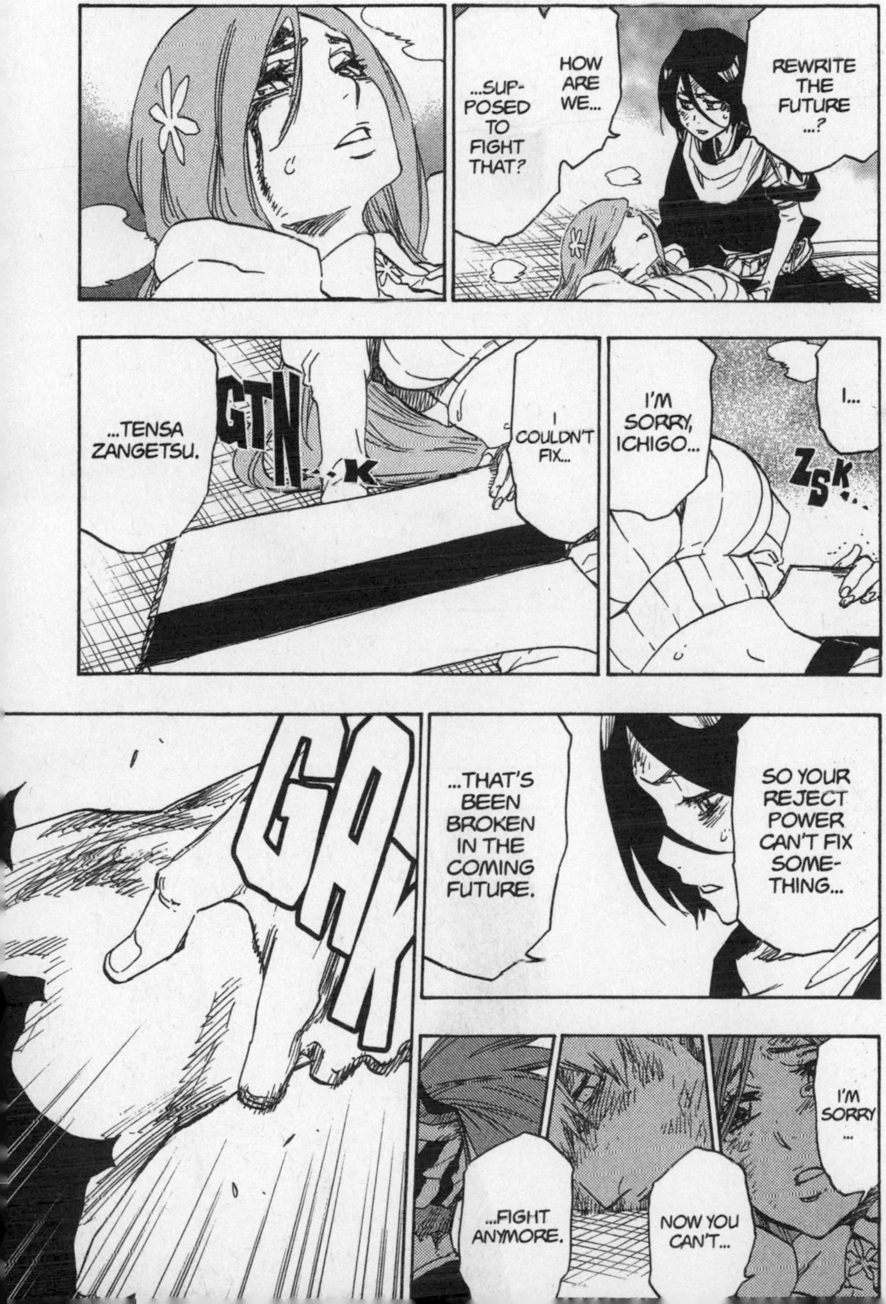

REWRITE THE FUTURE ...?
HOW ARE WE...
...SUP-POSED TO FIGHT THAT?
I...
ZSK..
I'M SORRY, ICHIGO...
I COULDN'T FIX...
GTN...K
...TENSA ZANGETSU.
SO YOUR REJECT POWER CAN'T FIX SOME-THING...
...THAT'S BEEN BROKEN IN THE COMING FUTURE.
I'M SORRY ...
NOW YOU CAN'T...
...FIGHT ANYMORE.
GA

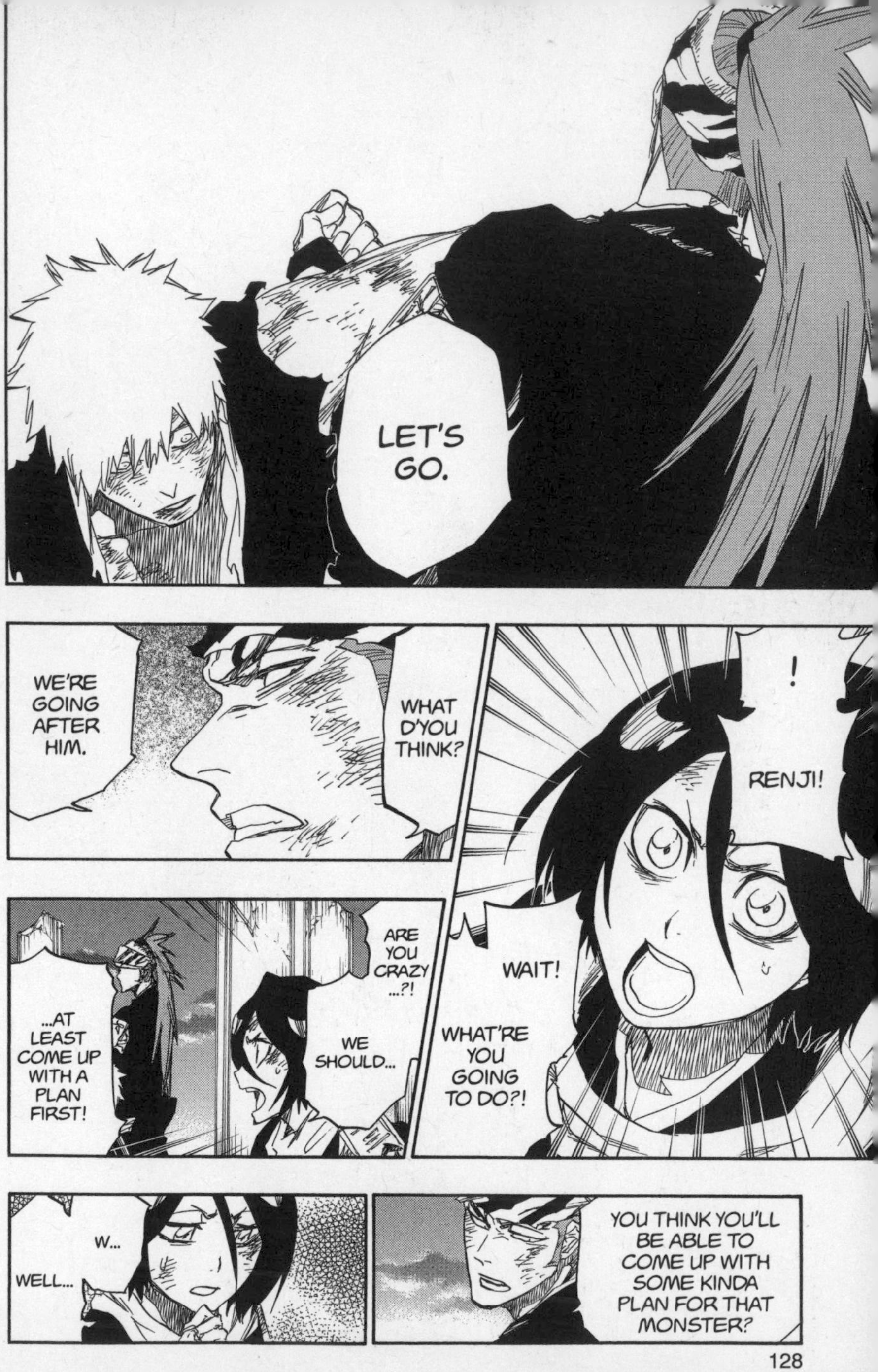
LET'S GO.
!
RENJI!
WAIT!
WHAT'RE YOU GOING TO DO?!
WHAT D'YOU THINK?
WE'RE GOING AFTER HIM.
ARE YOU CRAZY ...?!
WE SHOULD...
...AT LEAST COME UP WITH A PLAN FIRST!
YOU THINK YOU'LL BE ABLE TO COME UP WITH SOME KINDA PLAN FOR THAT MONSTER?
W...
WELL...

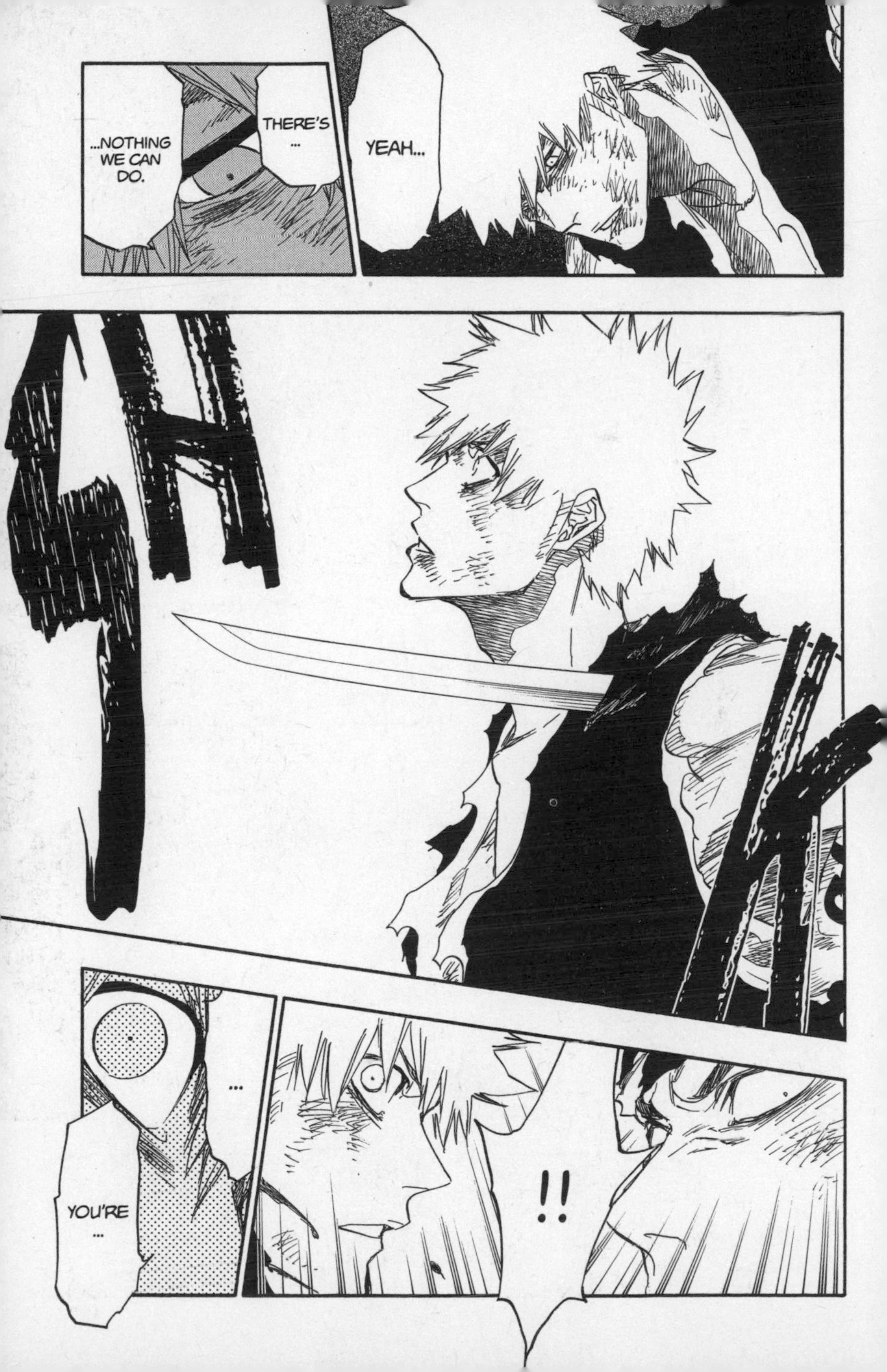
YEAH...
THERE'S ...
...NOTHING WE CAN DO.
!!
...
YOU'RE ...

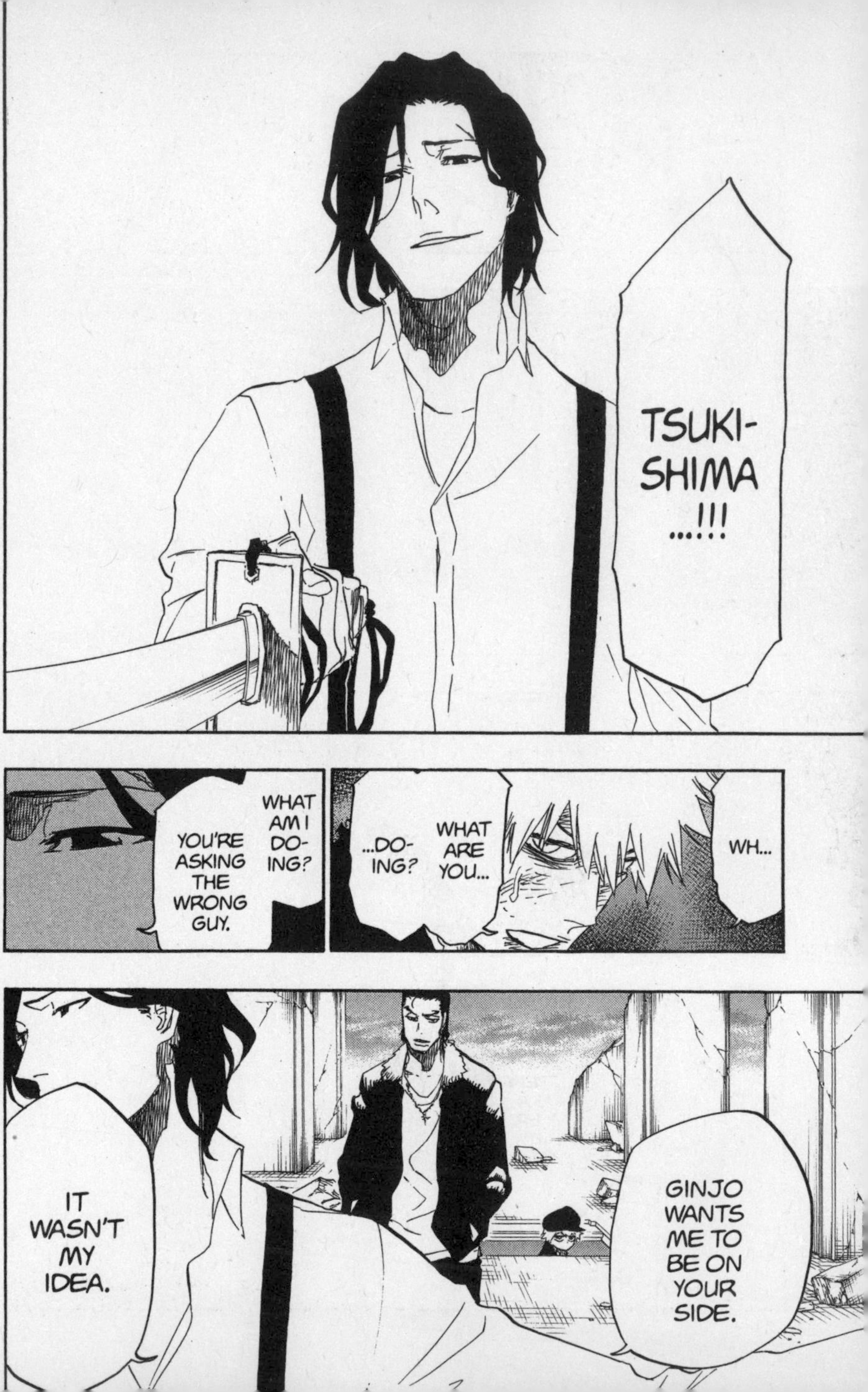
TSUKI-SHIMA ...!!!
WH...
WHAT ARE YOU...
...DO-ING?
WHAT AM I DO-ING?
YOU'RE ASKING THE WRONG GUY.
GINJO WANTS ME TO BE ON YOUR SIDE.
IT WASN'T MY IDEA.

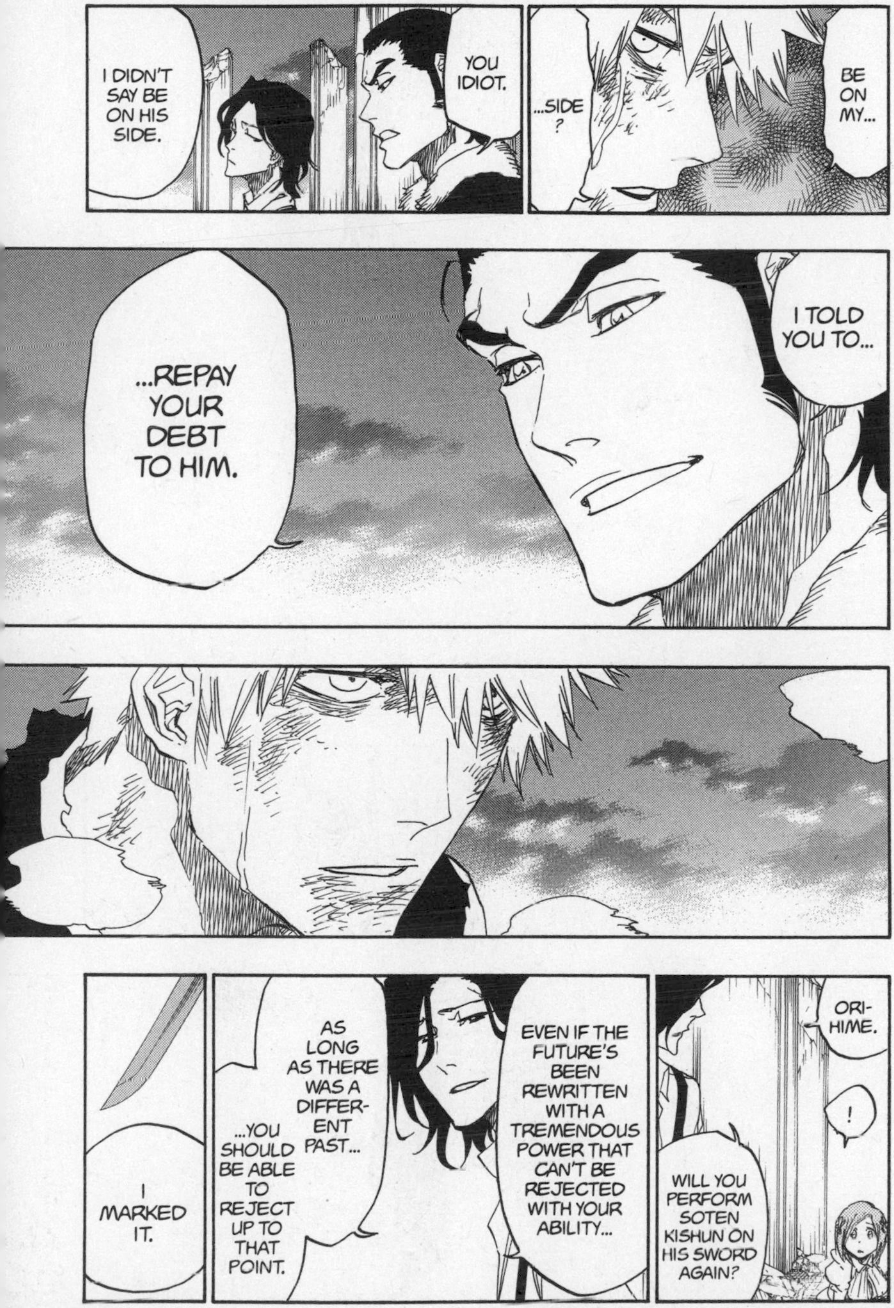
BE ON MY...
...SIDE ?
YOU IDIOT.
I DIDN'T SAY BE ON HIS SIDE.
I TOLD YOU TO...
...REPAY YOUR DEBT TO HIM.
ORIHIME.
!
WILL YOU PERFORM SOTEN KISHUN ON HIS SWORD AGAIN?
EVEN IF THE FUTURE'S BEEN REWRITTEN WITH A TREMENDOUS POWER THAT CAN'T BE REJECTED WITH YOUR ABILITY...
AS LONG AS THERE WAS A DIFFERENT PAST...
...YOU SHOULD BE ABLE TO REJECT UP TO THAT POINT.
I MARKED IT.

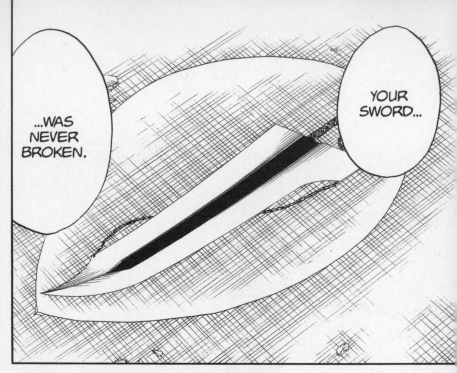

...WAS NEVER BROKEN.

YOUR SWORD...

NOW.

DOES THAT MAKE US EVEN?

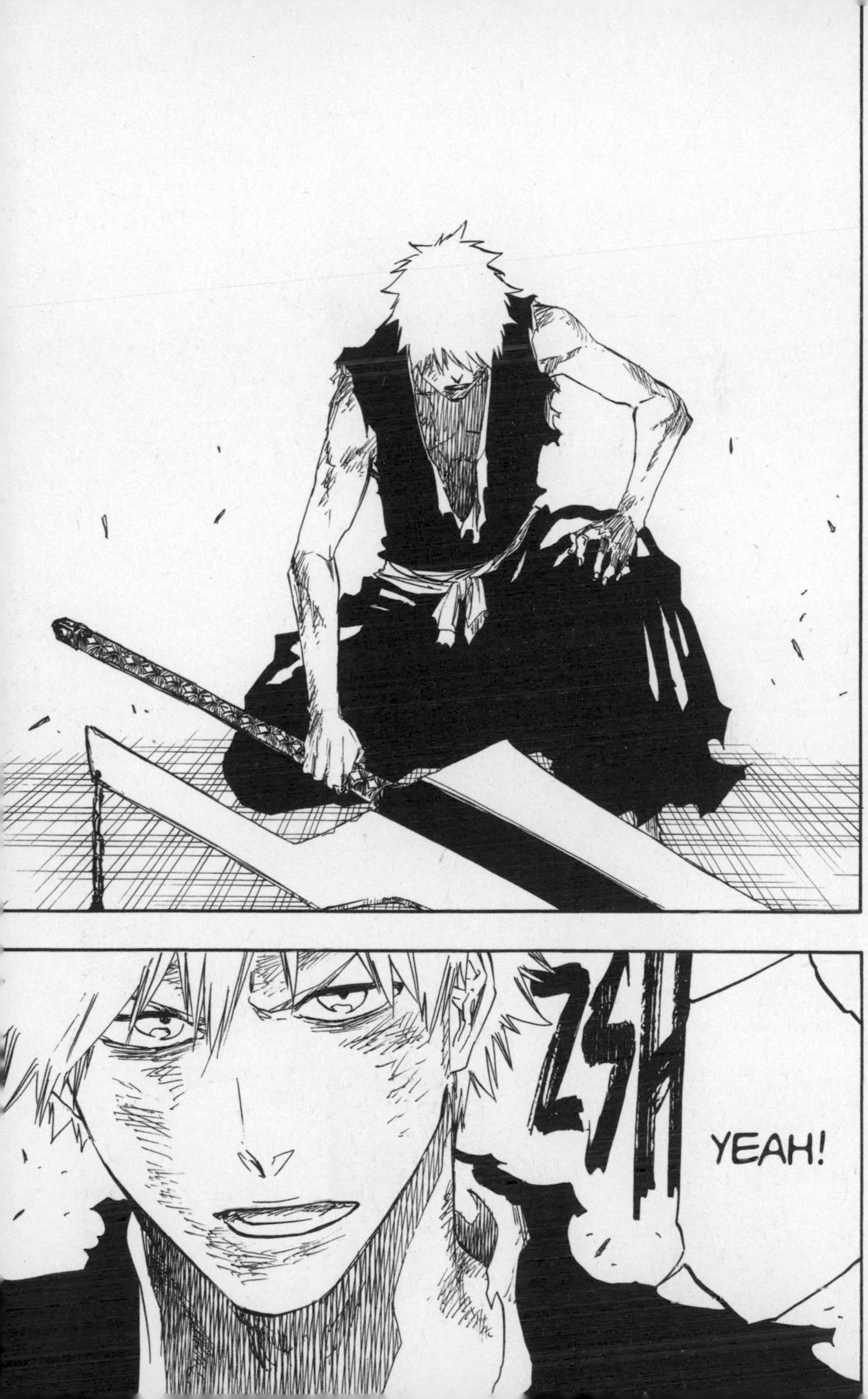
ZSH
YEAH!

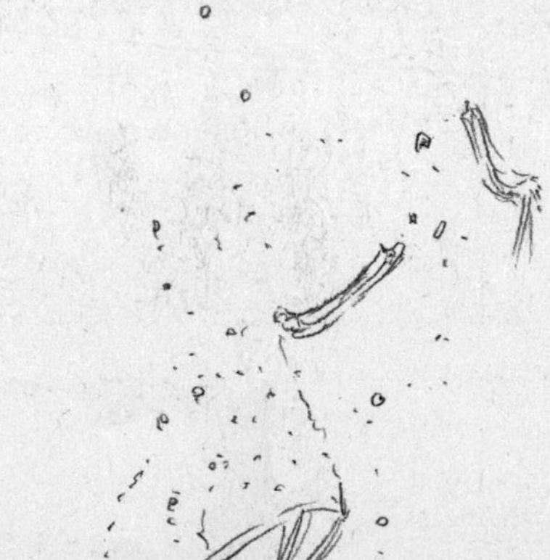

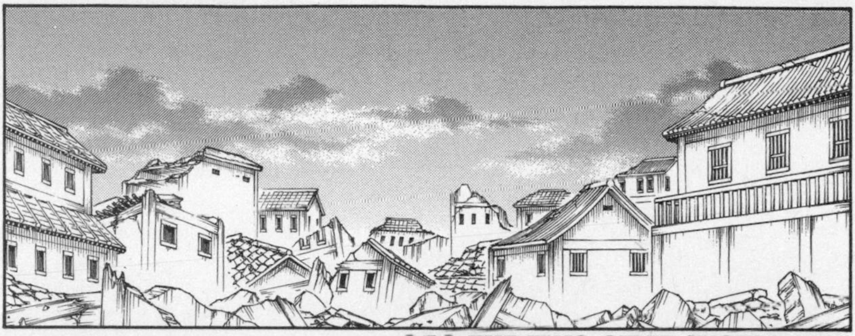

682. THE TWO SIDED WORLD END

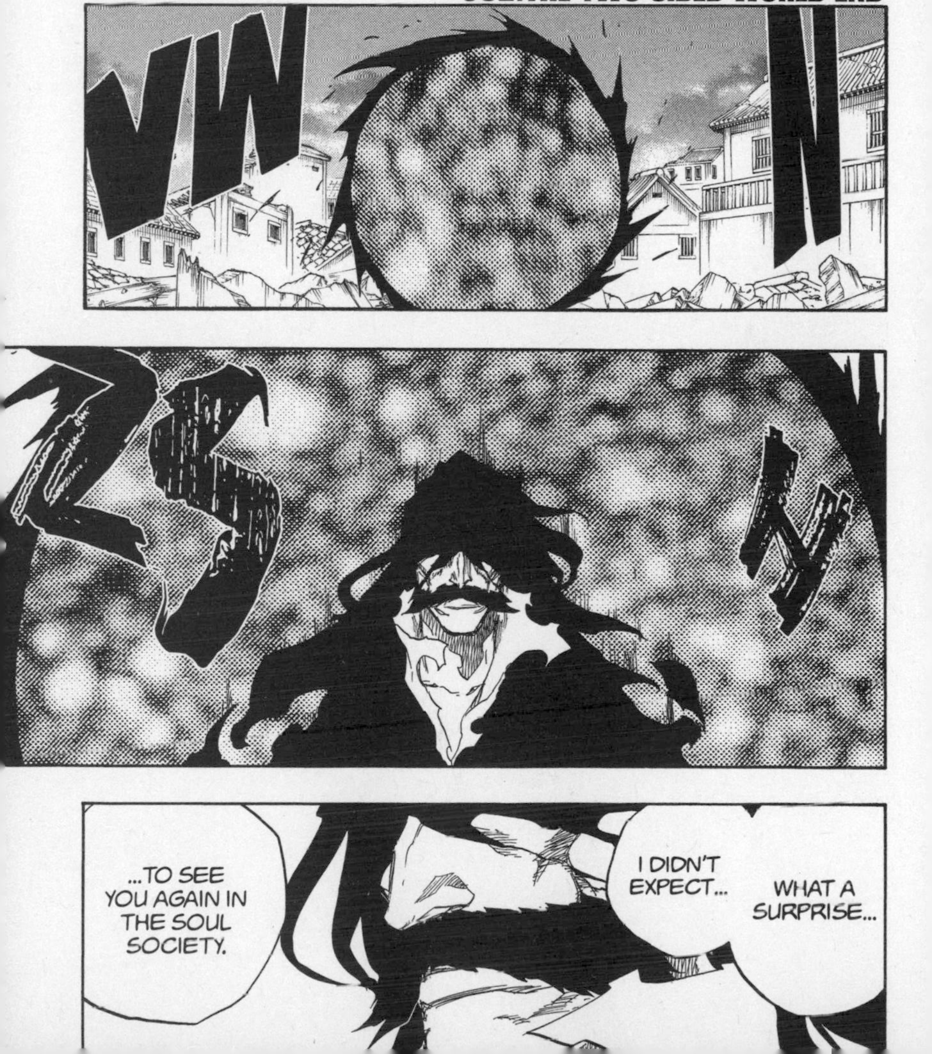
VWN
ZSN
WHAT A SURPRISE...
I DIDN'T EXPECT...
...TO SEE YOU AGAIN IN THE SOUL SOCIETY.

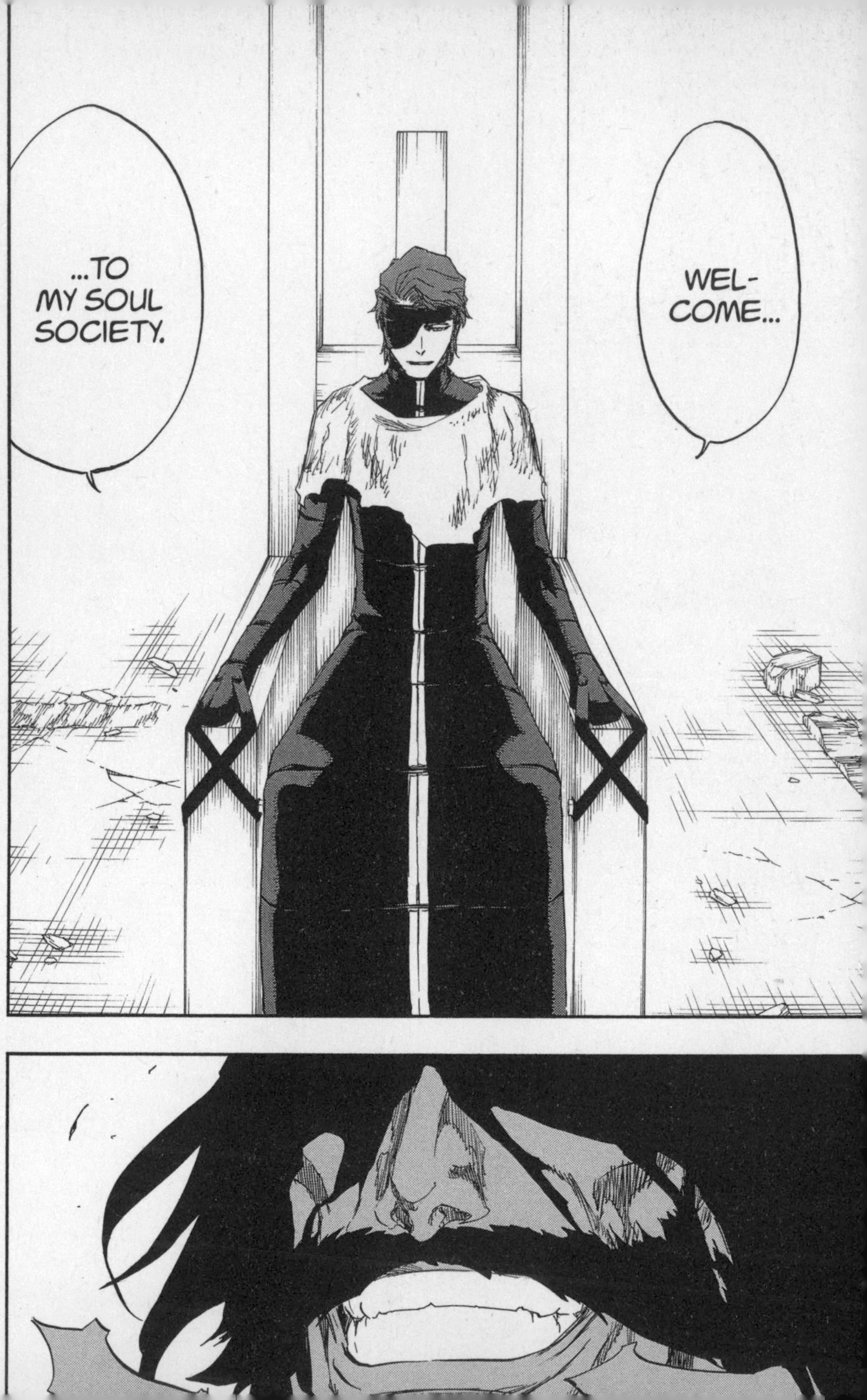
WEL-COME...
...TO MY SOUL SOCIETY.

BLEACH 682.

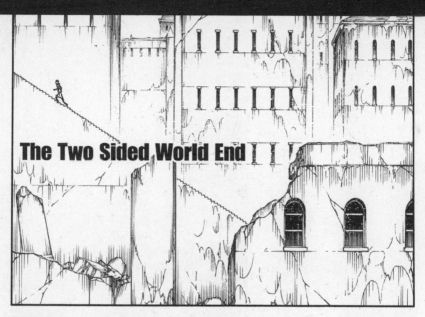

The Two Sided World End

WHO'S THERE ?!

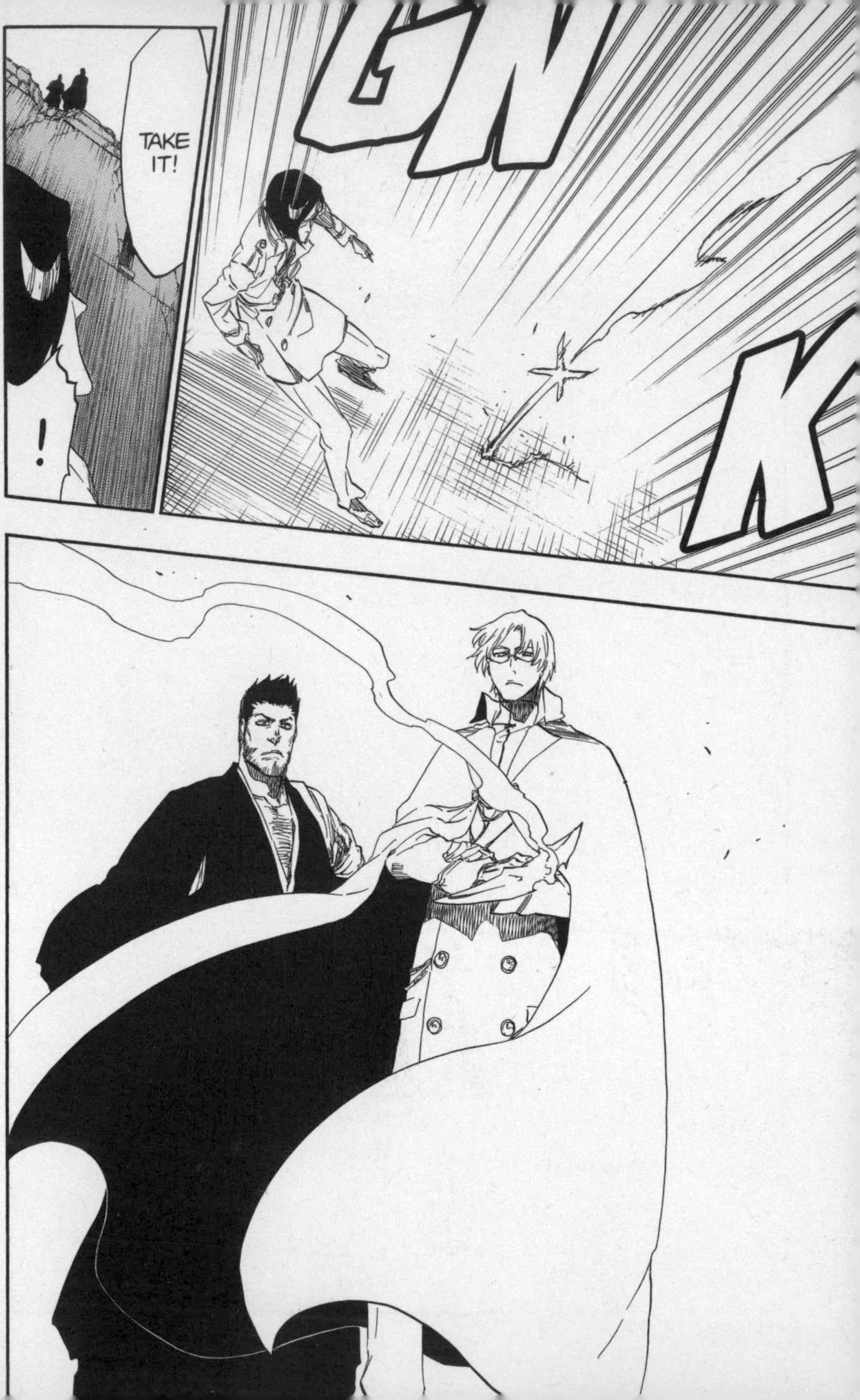
TAKE IT!
!

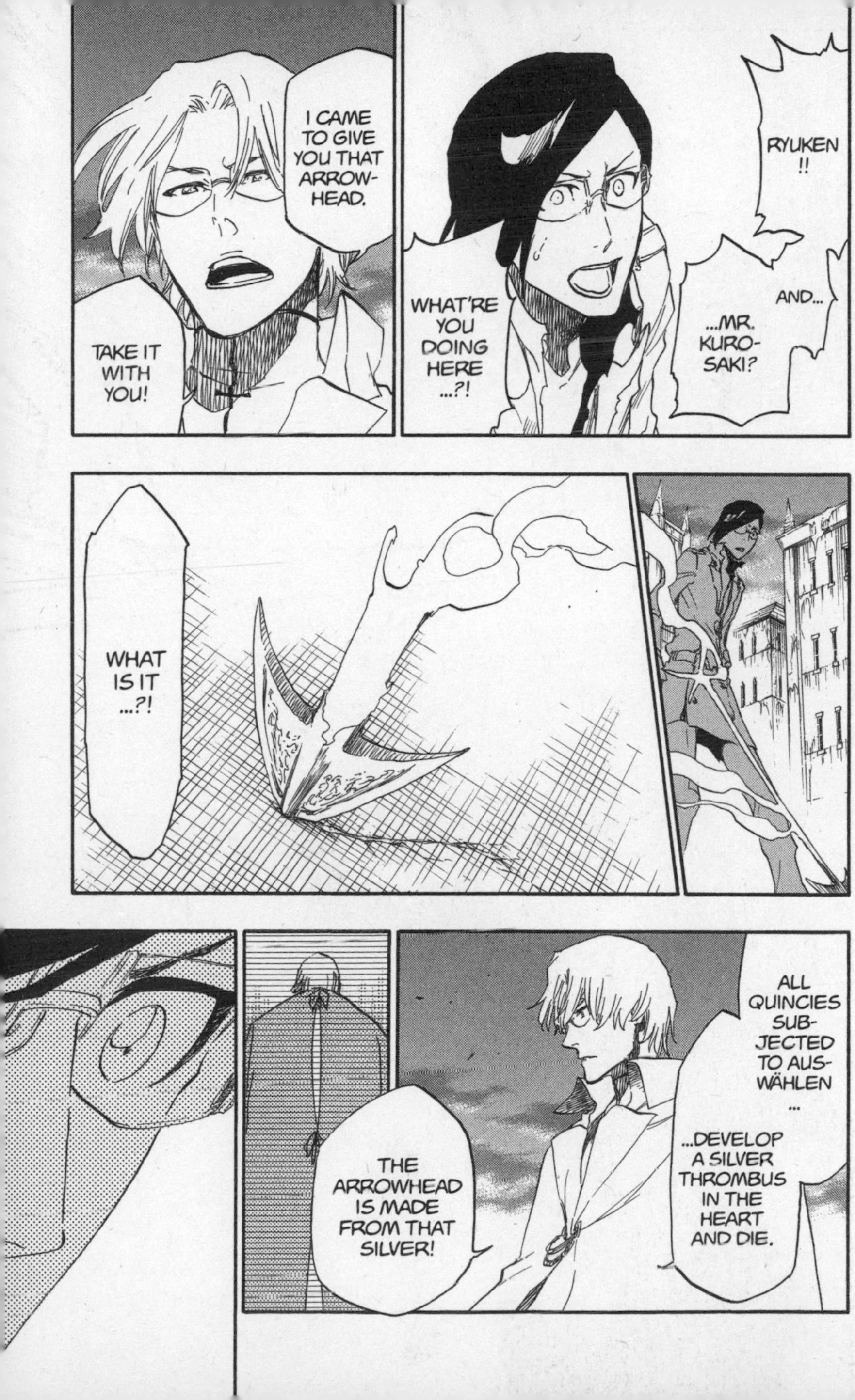
RYUKEN!!
AND...
...MR. KUROSAKI?
WHAT'RE YOU DOING HERE ...?!
I CAME TO GIVE YOU THAT ARROWHEAD.
TAKE IT WITH YOU!
WHAT IS IT ...?!
ALL QUINCIES SUBJECTED TO AUSWÄHLEN ...
...DEVELOP A SILVER THROMBUS IN THE HEART AND DIE.
THE ARROWHEAD IS MADE FROM THAT SILVER!

IT IS AN ARROW-HEAD...

...THAT SHOULD BE FIRED BY YOU.

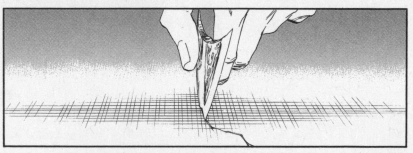

DS

SSH

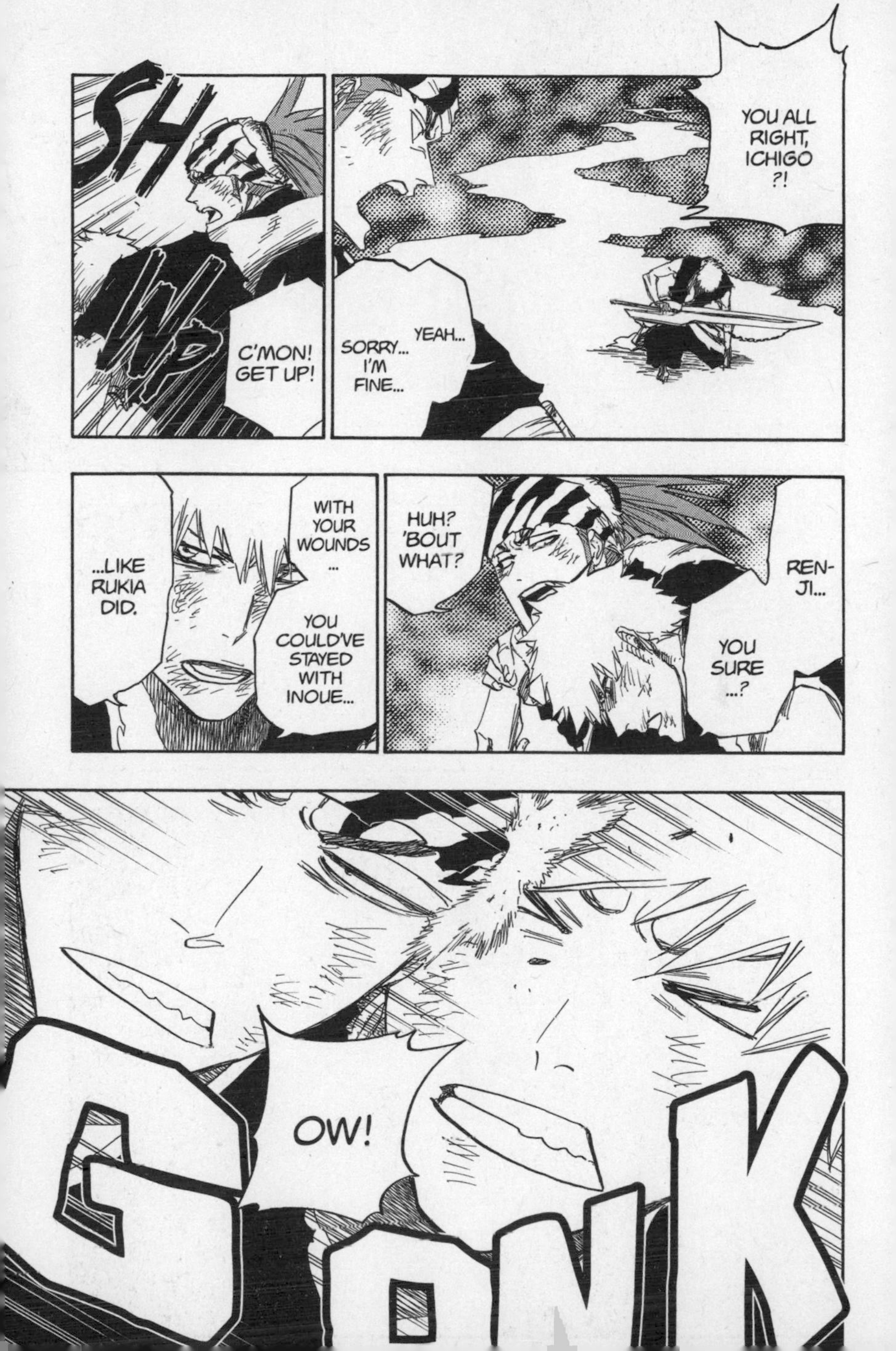
YOU ALL RIGHT, ICHIGO ?!
YEAH... SORRY... I'M FINE...
SHWP
C'MON! GET UP!
RENJI...
YOU SURE ...?
HUH? 'BOUT WHAT?
WITH YOUR WOUNDS ...
YOU COULD'VE STAYED WITH INOUE...
...LIKE RUKIA DID.
OW!
CONK

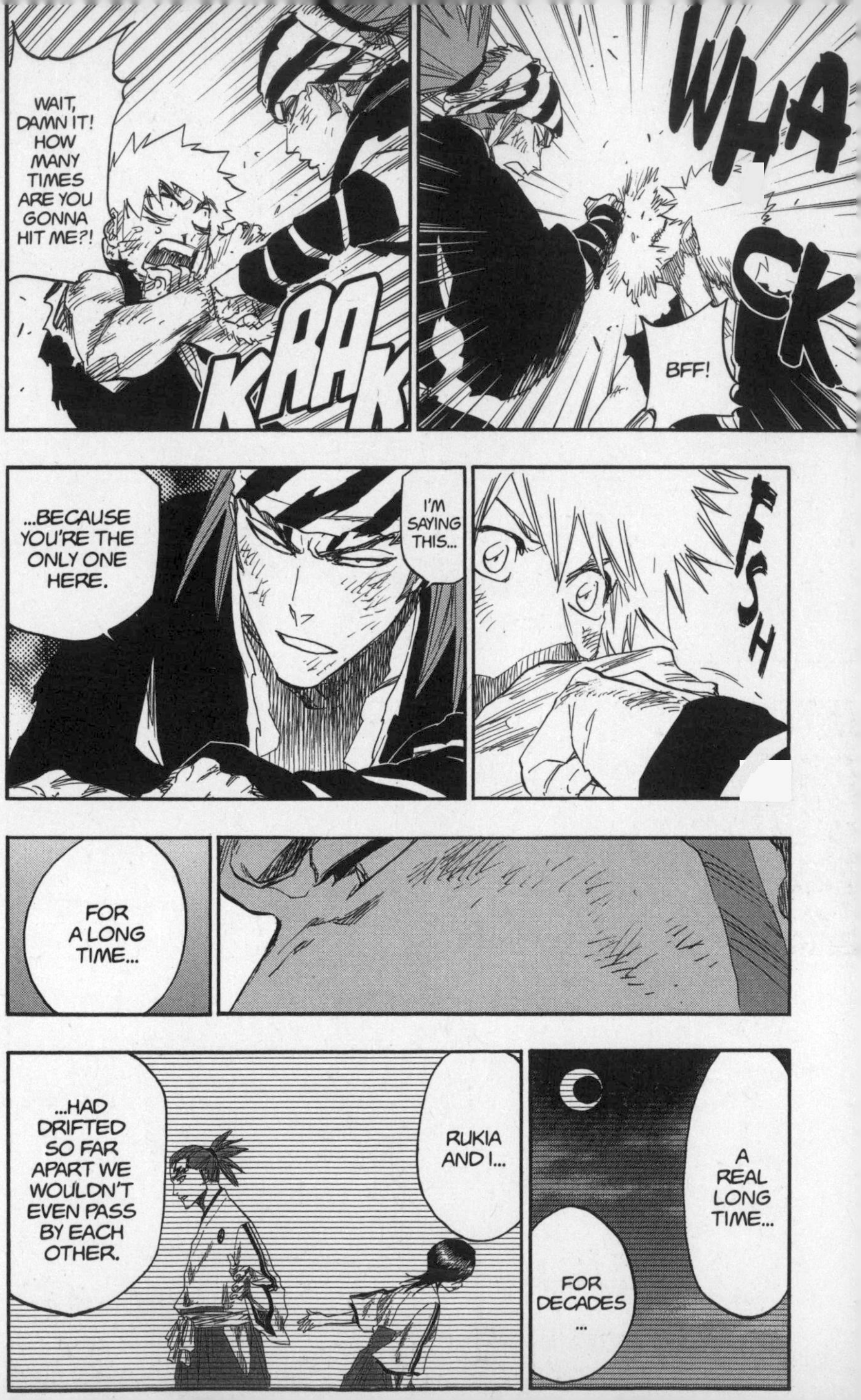
WHACK
BFF!
WAIT, DAMN IT! HOW MANY TIMES ARE YOU GONNA HIT ME?!
KRAAK
FSH
I'M SAYING THIS...
...BECAUSE YOU'RE THE ONLY ONE HERE.
FOR A LONG TIME...
A REAL LONG TIME...
FOR DECADES...
RUKIA AND I...
...HAD DRIFTED SO FAR APART WE WOULDN'T EVEN PASS BY EACH OTHER.

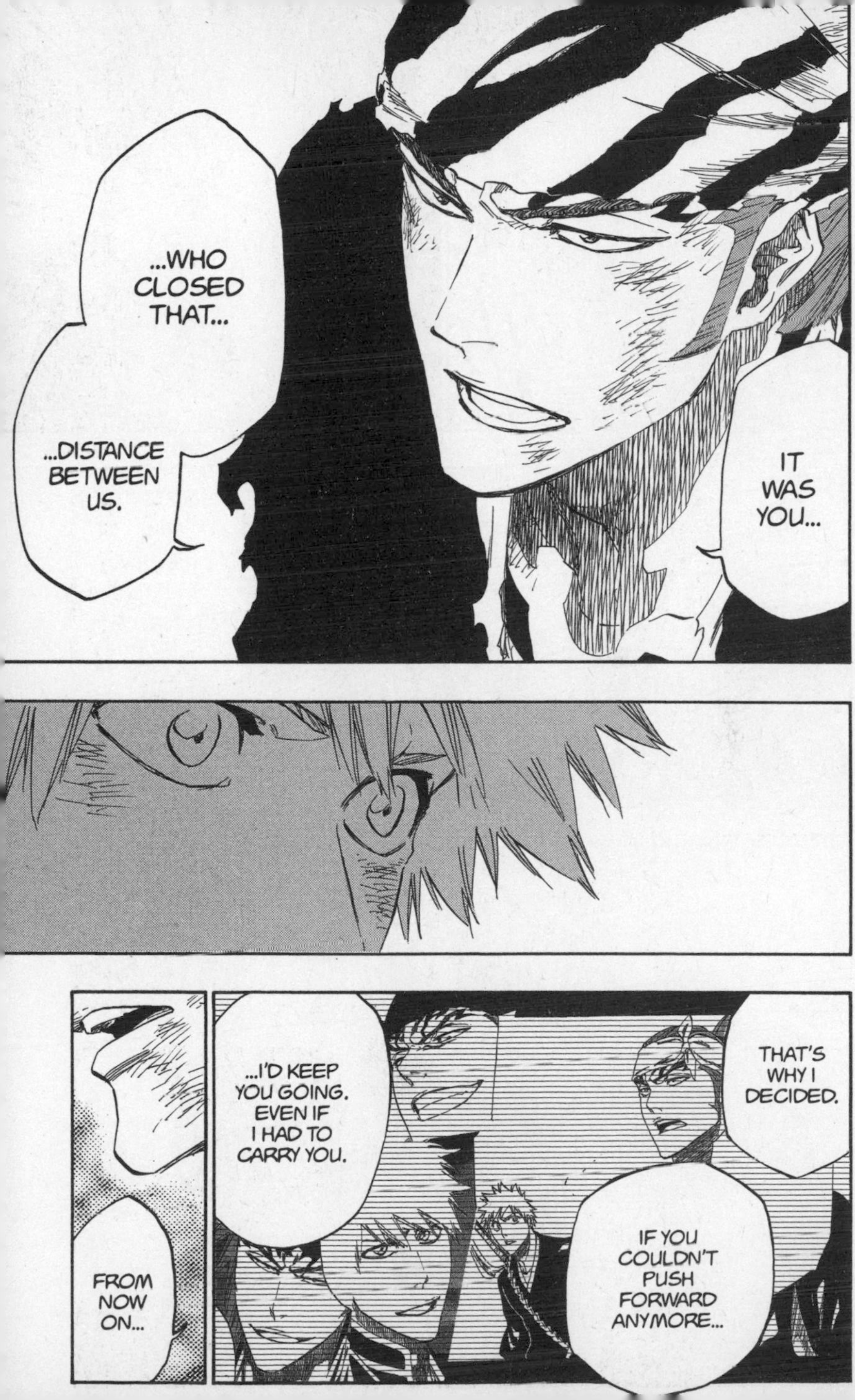
IT WAS YOU...
...WHO CLOSED THAT...
...DISTANCE BETWEEN US.
THAT'S WHY I DECIDED.
IF YOU COULDN'T PUSH FORWARD ANYMORE...
...I'D KEEP YOU GOING. EVEN IF I HAD TO CARRY YOU.
FROM NOW ON...

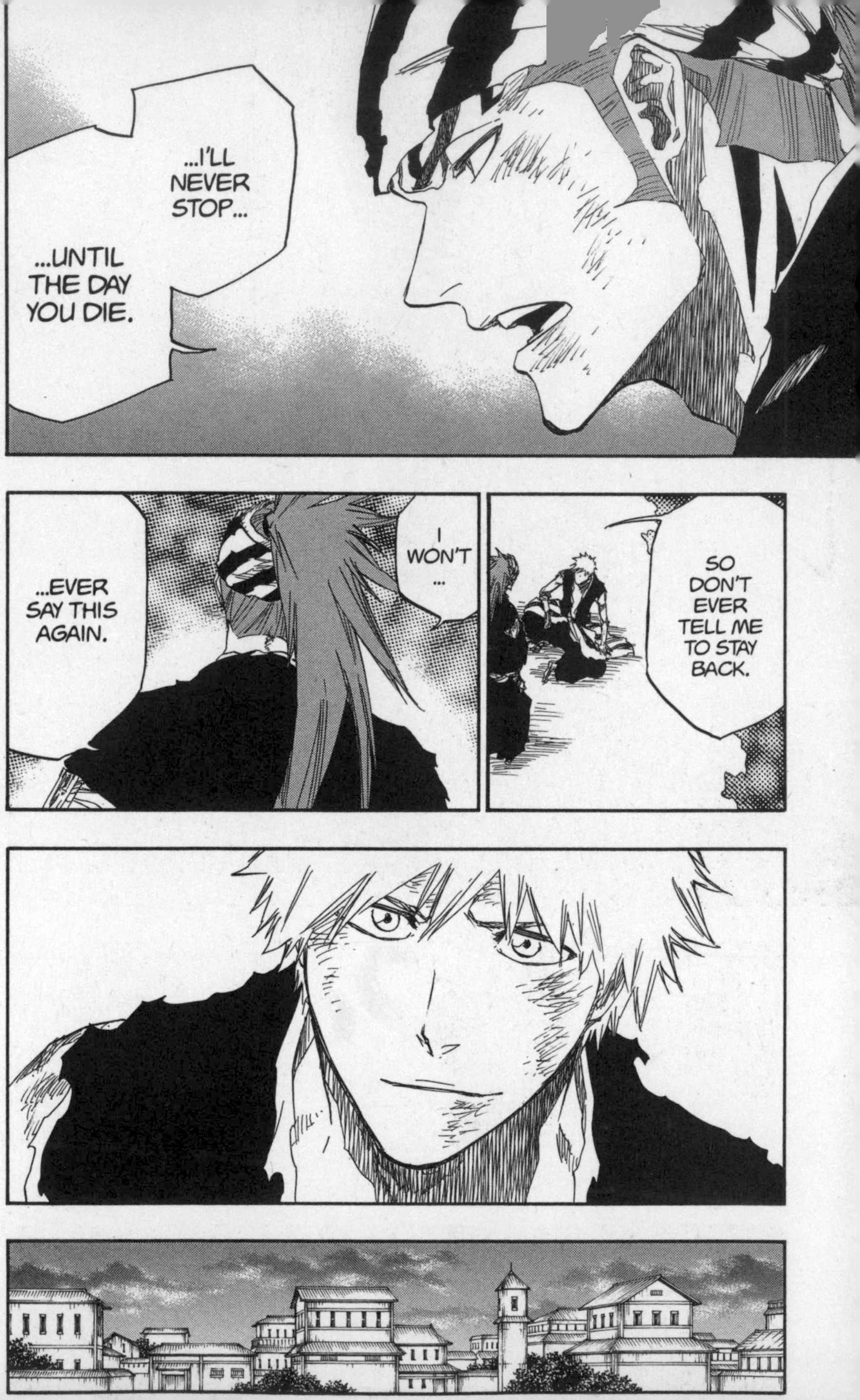
...I'LL NEVER STOP...
...UNTIL THE DAY YOU DIE.
SO DON'T EVER TELL ME TO STAY BACK.
I WON'T ...
...EVER SAY THIS AGAIN.

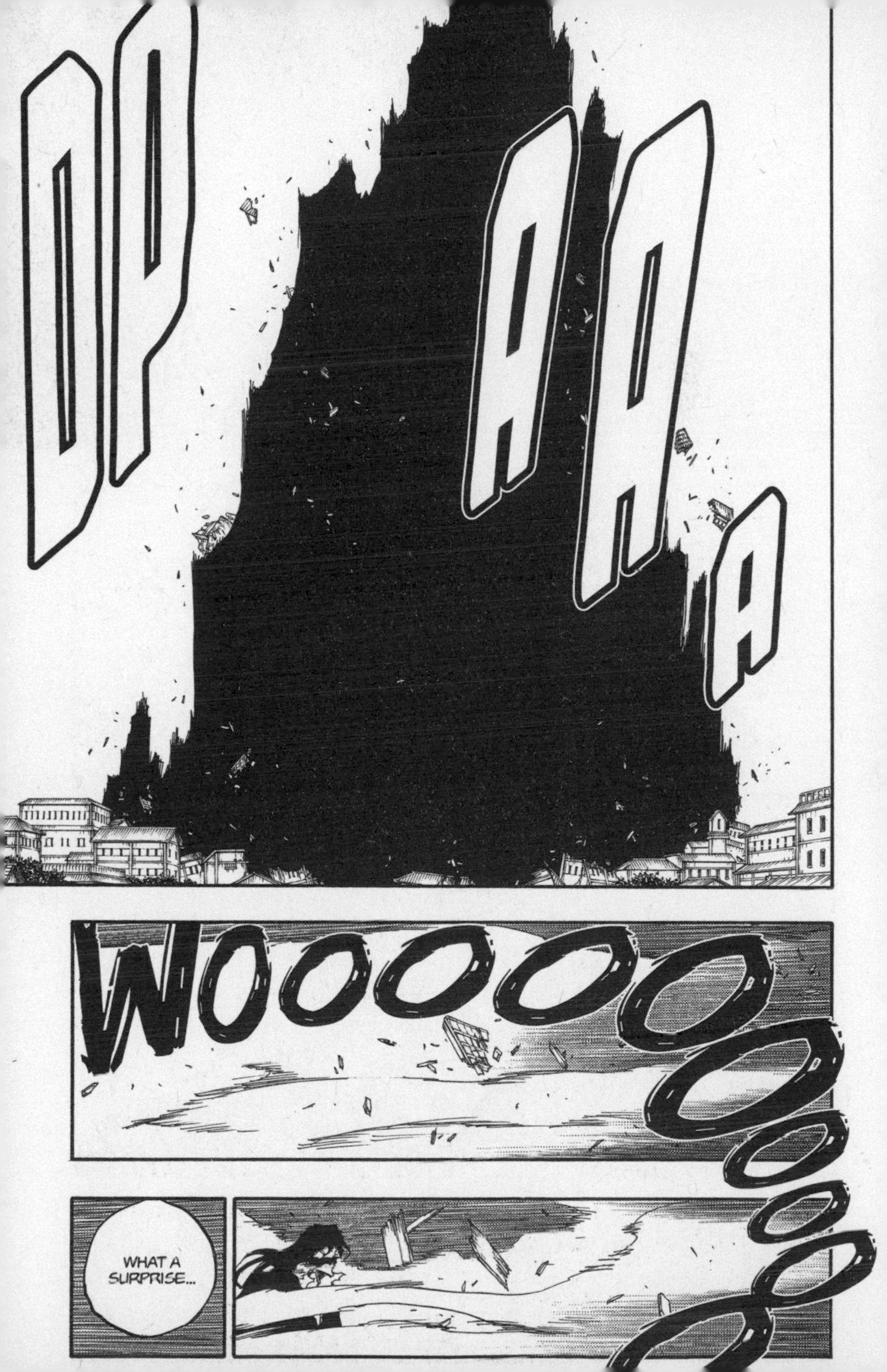
DOAAA
WOOOOOOOOOOO
WHAT A SURPRISE...

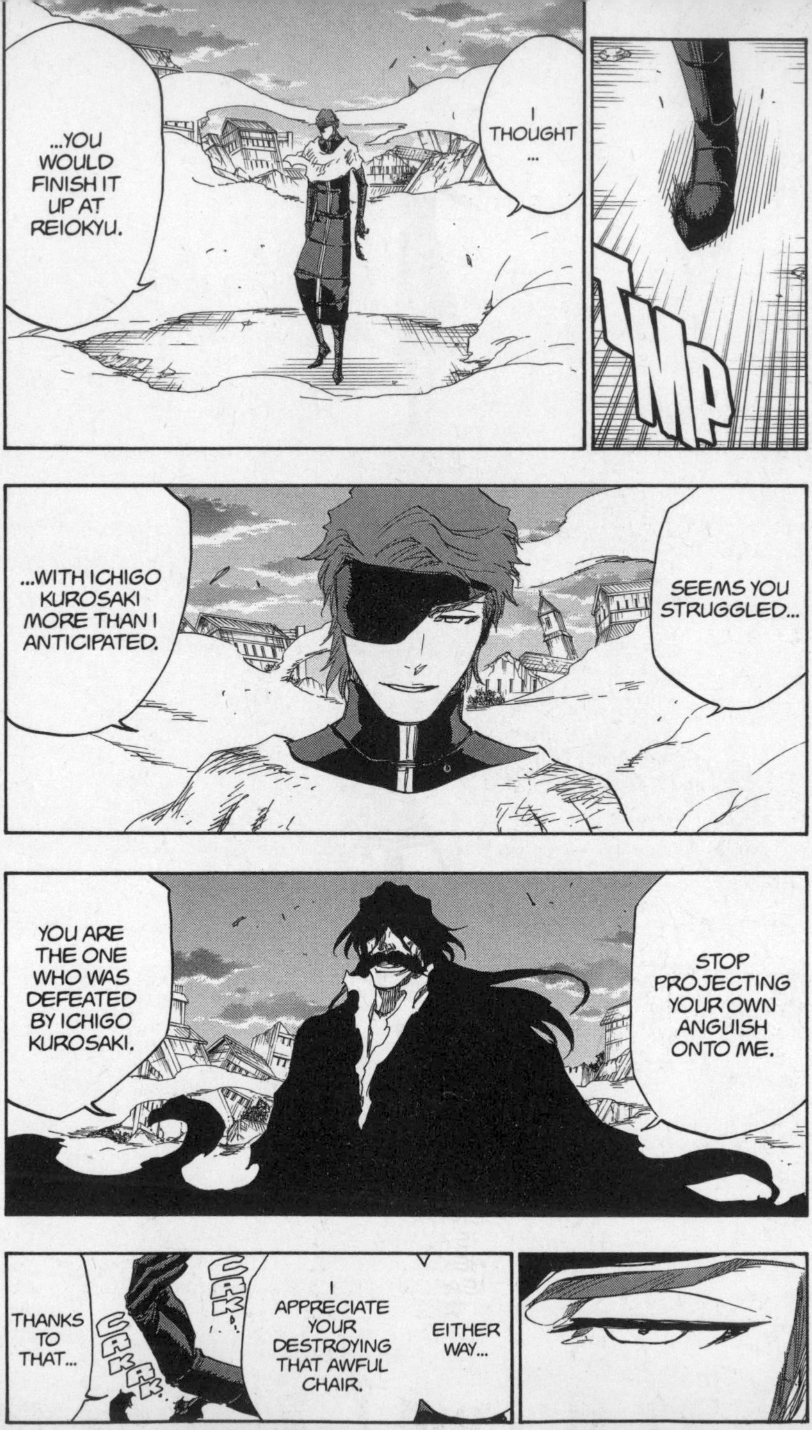
TMP
I THOUGHT ...
...YOU WOULD FINISH IT UP AT REIOKYU.
SEEMS YOU STRUGGLED...
...WITH ICHIGO KUROSAKI MORE THAN I ANTICIPATED.
STOP PROJECTING YOUR OWN ANGUISH ONTO ME.
YOU ARE THE ONE WHO WAS DEFEATED BY ICHIGO KUROSAKI.
EITHER WAY...
I APPRECIATE YOUR DESTROYING THAT AWFUL CHAIR.
CRK...
CRKRK...
THANKS TO THAT...

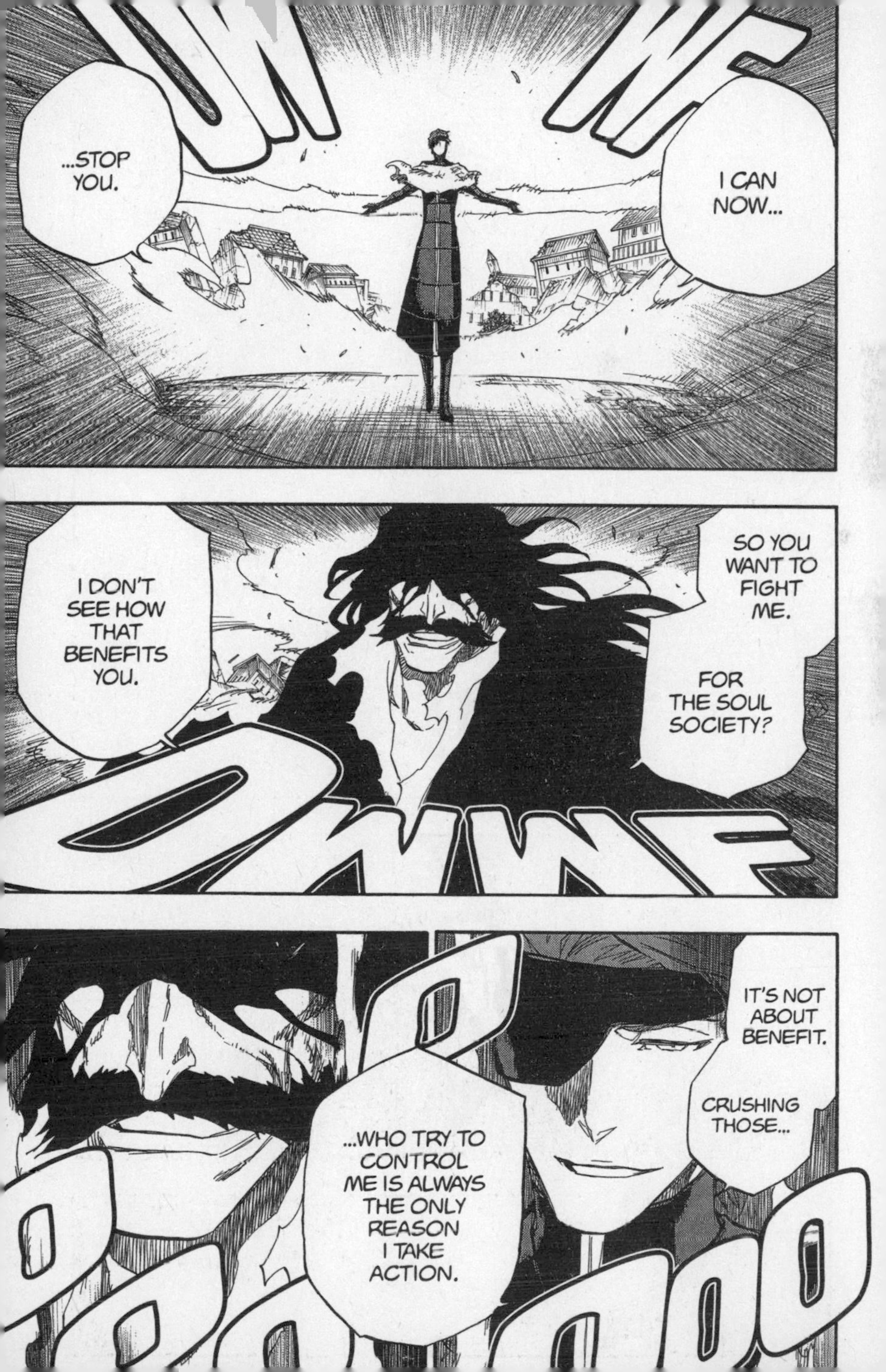
I CAN NOW...
...STOP YOU.
SO YOU WANT TO FIGHT ME.
FOR THE SOUL SOCIETY?
I DON'T SEE HOW THAT BENEFITS YOU.
IT'S NOT ABOUT BENEFIT.
CRUSHING THOSE...
...WHO TRY TO CONTROL ME IS ALWAYS THE ONLY REASON I TAKE ACTION.

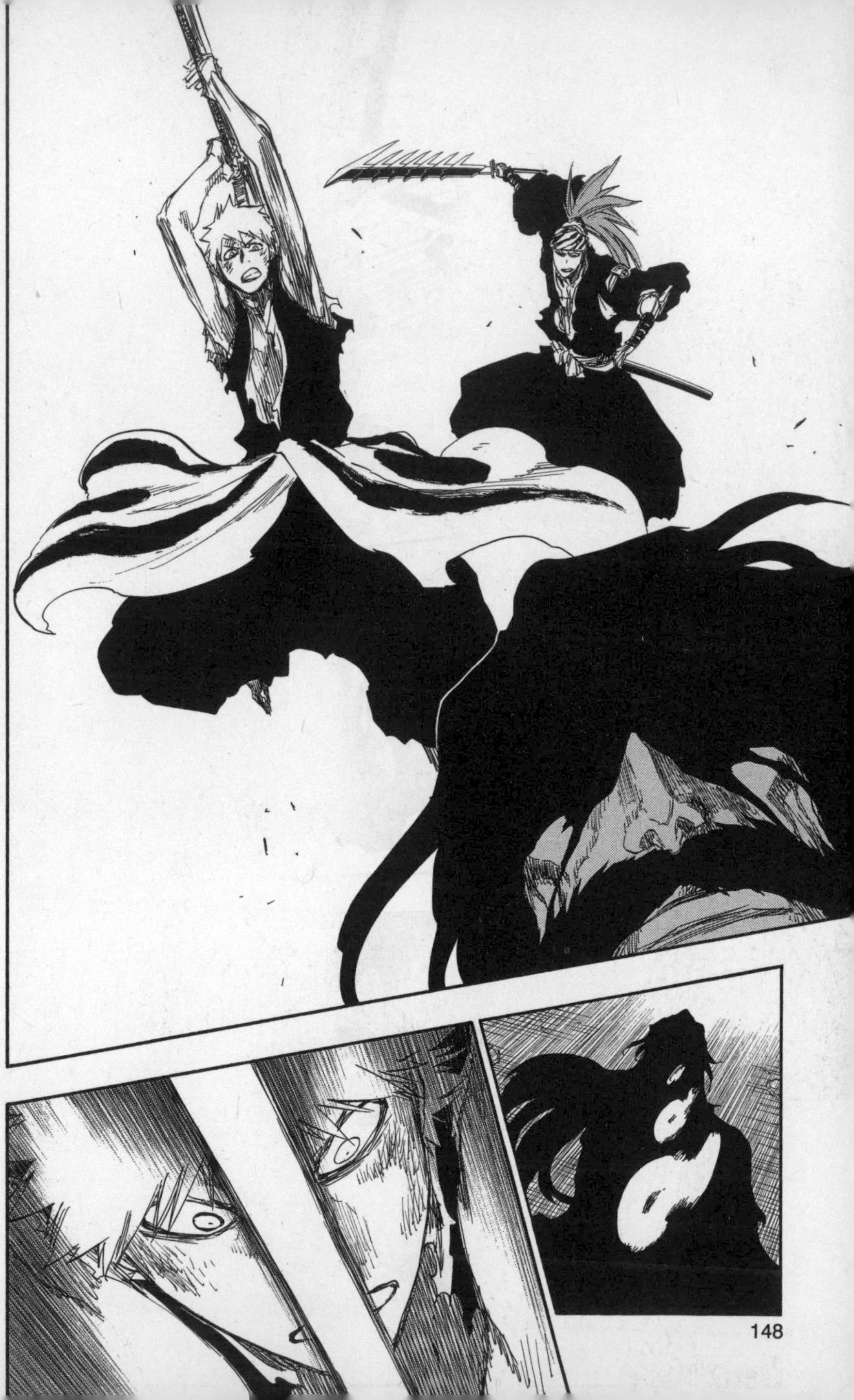

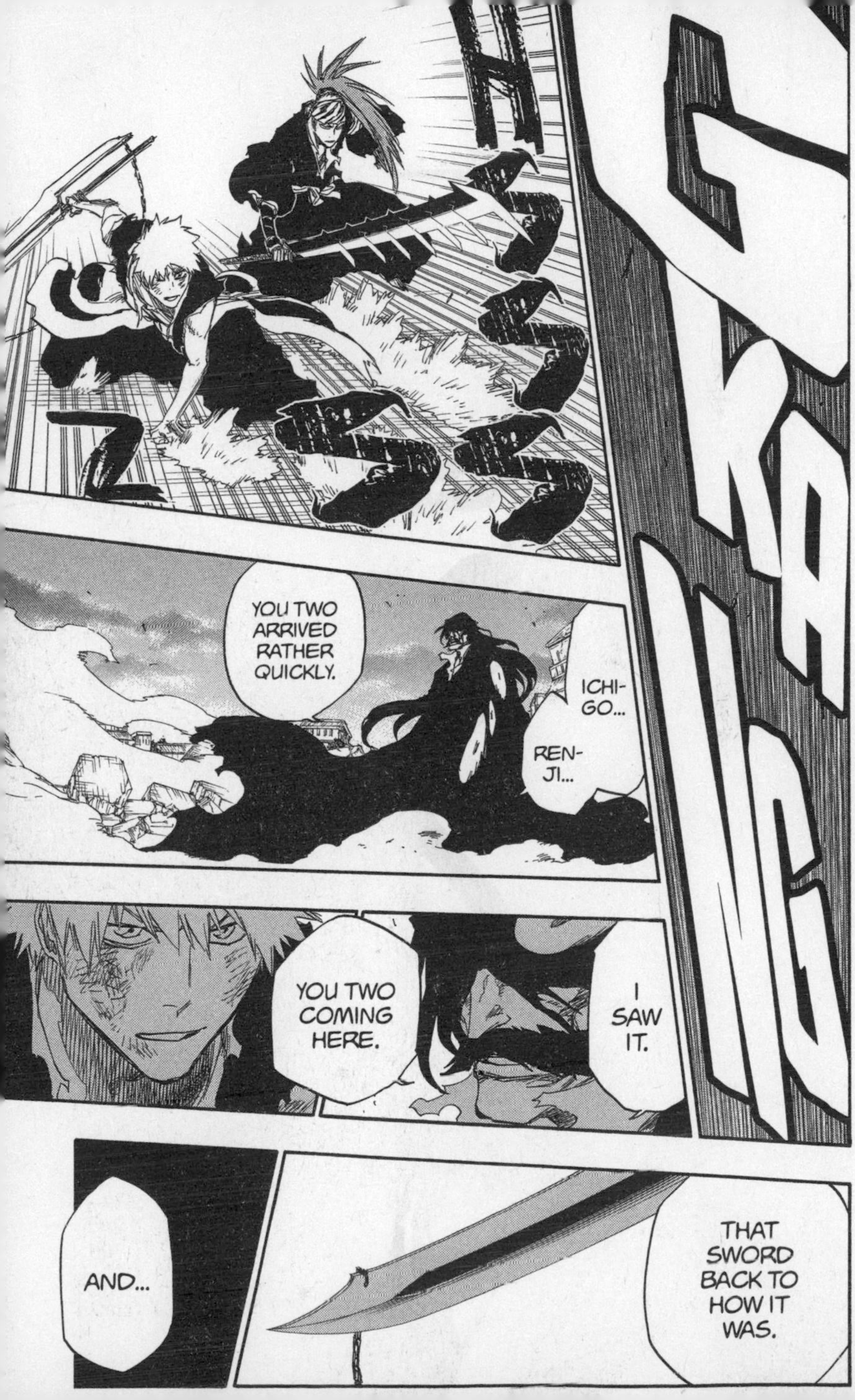
ICHI-GO...
REN-JI...
YOU TWO ARRIVED RATHER QUICKLY.
I SAW IT.
YOU TWO COMING HERE.
THAT SWORD BACK TO HOW IT WAS.
AND...

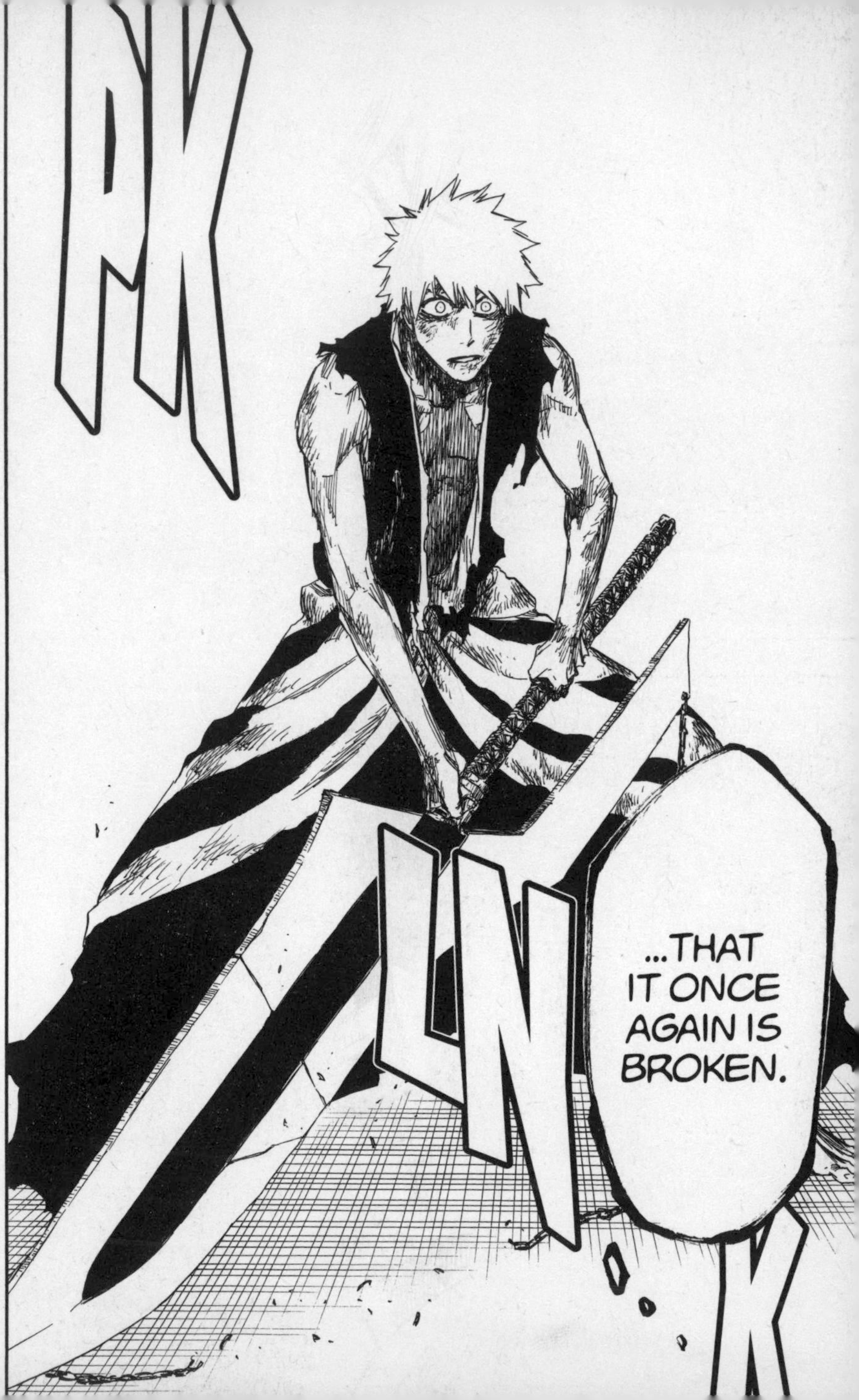
...THAT IT ONCE AGAIN IS BROKEN.
PK
LINK

HOW...

I THOUGHT I BROKE IT CLEAN...

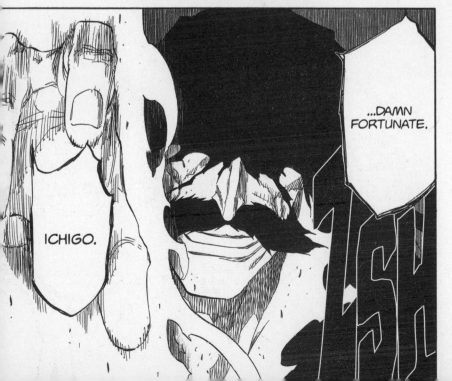

...DAMN FORTUNATE.

ICHIGO.

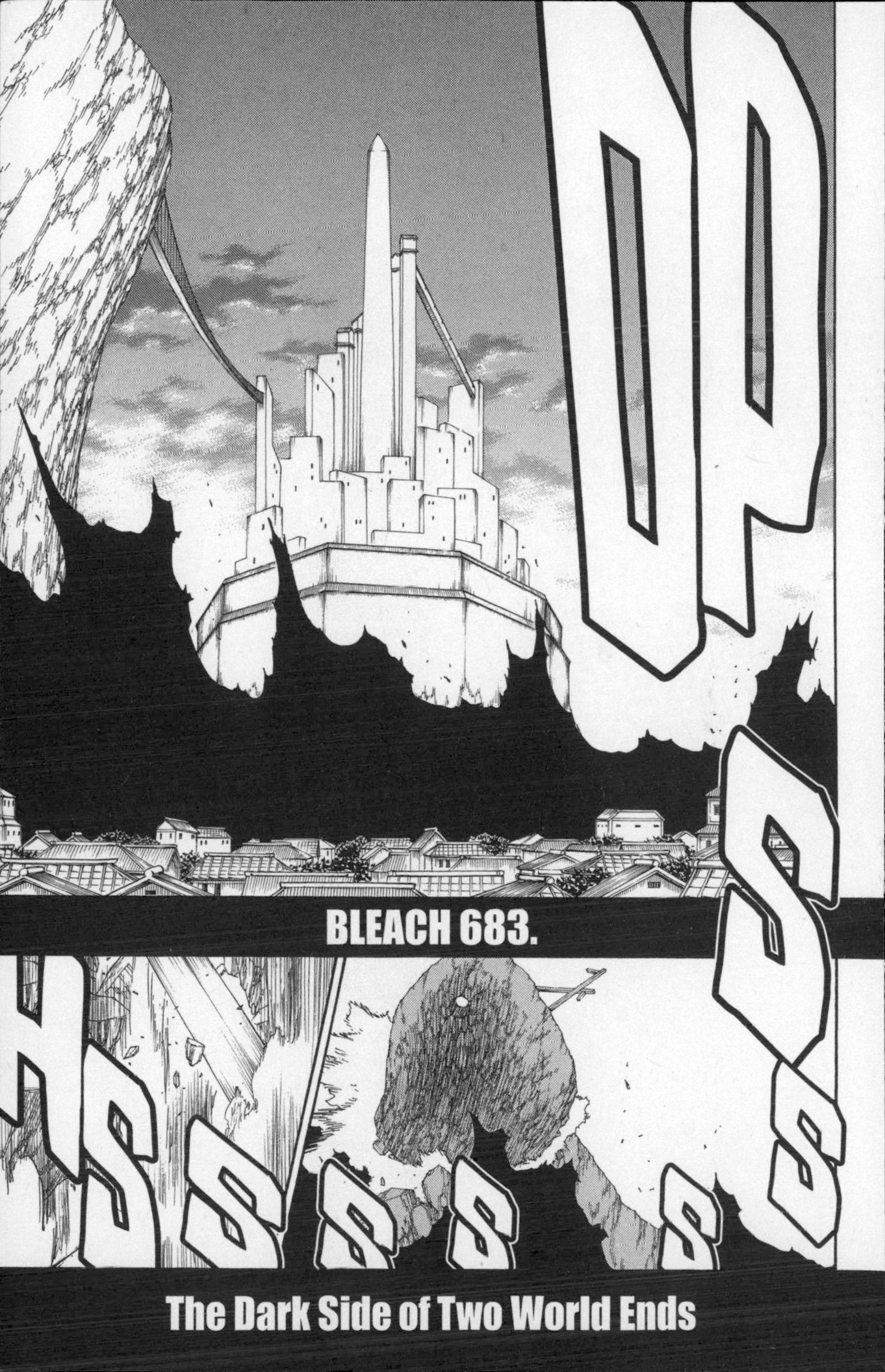
BLEACH 683.
The Dark Side of Two World Ends

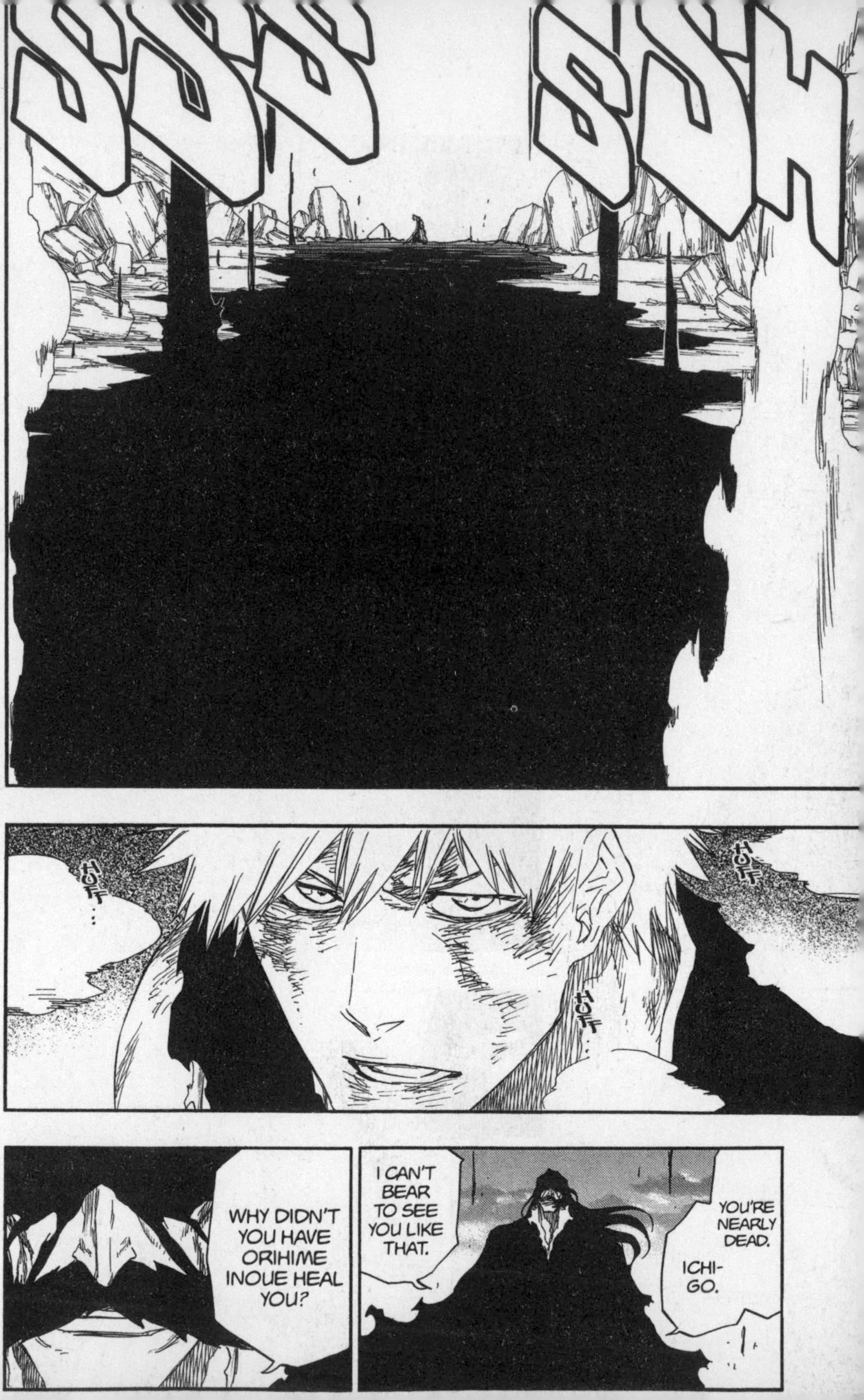
SSS
SSH
HUFF...
HUFF...
HUFF...
YOU'RE NEARLY DEAD.
ICHI-GO.
I CAN'T BEAR TO SEE YOU LIKE THAT.
WHY DIDN'T YOU HAVE ORIHIME INOUE HEAL YOU?

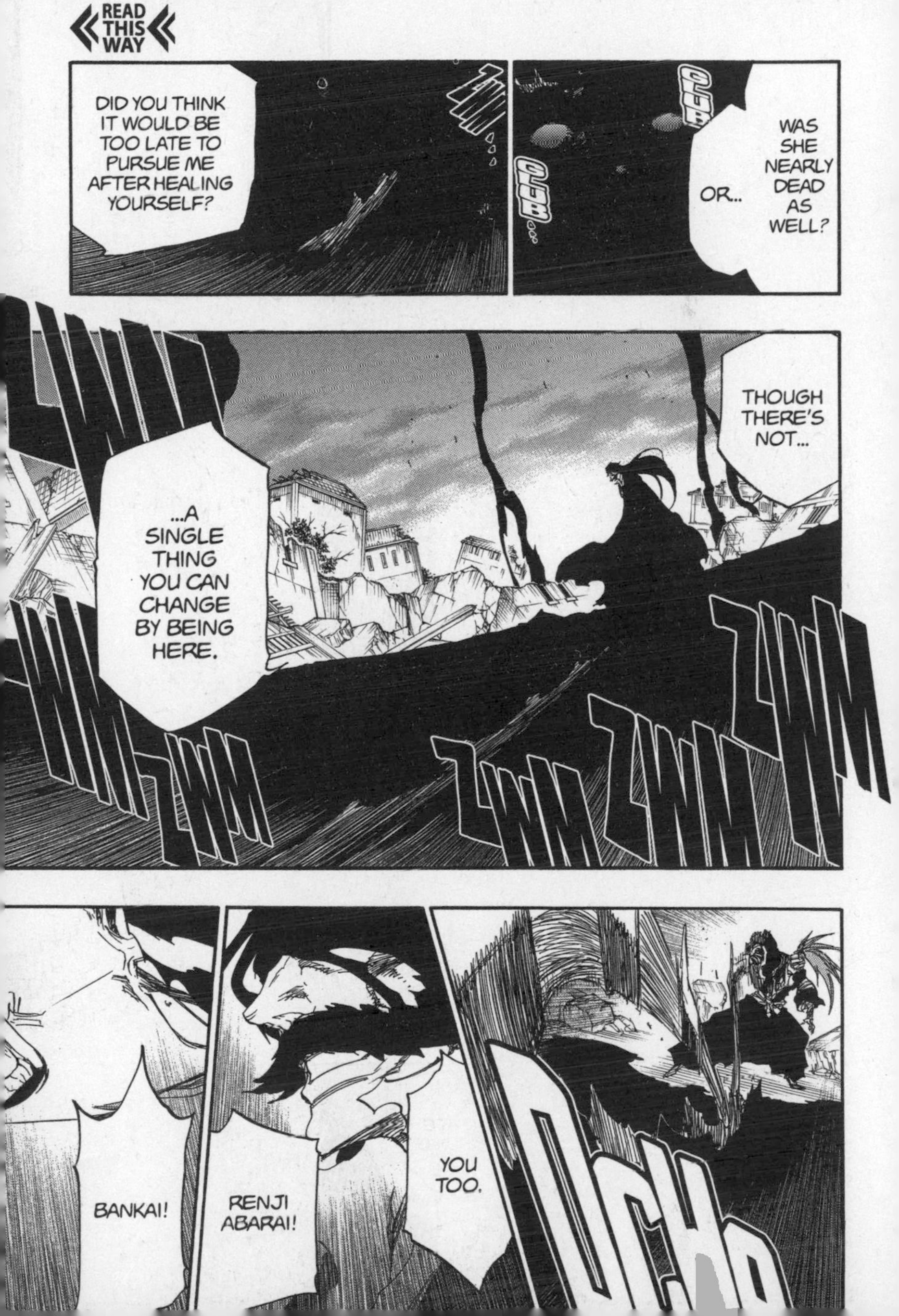
READ THIS WAY
GLUB
GLUB
WAS SHE NEARLY DEAD AS WELL?
OR...
DID YOU THINK IT WOULD BE TOO LATE TO PURSUE ME AFTER HEALING YOURSELF?
THOUGH THERE'S NOT...
...A SINGLE THING YOU CAN CHANGE BY BEING HERE.
YOU TOO.
RENJI ABARAI!
BANKAI!

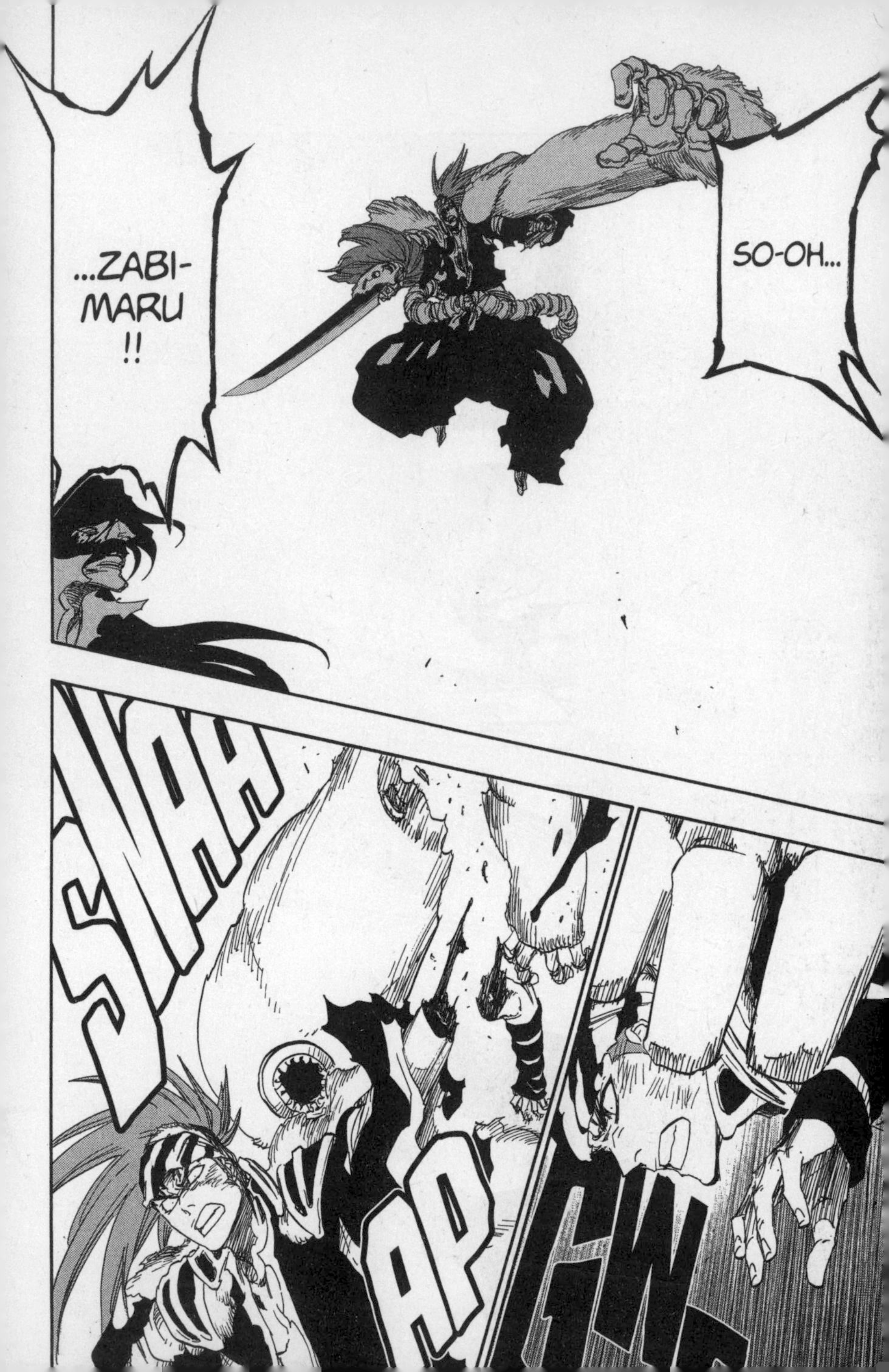
SO-OH...
...ZABI-
MARU
!!

READ THIS WAY

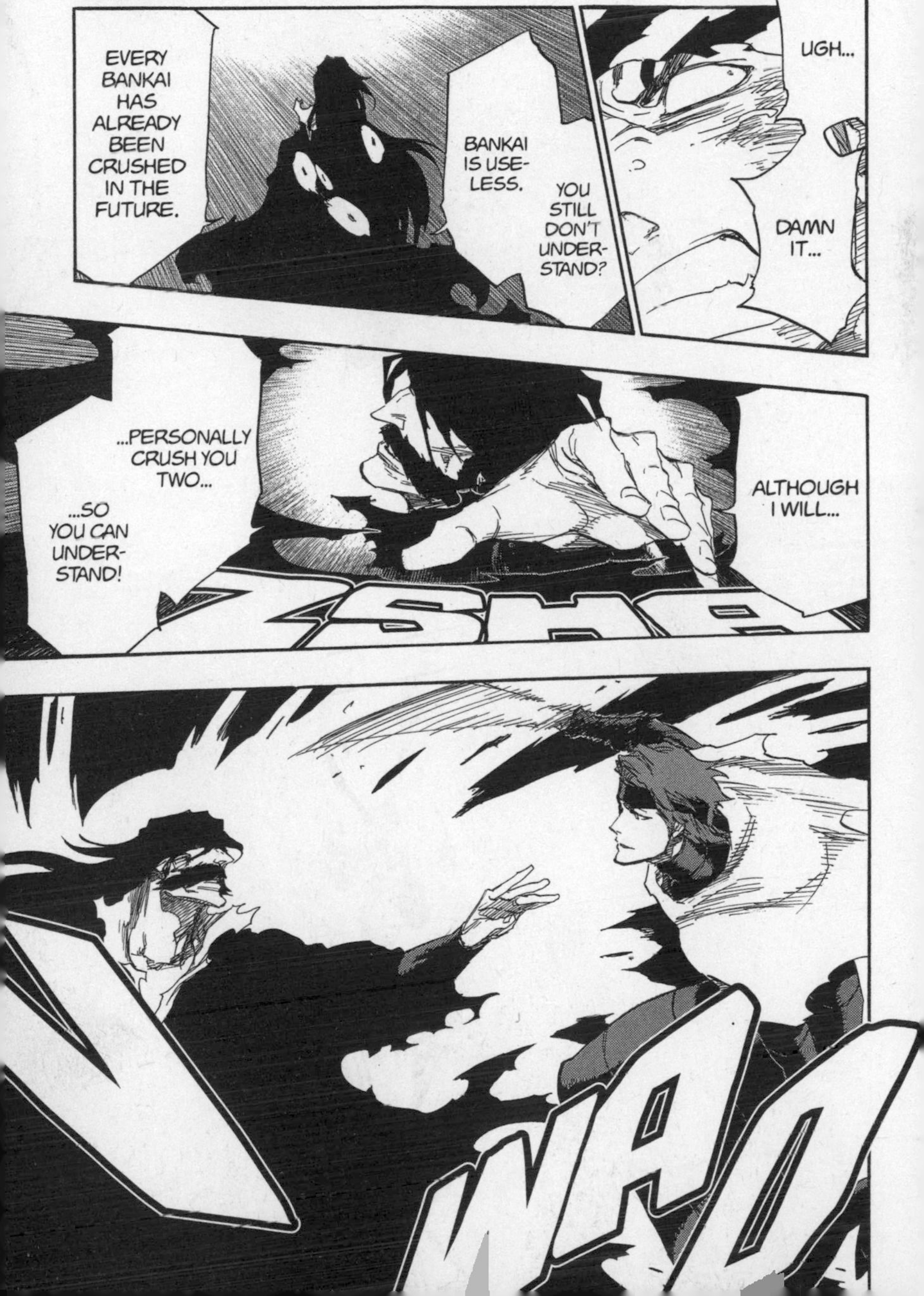
UGH...
DAMN IT...
YOU STILL DON'T UNDER-STAND?
BANKAI IS USE-LESS.
EVERY BANKAI HAS ALREADY BEEN CRUSHED IN THE FUTURE.
ALTHOUGH I WILL...
...PERSONALLY CRUSH YOU TWO...
...SO YOU CAN UNDER-STAND!

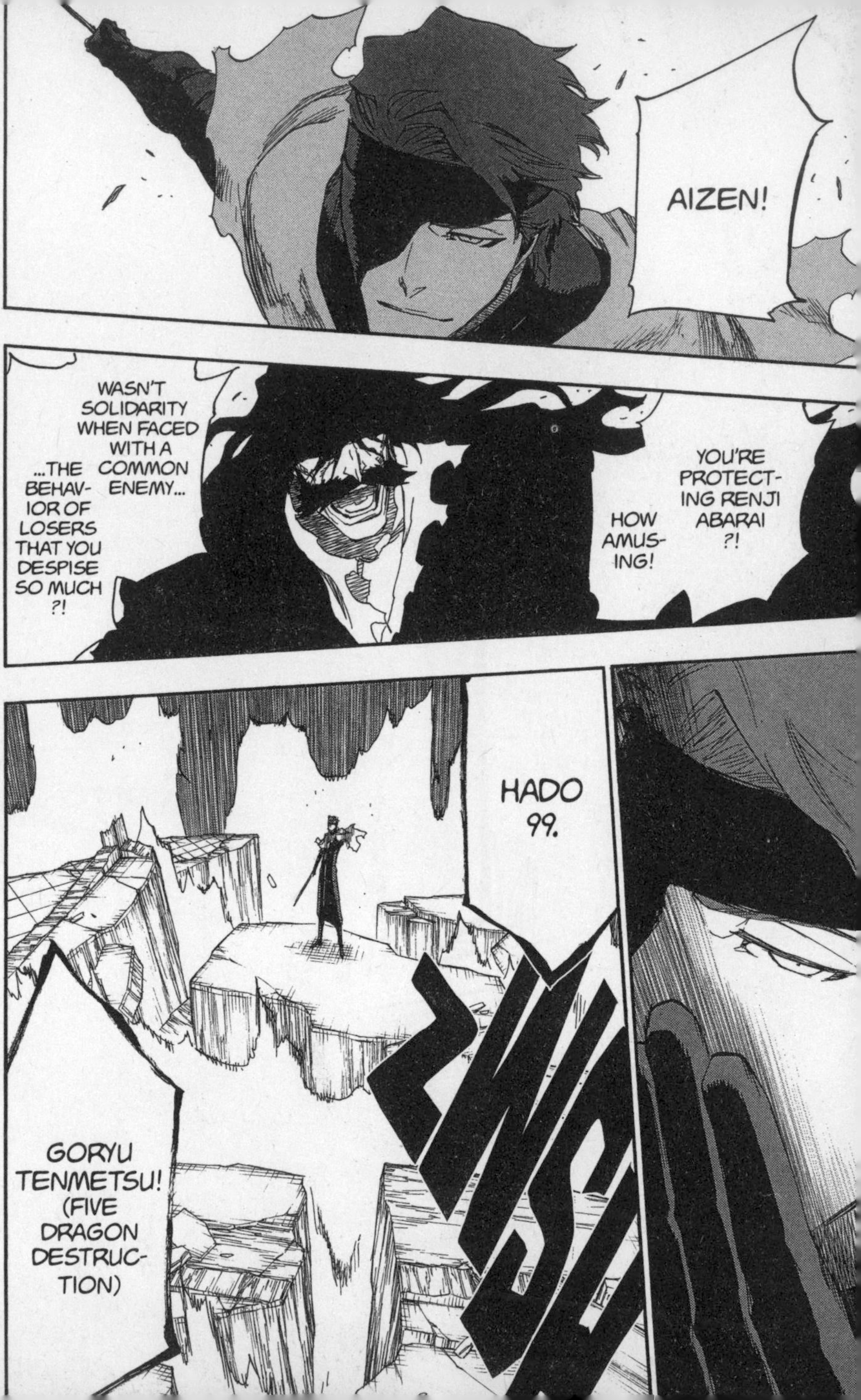
AIZEN!
YOU'RE PROTECTING RENJI ABARAI ?!
HOW AMUSING!
WASN'T SOLIDARITY WHEN FACED WITH A COMMON ENEMY...
...THE BEHAVIOR OF LOSERS THAT YOU DESPISE SO MUCH ?!
HADO 99.
GORYU TENMETSU! (FIVE DRAGON DESTRUCTION)

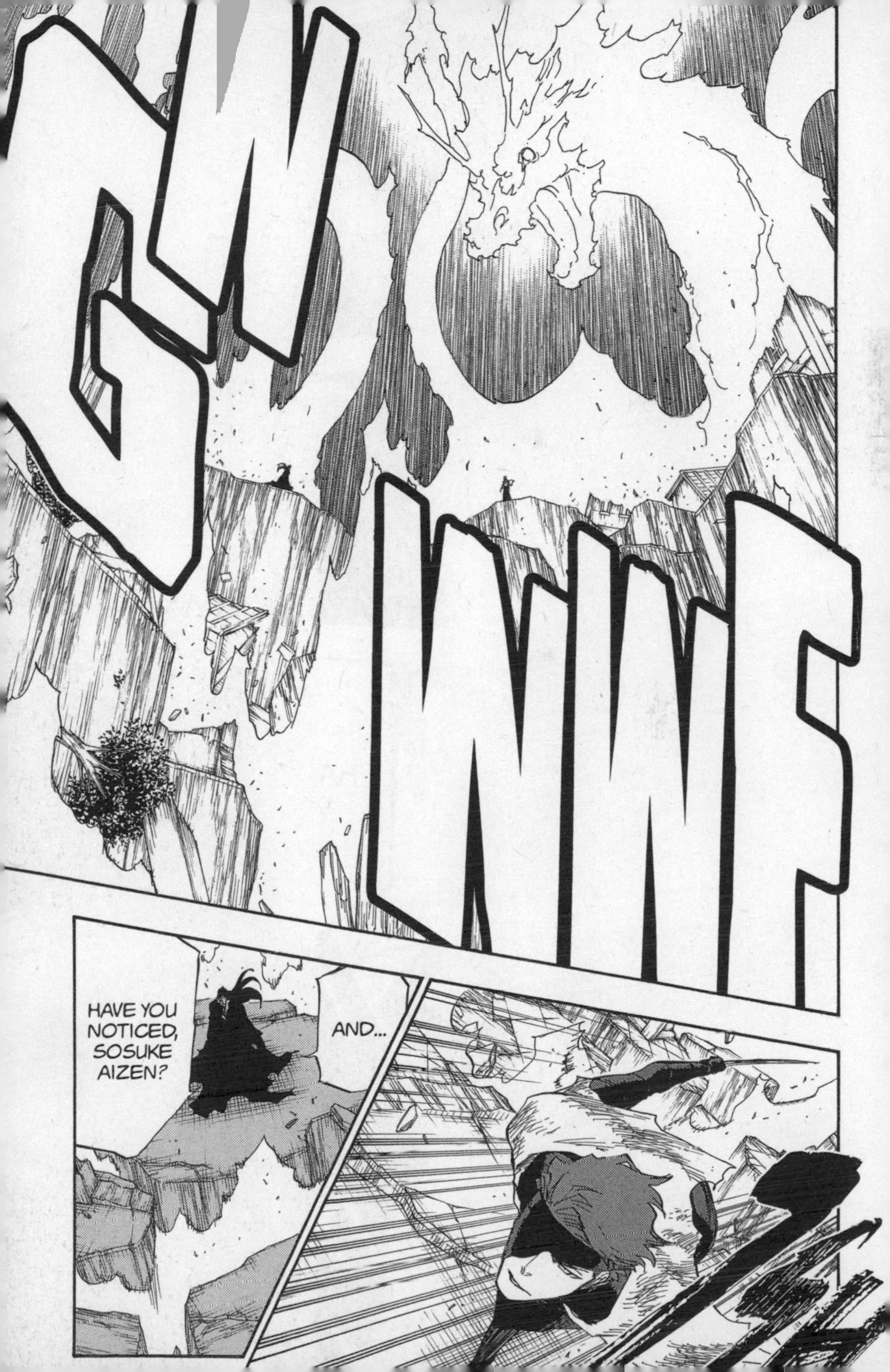
AND...
HAVE YOU NOTICED, SOSUKE AIZEN?

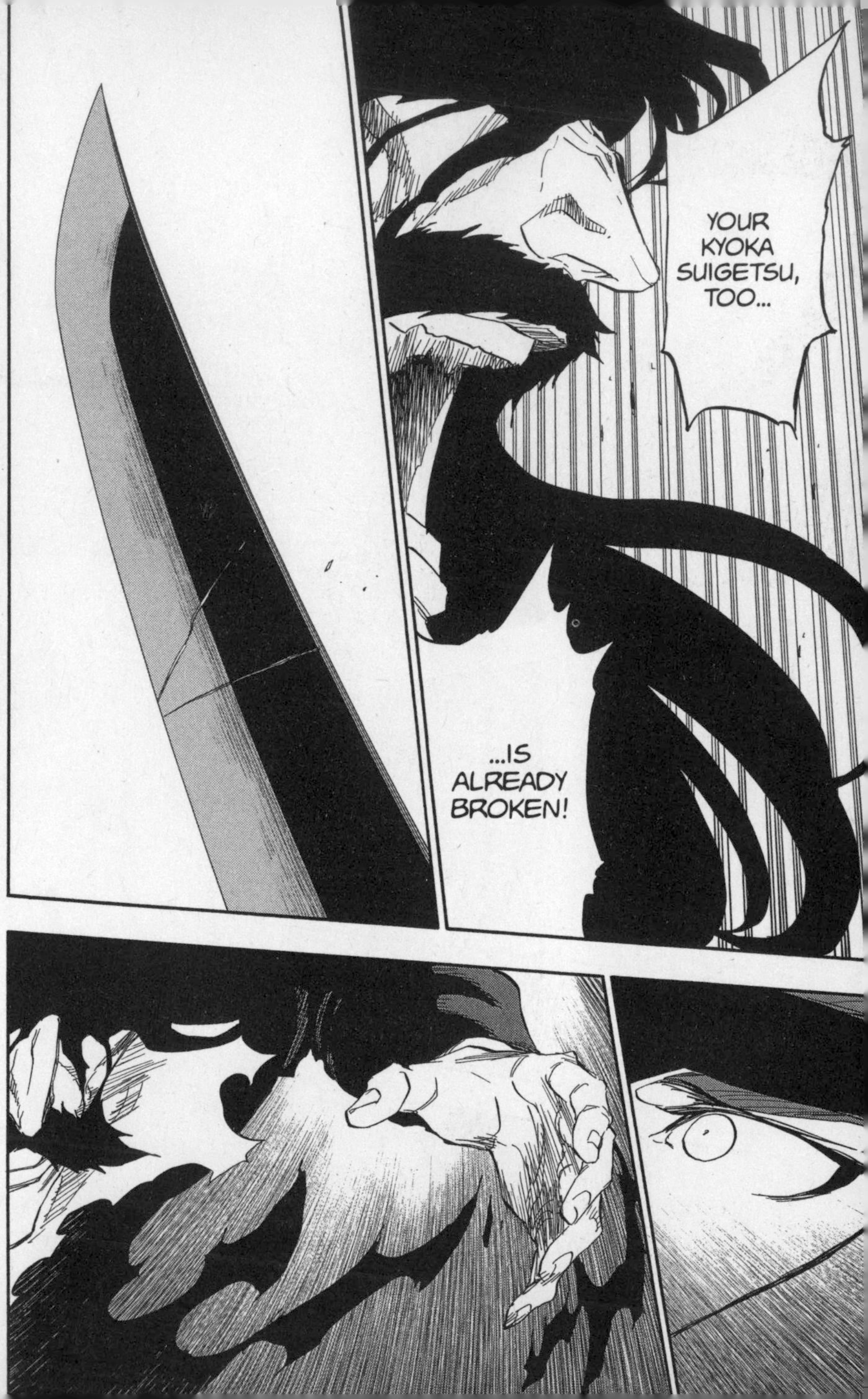
YOUR KYOKA SUIGETSU, TOO...
...IS ALREADY BROKEN!

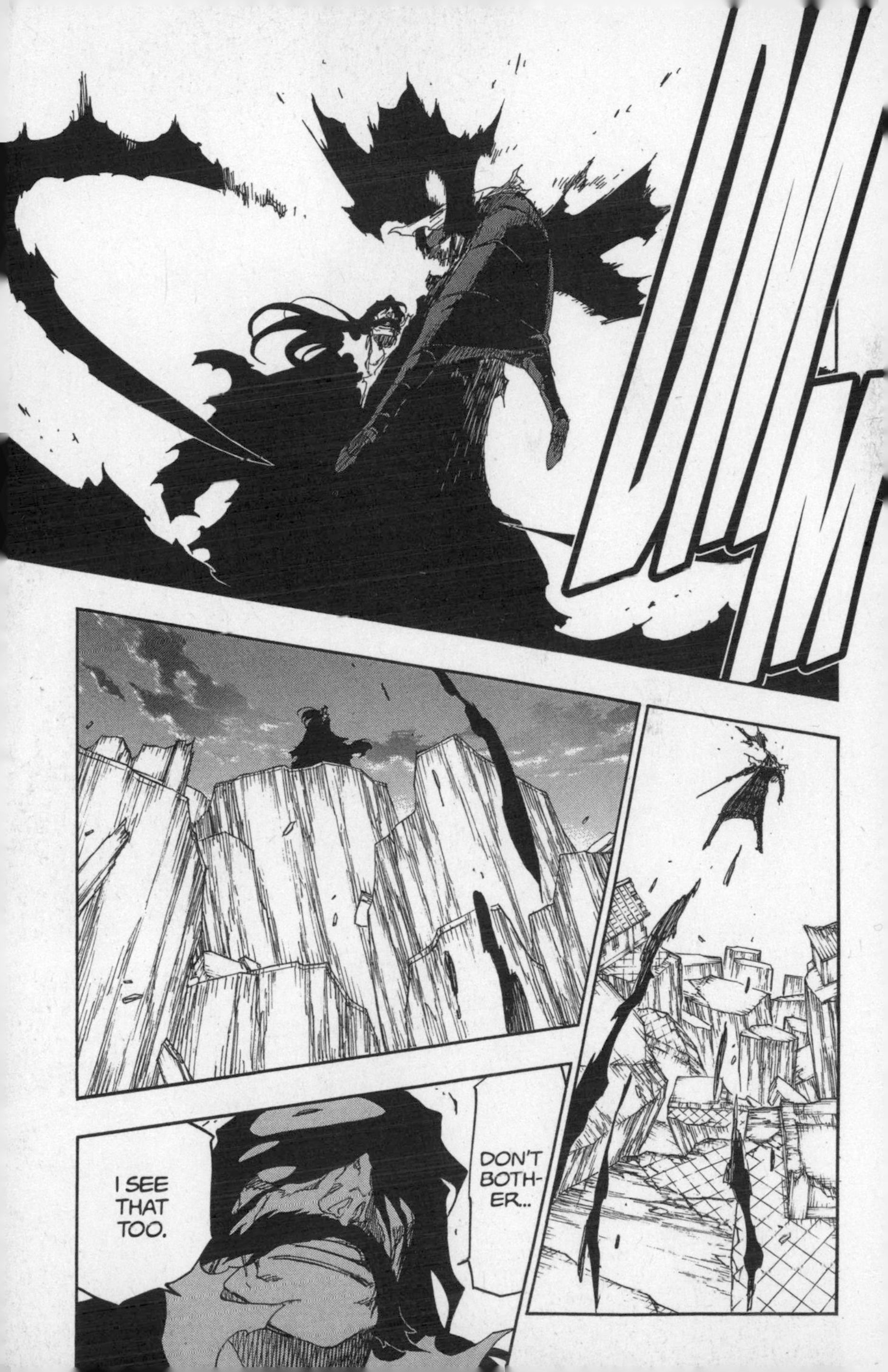
DON'T BOTHER...
I SEE THAT TOO.

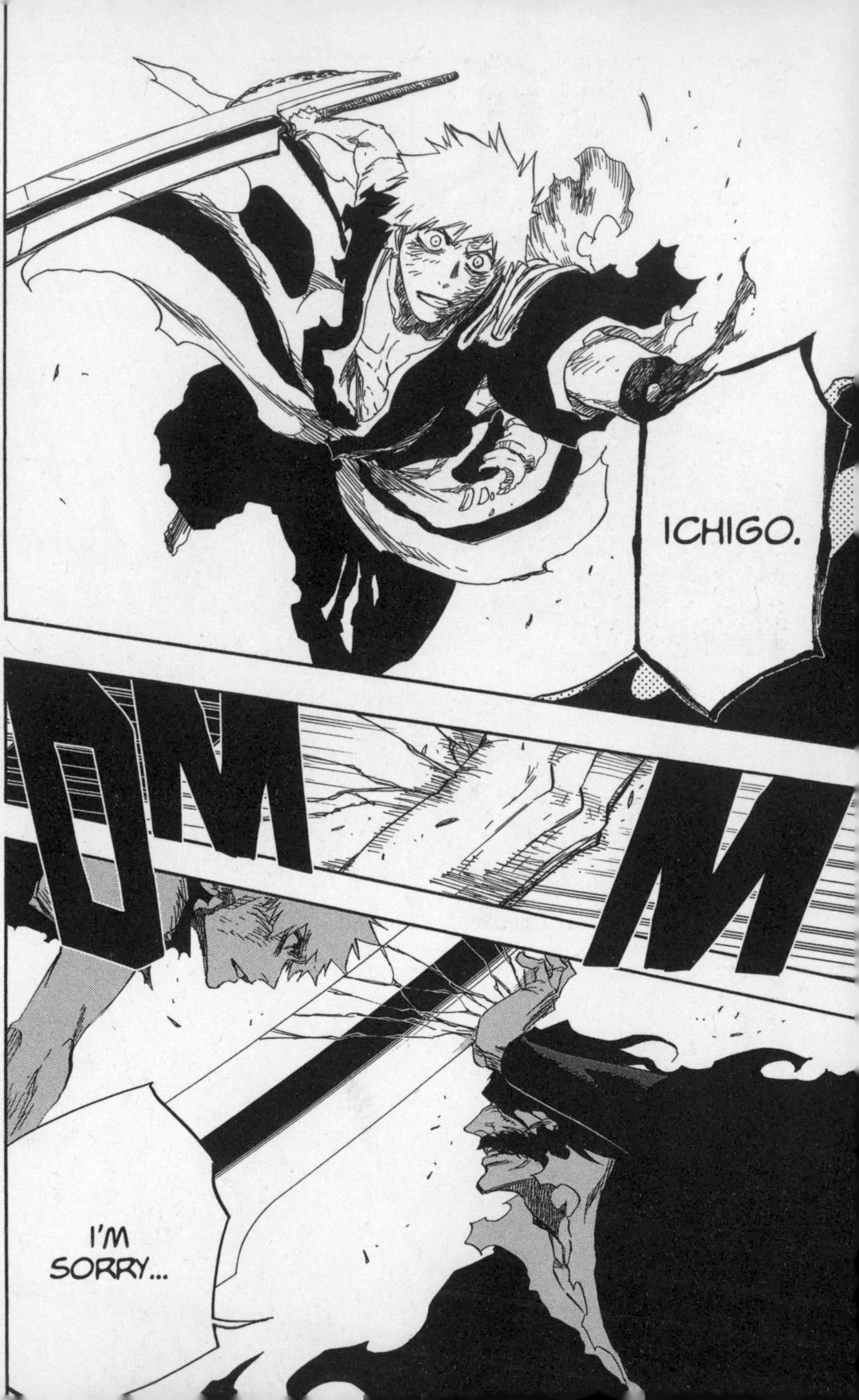
ICHIGO.
I'M SORRY...

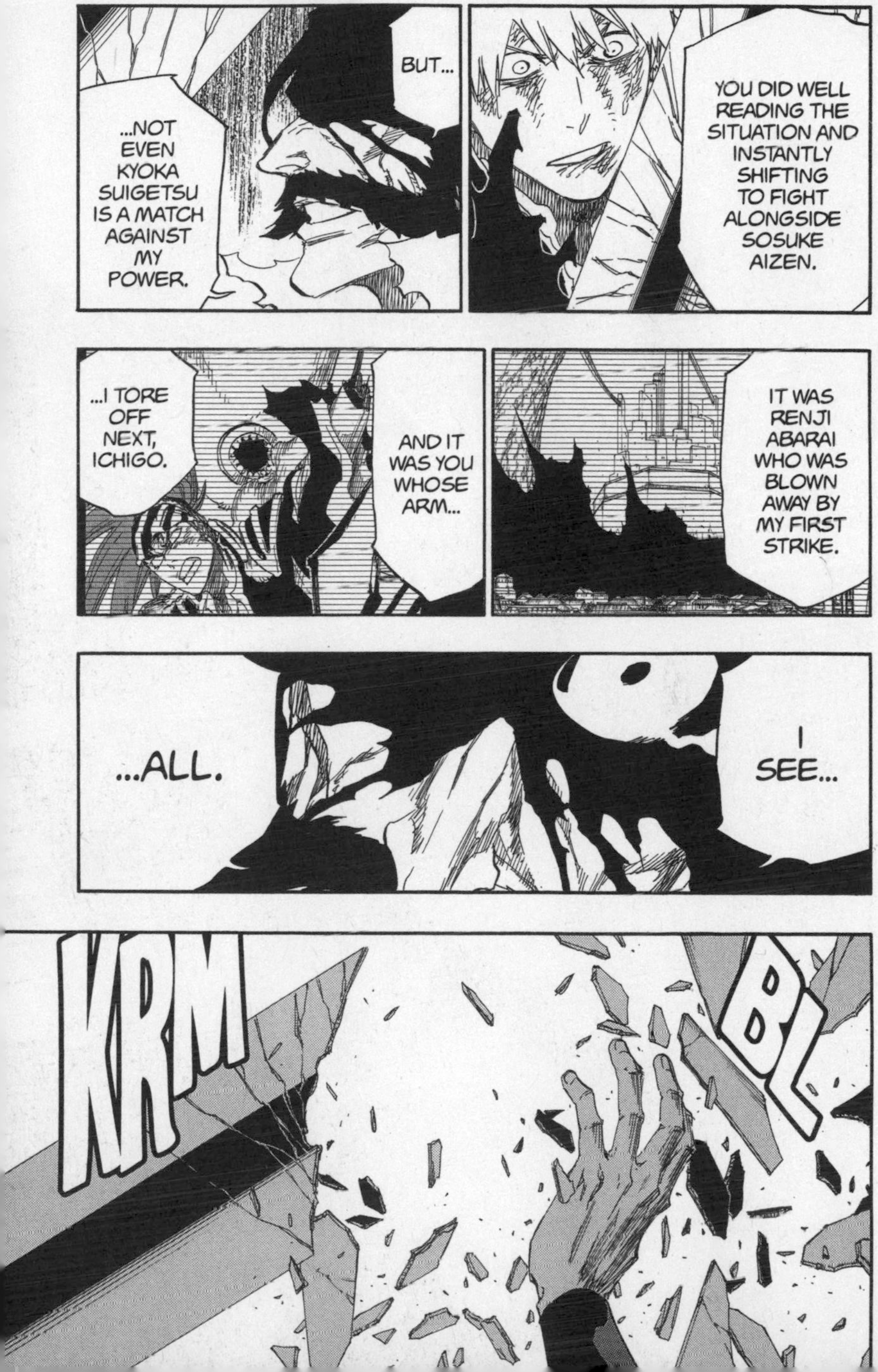
YOU DID WELL READING THE SITUATION AND INSTANTLY SHIFTING TO FIGHT ALONGSIDE SOSUKE AIZEN.
BUT...
...NOT EVEN KYOKA SUIGETSU IS A MATCH AGAINST MY POWER.
IT WAS RENJI ABARAI WHO WAS BLOWN AWAY BY MY FIRST STRIKE.
AND IT WAS YOU WHOSE ARM...
...I TORE OFF NEXT, ICHIGO.
I SEE...
...ALL.
BL
KRM

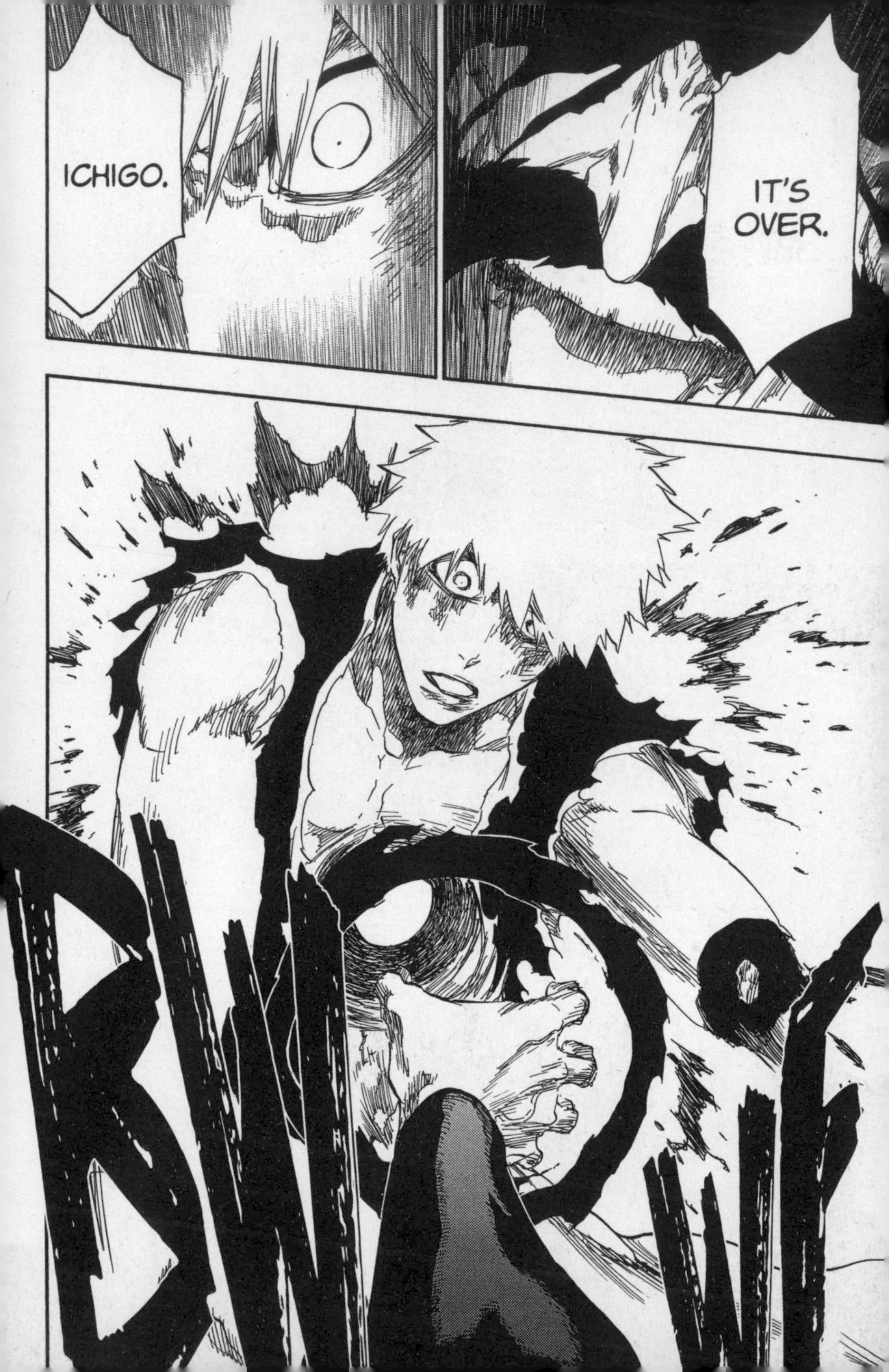
IT'S OVER.
ICHIGO.

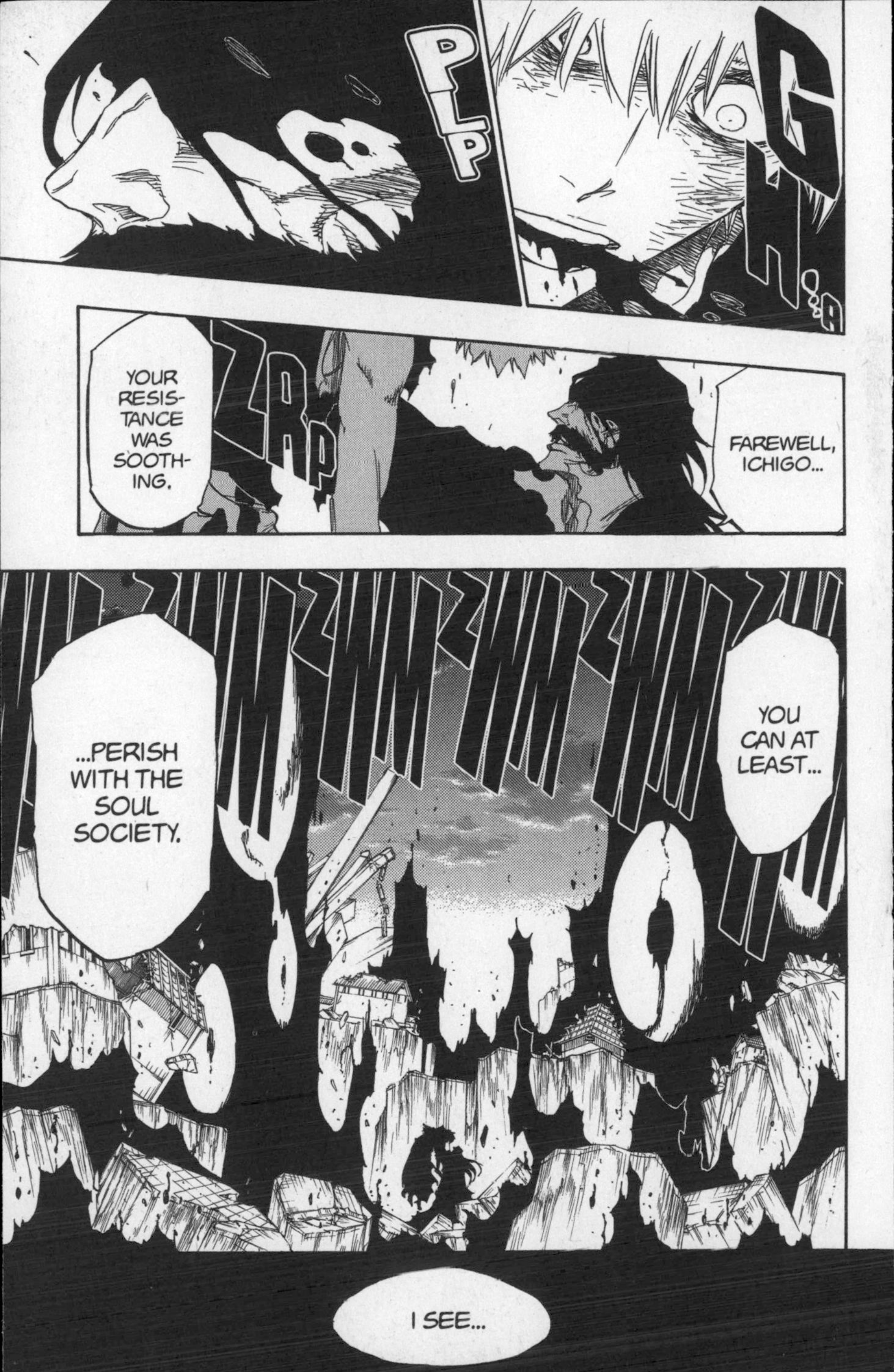
PLP
FAREWELL, ICHIGO...
ZRP
YOUR RESISTANCE WAS SOOTHING.
YOU CAN AT LEAST...
...PERISH WITH THE SOUL SOCIETY.
I SEE...

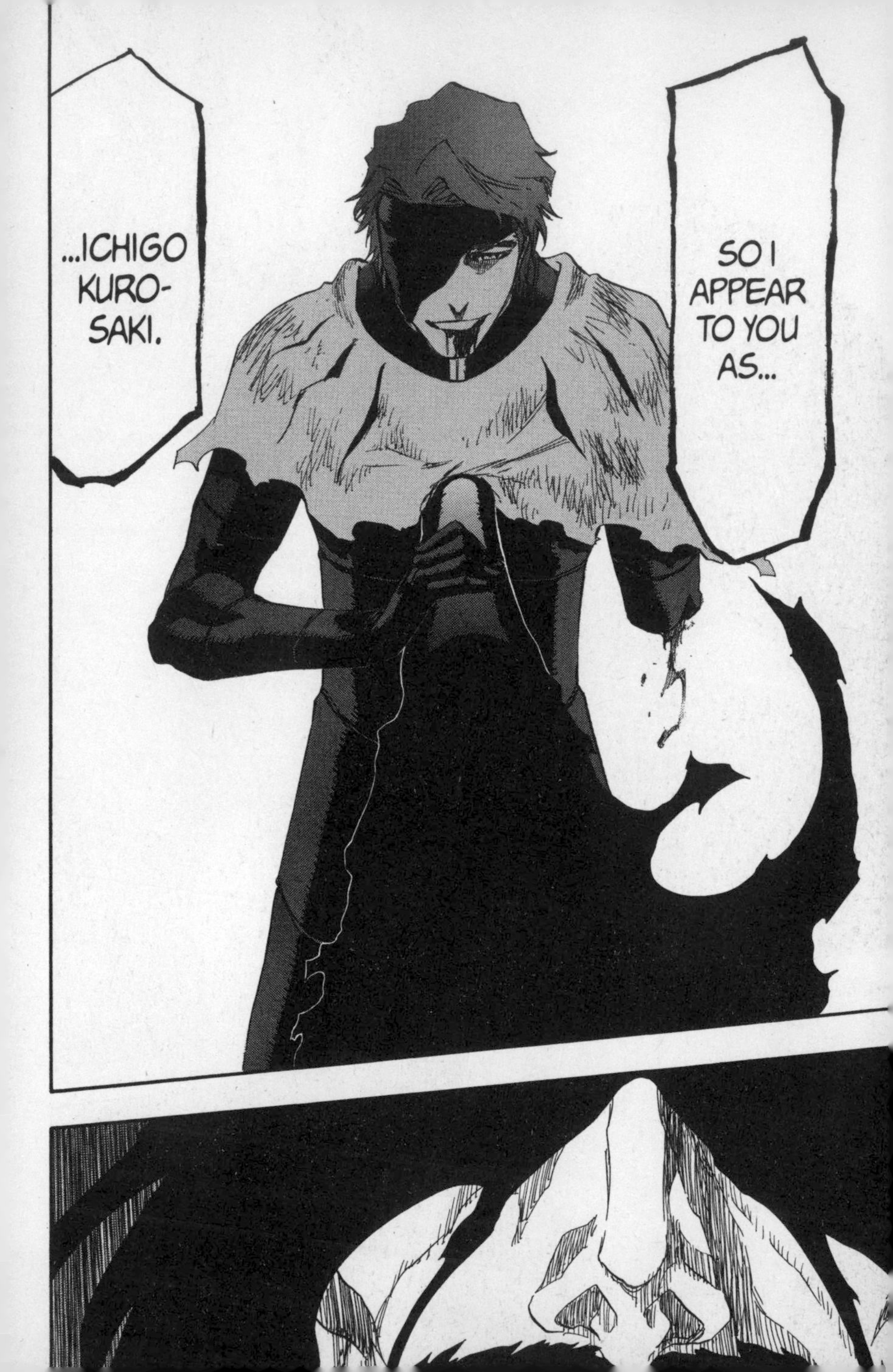
SO I APPEAR TO YOU AS...
...ICHIGO KURO-SAKI.

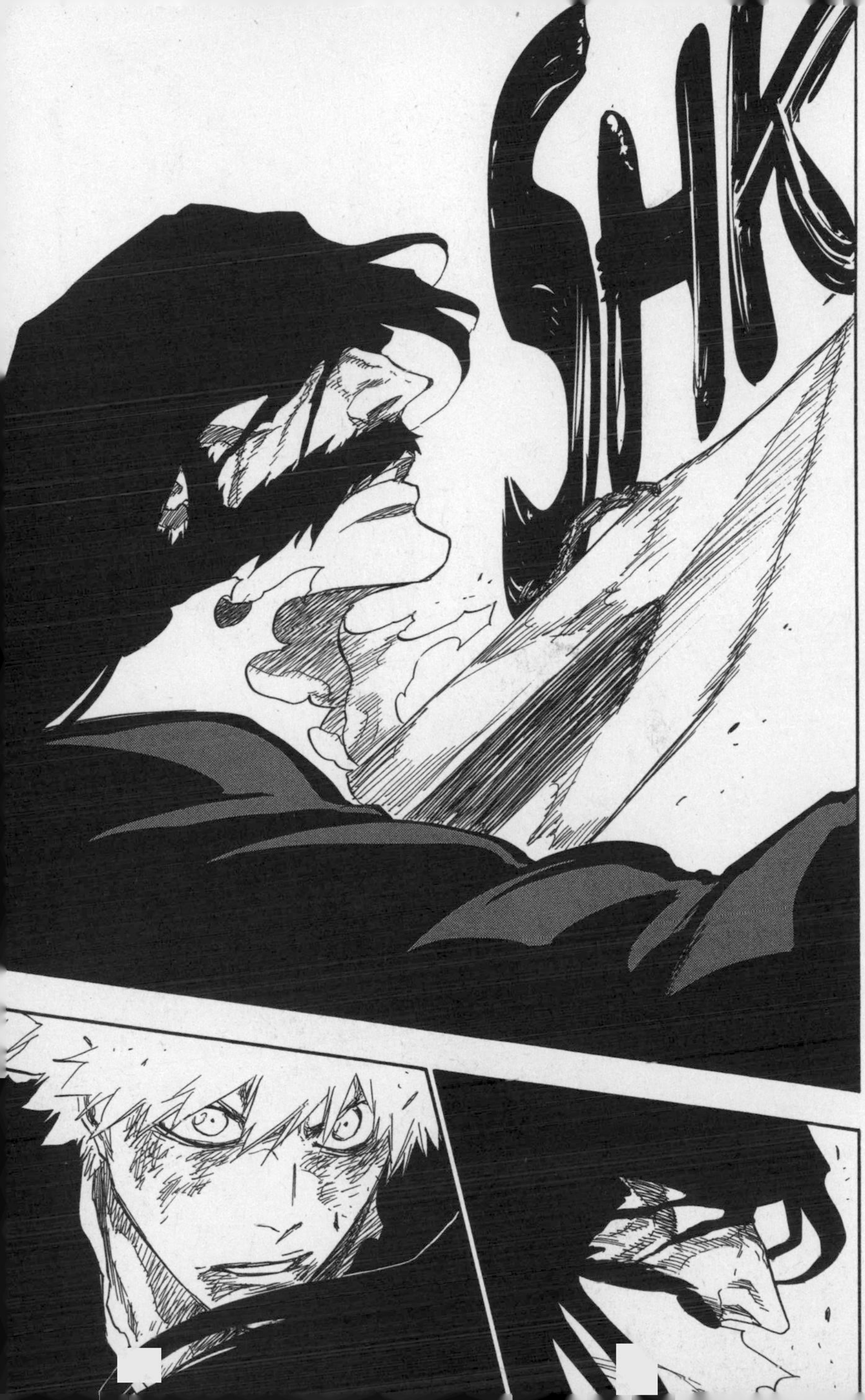
SHK

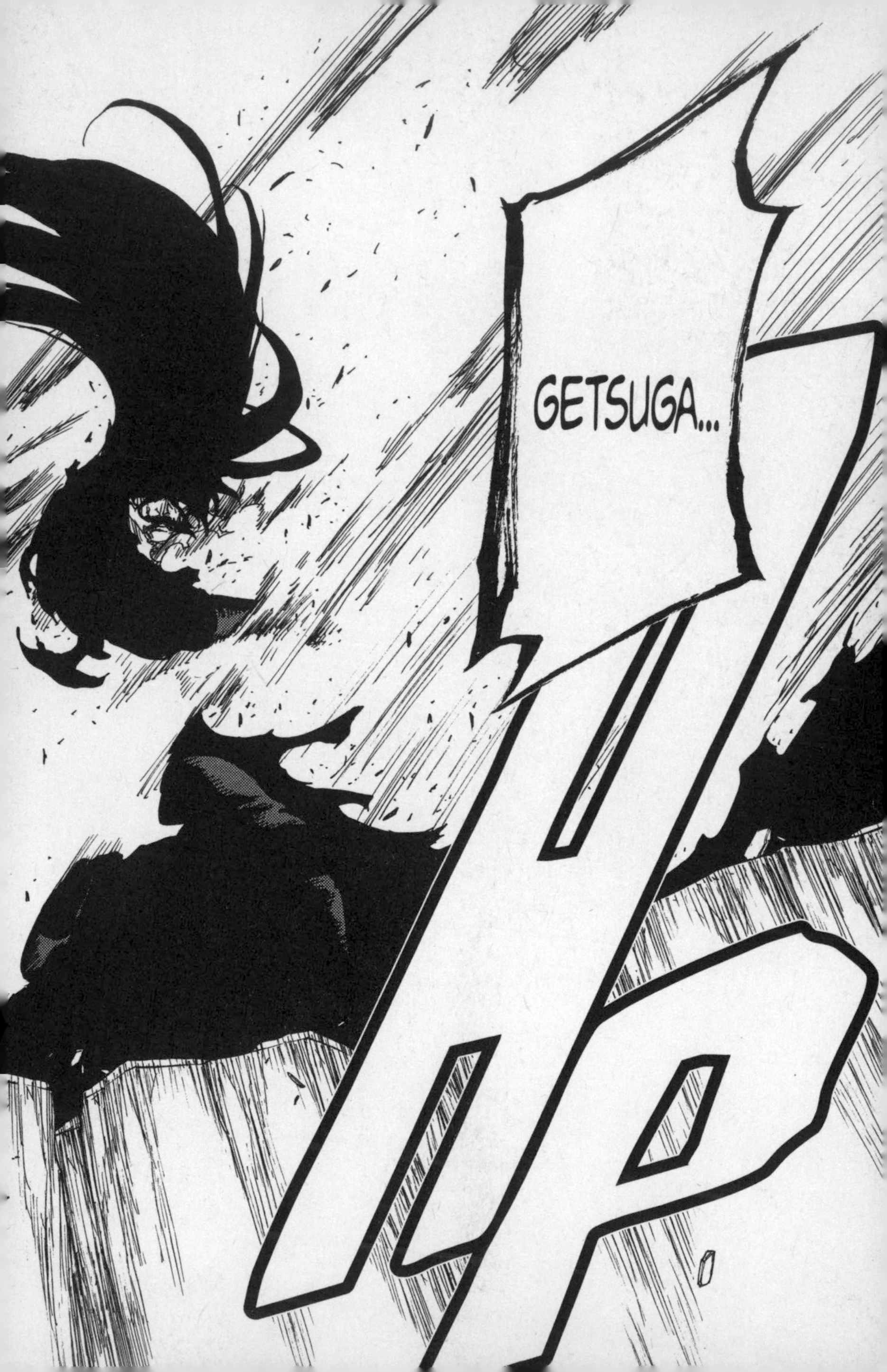
GETSUGA...

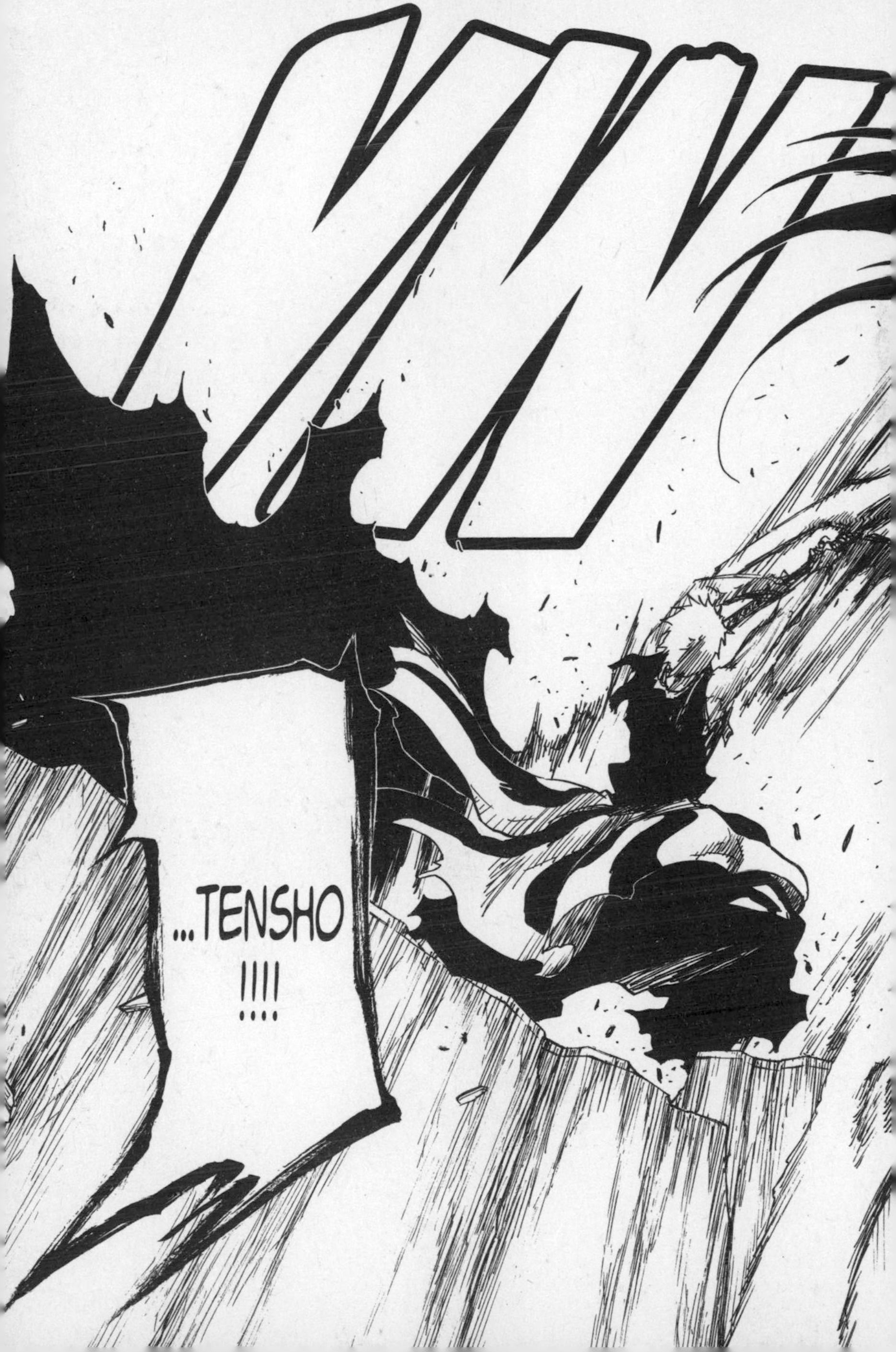
...TENSHO
!!!!

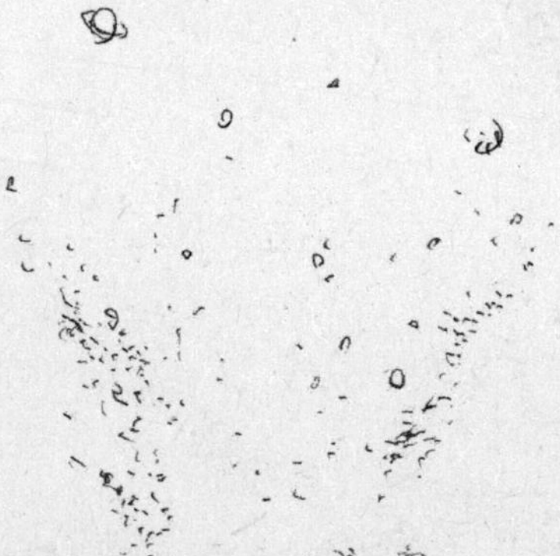

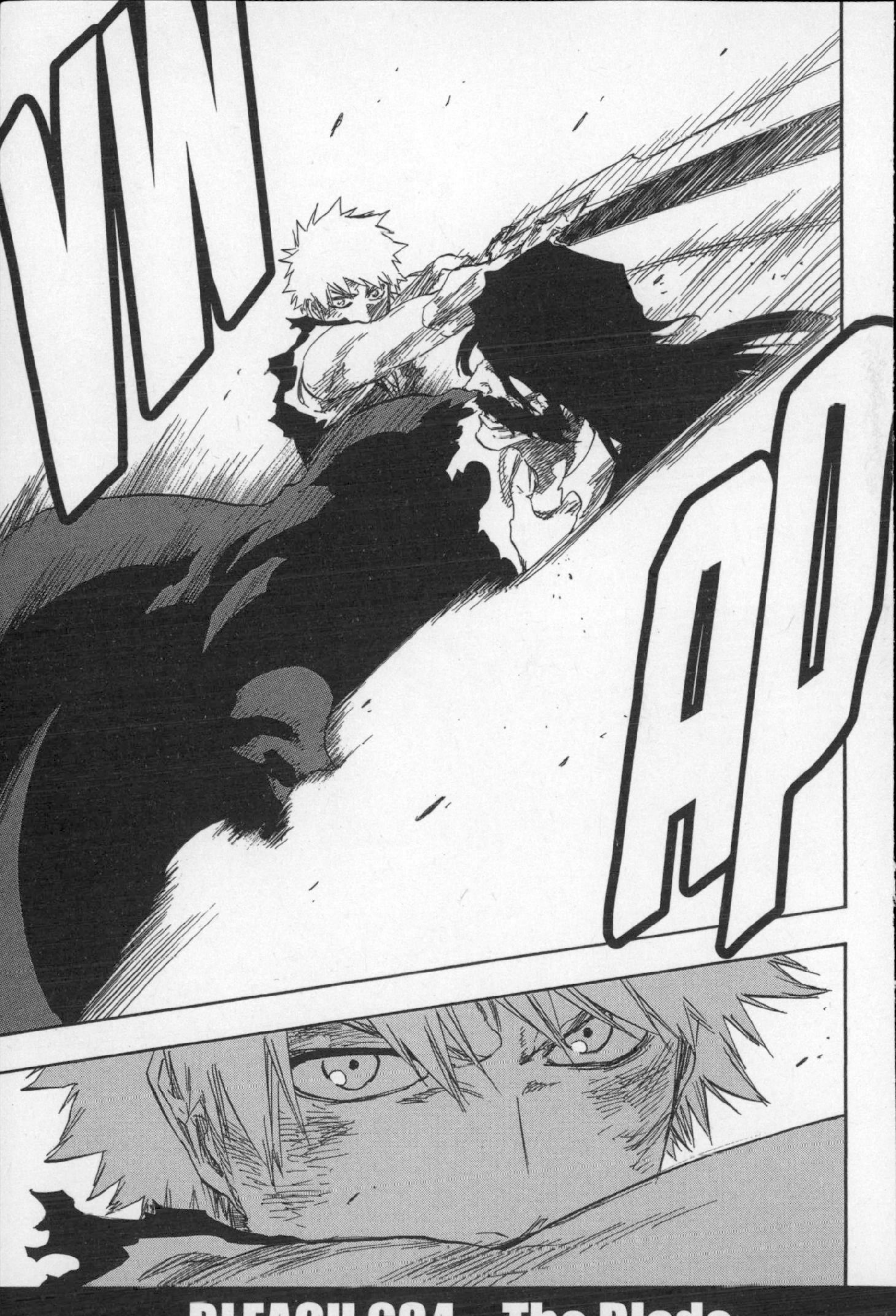

BLEACH 684. The Blade

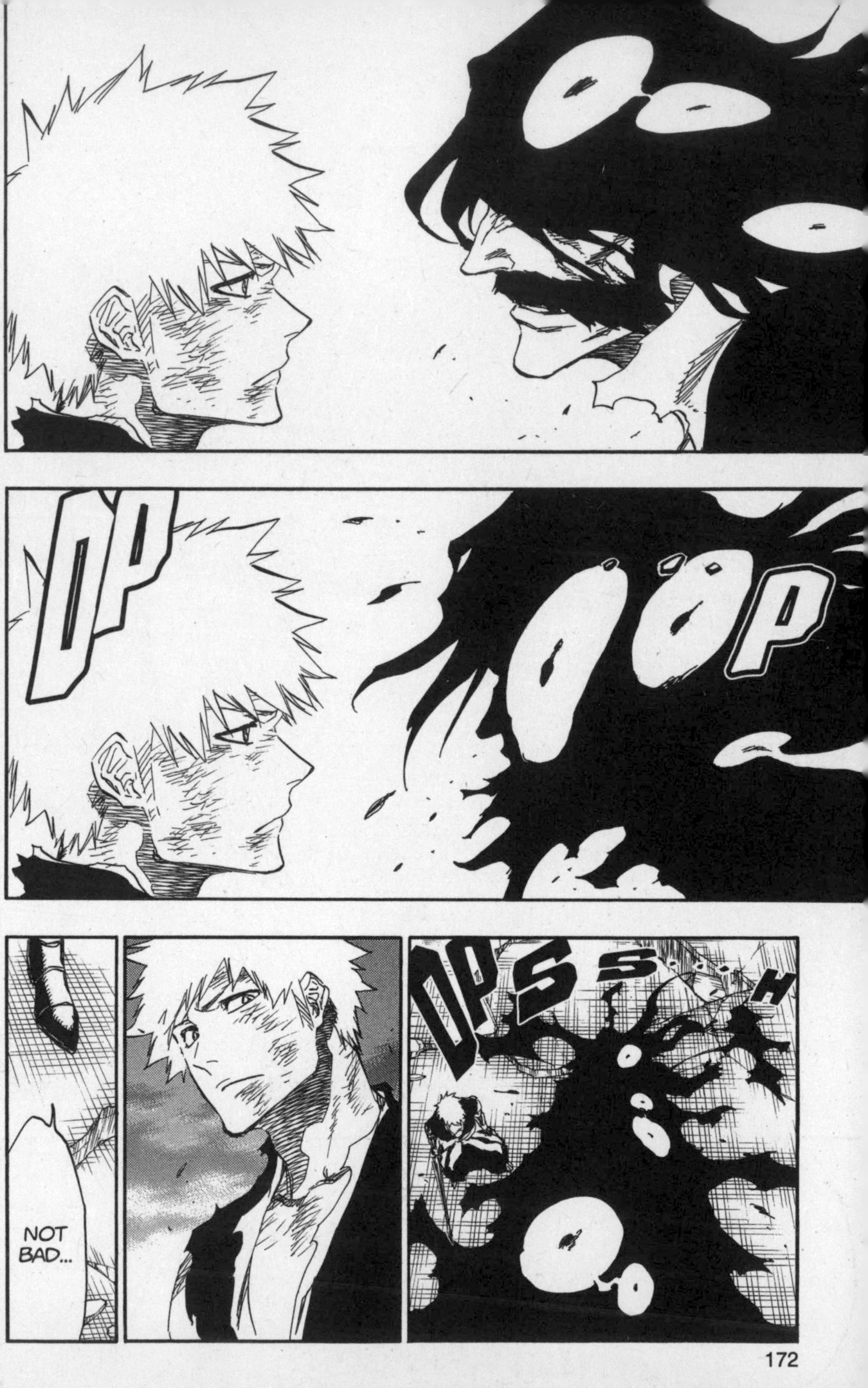
DOOOP
DOPSS...H
NOT BAD...

READ THIS WAY

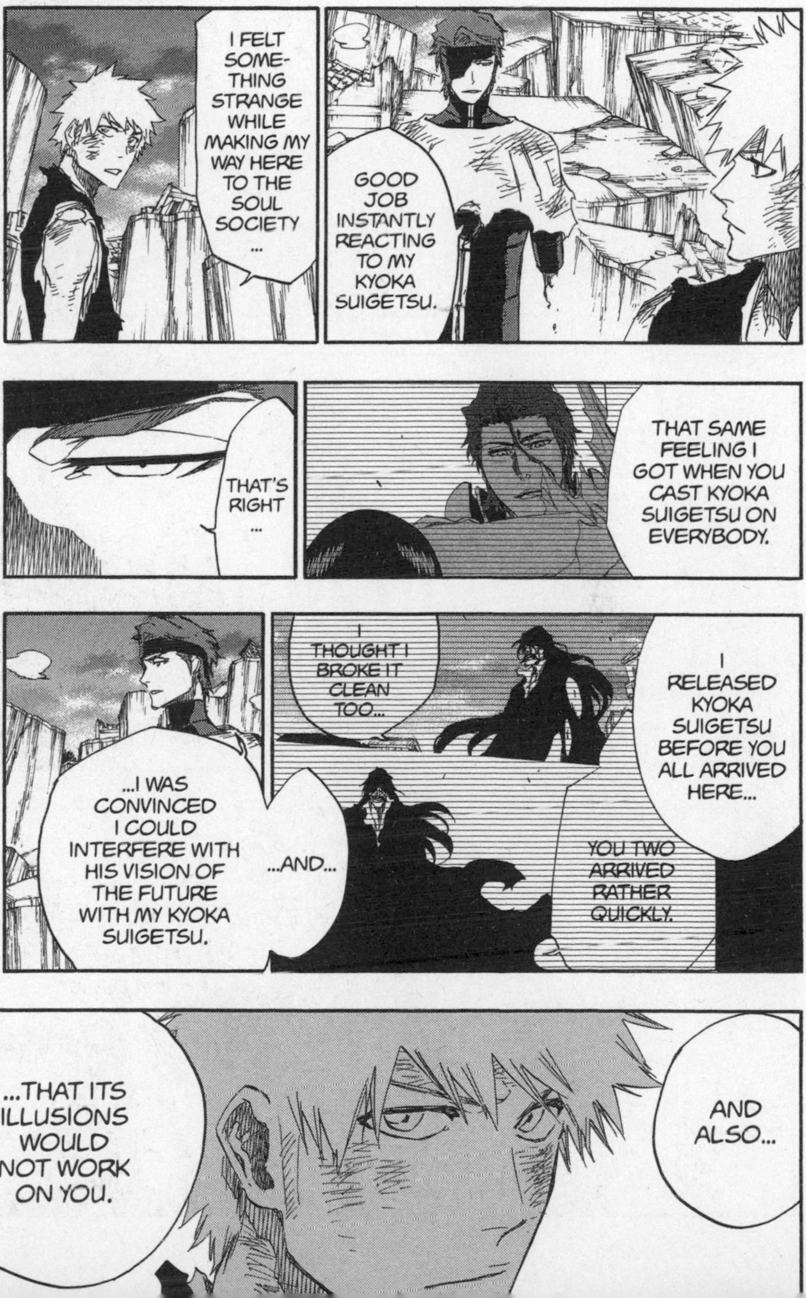
GOOD JOB INSTANTLY REACTING TO MY KYOKA SUIGETSU.
I FELT SOME-THING STRANGE WHILE MAKING MY WAY HERE TO THE SOUL SOCIETY ...
THAT SAME FEELING I GOT WHEN YOU CAST KYOKA SUIGETSU ON EVERYBODY.
THAT'S RIGHT ...
I RELEASED KYOKA SUIGETSU BEFORE YOU ALL ARRIVED HERE...
I THOUGHT I BROKE IT CLEAN TOO...
YOU TWO ARRIVED RATHER QUICKLY.
...AND...
...I WAS CONVINCED I COULD INTERFERE WITH HIS VISION OF THE FUTURE WITH MY KYOKA SUIGETSU.
AND ALSO...
...THAT ITS ILLUSIONS WOULD NOT WORK ON YOU.

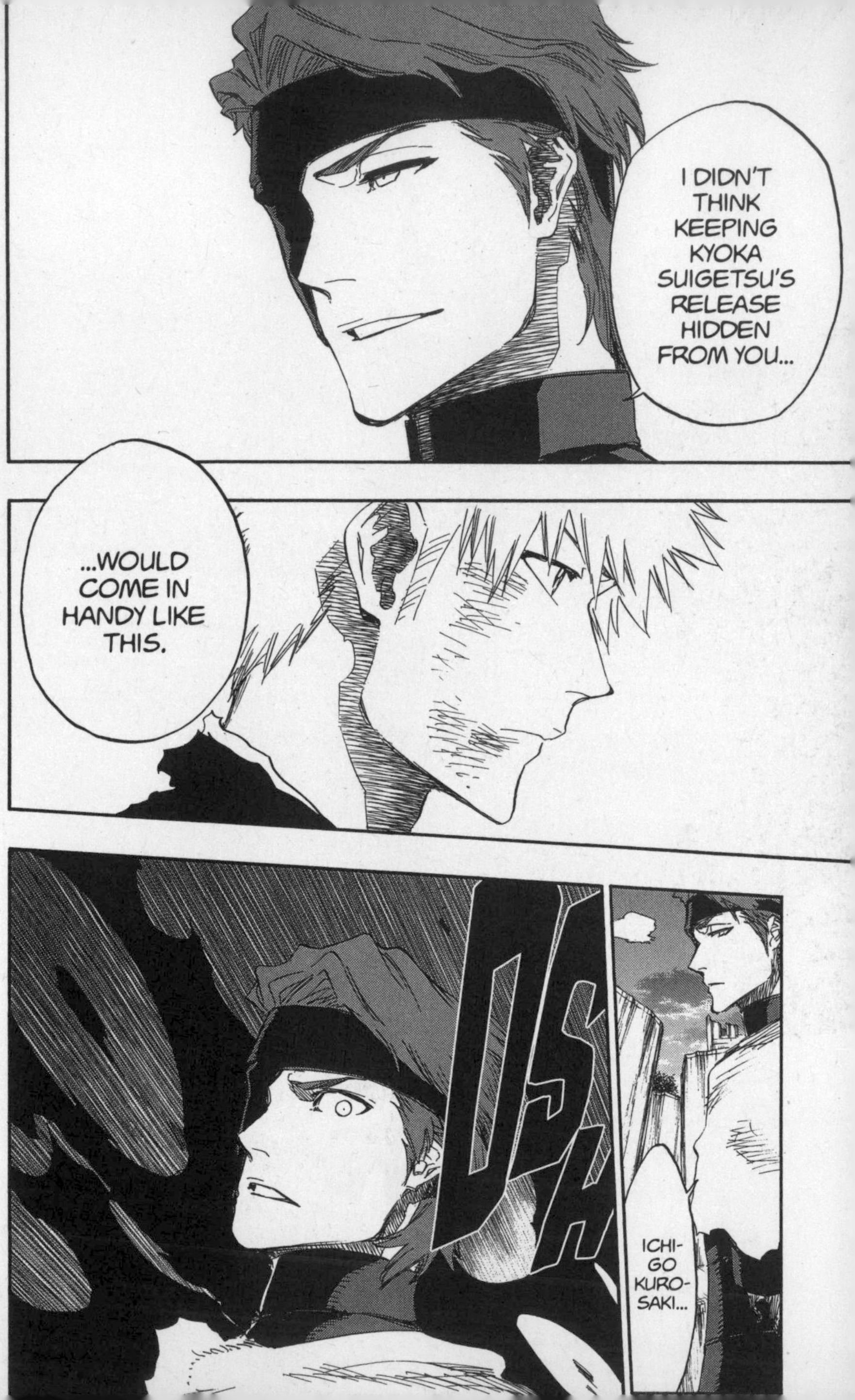
I DIDN'T THINK KEEPING KYOKA SUIGETSU'S RELEASE HIDDEN FROM YOU...
...WOULD COME IN HANDY LIKE THIS.
ICHI-GO KURO-SAKI...

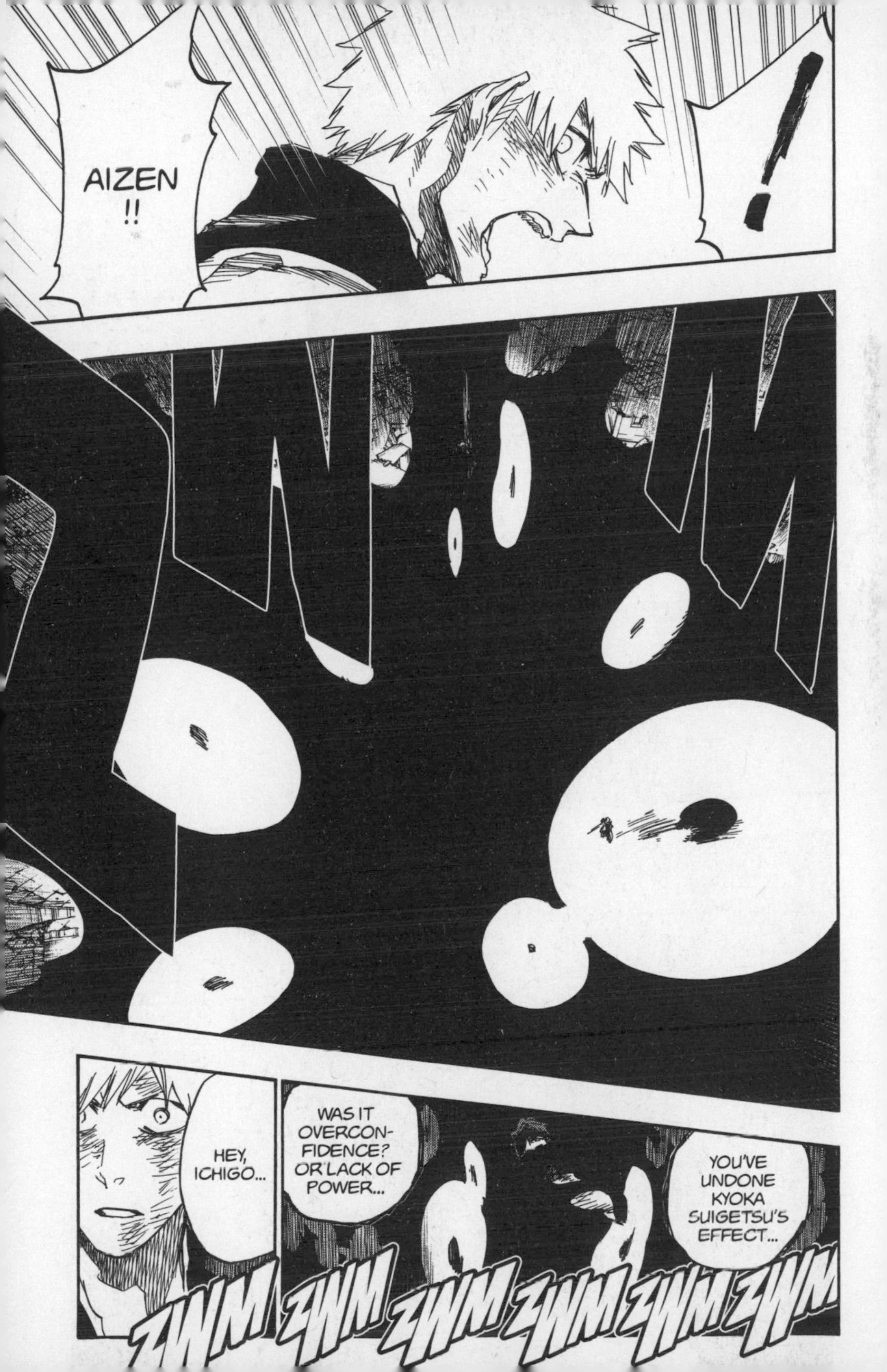
AIZEN !!
YOU'VE UNDONE KYOKA SUIGETSU'S EFFECT...
WAS IT OVERCONFIDENCE? OR LACK OF POWER...
HEY, ICHIGO...
ZWM ZWM ZWM ZWM ZWM ZWM

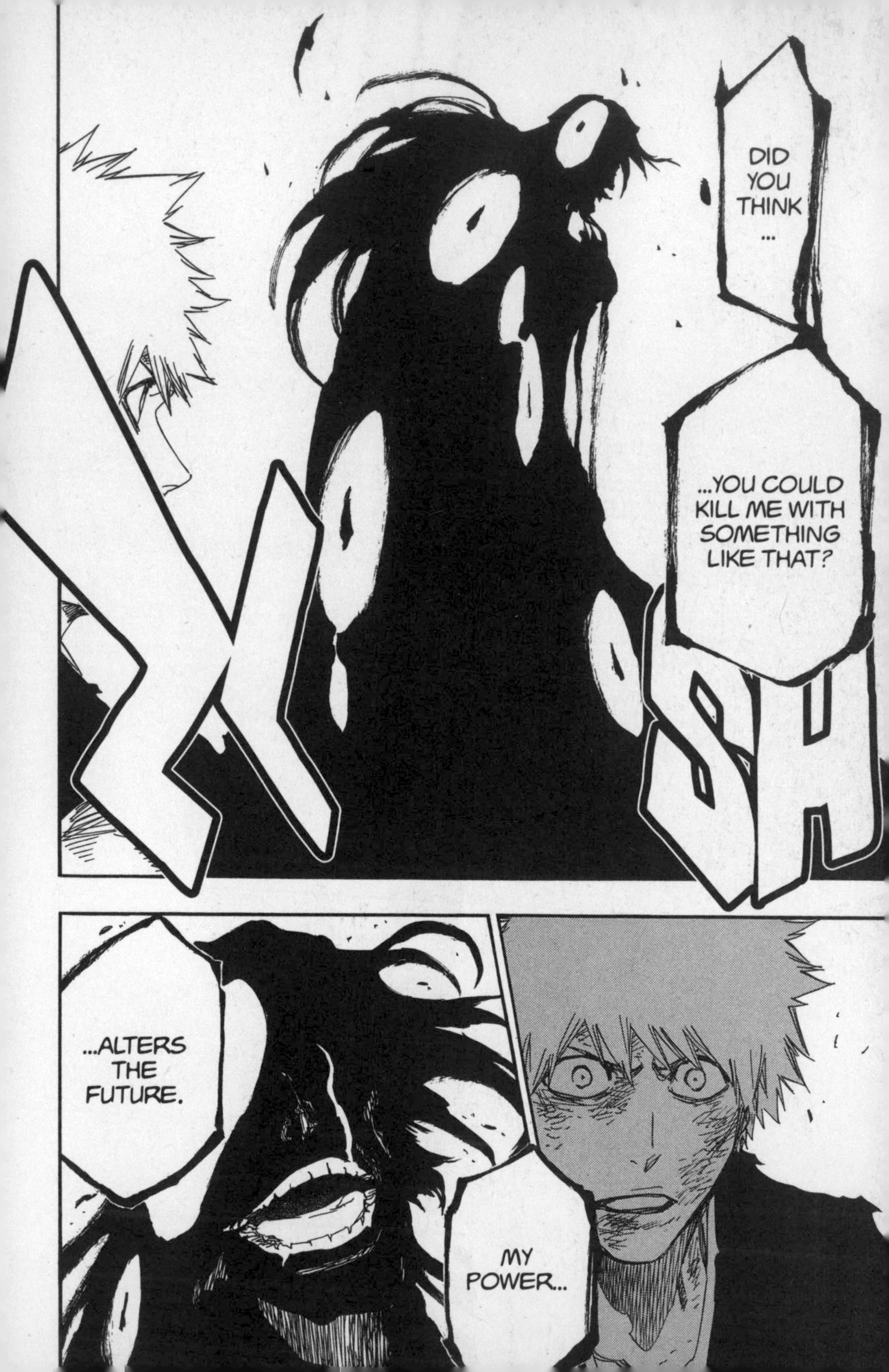
DID YOU THINK ...
...YOU COULD KILL ME WITH SOMETHING LIKE THAT?
MY POWER...
...ALTERS THE FUTURE.

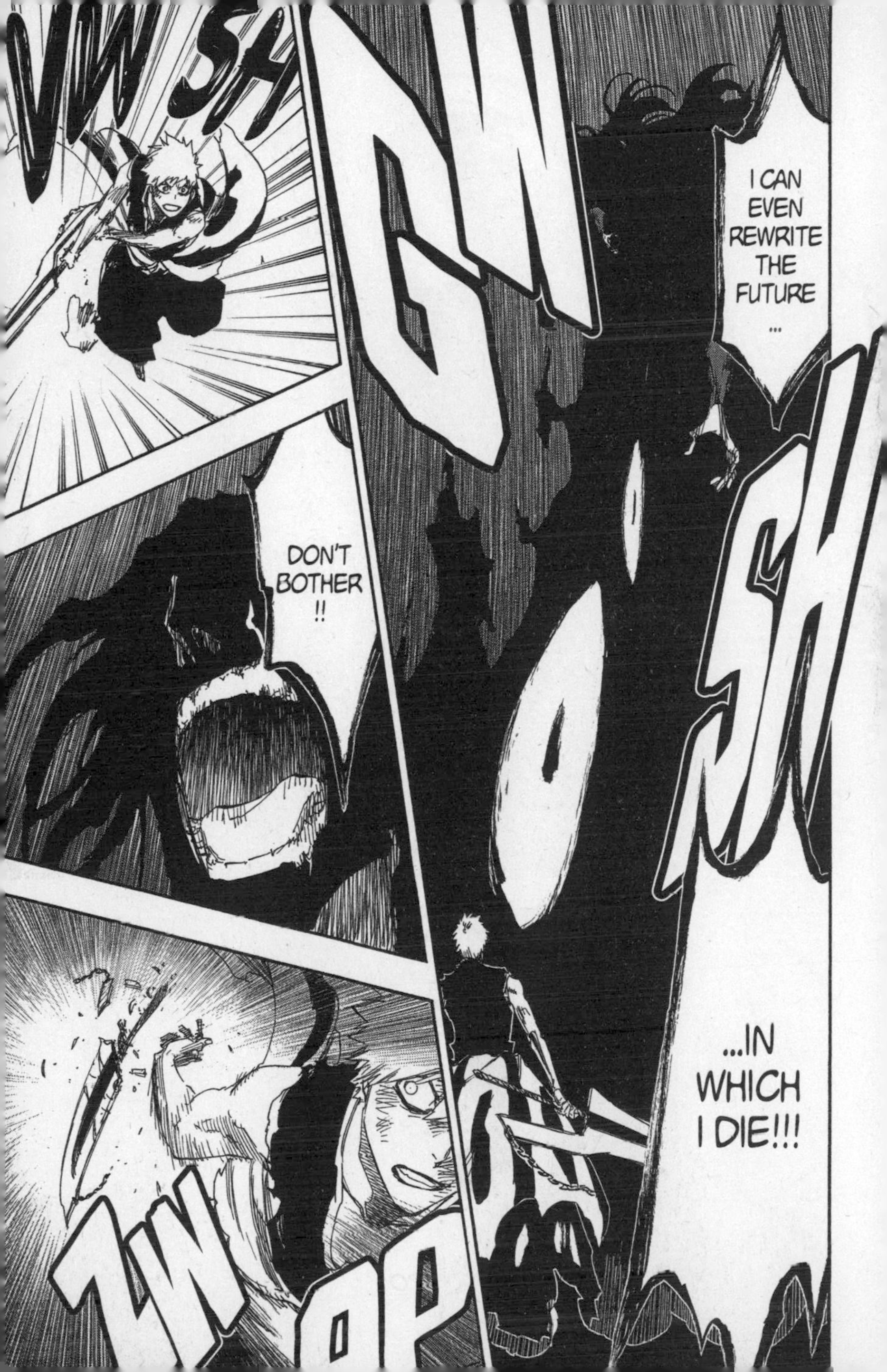
I CAN EVEN REWRITE THE FUTURE ...
...IN WHICH I DIE!!!
VWSH
DON'T BOTHER !!

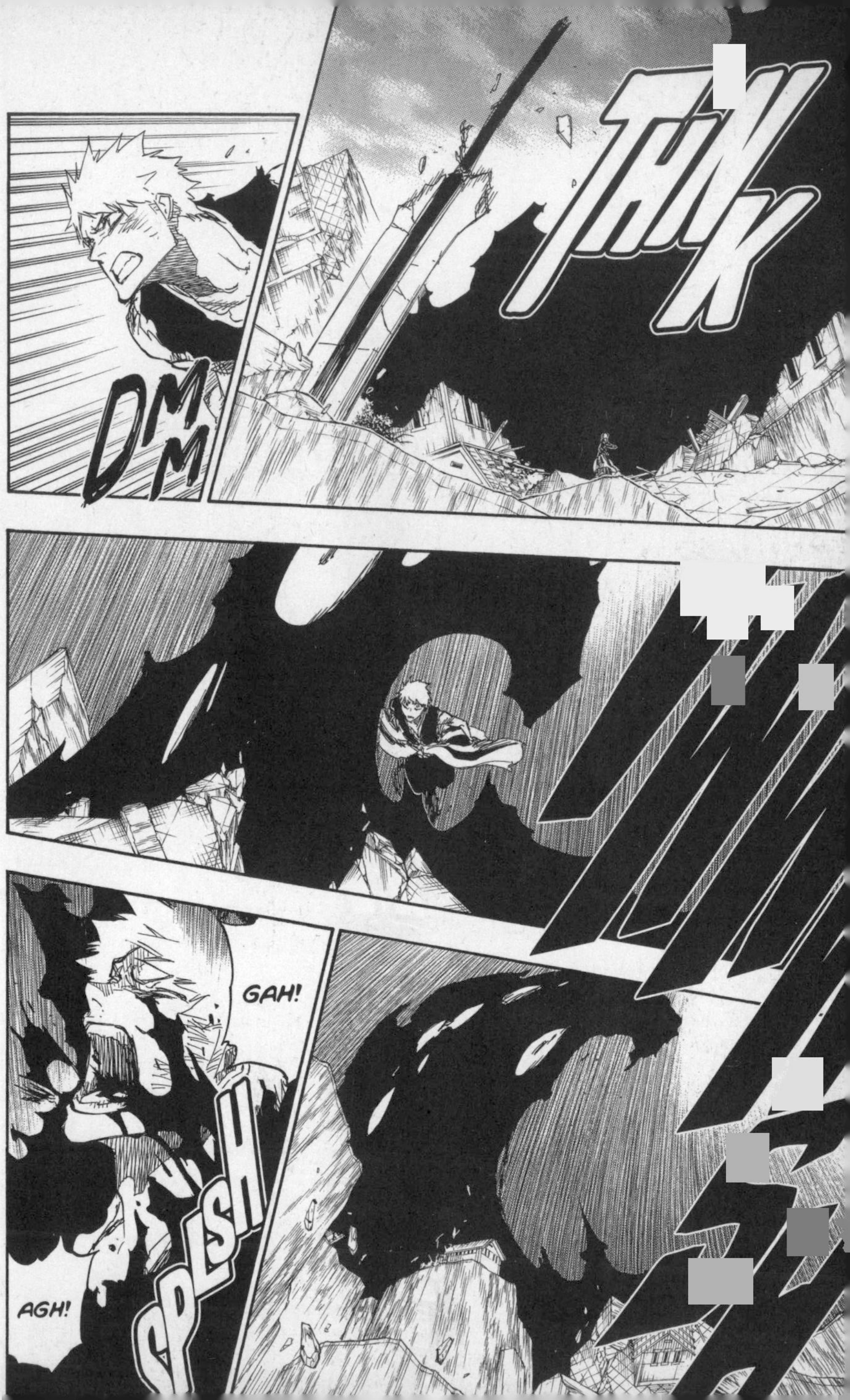
THNK
DMM
GAH!
SPLSH
AGH!

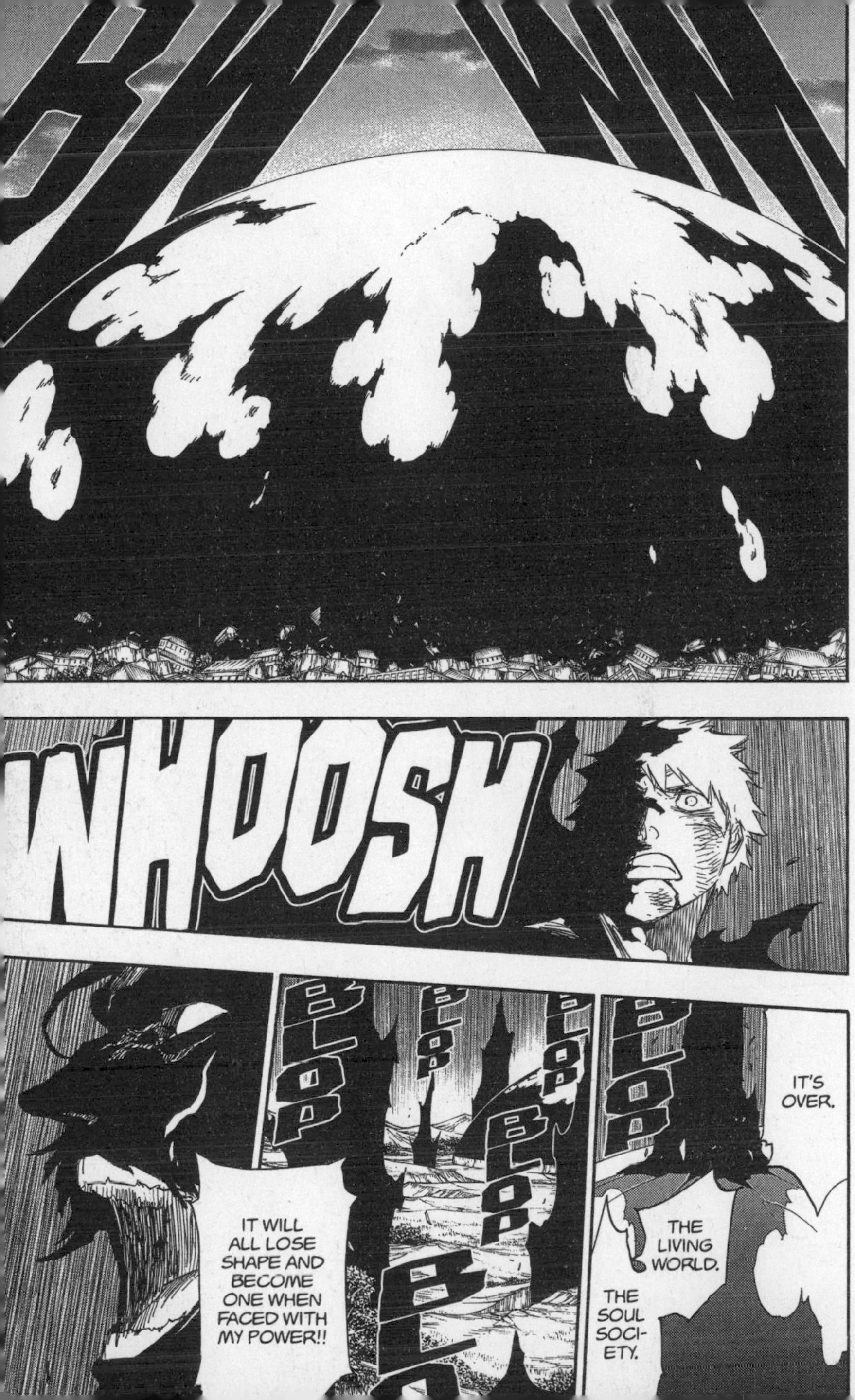
WHOOSH
IT'S OVER.
THE LIVING WORLD.
THE SOUL SOCI-ETY.
IT WILL ALL LOSE SHAPE AND BECOME ONE WHEN FACED WITH MY POWER!!

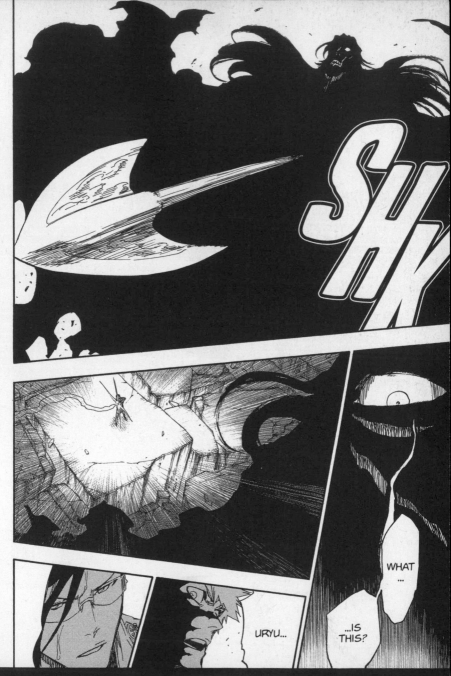

WHAT
...

...IS
THIS?

URYU...

SOKEN ONCE TOLD ME...

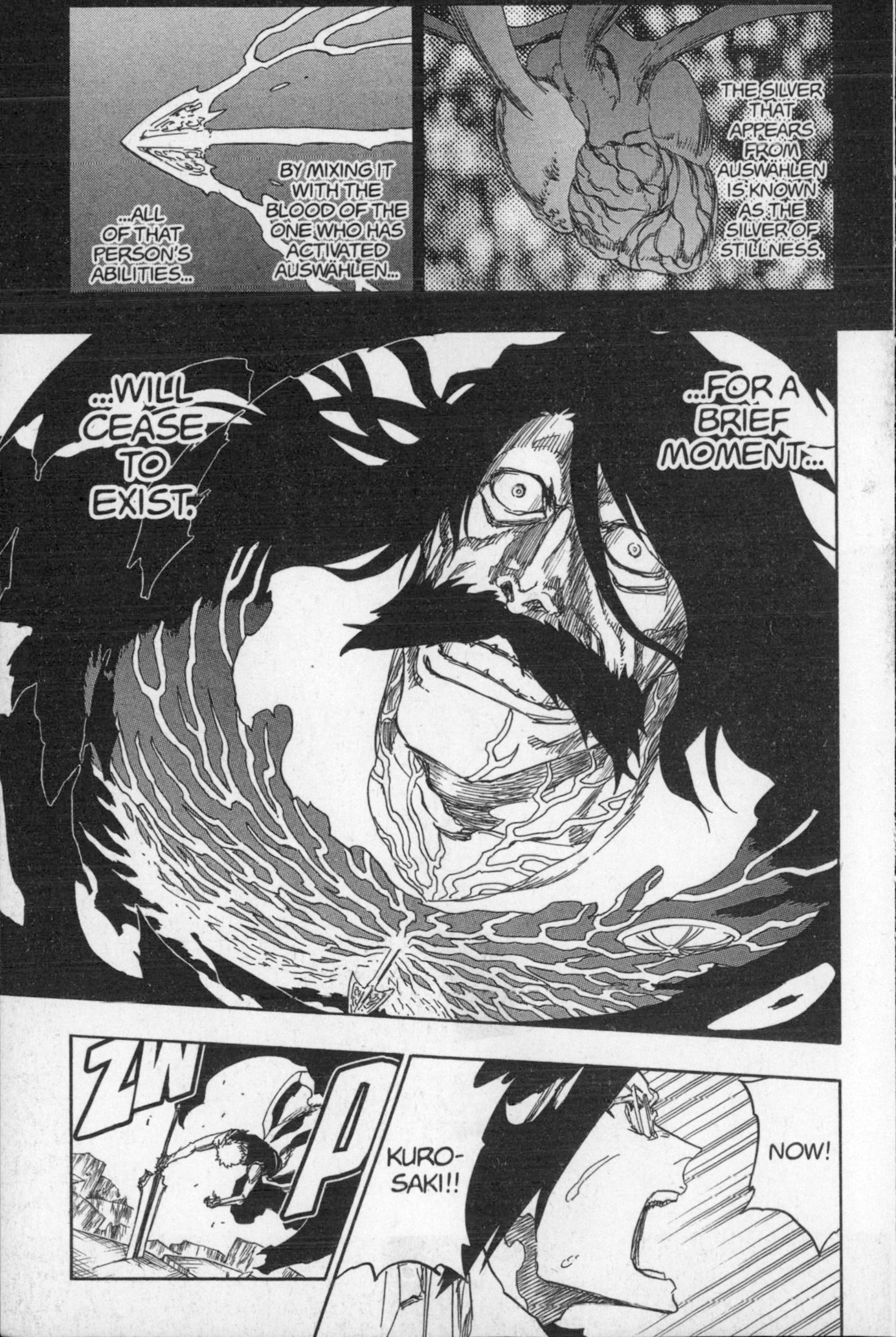
THE SILVER THAT APPEARS FROM AUSWÄHLEN IS KNOWN AS THE SILVER OF STILLNESS.
BY MIXING IT WITH THE BLOOD OF THE ONE WHO HAS ACTIVATED AUSWÄHLEN...
...ALL OF THAT PERSON'S ABILITIES...
...FOR A BRIEF MOMENT...
...WILL CEASE TO EXIST.
NOW!
KURO-SAKI!!
ZWP

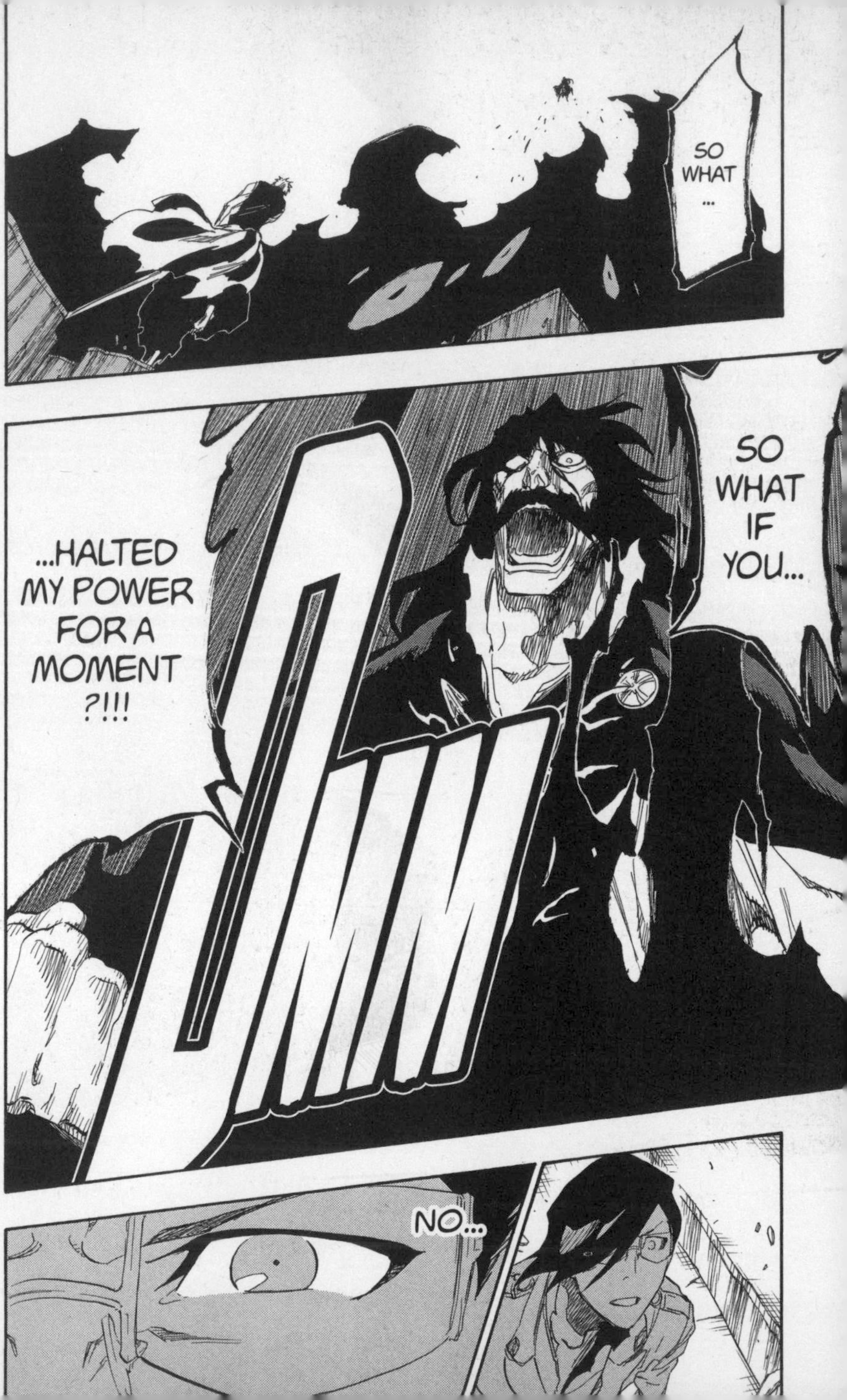
SO WHAT ...
SO WHAT IF YOU...
...HALTED MY POWER FOR A MOMENT ?!!!
NO...

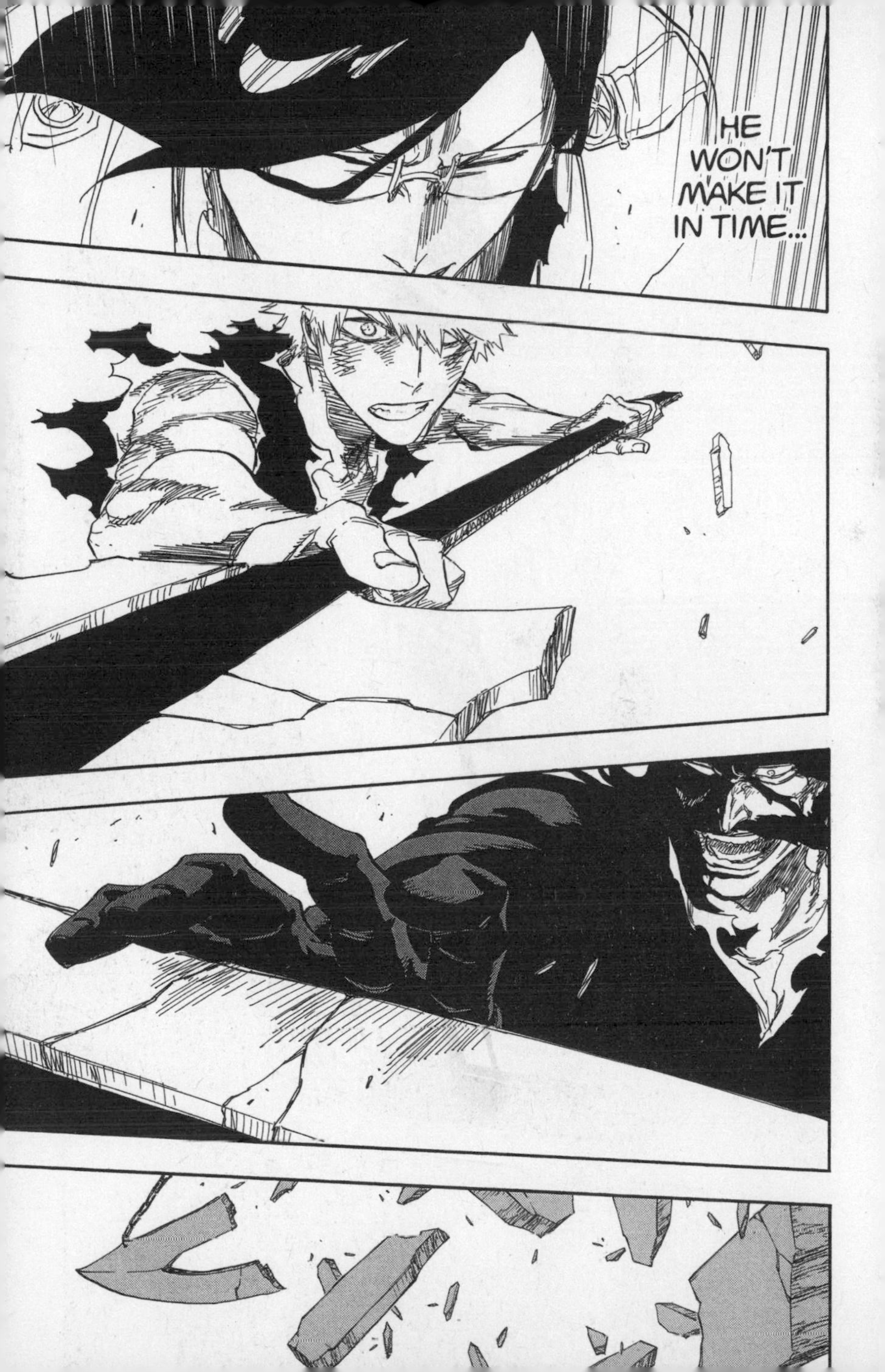
HE WON'T MAKE IT IN TIME...

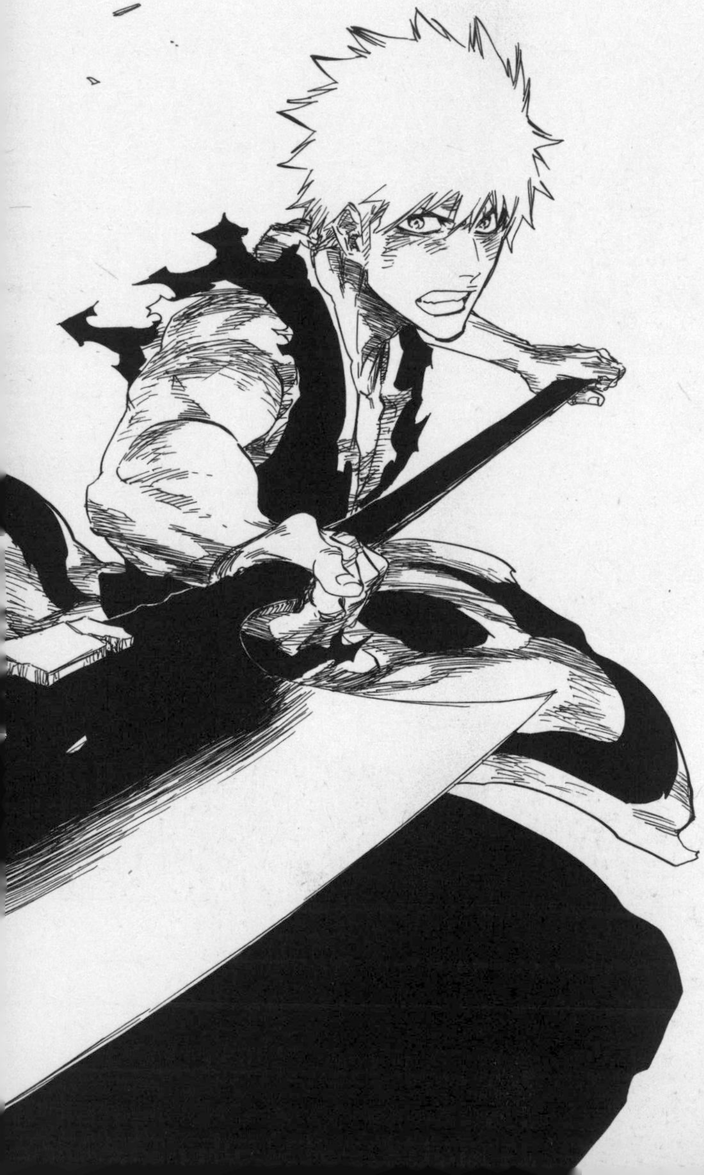

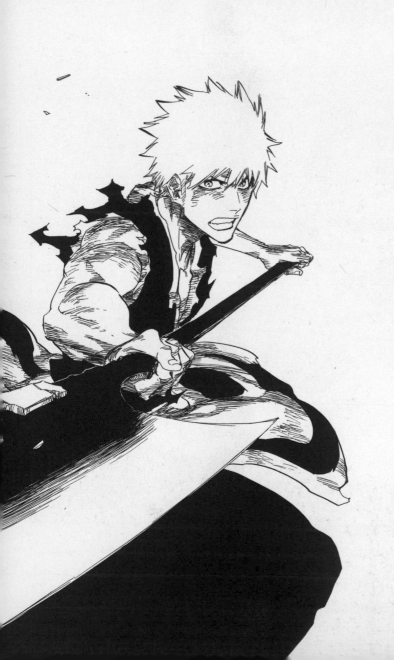

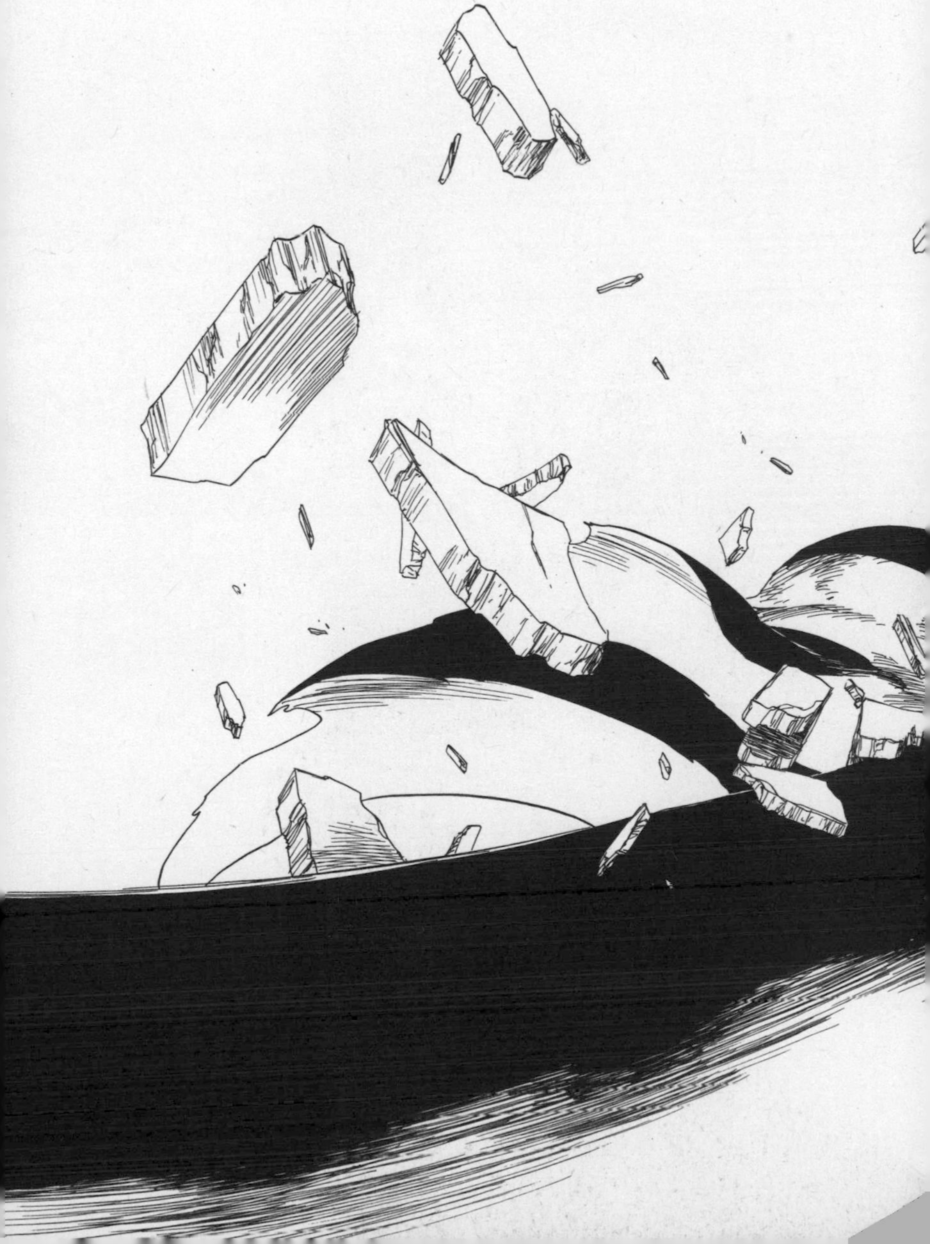

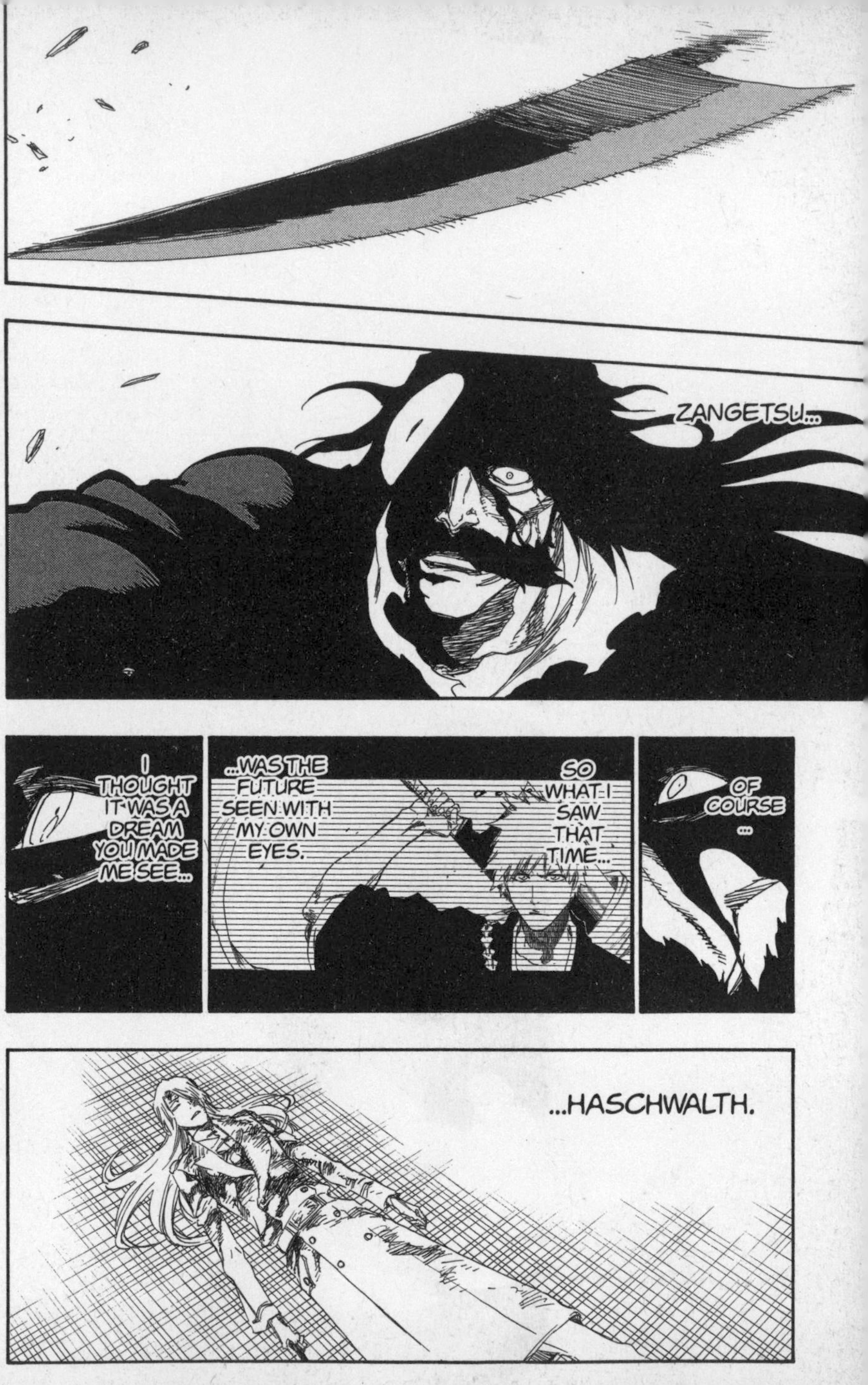
ZANGETSU...
OF COURSE...
SO WHAT I SAW THAT TIME...
...WAS THE FUTURE SEEN WITH MY OWN EYES.
I THOUGHT IT WAS A DREAM YOU MADE ME SEE...
...HASCHWALTH.

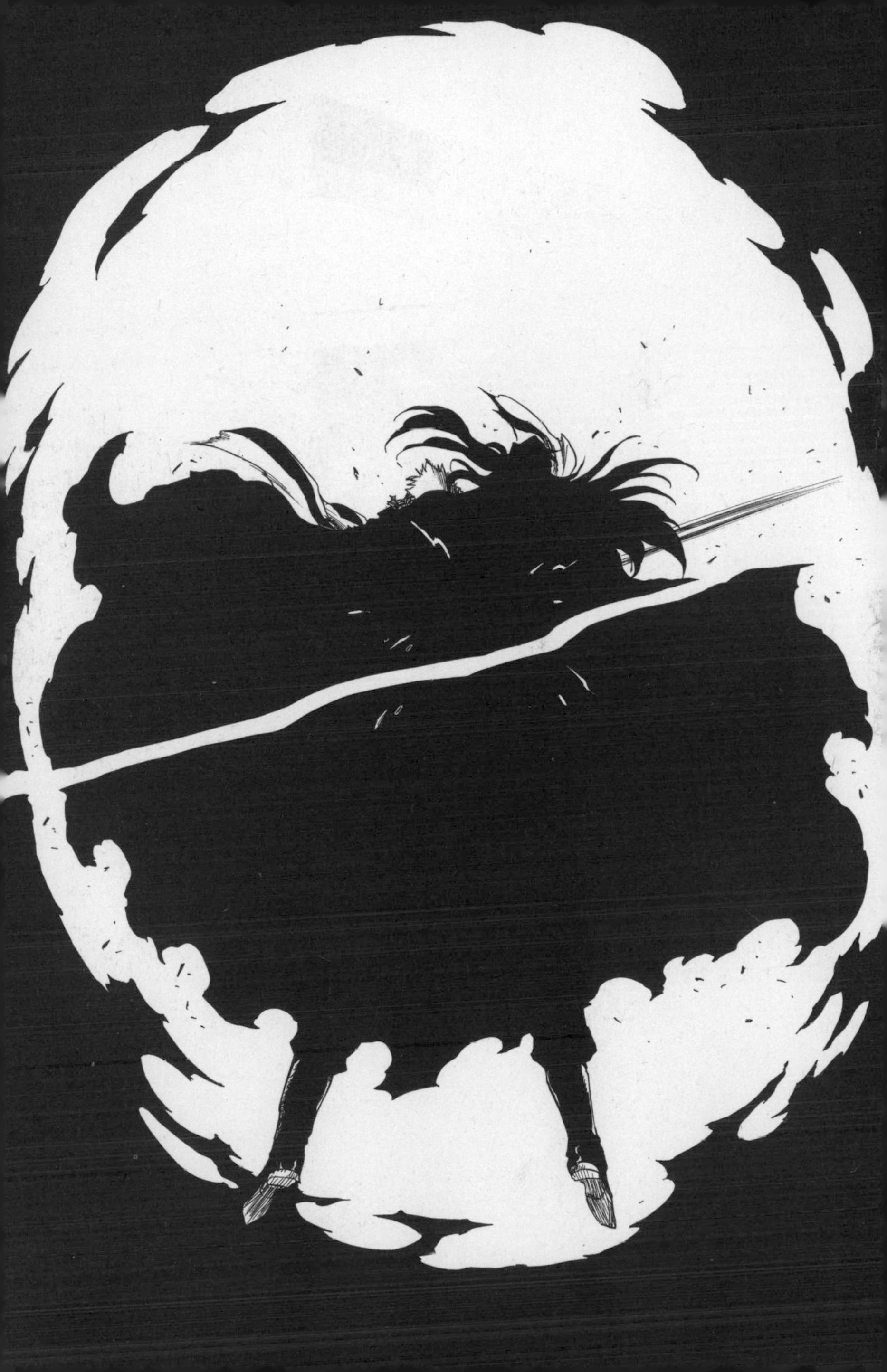

despair

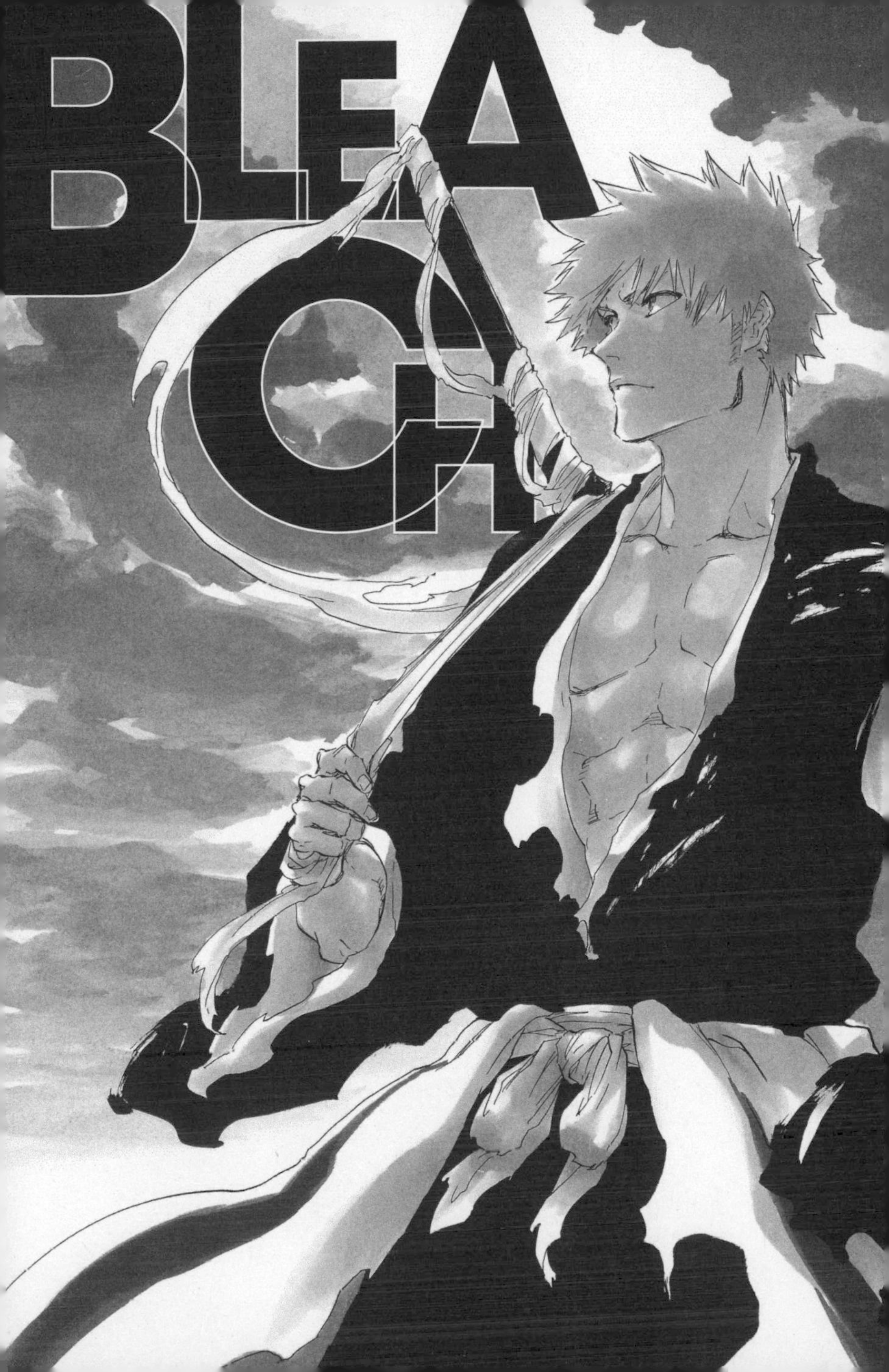
BLEACH

BLEACH
ブリーチ

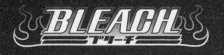

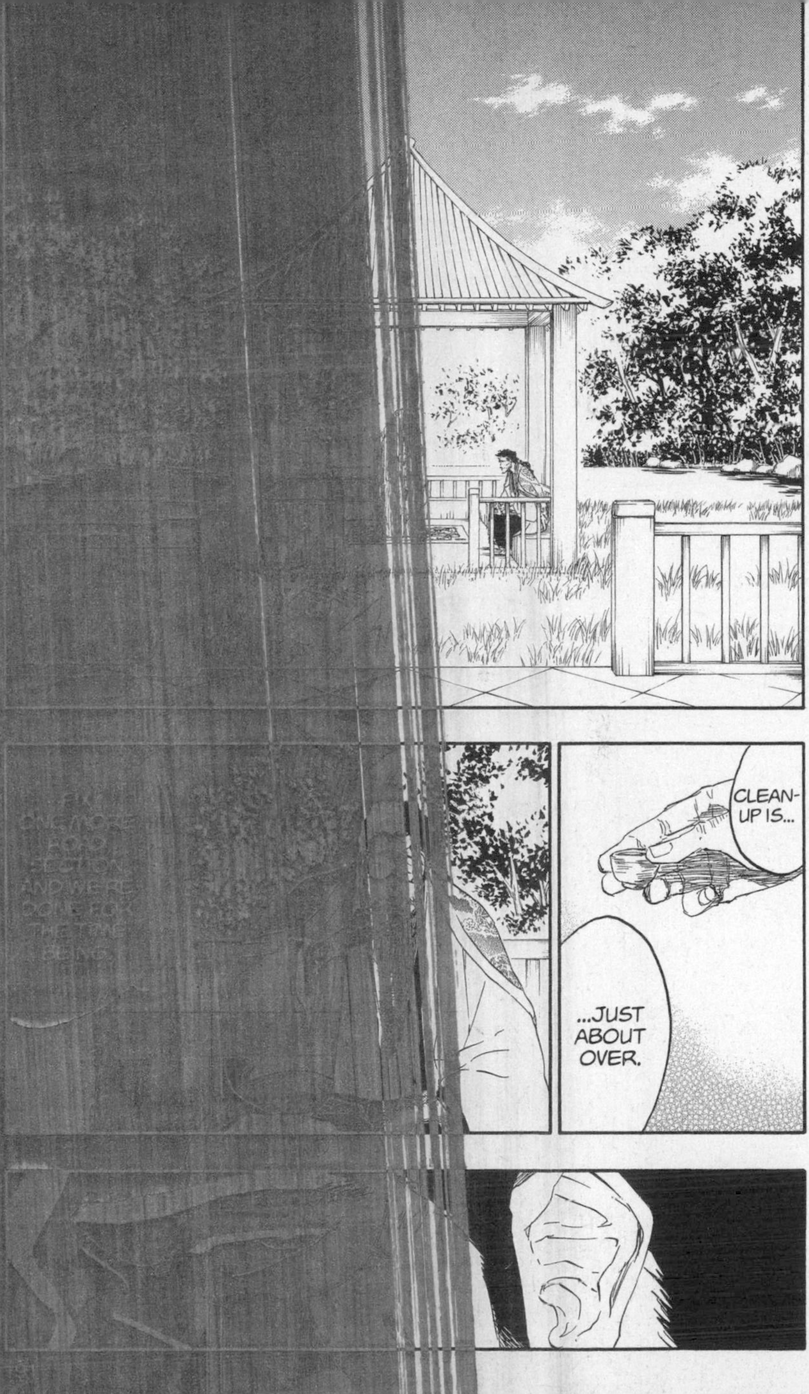
CLEAN-UP IS...
...JUST ABOUT OVER.

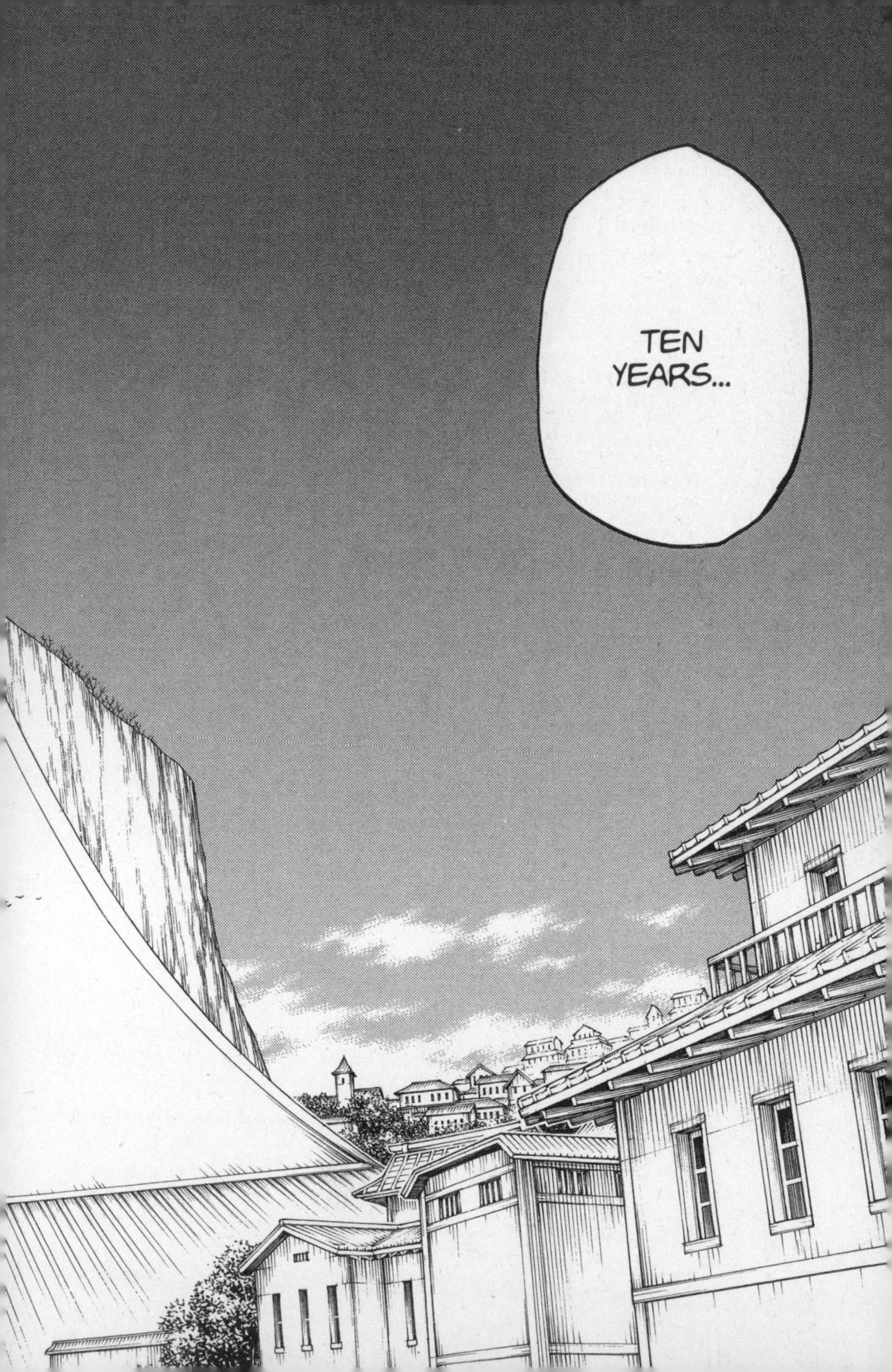
TEN YEARS...

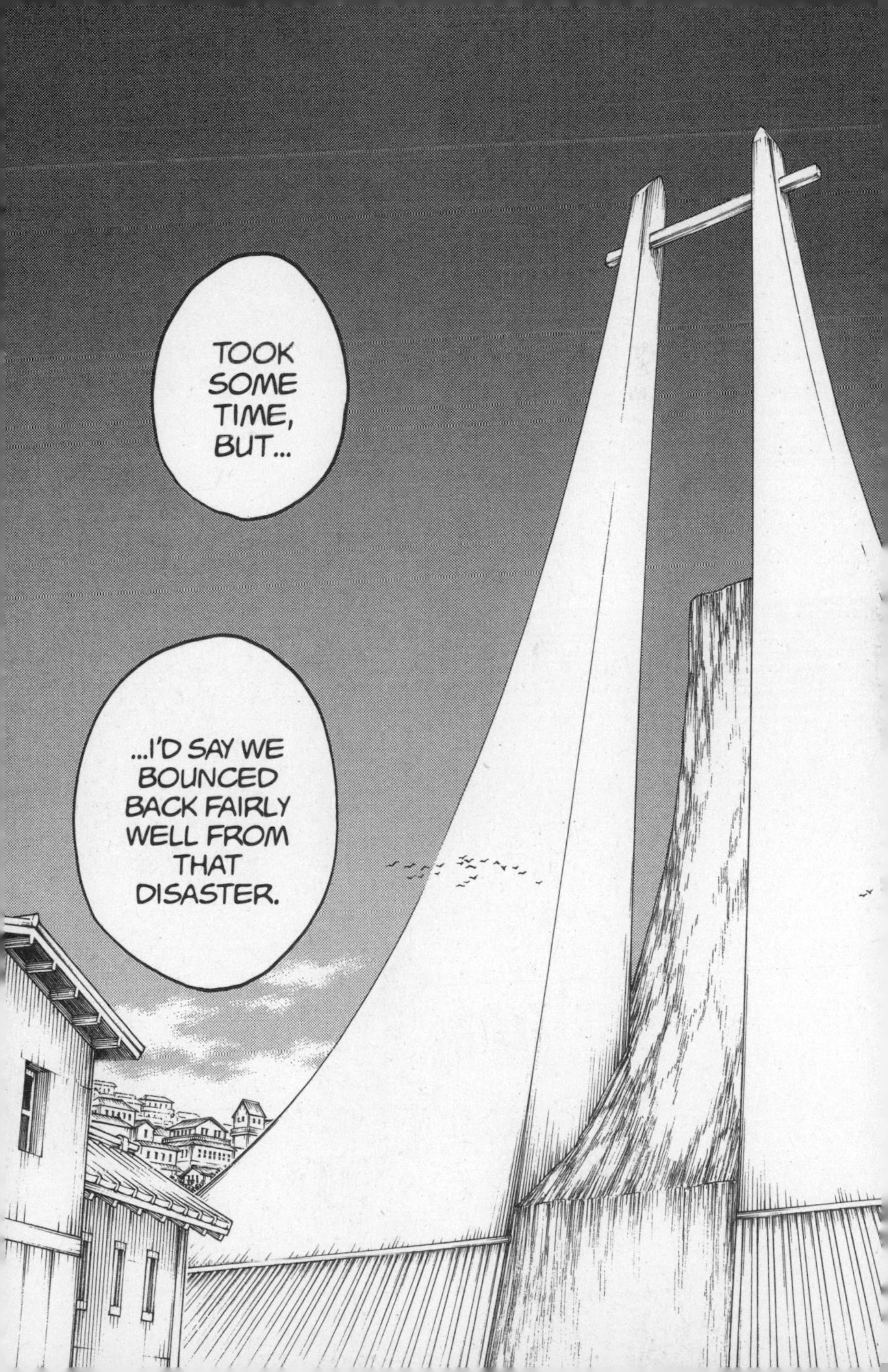
TOOK SOME TIME, BUT...
...I'D SAY WE BOUNCED BACK FAIRLY WELL FROM THAT DISASTER.

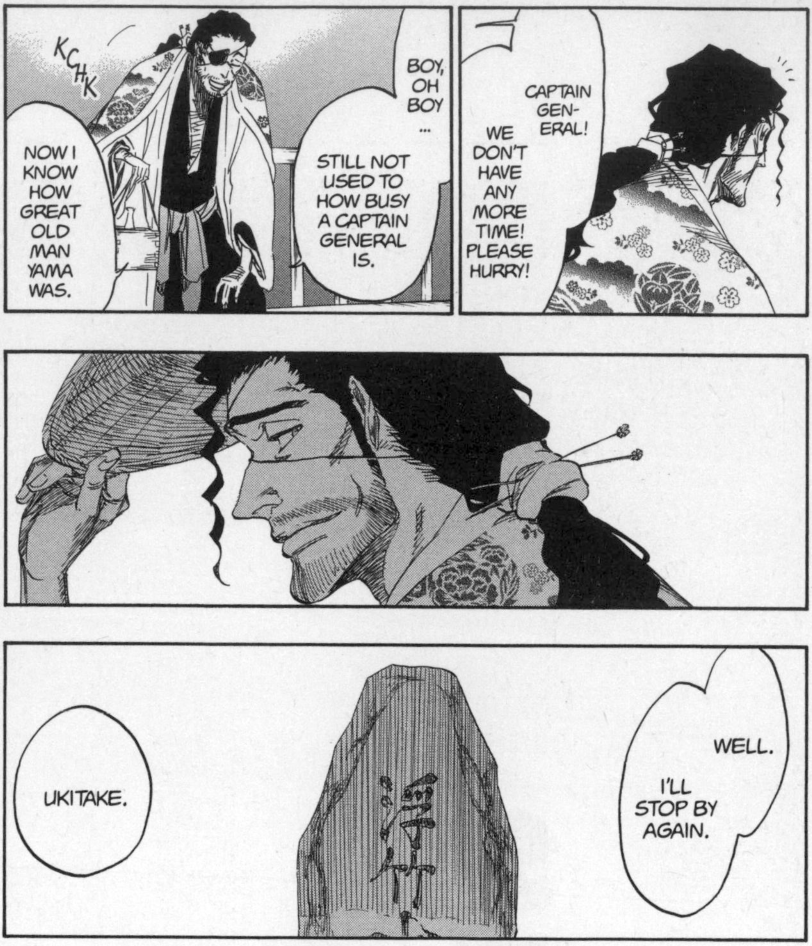
CAPTAIN GEN-ERAL!
WE DON'T HAVE ANY MORE TIME! PLEASE HURRY!
BOY, OH BOY ...
STILL NOT USED TO HOW BUSY A CAPTAIN GENERAL IS.
KCHK
NOW I KNOW HOW GREAT OLD MAN YAMA WAS.
WELL.
I'LL STOP BY AGAIN.
UKITAKE.

BLEACH 685.

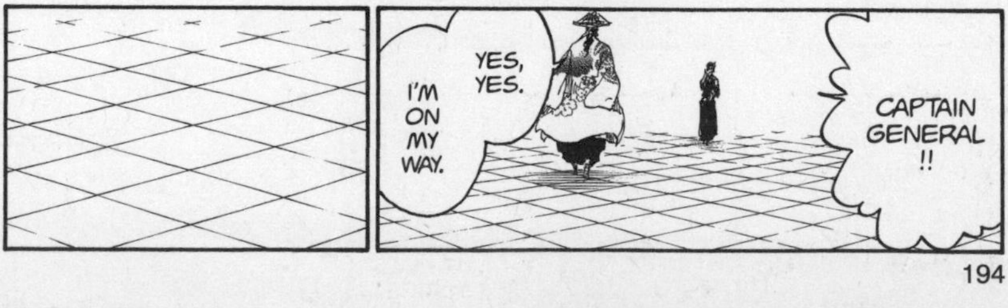
CAPTAIN GENERAL !!
YES, YES.
I'M ON MY WAY.

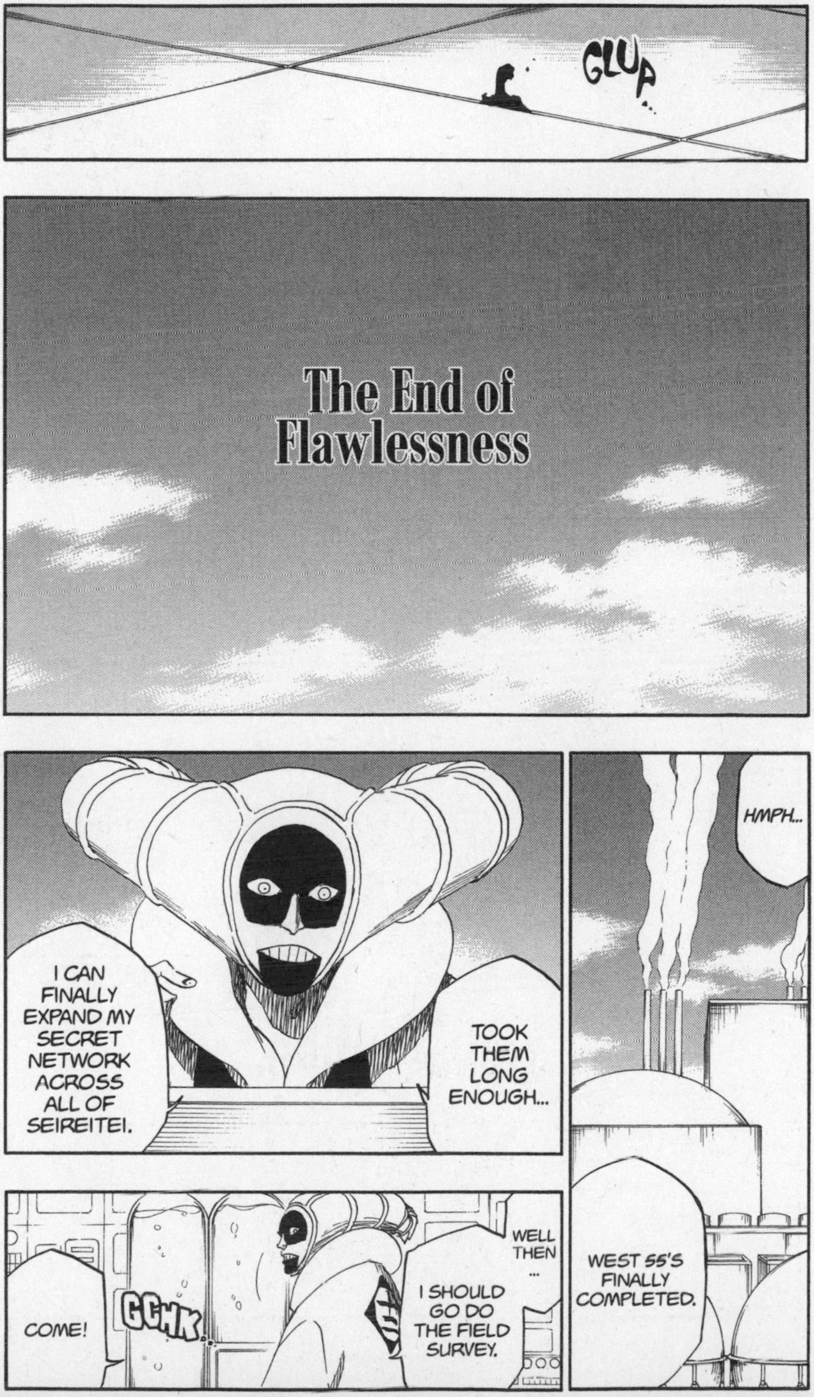
GLUP...
The End of Flawlessness
HMPH...
WEST 55'S FINALLY COMPLETED.
TOOK THEM LONG ENOUGH...
I CAN FINALLY EXPAND MY SECRET NETWORK ACROSS ALL OF SEIREITEI.
WELL THEN...
I SHOULD GO DO THE FIELD SURVEY.
GCHK..
COME!

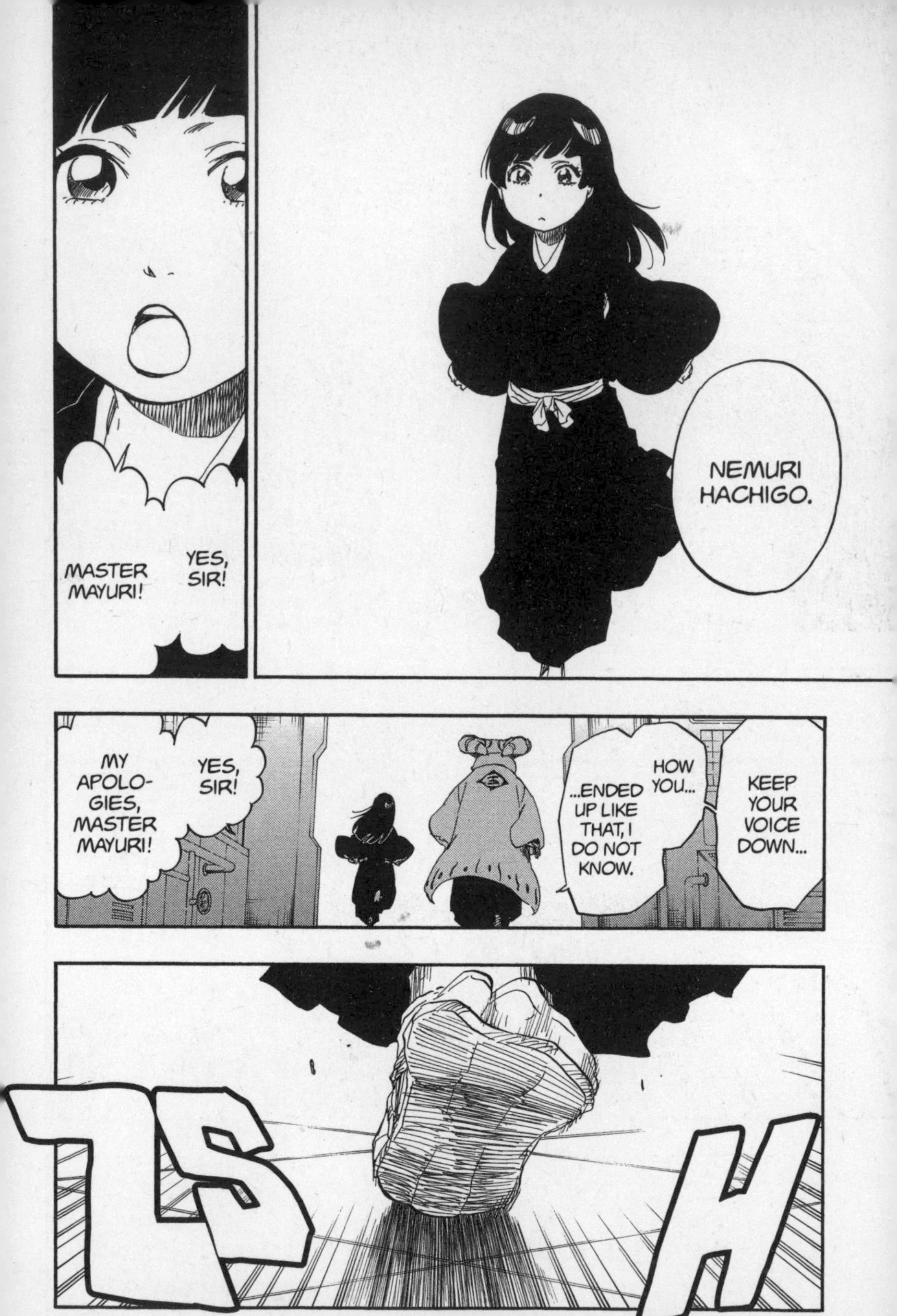
NEMURI HACHIGO.
YES, SIR!
MASTER MAYURI!
KEEP YOUR VOICE DOWN...
HOW YOU...
...ENDED UP LIKE THAT, I DO NOT KNOW.
YES, SIR!
MY APOLOGIES, MASTER MAYURI!
TSH

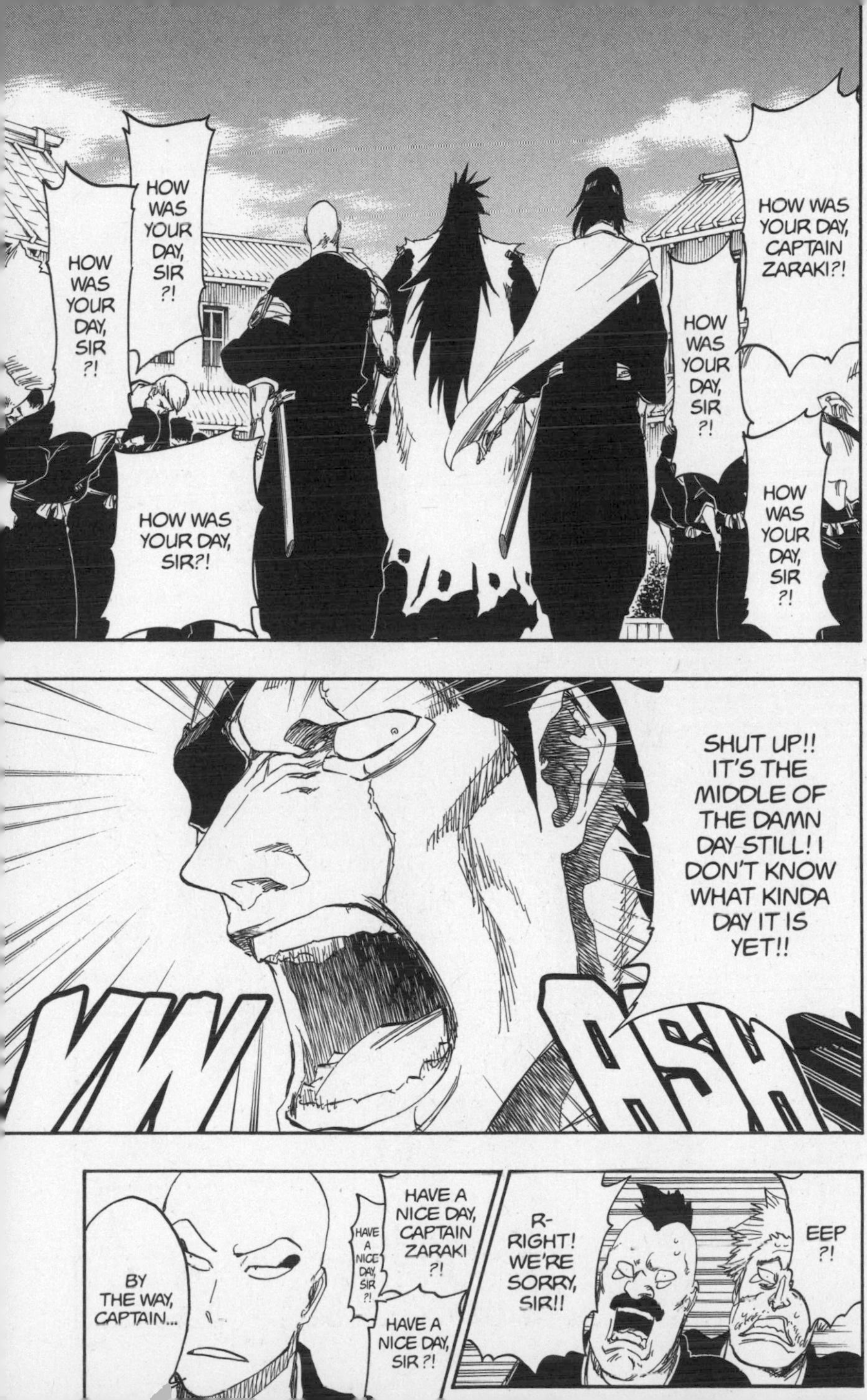
HOW WAS YOUR DAY, CAPTAIN ZARAKI?!
HOW WAS YOUR DAY, SIR?!
HOW WAS YOUR DAY, SIR?!
HOW WAS YOUR DAY, SIR?!
HOW WAS YOUR DAY, SIR?!
HOW WAS YOUR DAY, SIR?!
SHUT UP!! IT'S THE MIDDLE OF THE DAMN DAY STILL! I DON'T KNOW WHAT KINDA DAY IT IS YET!!
EEP?!
R-RIGHT! WE'RE SORRY, SIR!!
HAVE A NICE DAY, CAPTAIN ZARAKI?!
HAVE A NICE DAY, SIR?!
HAVE A NICE DAY, SIR?!
BY THE WAY, CAPTAIN...

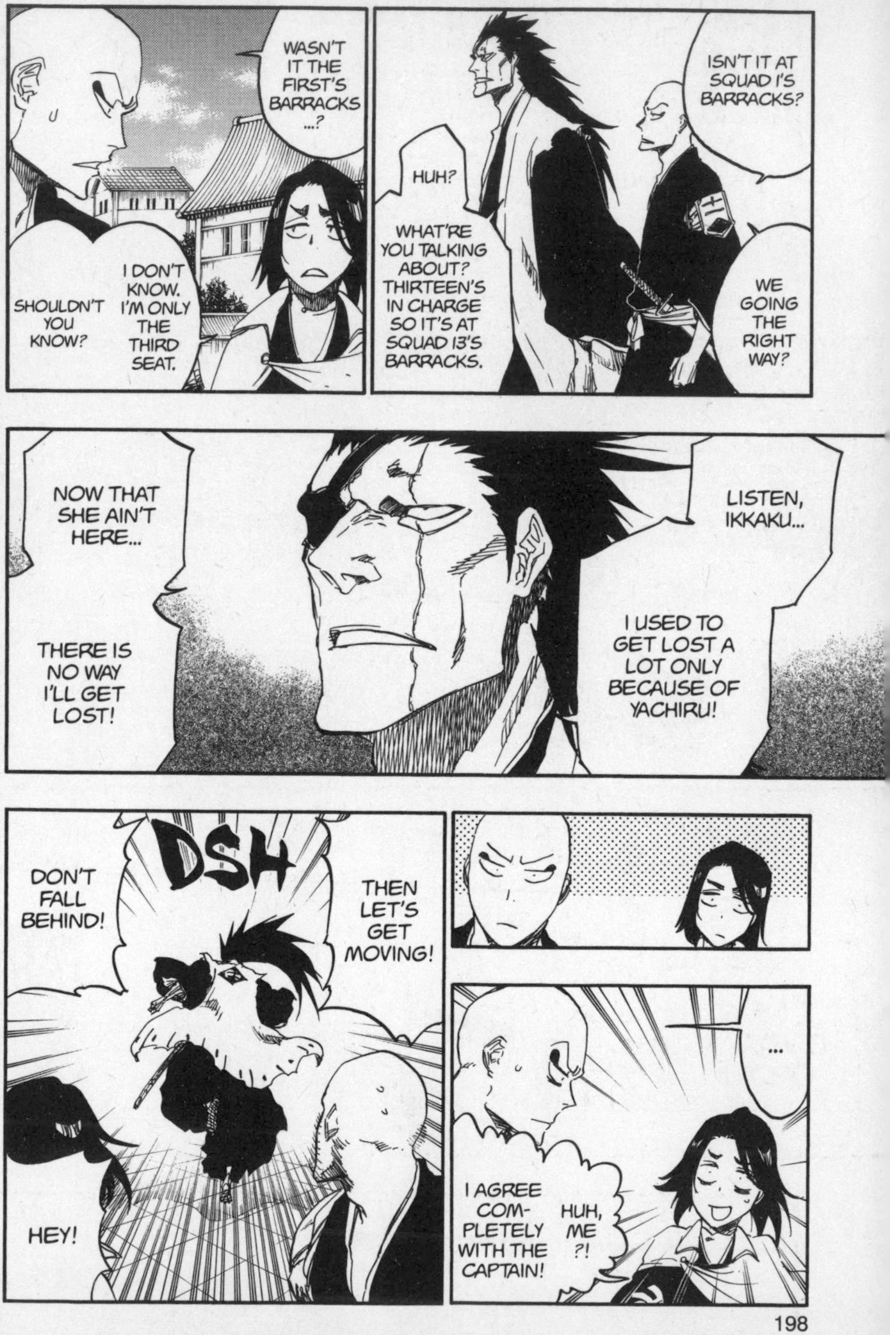
ISN'T IT AT SQUAD 1'S BARRACKS?
HUH?
WHAT'RE YOU TALKING ABOUT? THIRTEEN'S IN CHARGE SO IT'S AT SQUAD 13'S BARRACKS.
WE GOING THE RIGHT WAY?
WASN'T IT THE FIRST'S BARRACKS ...?
I DON'T KNOW. I'M ONLY THE THIRD SEAT.
SHOULDN'T YOU KNOW?
LISTEN, IKKAKU...
I USED TO GET LOST A LOT ONLY BECAUSE OF YACHIRU!
NOW THAT SHE AIN'T HERE...
THERE IS NO WAY I'LL GET LOST!
...
HUH, ME ?!
I AGREE COM-PLETELY WITH THE CAPTAIN!
DSH
THEN LET'S GET MOVING!
DON'T FALL BEHIND!
HEY!

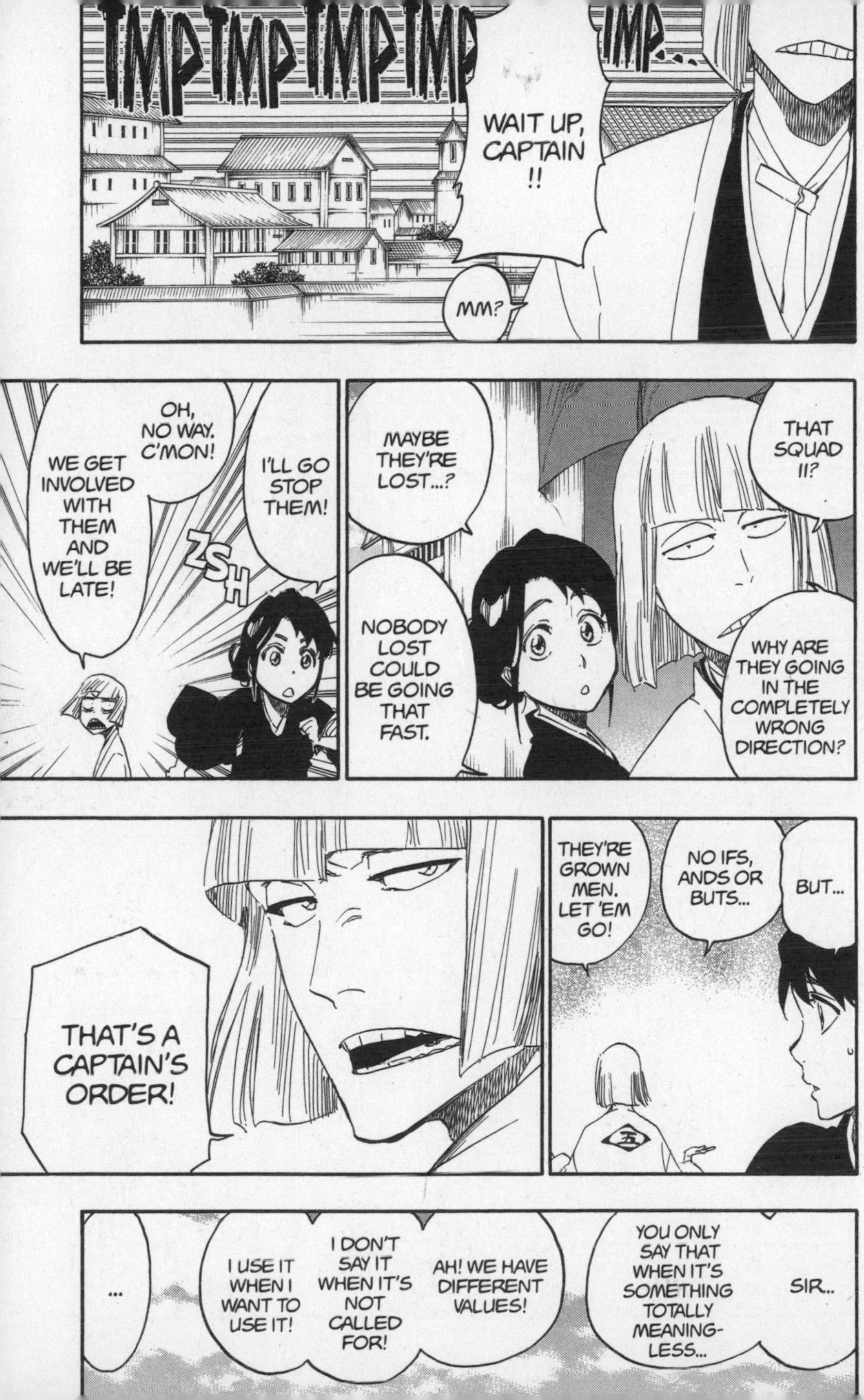
TMP TMP TMP TMP TMP...
WAIT UP, CAPTAIN !!
MM?
THAT SQUAD !!?
WHY ARE THEY GOING IN THE COMPLETELY WRONG DIRECTION?
MAYBE THEY'RE LOST...?
NOBODY LOST COULD BE GOING THAT FAST.
I'LL GO STOP THEM!
ZSH
OH, NO WAY. C'MON!
WE GET INVOLVED WITH THEM AND WE'LL BE LATE!
BUT...
NO IFS, ANDS OR BUTS...
THEY'RE GROWN MEN. LET 'EM GO!
THAT'S A CAPTAIN'S ORDER!
SIR...
YOU ONLY SAY THAT WHEN IT'S SOMETHING TOTALLY MEANING-LESS...
AH! WE HAVE DIFFERENT VALUES!
I DON'T SAY IT WHEN IT'S NOT CALLED FOR!
I USE IT WHEN I WANT TO USE IT!
...

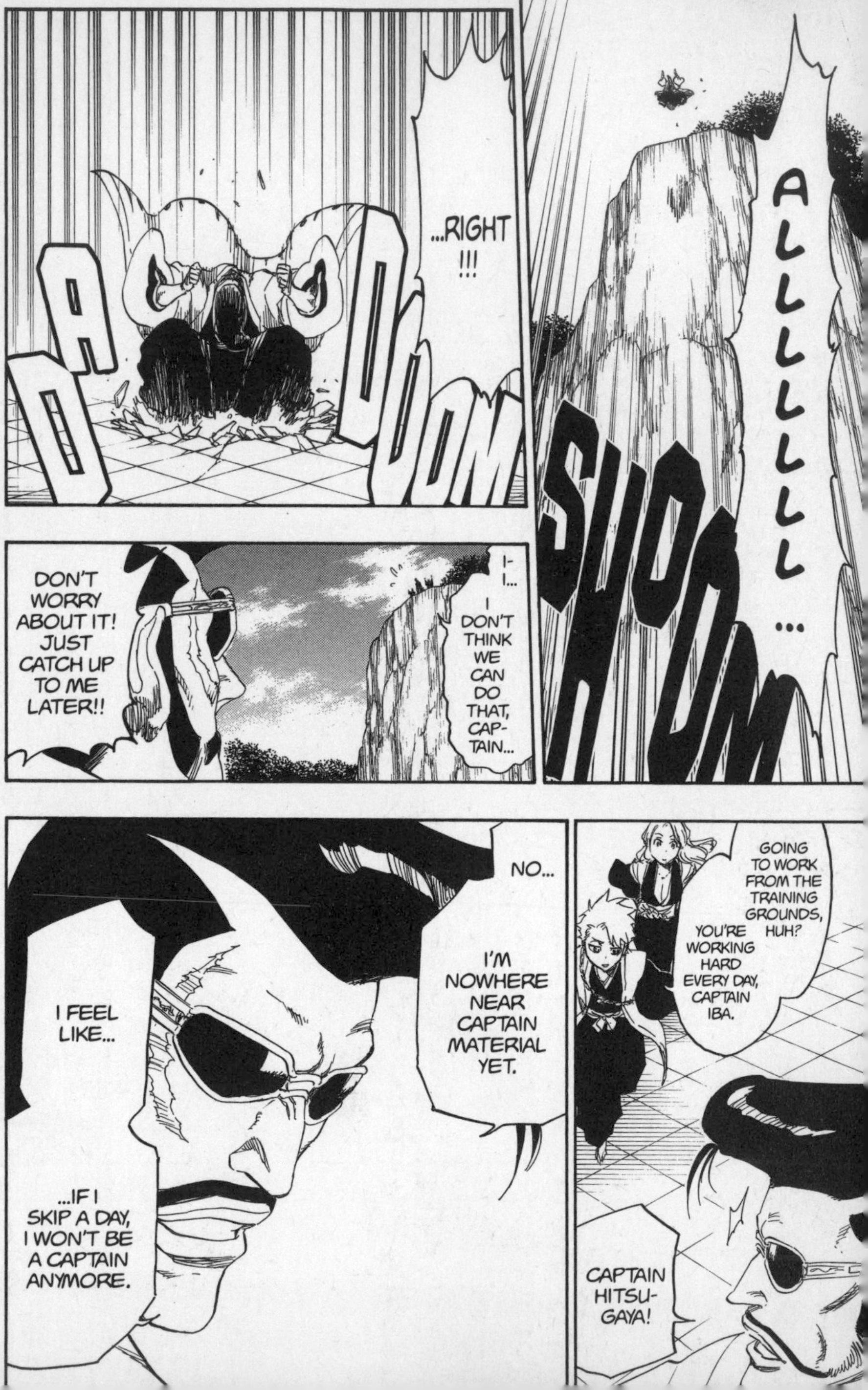
ALLLLLLL...
SHOOOM
DADOOM
...RIGHT !!!
I- I... I DON'T THINK WE CAN DO THAT, CAP- TAIN...
DON'T WORRY ABOUT IT! JUST CATCH UP TO ME LATER!!
GOING TO WORK FROM THE TRAINING GROUNDS, HUH?
YOU'RE WORKING HARD EVERY DAY, CAPTAIN IBA.
CAPTAIN HITSU- GAYA!
NO...
I'M NOWHERE NEAR CAPTAIN MATERIAL YET.
I FEEL LIKE...
...IF I SKIP A DAY, I WON'T BE A CAPTAIN ANYMORE.

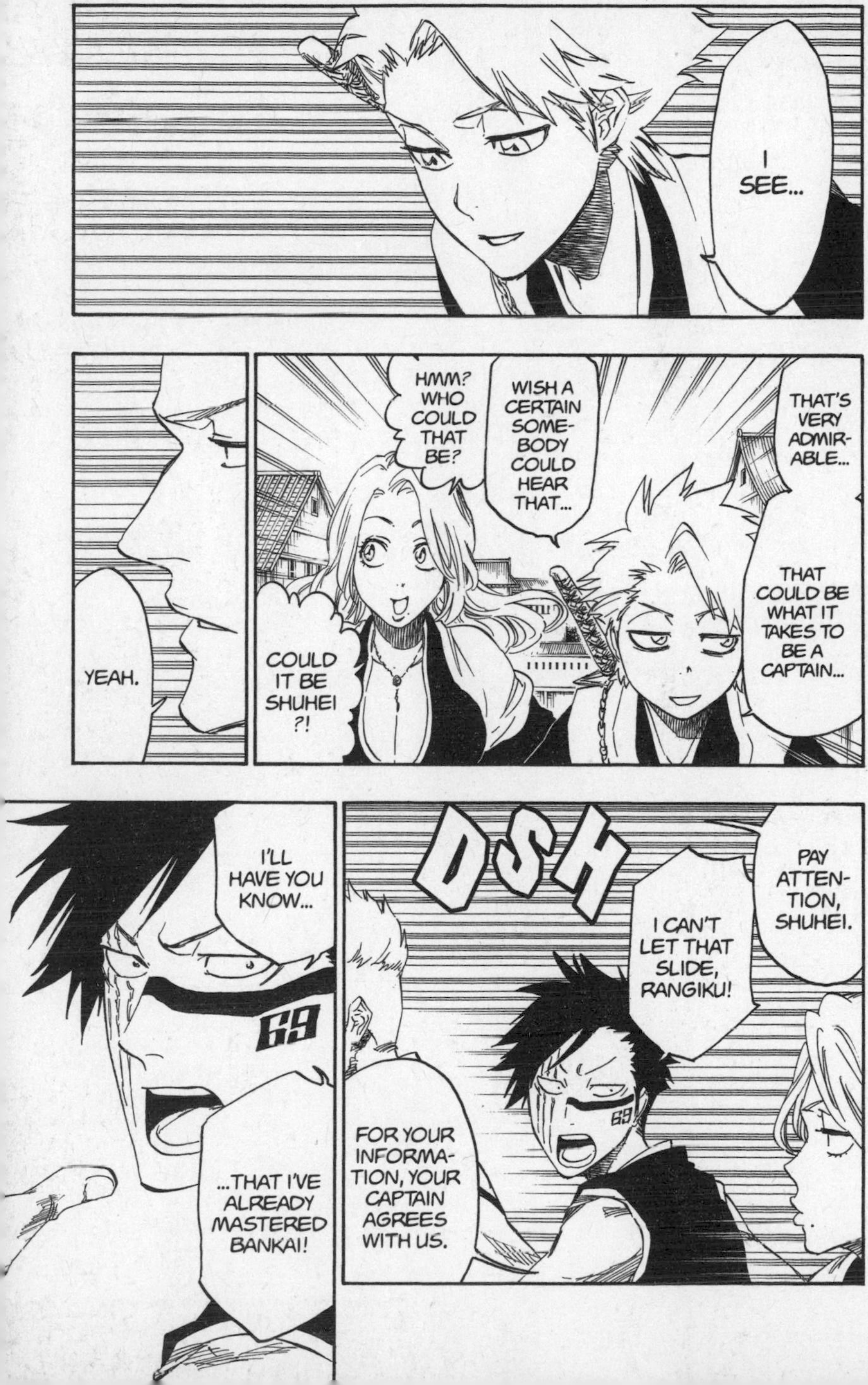
I SEE...
THAT'S VERY ADMIRABLE...
THAT COULD BE WHAT IT TAKES TO BE A CAPTAIN...
WISH A CERTAIN SOMEBODY COULD HEAR THAT...
HMM? WHO COULD THAT BE?
COULD IT BE SHUHEI?!
YEAH.
DSH
PAY ATTENTION, SHUHEI.
I CAN'T LET THAT SLIDE, RANGIKU!
FOR YOUR INFORMATION, YOUR CAPTAIN AGREES WITH US.
I'LL HAVE YOU KNOW...
...THAT I'VE ALREADY MASTERED BANKAI!

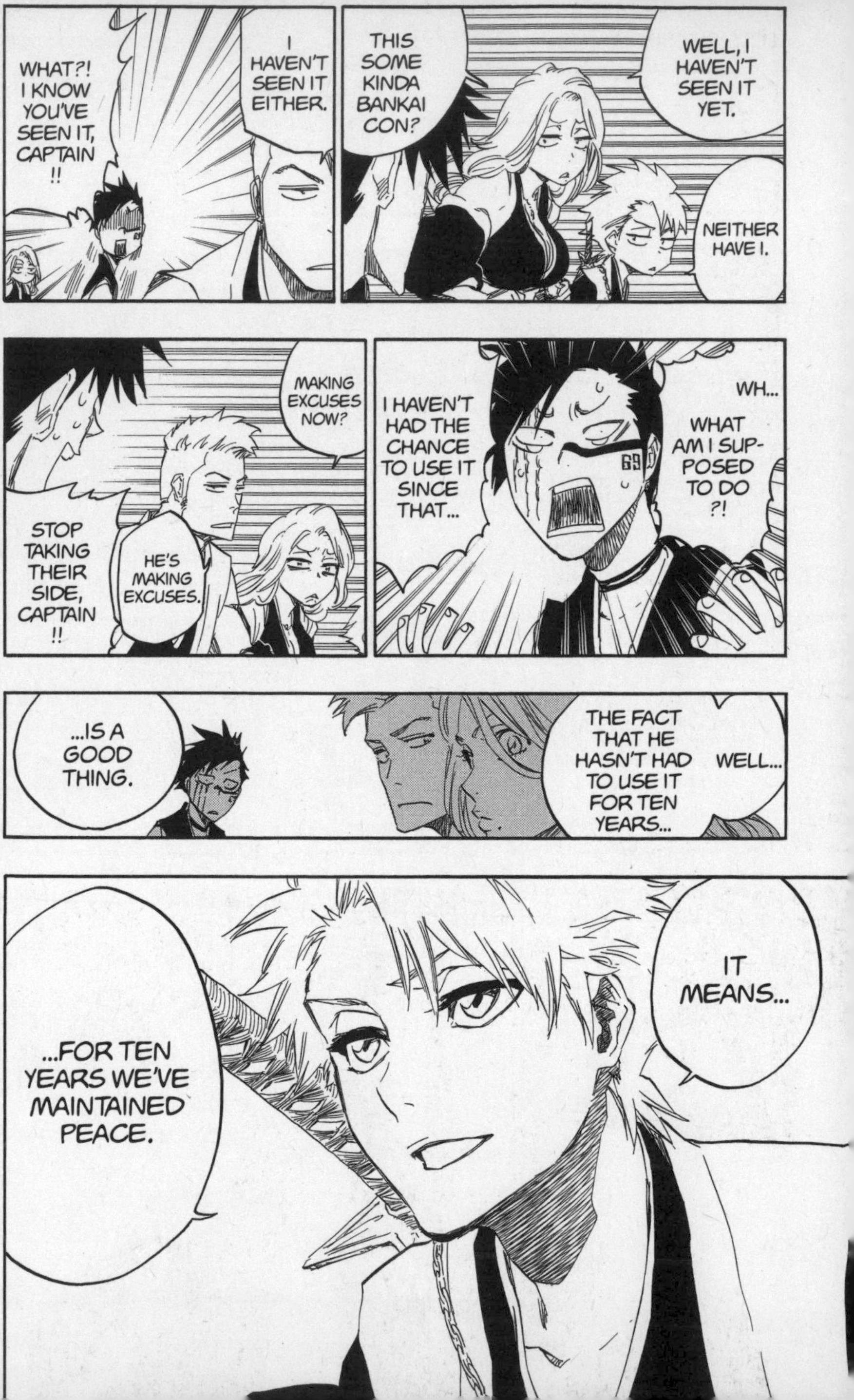
WELL, I HAVEN'T SEEN IT YET.
NEITHER HAVE I.
THIS SOME KINDA BANKAI CON?
I HAVEN'T SEEN IT EITHER.
WHAT?! I KNOW YOU'VE SEEN IT, CAPTAIN!!
WH...
WHAT AM I SUPPOSED TO DO?!
I HAVEN'T HAD THE CHANCE TO USE IT SINCE THAT...
MAKING EXCUSES NOW?
HE'S MAKING EXCUSES.
STOP TAKING THEIR SIDE, CAPTAIN!!
WELL...
THE FACT THAT HE HASN'T HAD TO USE IT FOR TEN YEARS...
...IS A GOOD THING.
IT MEANS...
...FOR TEN YEARS WE'VE MAINTAINED PEACE.

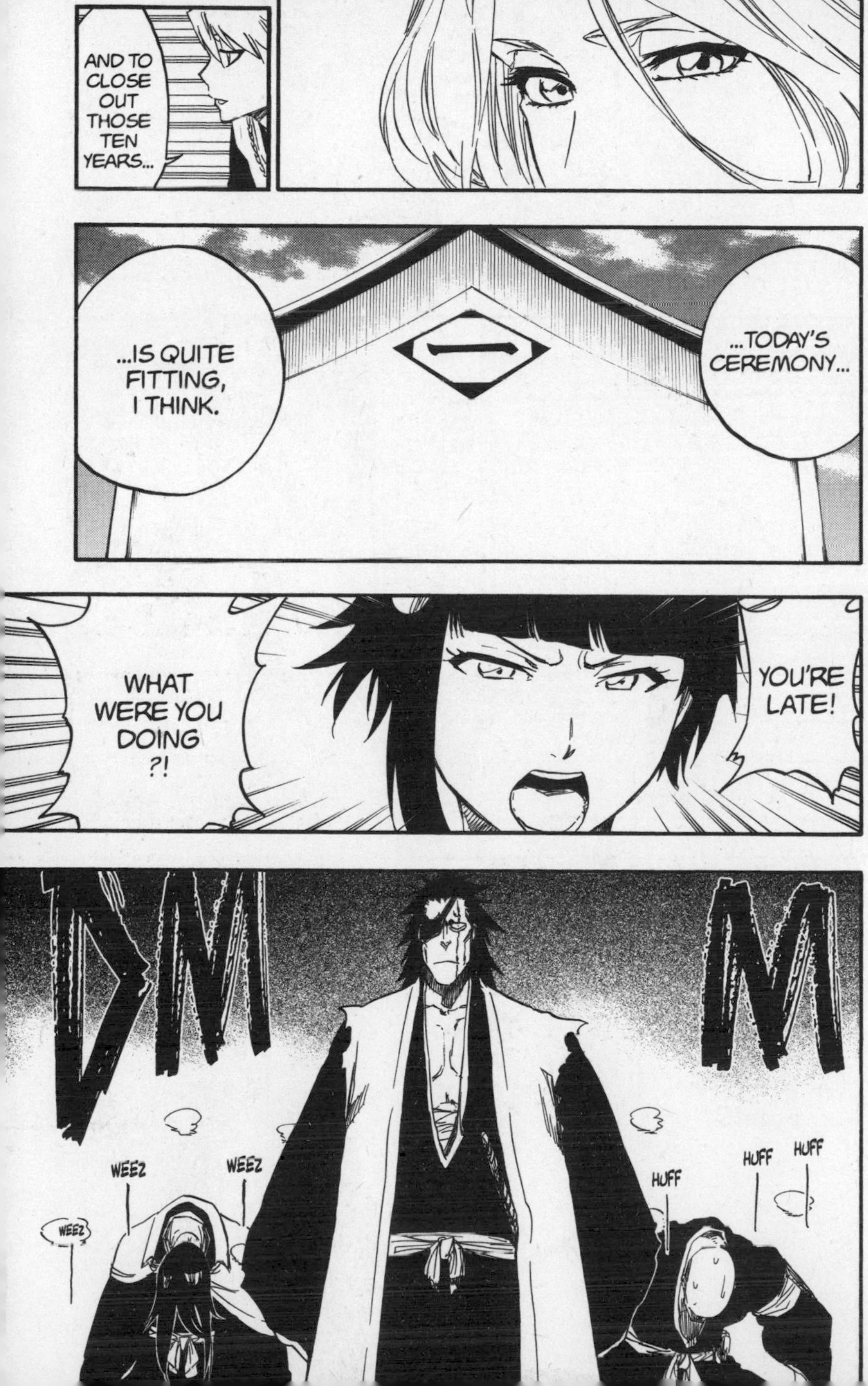
AND TO CLOSE OUT THOSE TEN YEARS...
...TODAY'S CEREMONY...
...IS QUITE FITTING, I THINK.
YOU'RE LATE!
WHAT WERE YOU DOING?!
DMM
HUFF
HUFF
HUFF
WEEZ
WEEZ
WEEZ

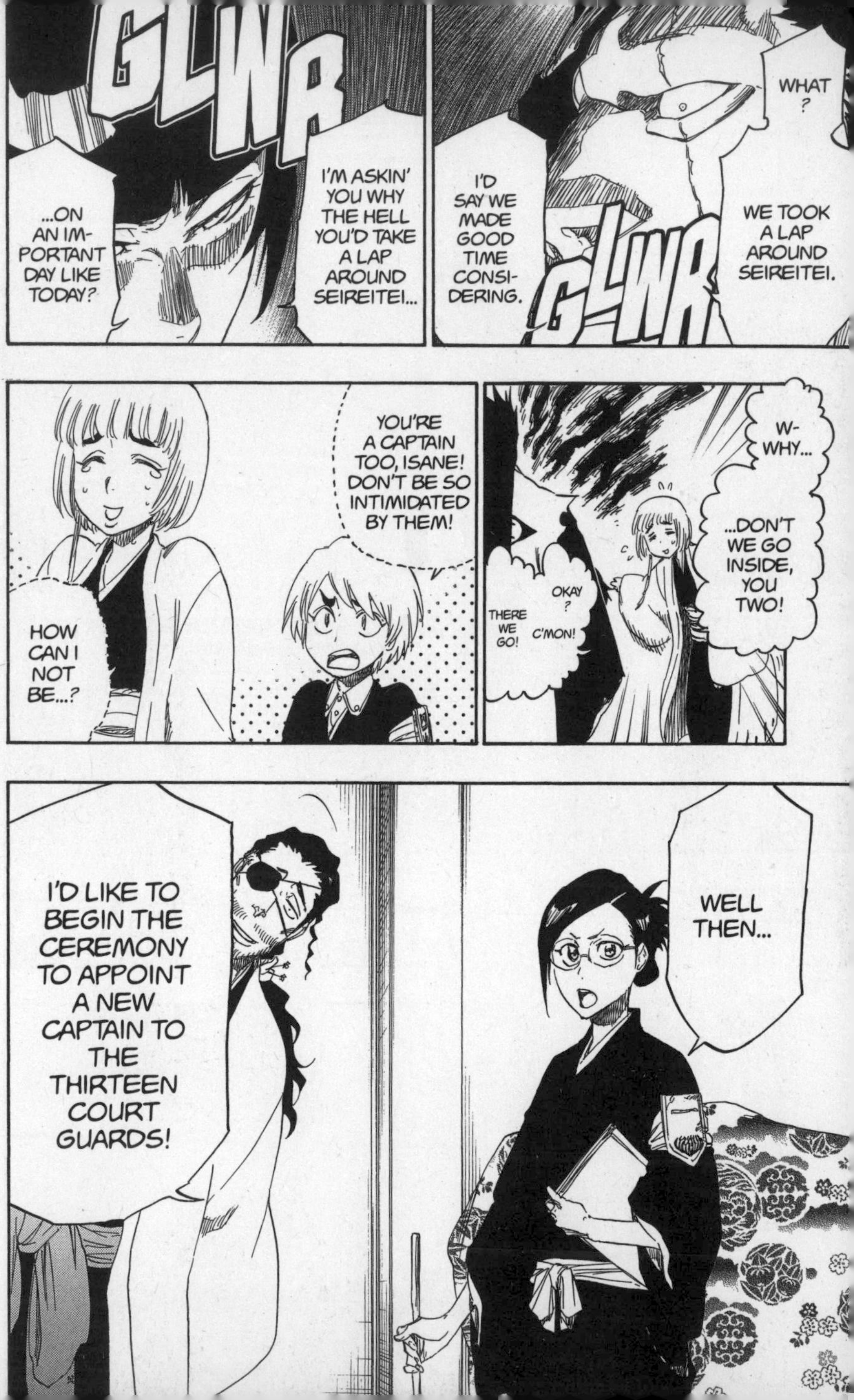
WHAT?
WE TOOK A LAP AROUND SEIREITEI.
GLWA
I'D SAY WE MADE GOOD TIME CONSIDERING.
GLWA
I'M ASKIN' YOU WHY THE HELL YOU'D TAKE A LAP AROUND SEIREITEI...
...ON AN IMPORTANT DAY LIKE TODAY?
W-WHY...
...DON'T WE GO INSIDE, YOU TWO!
OKAY?
C'MON!
THERE WE GO!
YOU'RE A CAPTAIN TOO, ISANE! DON'T BE SO INTIMIDATED BY THEM!
HOW CAN I NOT BE...?
WELL THEN...
I'D LIKE TO BEGIN THE CEREMONY TO APPOINT A NEW CAPTAIN TO THE THIRTEEN COURT GUARDS!

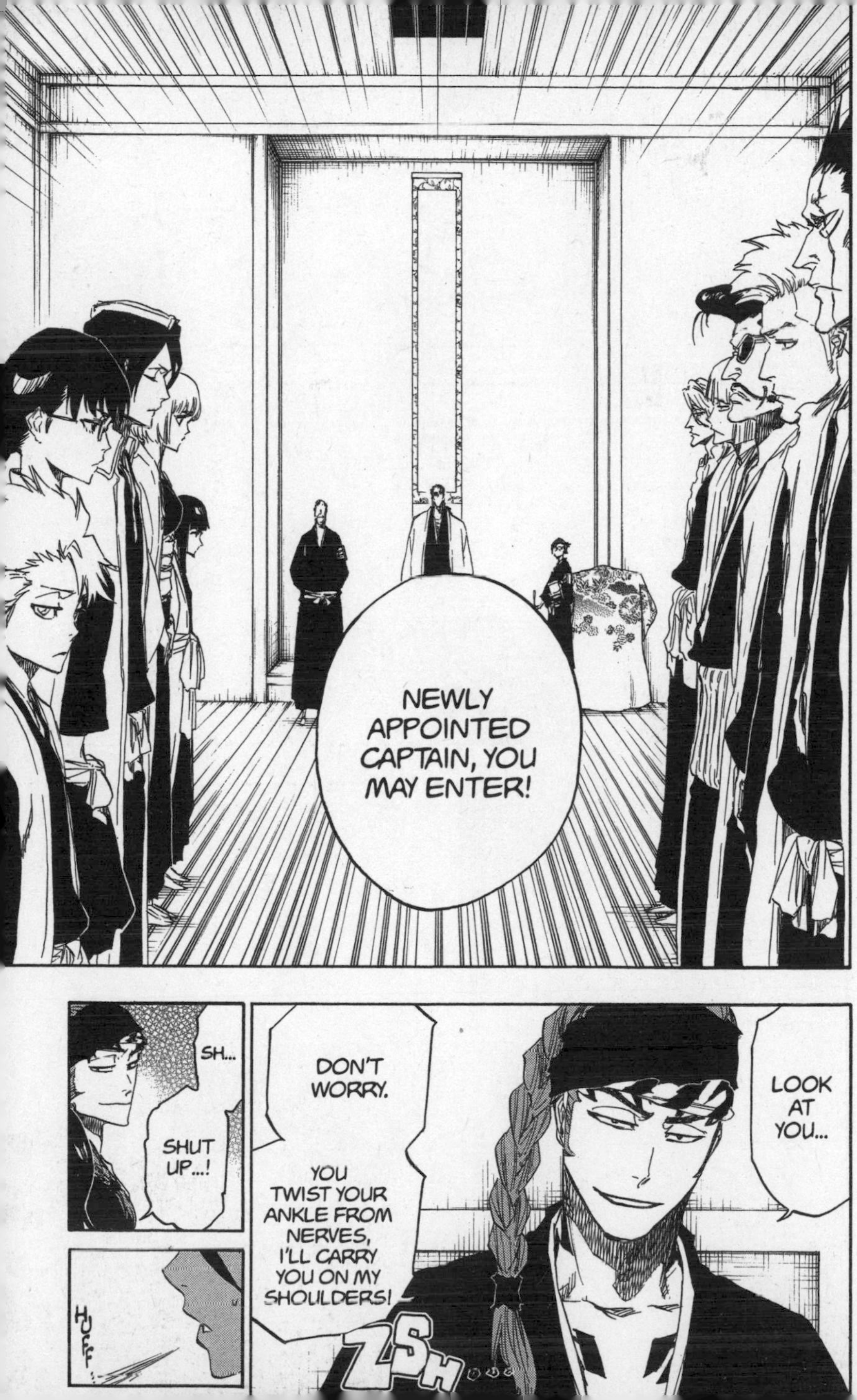
NEWLY APPOINTED CAPTAIN, YOU MAY ENTER!
LOOK AT YOU...
DON'T WORRY.
YOU TWIST YOUR ANKLE FROM NERVES, I'LL CARRY YOU ON MY SHOULDERS!
ZSH
SH...
SHUT UP...!
HUFF

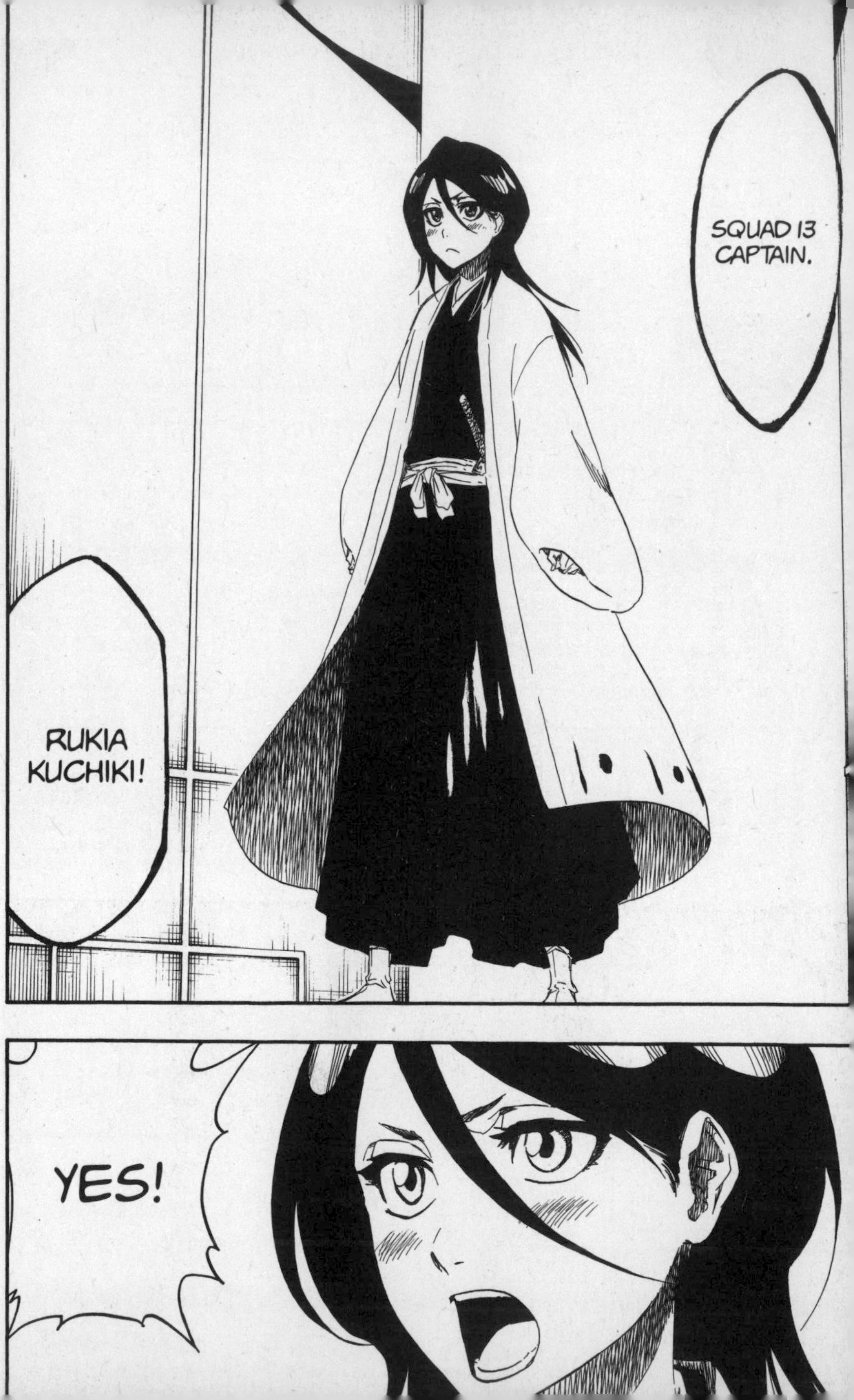
SQUAD 13 CAPTAIN.
RUKIA KUCHIKI!
YES!

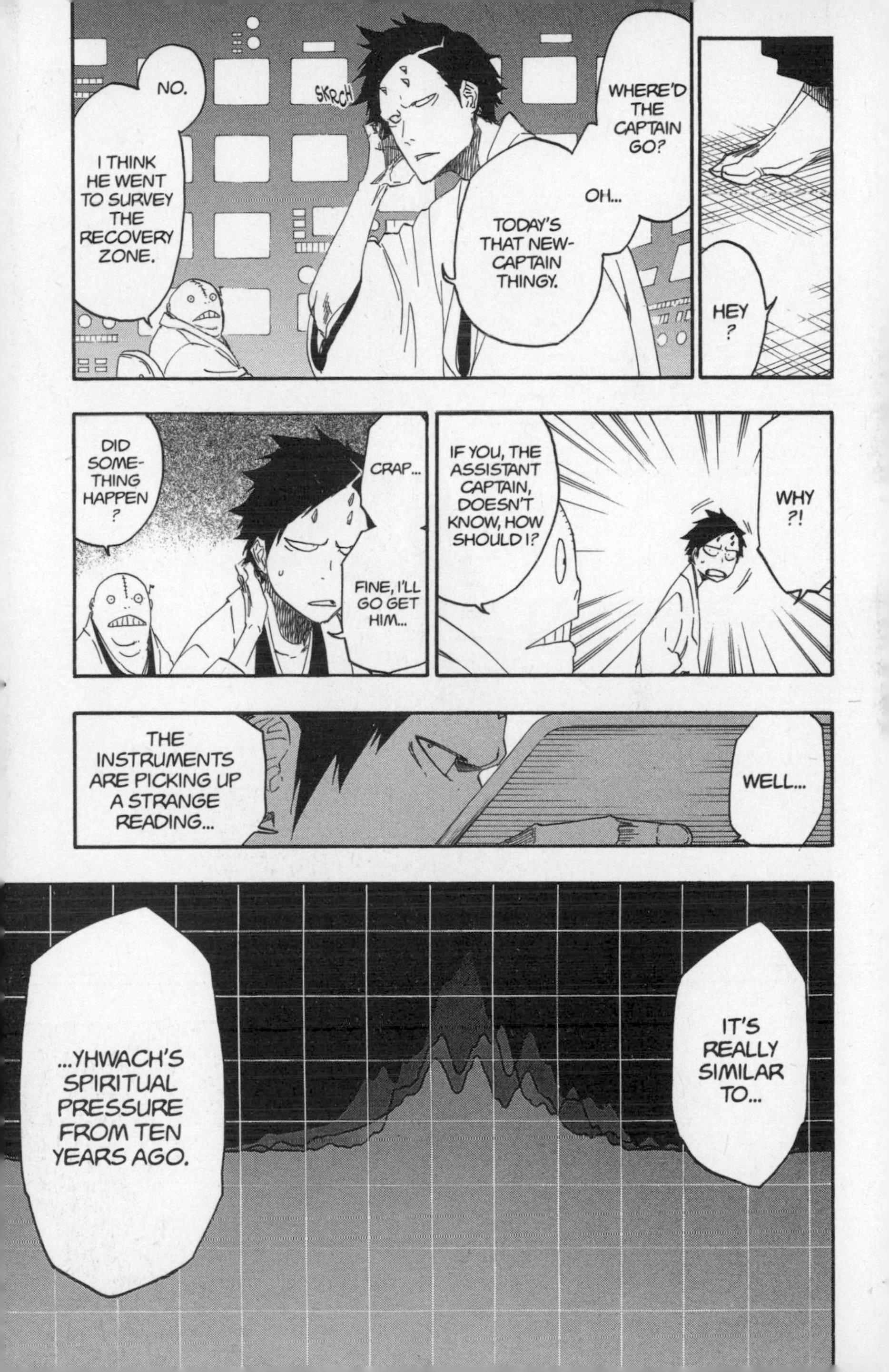
HEY?
WHERE'D THE CAPTAIN GO?
SKRCH
NO.
I THINK HE WENT TO SURVEY THE RECOVERY ZONE.
OH...
TODAY'S THAT NEW-CAPTAIN THINGY.
WHY?!
IF YOU, THE ASSISTANT CAPTAIN, DOESN'T KNOW, HOW SHOULD I?
CRAP...
FINE, I'LL GO GET HIM...
DID SOMETHING HAPPEN?
WELL...
THE INSTRUMENTS ARE PICKING UP A STRANGE READING...
IT'S REALLY SIMILAR TO...
...YHWACH'S SPIRITUAL PRESSURE FROM TEN YEARS AGO.

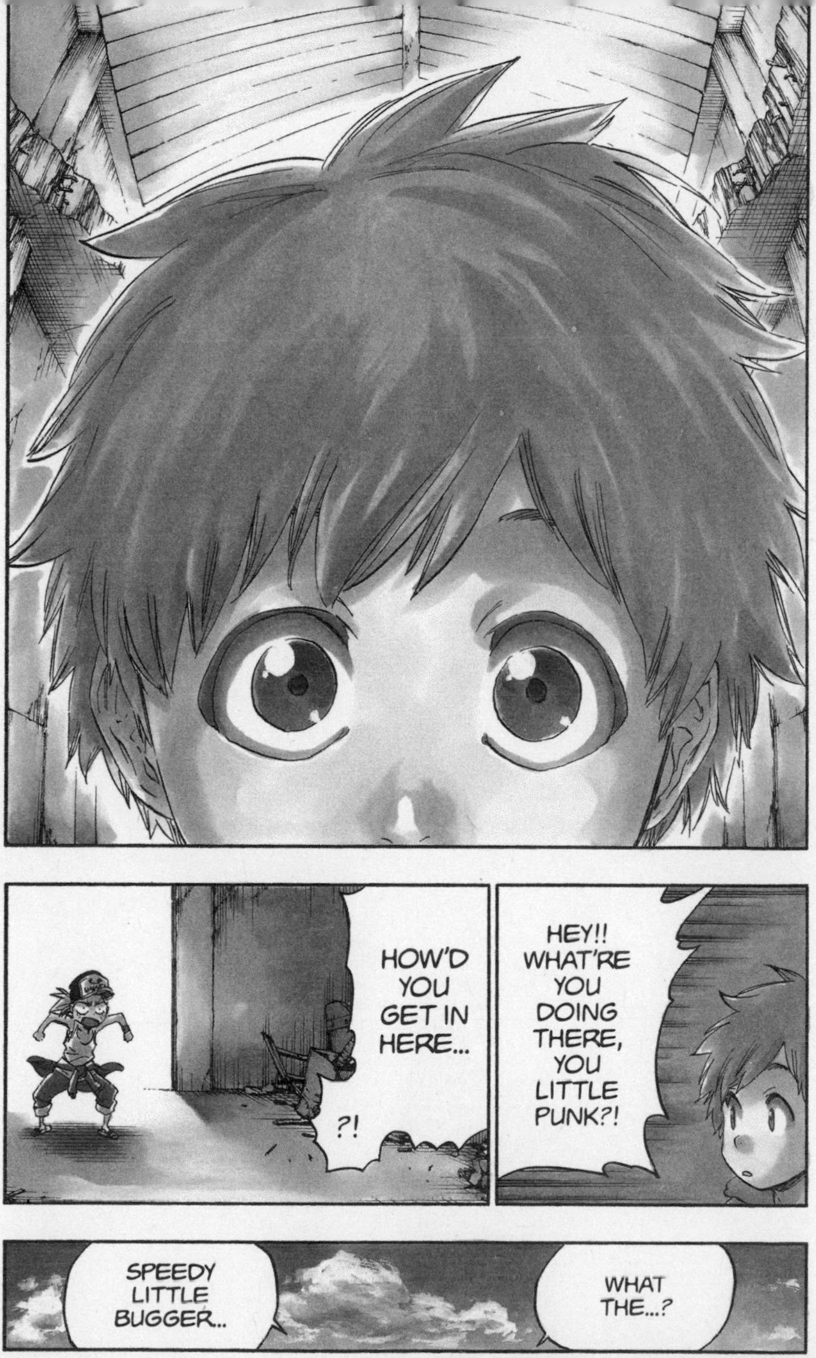
HEY!! WHAT'RE YOU DOING THERE, YOU LITTLE PUNK?!
HOW'D YOU GET IN HERE...
?!
WHAT THE...?
SPEEDY LITTLE BUGGER...

686. DEATH & STRAWBERRY

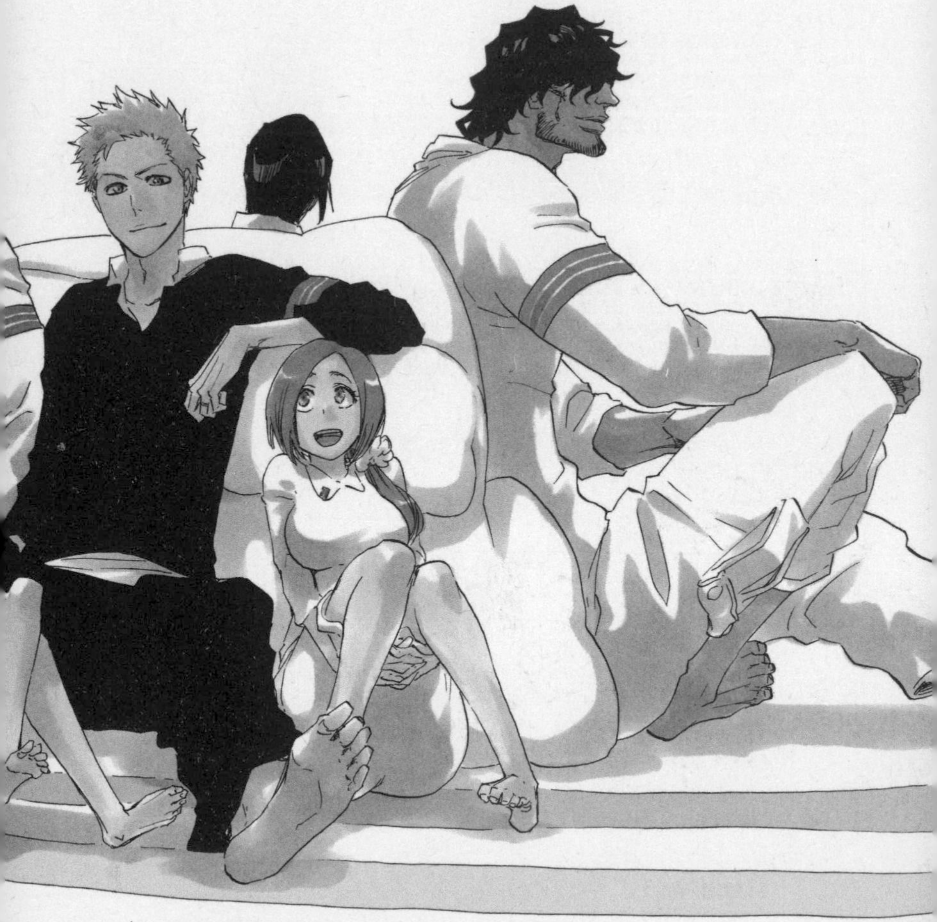

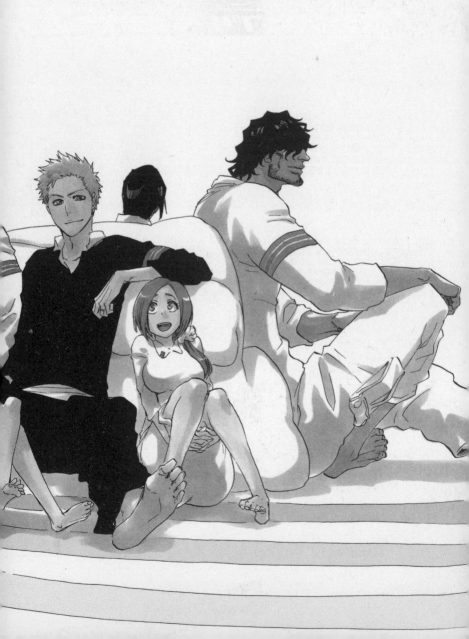

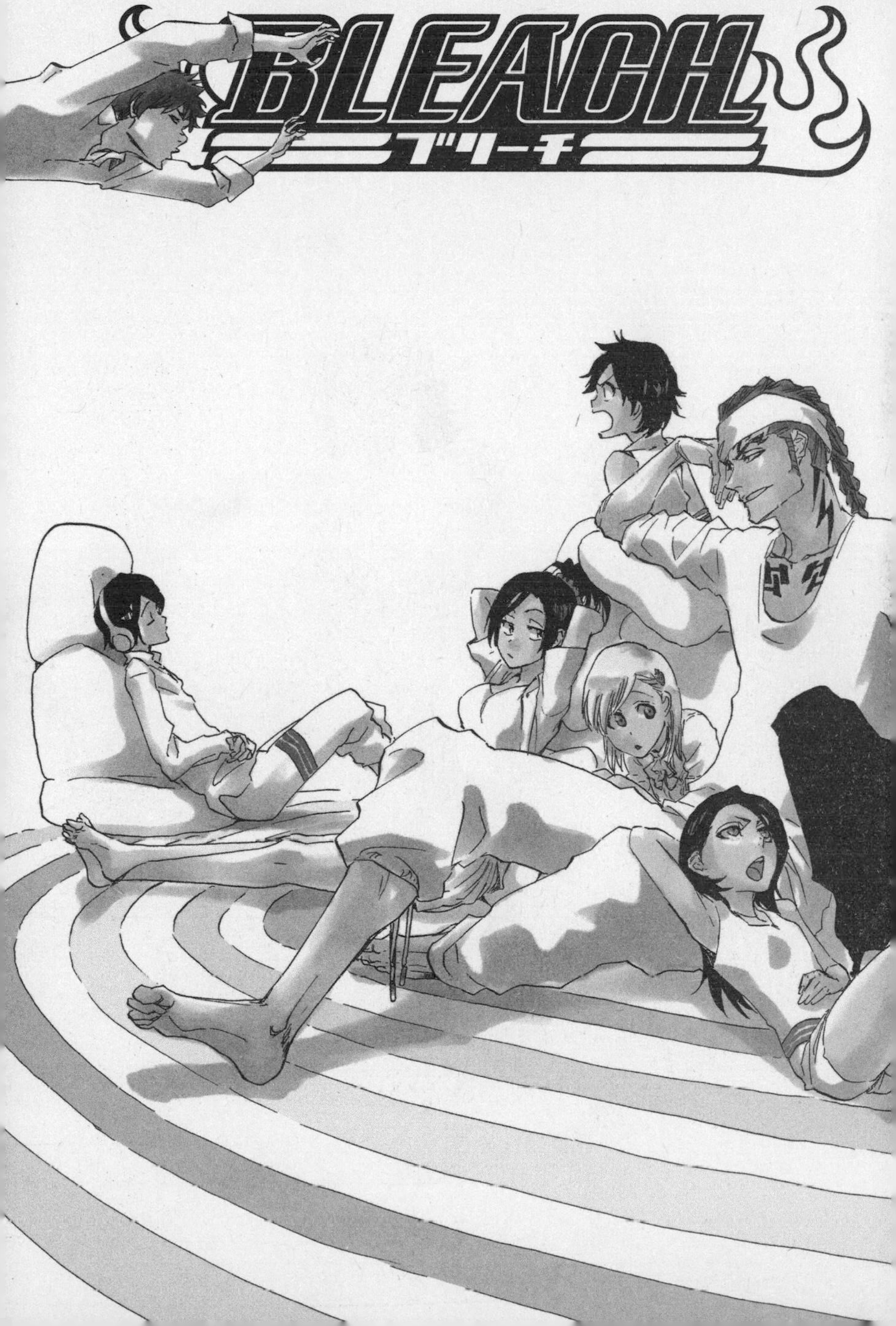
BLEACH
ブリーチ

BLEACH
ブリーチ

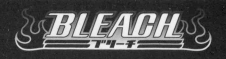

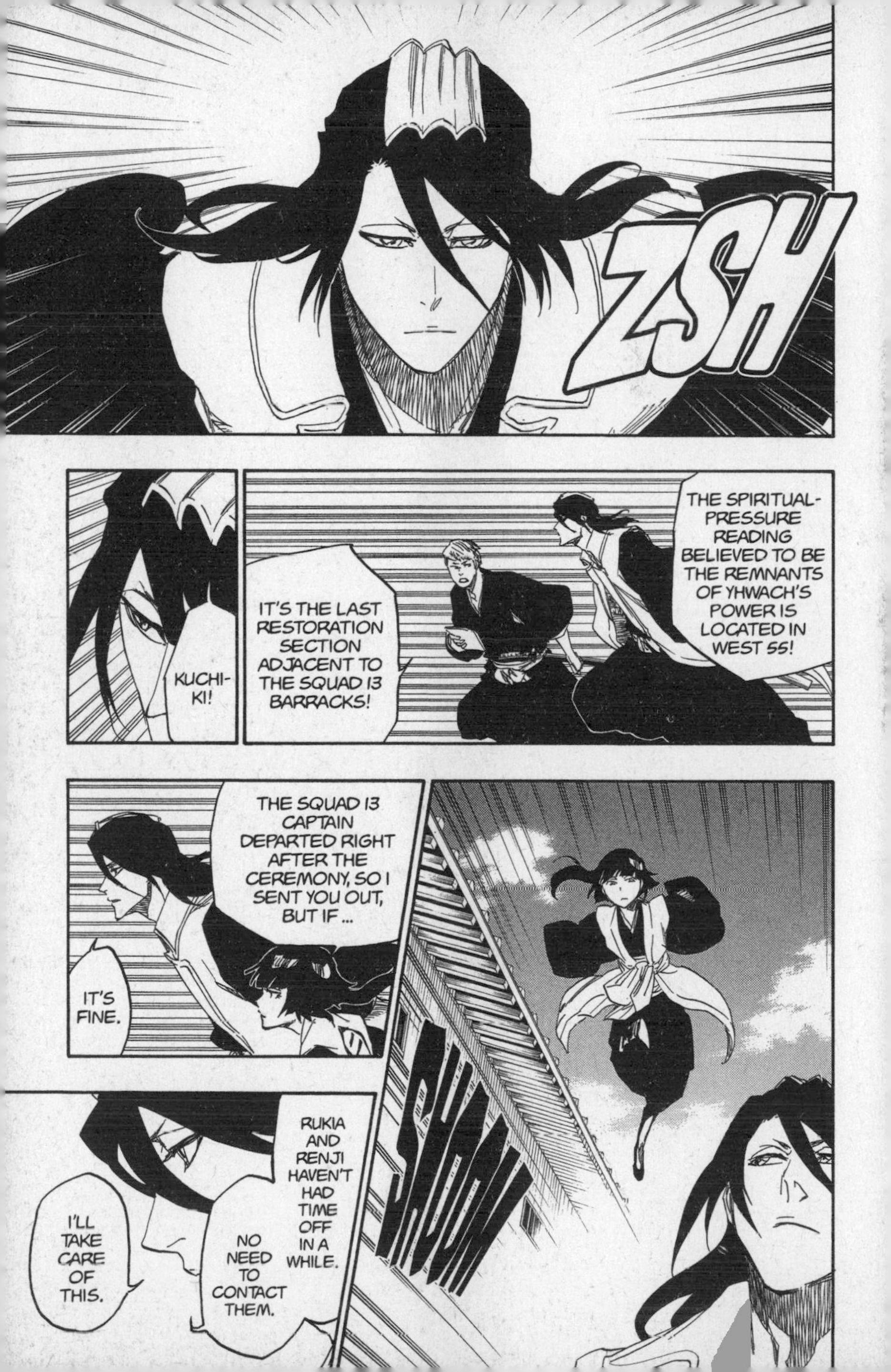
ZSH
THE SPIRITUAL-PRESSURE READING BELIEVED TO BE THE REMNANTS OF YHWACH'S POWER IS LOCATED IN WEST 55!
IT'S THE LAST RESTORATION SECTION ADJACENT TO THE SQUAD 13 BARRACKS!
KUCHI-KI!
THE SQUAD 13 CAPTAIN DEPARTED RIGHT AFTER THE CEREMONY, SO I SENT YOU OUT, BUT IF ...
IT'S FINE.
RUKIA AND RENJI HAVEN'T HAD TIME OFF IN A WHILE.
NO NEED TO CONTACT THEM.
I'LL TAKE CARE OF THIS.

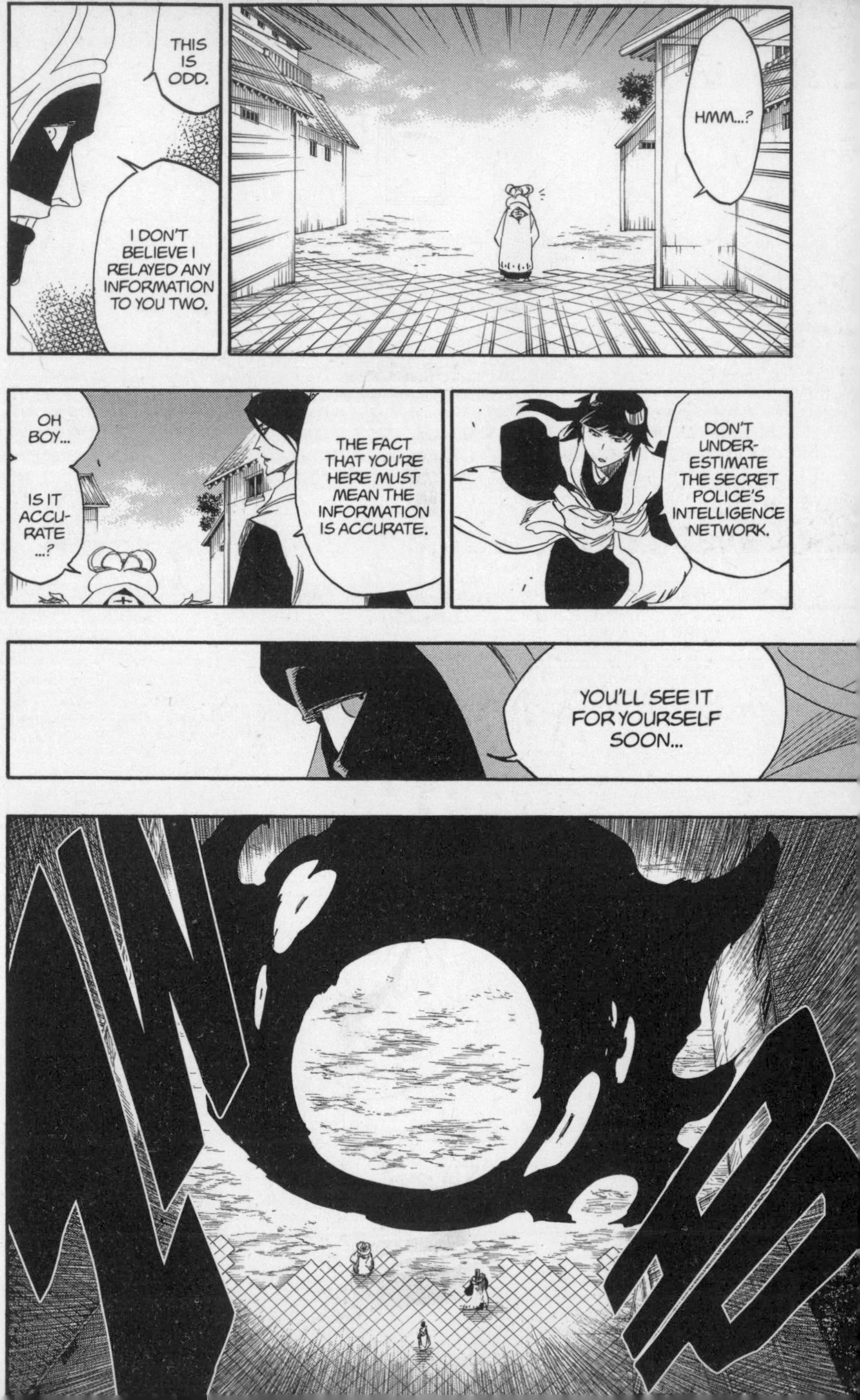
HMM...?
THIS IS ODD.
I DON'T BELIEVE I RELAYED ANY INFORMATION TO YOU TWO.
DON'T UNDER-ESTIMATE THE SECRET POLICE'S INTELLIGENCE NETWORK.
THE FACT THAT YOU'RE HERE MUST MEAN THE INFORMATION IS ACCURATE.
OH BOY...
IS IT ACCU-RATE ...?
YOU'LL SEE IT FOR YOURSELF SOON...

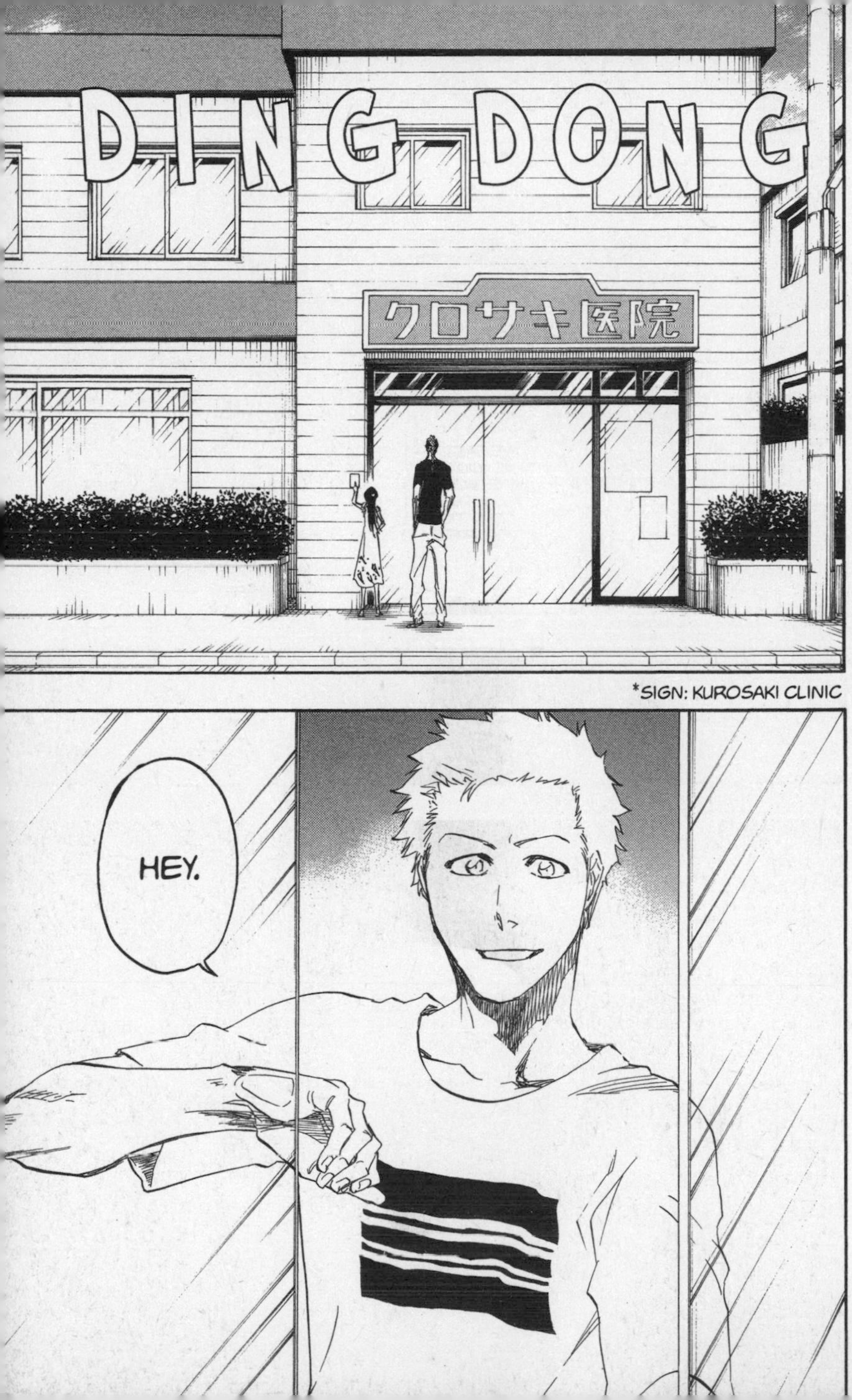
DING DONG
クロサキ医院
*SIGN: KUROSAKI CLINIC
HEY.

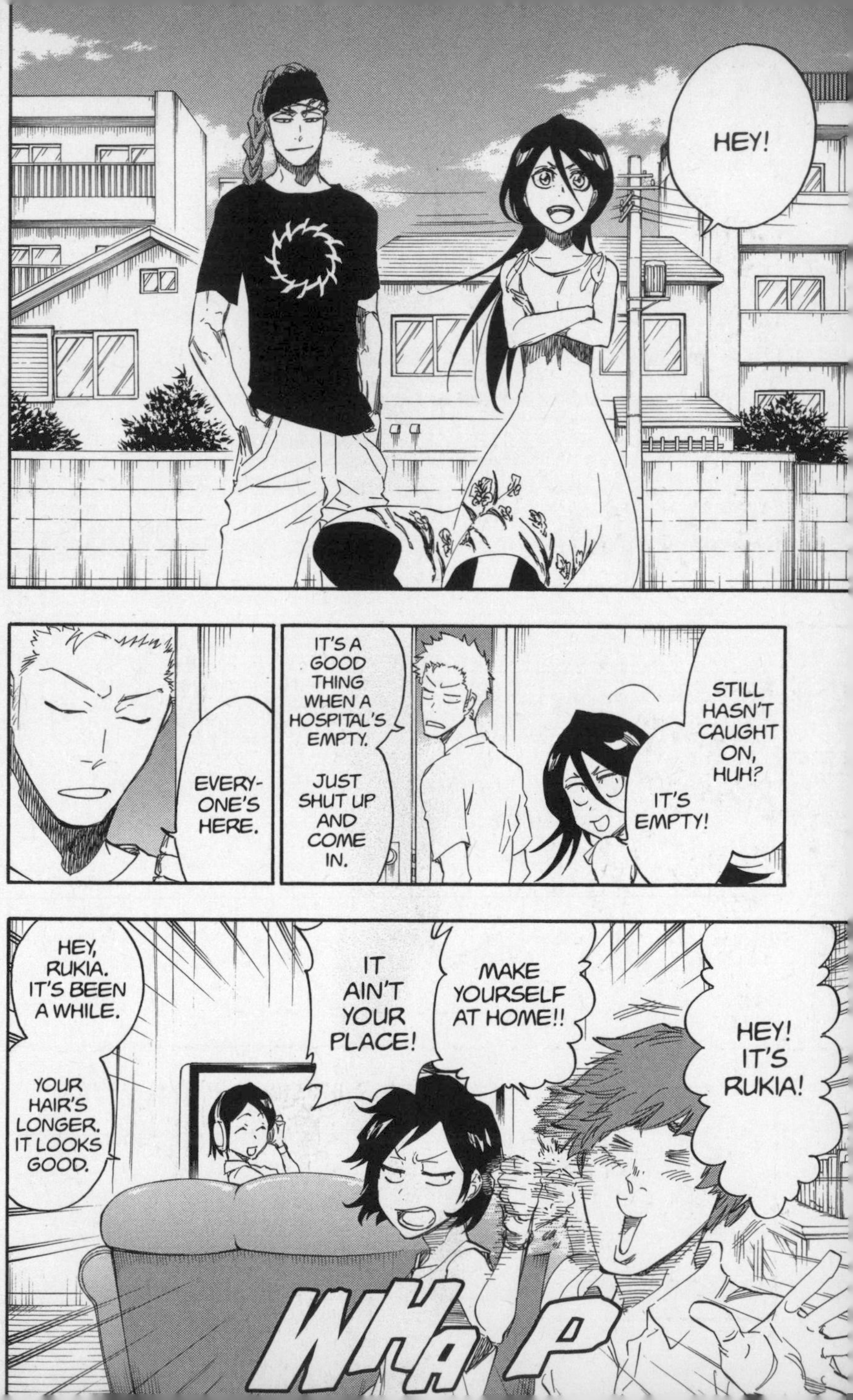
HEY!
STILL HASN'T CAUGHT ON, HUH?
IT'S EMPTY!
IT'S A GOOD THING WHEN A HOSPITAL'S EMPTY.
JUST SHUT UP AND COME IN.
EVERY-ONE'S HERE.
HEY! IT'S RUKIA!
MAKE YOURSELF AT HOME!!
IT AIN'T YOUR PLACE!
HEY, RUKIA. IT'S BEEN A WHILE.
YOUR HAIR'S LONGER. IT LOOKS GOOD.
WHAP

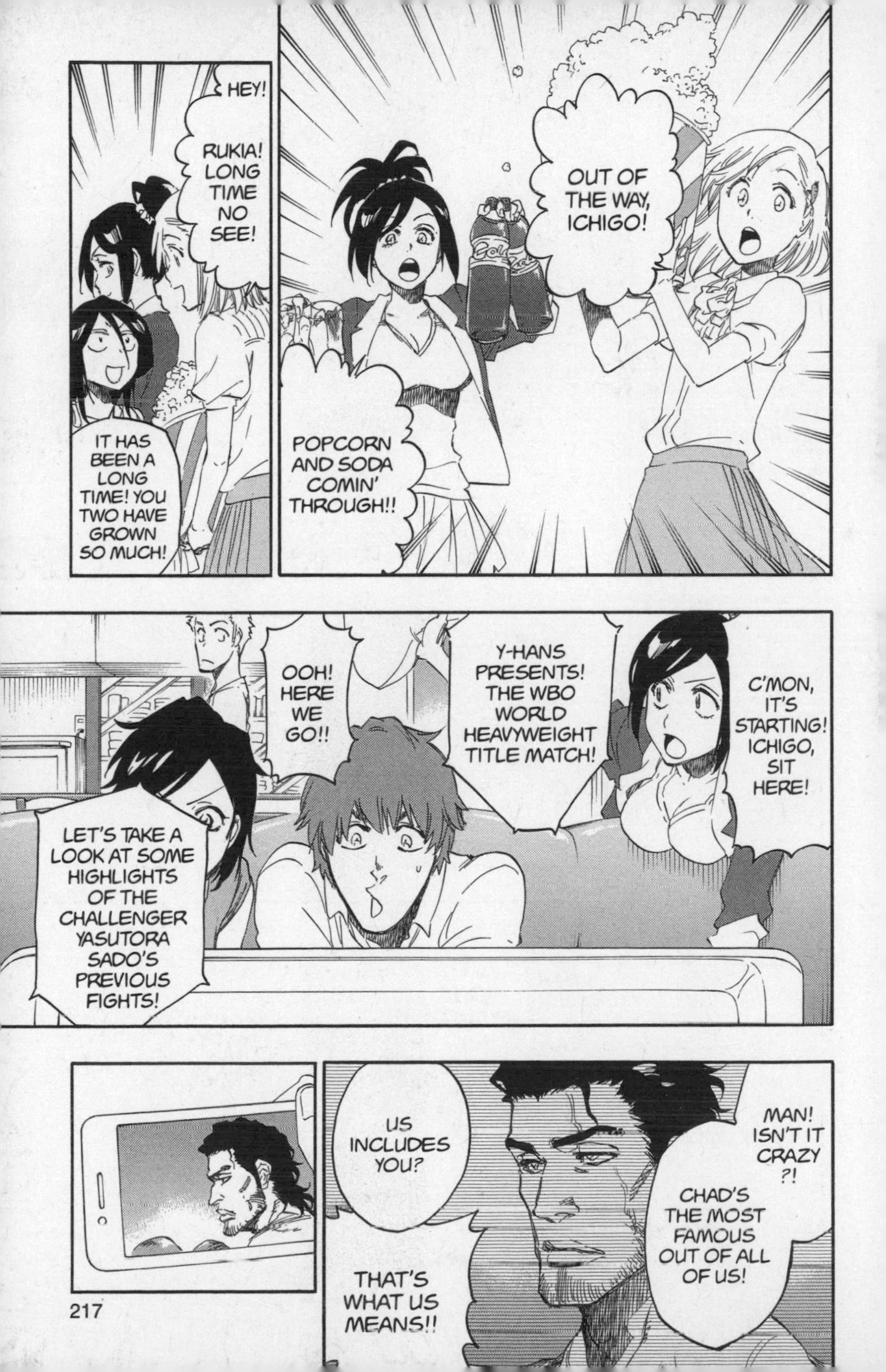
OUT OF THE WAY, ICHIGO!
POPCORN AND SODA COMIN' THROUGH!!
HEY!
RUKIA! LONG TIME NO SEE!
IT HAS BEEN A LONG TIME! YOU TWO HAVE GROWN SO MUCH!
C'MON, IT'S STARTING! ICHIGO, SIT HERE!
Y-HANS PRESENTS! THE WBO WORLD HEAVYWEIGHT TITLE MATCH!
OOH! HERE WE GO!!
LET'S TAKE A LOOK AT SOME HIGHLIGHTS OF THE CHALLENGER YASUTORA SADO'S PREVIOUS FIGHTS!
MAN! ISN'T IT CRAZY?!
CHAD'S THE MOST FAMOUS OUT OF ALL OF US!
US INCLUDES YOU?
THAT'S WHAT US MEANS!!

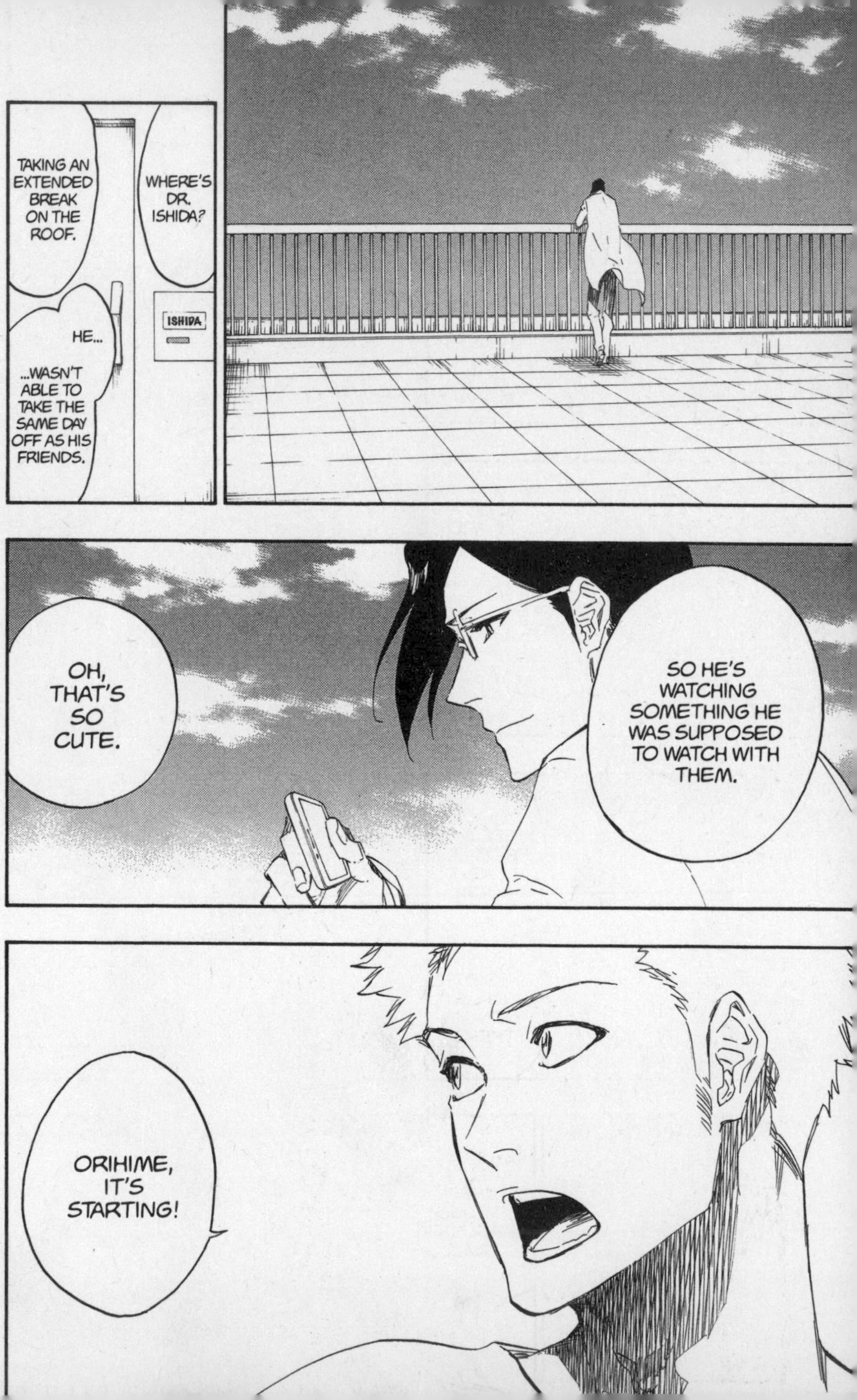
WHERE'S DR. ISHIDA?
TAKING AN EXTENDED BREAK ON THE ROOF.
HE...
...WASN'T ABLE TO TAKE THE SAME DAY OFF AS HIS FRIENDS.
ISHIDA
SO HE'S WATCHING SOMETHING HE WAS SUPPOSED TO WATCH WITH THEM.
OH, THAT'S SO CUTE.
ORIHIME, IT'S STARTING!

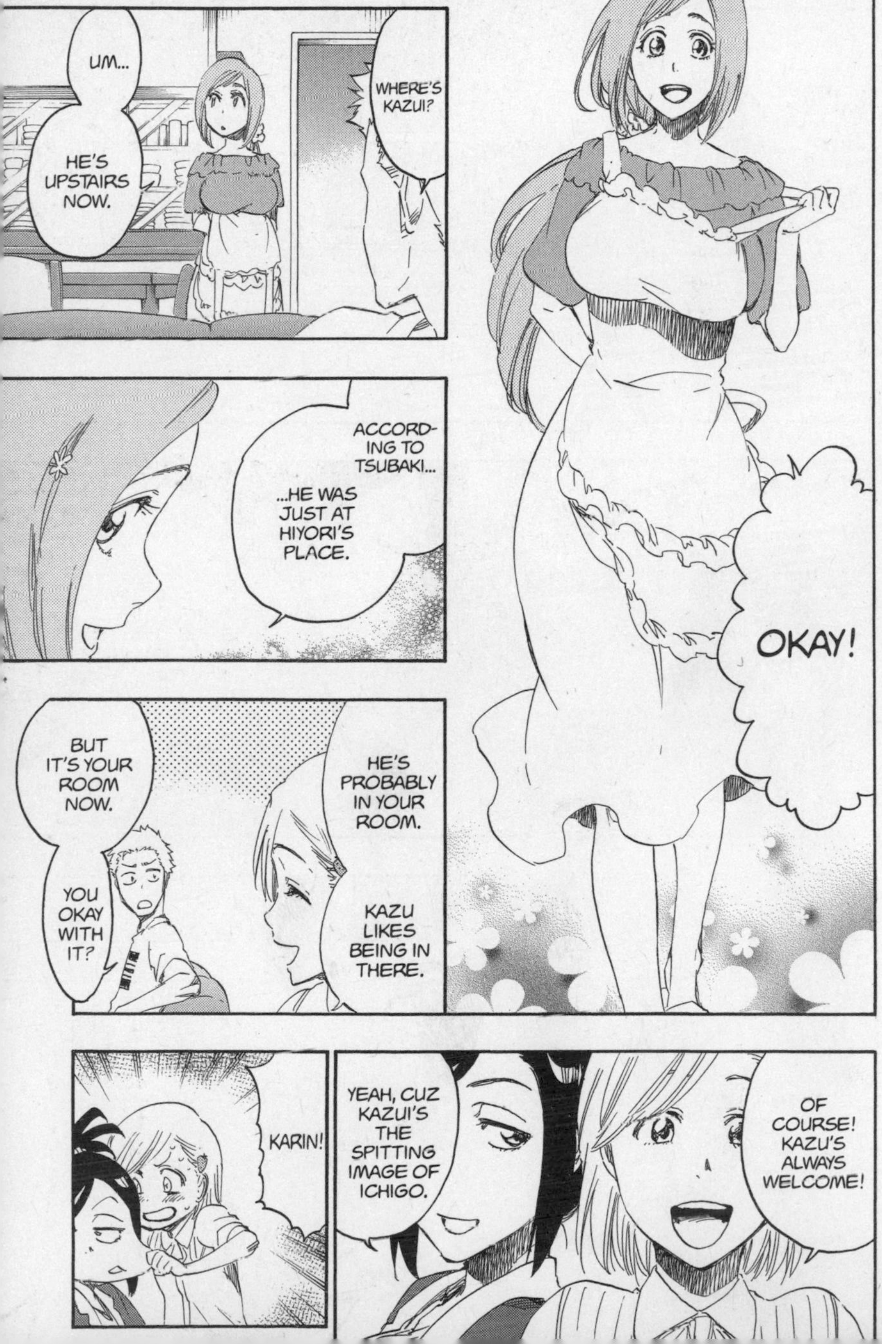
OKAY!
WHERE'S KAZUI?
UM...
HE'S UPSTAIRS NOW.
ACCORDING TO TSUBAKI...
...HE WAS JUST AT HIYORI'S PLACE.
HE'S PROBABLY IN YOUR ROOM.
BUT IT'S YOUR ROOM NOW.
KAZU LIKES BEING IN THERE.
YOU OKAY WITH IT?
OF COURSE! KAZU'S ALWAYS WELCOME!
YEAH, CUZ KAZUI'S THE SPITTING IMAGE OF ICHIGO.
KARIN!

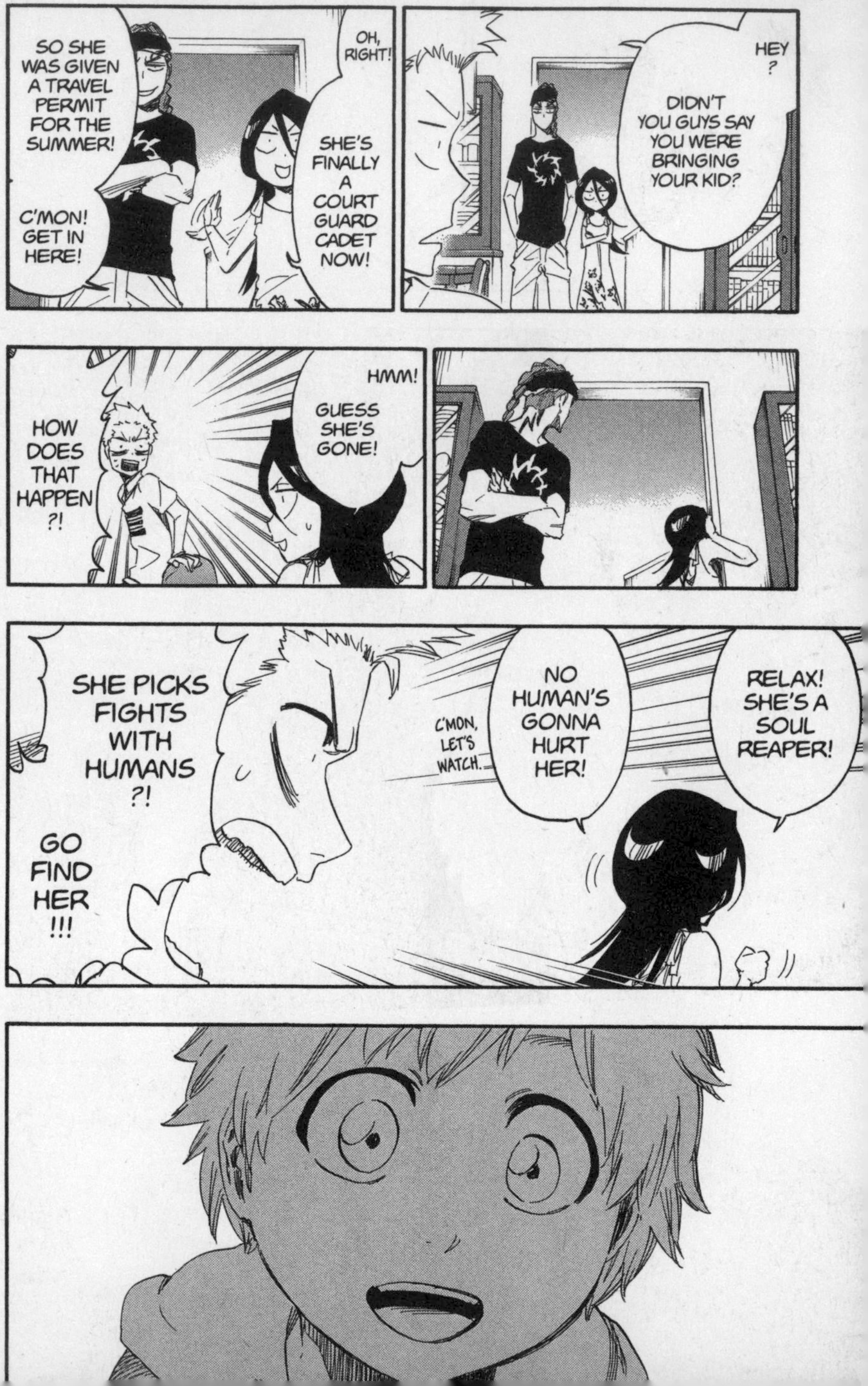
HEY ?
DIDN'T YOU GUYS SAY YOU WERE BRINGING YOUR KID?
OH, RIGHT!
SHE'S FINALLY A COURT GUARD CADET NOW!
SO SHE WAS GIVEN A TRAVEL PERMIT FOR THE SUMMER!
C'MON! GET IN HERE!
HMM!
GUESS SHE'S GONE!
HOW DOES THAT HAPPEN ?!
RELAX! SHE'S A SOUL REAPER!
NO HUMAN'S GONNA HURT HER!
C'MON, LET'S WATCH.
SHE PICKS FIGHTS WITH HUMANS ?!
GO FIND HER !!!

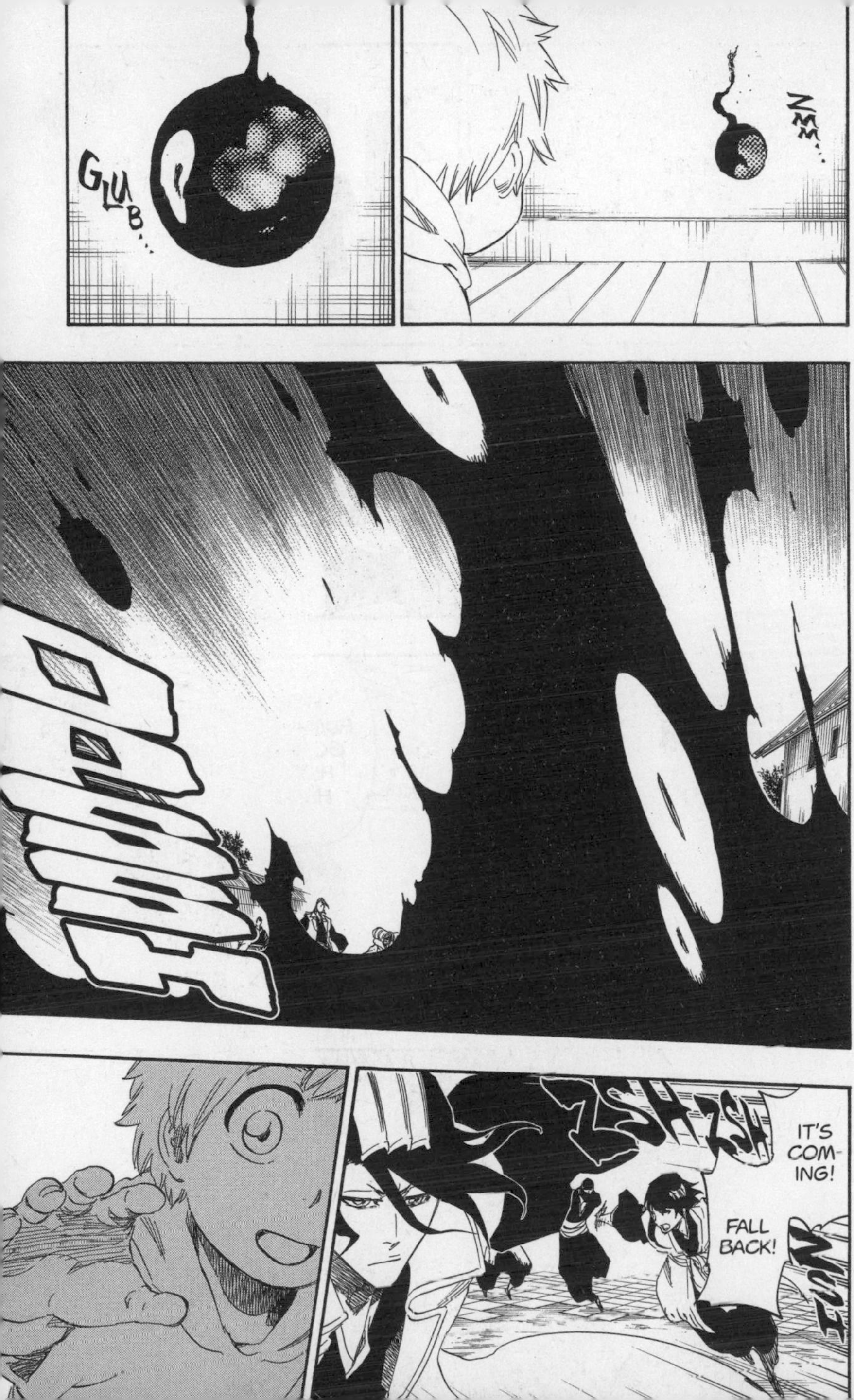
ZMM...
GLUB...
ZSH ZSH
IT'S COMING!
FALL BACK!

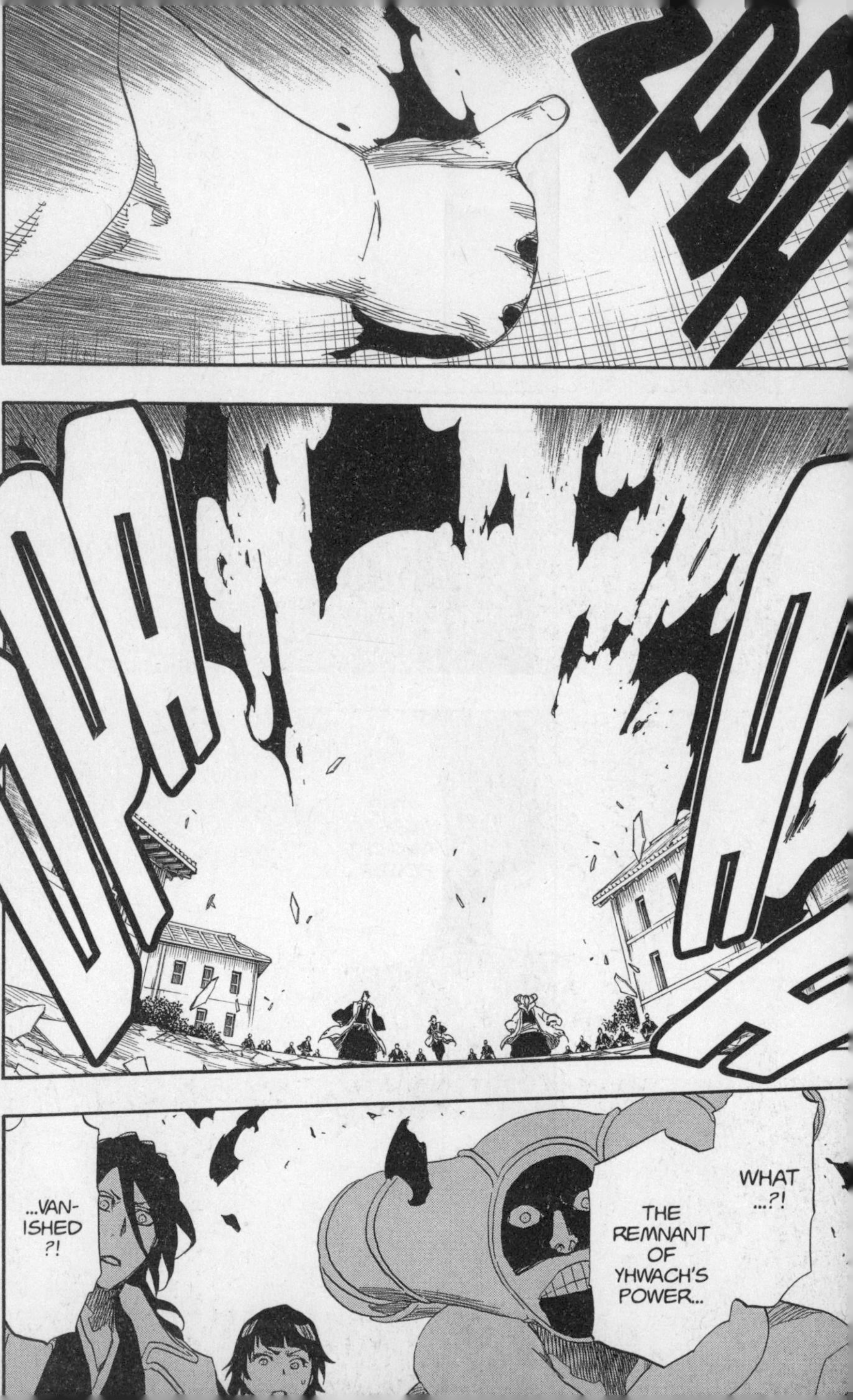
WHAT ...?!
THE REMNANT OF YHWACH'S POWER...
...VAN-ISHED ?!

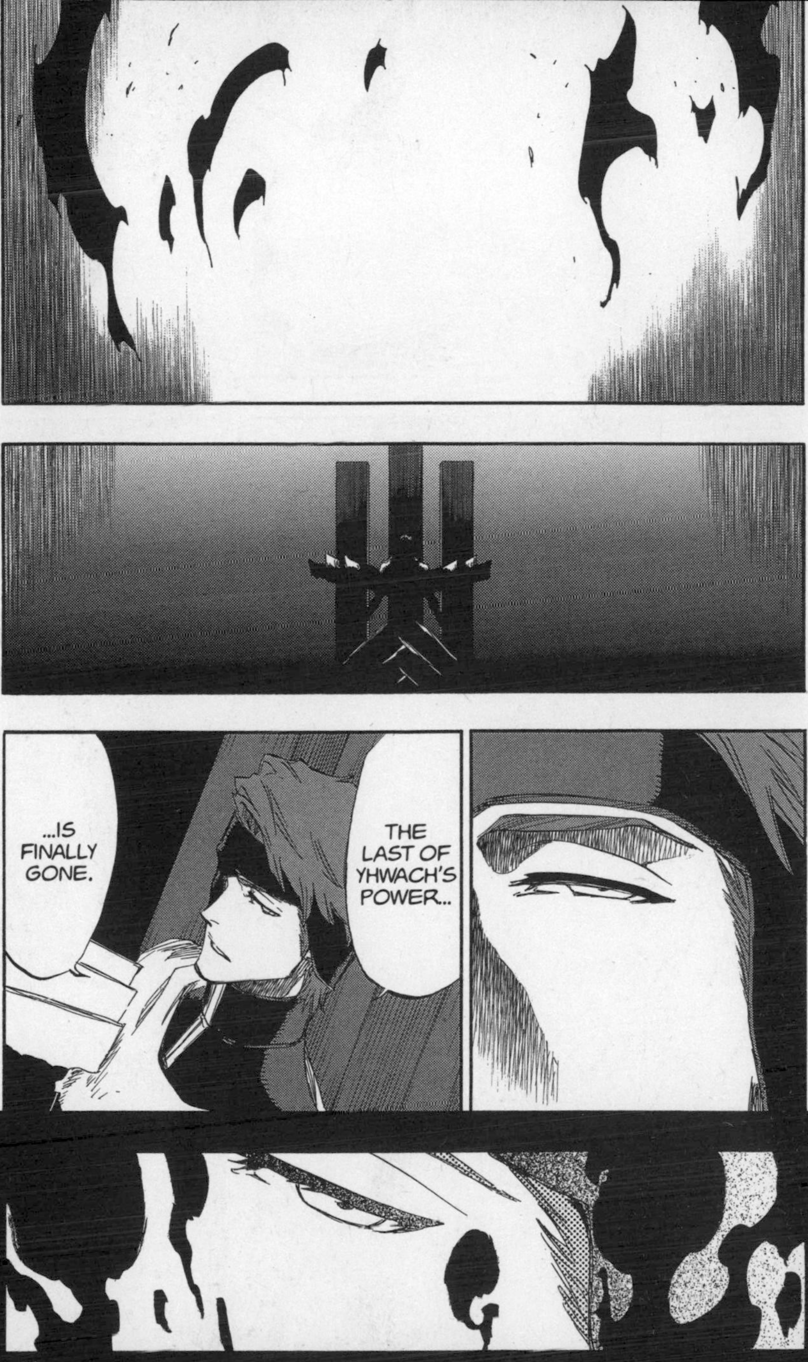
THE LAST OF YHWACH'S POWER...
...IS FINALLY GONE.

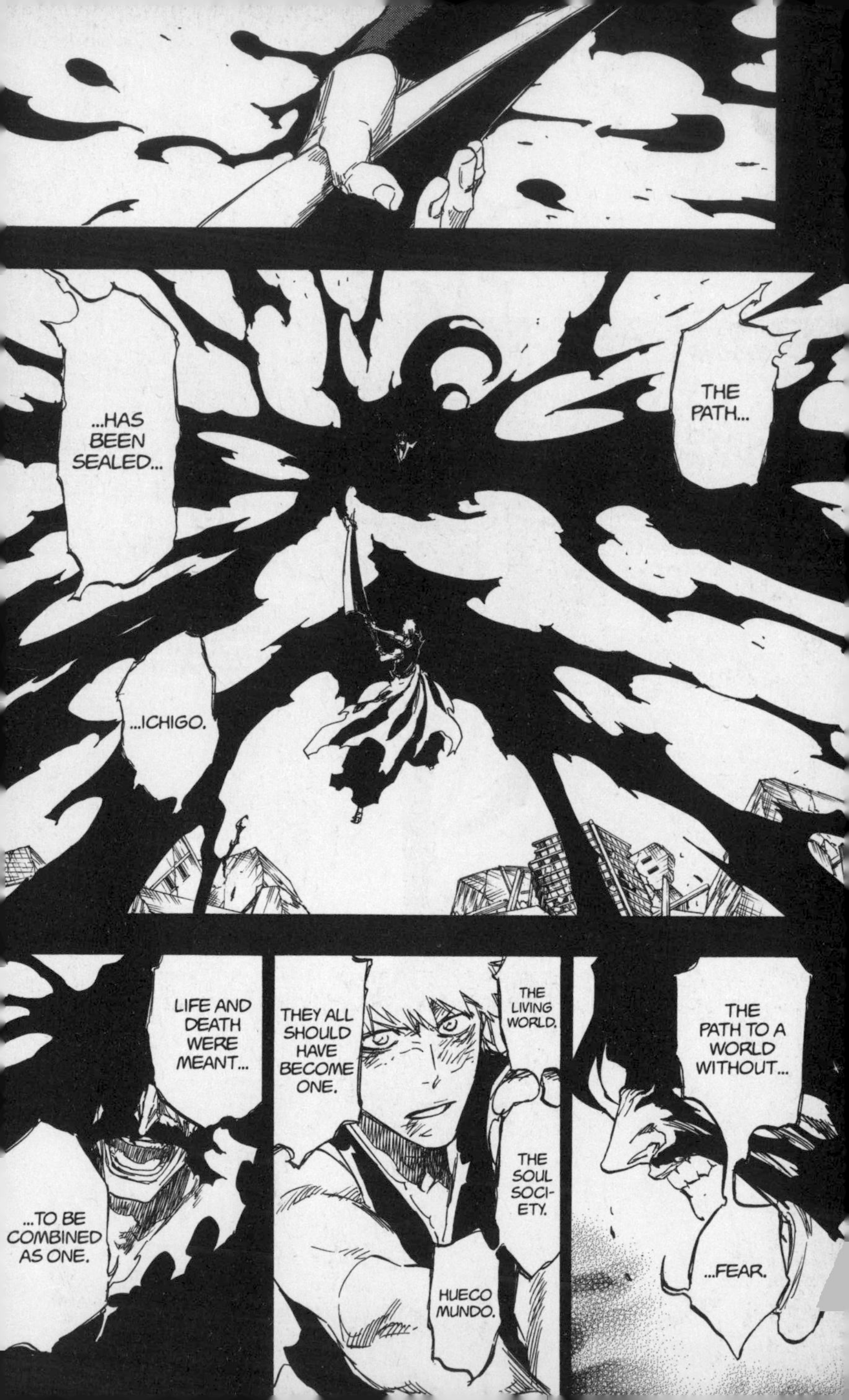
THE PATH...
...HAS BEEN SEALED...
...ICHIGO.
THE PATH TO A WORLD WITHOUT...
...FEAR.
THE LIVING WORLD.
THE SOUL SOCI-ETY.
HUECO MUNDO.
THEY ALL SHOULD HAVE BECOME ONE.
LIFE AND DEATH WERE MEANT...
...TO BE COMBINED AS ONE.

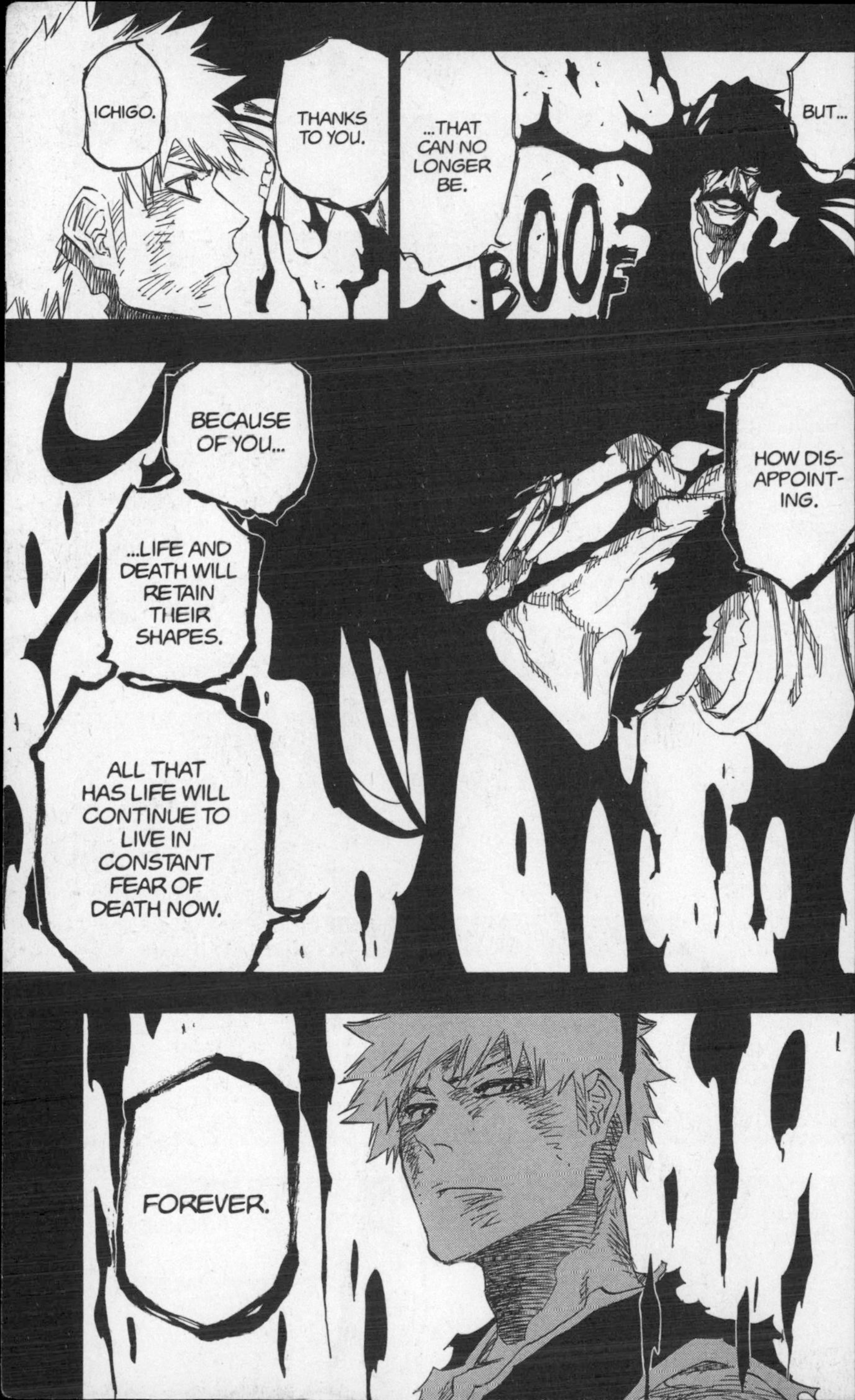
BUT...
...THAT CAN NO LONGER BE.
BOOF
THANKS TO YOU.
ICHIGO.
HOW DIS-APPOINT-ING.
BECAUSE OF YOU...
...LIFE AND DEATH WILL RETAIN THEIR SHAPES.
ALL THAT HAS LIFE WILL CONTINUE TO LIVE IN CONSTANT FEAR OF DEATH NOW.
FOREVER.

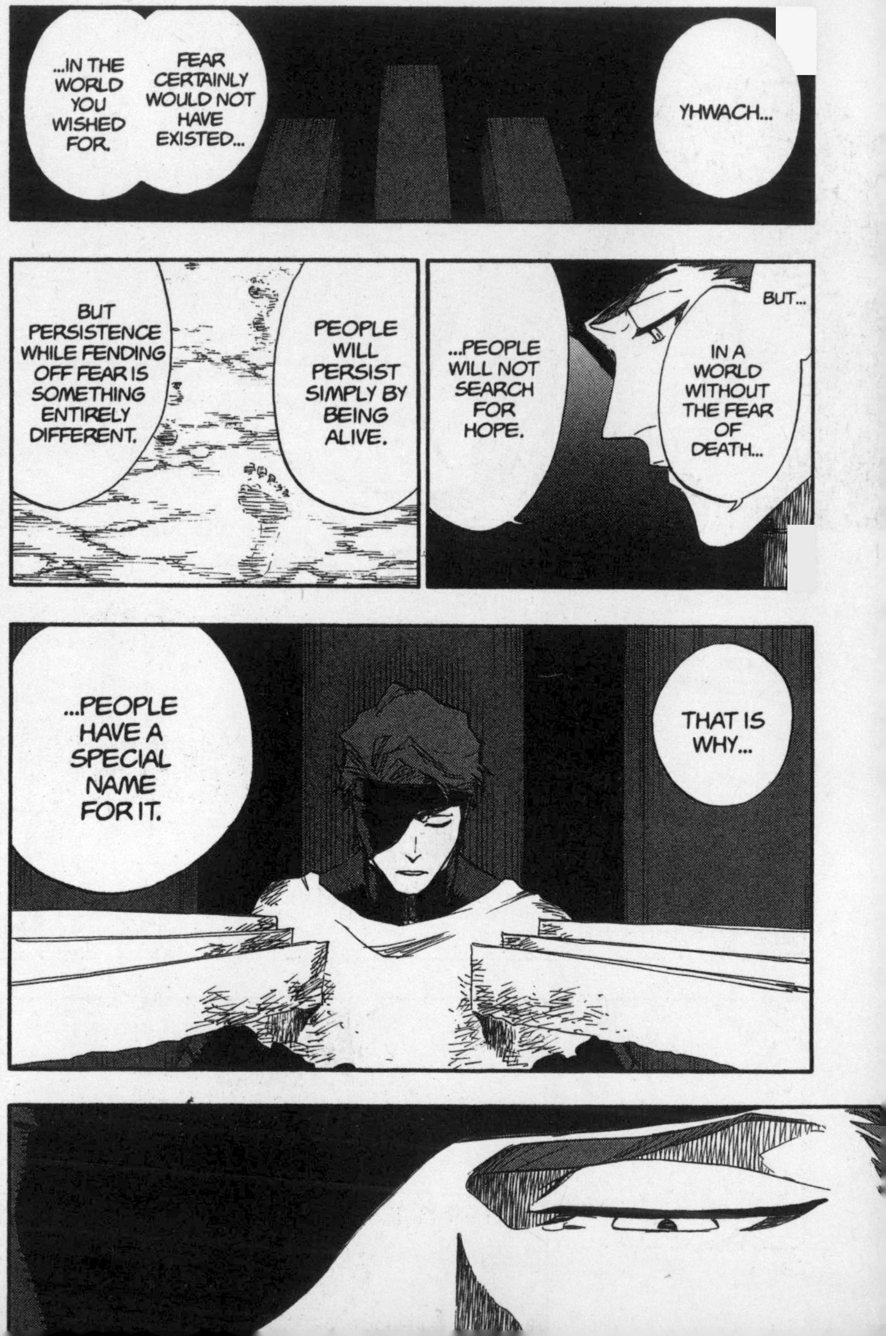
YHWACH...
FEAR CERTAINLY WOULD NOT HAVE EXISTED...
...IN THE WORLD YOU WISHED FOR.
BUT...
IN A WORLD WITHOUT THE FEAR OF DEATH...
...PEOPLE WILL NOT SEARCH FOR HOPE.
PEOPLE WILL PERSIST SIMPLY BY BEING ALIVE.
BUT PERSISTENCE WHILE FENDING OFF FEAR IS SOMETHING ENTIRELY DIFFERENT.
THAT IS WHY...
...PEOPLE HAVE A SPECIAL NAME FOR IT.

THEY CALL IT COURAGE.

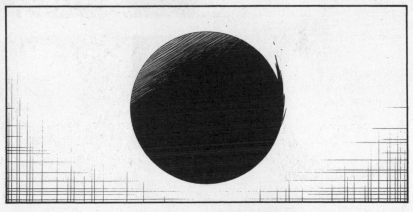

WHO'S THERE?

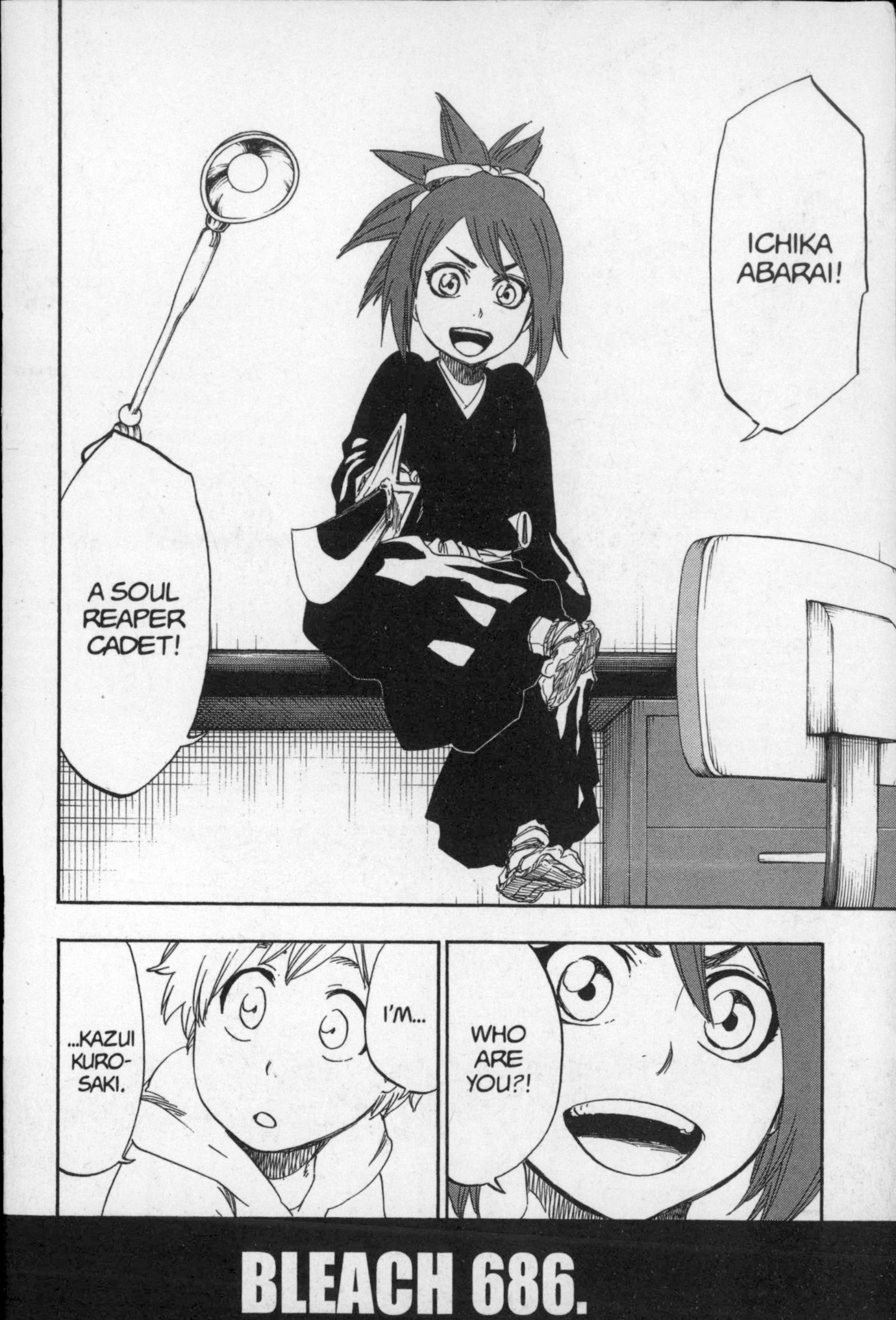
ICHIKA ABARAI!
A SOUL REAPER CADET!
WHO ARE YOU?!
I'M...
...KAZUI KURO-SAKI.

BLEACH 686.

THE END

BRAVE

THE STORIES OF

BLEACH

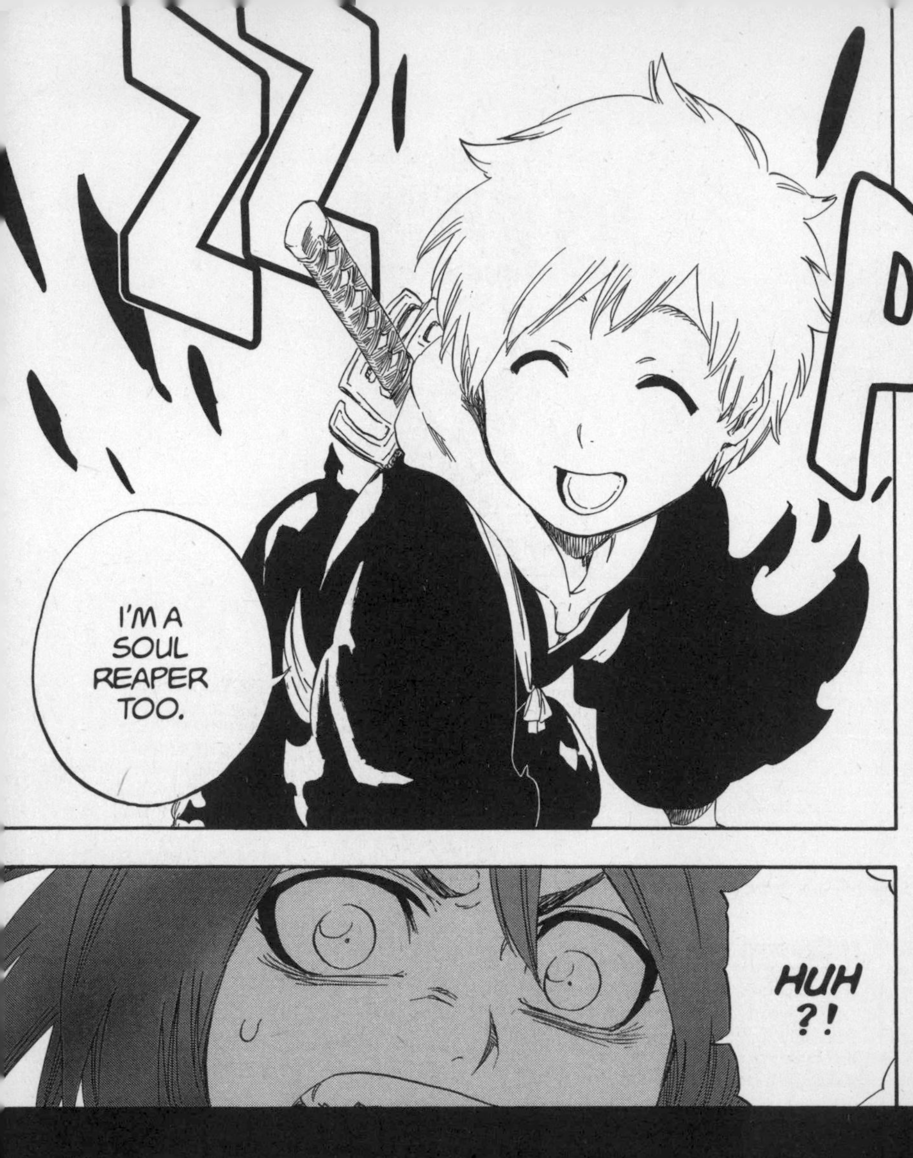
I'M A SOUL REAPER TOO.
HUH ?!

Death & Strawberry

15 YEARS OF THE BLEACH CREW

Abiko Yuki

Aimoto Shou

Funatsu Hajime

Imoto Hitoshi

Iwata Shogo

Kurimoto Kentaro

Matsuo Aisuke

Narita Koichi

Nawashirozawa Haruto

Okada Kasumi

Sato Atsuhiro

Sato Yoshitaka

Shiromoto Sho

Tatsushima Shiori

Yamakoshi Reiko

Yoshioka Yasuhiro

And Your Soul

You're Reading in the Wrong Direction!!

Whoops! Guess what? You're starting at the wrong end of the comic!

...It's true! In keeping with the original Japanese format, **Bleach** is meant to be read from right to left, starting in the upper-right corner.

Unlike English, which is read from left to right, Japanese is read from right to left, meaning that action, sound effects and word-balloon order are completely reversed... something which can make readers unfamiliar with Japanese feel pretty backwards themselves. For this reason, manga or Japanese comics published in the U.S. in English have sometimes been published "flopped"—that is, printed in exact reverse order, as though seen from the other side of a mirror.

By flopping pages, U.S. publishers can avoid confusing readers, but the compromise is not without its downside. For one thing, a character in a flopped manga series who once wore in the original Japanese version a T-shirt emblazoned with "M A Y" (as in "the merry month of") now wears one which reads "Y A M"! Additionally, many manga creators in Japan are themselves unhappy with the process, as some feel the mirror-imaging of their art skews their original intentions.

We are proud to bring you Tite Kubo's **Bleach** in the original unflopped format. For now, though, turn to the other side of the book and let the adventure begin...!

—Editor

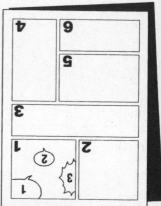